Human Resource Management

IN LOCAL GOVERNMENT

AN ESSENTIAL GUIDE

Third Edition

Human Resource Management
IN LOCAL GOVERNMENT

AN ESSENTIAL GUIDE

Third Edition

Edited by Siegrun Fox Freyss

Leaders at the Core of Better Communities

ICMA advances professional local government worldwide. Its mission is to create excellence in local governance by developing and advancing professional management of local government. ICMA, the International City/County Management Association, provides member support; publications, data, and information; peer and results-oriented assistance; and training and professional development to more than 9,000 city, town, and county experts and other individuals and organizations throughout the world. The management decisions made by ICMA's members affect 185 million individuals living in thousands of communities, from small villages and towns to large metropolitan areas.

Library of Congress Cataloging-in-Publication Data

Human resource management in local government : an essential guide / edited by Siegrun Fox Freyss. -- 3rd ed.
    p. cm.
  Includes bibliographical references and index.
  ISBN 978-0-87326-186-9 (alk. paper)
  1. Local officials and employees--United States. 2. Personnel management--United States. 3. Local government--United States. I. Freyss, Siegrun Fox. II. International City/County Management Association.
  JS331.H86 2009
  352.6'2140973--dc22

2009020652

Design and Composition: Will Kemp

Printed in the United States of America
2016 2015 2014 2013 2012 2011 2010 2009
5 4 3 2 1

About the editor

Siegrun Fox Freyss (also author of the Preface, Introduction, and Chapters 1, 2, and 8) is professor of political science and director of the master of science in public administration program at the California State University, Los Angeles. Her research interests include local politics, urban policies, and municipal management. In addition to having edited the first and second editions of *Human Resource Management in Local Government*, she is also the author of numerous articles published in academic journals and as book chapters. She holds a PhD in government from Claremont Graduate University in Southern California and received her bachelor's as well as master's degrees in urban planning from Technical University of Munich, Germany.

Recent Titles from ICMA Press

Citizen Surveys for Local Government: A Comprehensive Guide to Making Them Matter
The Effective Local Government Manager
Effective Supervisory Practices
Leading Your Community: A Guide for Local Elected Leaders
Managing Local Government: Cases in Effectiveness
Managing Local Government Services: A Practical Guide
Service Contracting: A Local Government Guide

Green Books—Authoritative source books on local government management

Emergency Management: Principles and Practice for Local Government
Local Government Police Management
Local Planning: Contemporary Principles and Practice
Management Policies in Local Government Finance
Managing Fire and Rescue Services

Contents

Online supplements
icma.org/press/HRsupplements

Human resource management in context: A theoretical perspective
Sample job descriptions
    Accounting clerk
    Administrative assistant
    Administrative office manager
    Library director
    Manager of information systems

Reasons for a complete compensation and classification study
Classification rating factors
Clerical/secretarial matrix
Points assigned to factor degrees
Products and services for the human resource manager in local government

Exhibits

Foreword

State and local governments are facing unprecedented challenges as the baby boomers begin to retire, taking years of knowledge and experience with them. Attracting, retaining, and developing the talent that governments need is a major undertaking. Doing so in a time of fiscal constraints makes it even more important to understand the rapidly changing world of human resources.

More than one-third of all state and local government workers are now age fifty or older, compared with a little less than a quarter of private sector workers. But while only 32 percent of private sector workers are classified as knowledge workers, almost 70 percent of public sector employees fall into that category. Thus, the retirement of these employees will have a significant impact on the continuing ability of state and local governments to meet the public's needs in an increasingly complex world.

Most local government leaders have not begun to address this workforce challenge. Fiscal realities have shifted the focus away from the workforce of the future to the question of how to balance their budgets today. But when local government leaders consider the experience they may lose when knowledgeable individuals start to retire, the focus will shift back again.

This book provides an up-to-date framework of today's human resource issues and best practices. Readers, both local government managers and human resource professionals, will gain insight on how to address long-term workforce needs, how to recruit and maintain a high-performance team, and what it takes to create an environment where excellence thrives.

At a time when compensation and benefits are being closely scrutinized, local government managers will want to be sure they are providing high-quality benefits that are also cost-effective. This book takes a principle-based approach to human resources, emphasizing fairness to employees and competitive compensation practices. Whether employers are dealing with labor negotiations or setting high performance goals, the key is to build and maintain positive relationships with employees.

The evolving workforce requires creativity and flexibility. Experienced employees who are eligible to retire may be persuaded to stay on the job longer to help mentor new hires. Older employees, as well as younger employees with family obligations, may be interested in part-time rather than full-time work.

Having good health insurance and retirement benefits has been a traditional strength of the public sector and will be important in the years ahead as the competition for talent intensifies for some skilled jobs. Equally important is having a plan to meet the workforce challenges of the future.

Whether we are addressing fiscal challenges, environmental issues, public safety, or a crisis, we know that having the right people in the job will pay off for our communities.

Elizabeth K. Kellar
Executive Director
Center for State and Local Government Excellence
Washington, D.C.

Preface

The third edition of this book has been revised to meet the information needs of a growing number of users. Originally, this guide was written to provide a solid reference for chief administrative officers and department heads employed in local governments that are too small to have a separate human resource department staffed with its own experts. In such cities and counties the city manager or department head may fulfill personnel duties, such as recruitment or promotions, as the need for such functions arises. For this latest edition, *Human Resource Management in Local Government* has been updated to ensure that it continues to serve as a comprehensive resource on how to manage the most common personnel actions. An online supplement was added as well to make personnel forms more readily available and to simplify access to the many Web resources that are in the area of public personnel management.

The table below shows the relationship between the size of the jurisdiction and the employment of a human resource director. ICMA's 2000 survey of local government personnel practices found that as the population increased, so did the likelihood that the jurisdiction employed a full-time human resource administrator.

This book is also being used by administrators in larger jurisdictions that have a separate human resource department. Managers and supervisors in line agencies need to know about many aspects of personnel administration in order to collaborate effectively with the specialists from human resources. Most personnel functions—from planning future positions, hiring new personnel, and evaluating employees' performance, to disciplining and terminating employees—are accomplished in joint efforts involving line managers and human resource staff. However, the work of public personnel departments is circumscribed in many different ways—by federal laws, Supreme Court rulings, state statutes, local ordinances, and professional standards, which may at times appear as unreasonable red tape to persons not trained in personnel management. This guide, a handy reference of the

Percentages of small and medium-size municipalities employing a human resource director

Population	Has a human resource director (%)
100,000–249,999	93
50,000–99,999	83
25,000–49,999	74
10,000–24,999	47

Source: 2000 ICMA Survey of Local Government Human Resource Functions.

accumulated principles and practices, will help line managers understand why staff from human resources insist on certain procedures, while staff in human resources can use it to update their knowledge about best practices in their field.

Increasingly, faculty and students in master of public administration programs are finding this guide to be a good alternative to a traditional textbook. It is written for mature adults and appeals to graduate students precisely because it does not have the feel of a textbook. In many instances, students are already working in, or aspiring to, supervisory positions, and the book meets their current and emerging information needs. But for educational purposes, the book requires contexts; thus, we added a new introductory chapter to provide the historical background and an online supplement to provide the theoretical background. Most of the chapters answer the questions of *how* to administer the various personnel functions. The introduction and the theoretical article in the online supplement tell *why* certain approaches gained the status of best practices.

In addition to the new introduction, each chapter was carefully reviewed and new material added as warranted. Chapter 1 was expanded to include a section on succession planning; Chapter 2 gives more attention to the issues of equal employment opportunity, affirmative action, and reverse discrimination; Chapter 3 takes a fresh look at the impact of generational differences in work motivation; Chapter 4 includes the latest union developments in the public sector; Chapter 5 was updated and new case law has been added; Chapter 6 now includes a systematic discussion of pay policies in addition to benefits; Chapter 7 emphasizes the importance of ethics with a new section on a code of ethics; and because "when things go wrong" it may involve not only problem employees but also a problem economy, Chapter 8 has a new section on cutback management. The old Chapter 9, which covered products and services for human resource management, has been moved to the online supplement to make the many Web resources more readily available to administrators and researchers.

To ensure that the various groups of users are represented, each chapter was written by a team of practitioners and academicians. The team arrangement made it possible to draw on the best applied and theoretical knowledge in the human resource management field. Some of the contributors are actually "pracademicians," having entered academia after years of practical service or having chosen government work after years of teaching and research.

The presentation of the information in sidebars signals the degree to which personnel policies are settled. Well-established legal and professional standards are presented as "guiding principles" and reinforced as "tips" for the successful implementation of the policy. Conversely, readers are alerted to clearly unprofessional or illegal personnel practices in sidebars that are labeled "caution." In between these two extremes are the many gray areas, which are listed under "challenges." Often these are instances in which human resource researchers and consultants cannot give a definitive answer. The authors of the chapters cannot prescribe or proscribe proper or improper practices because the lines are not clearly drawn. Moreover, in some cases, two equally defensible standards are in conflict. In such circumstances, the manager is asked to exercise judgment and leadership.

Since the second edition of this book was published five years ago, several developments have made human resource management in local government more challenging. Severe fiscal stress has become a painful reality, affecting personnel administration in several fundamental ways. Whether it involves position planning or the recruitment, development, or disciplining of employees, cost has become a central consideration for many personnel decisions; and to limit expenditures, many jurisdictions are implementing reduction-in-force procedures or other revenue-saving measures. And since the bursting of bubbles in the private sector usually means the greater availability of highly qualified applicants who are willing to forgo the higher compensation in the private sector for job security in the public sector, the inability of cities and counties to hire during a recession is that much more unfortunate.

Another change can be summed up under the term "globalization." Even though the worldwide recession has slowed the flow of goods across national boundaries, the integration of world markets has left its mark on local governments. Cities and counties, no matter what their size, have been affected by the high mobility of capital, goods, and people around the globe. More sophisticated financial markets, more international production processes, and a more diverse workforce have increased the complexity of human capital management.[1] Unfortunately, the global movements are not exclusively commercial in nature; they have also brought terrorism to U.S. shores. The heightened insecurity requires local governments to divert scarce resources from traditional government functions to fund the increased safety needs in their jurisdictions.

In conclusion, human capital management is in flux because of ongoing changes in laws, court rulings, demographics, technology, practical insights, and theoretical knowledge, as well as the impact of economic and global upheavals. This guide represents an effort to identify the principles and practices in human resource management that have been developed in the face of other challenging times and have enabled employers to hire, develop, and promote a most competent workforce, which is the backbone for excellence in service to the public.

Siegrun Fox Freyss
Department of Political Science
Director, Master of Science in Public Administration Program
California State University, Los Angeles

---

1 The summary term for the administration of the workforce has progressed historically from "personnel management" to "human resource management" and now to "human capital management," reflecting changes in the functions of personnel administrators. However, these changes are so subtle that the distinctions become blurred; therefore, this book uses the three terms interchangeably. See Kay Coles James, "The HR Paradigm Shift and the Federal Human Capital Opportunity," *Public Manager* 30, (Winter 2001–2002): 13–16.

Introduction

Siegrun Fox Freyss

Hiring, developing, and promoting a competent workforce creates the backbone for excellence in service to the public. This book is intended to assist city and county executives, department heads, and other supervisory employees of relatively small jurisdictions, as well as students who will be serving in smaller local governments, in implementing sound human resource management practices.

Guiding principles

- Public sector human resource policies should be based on professional principles and practices as they have developed over more than a hundred years.
- Public sector human resource procedures should comply with applicable federal statutes, case law, state laws, local ordinances, and standards set by professional associations.
- Historical and theoretical developments provide a rich tradition that should guide professional public personnel administration.

Challenges

- Identifying, retaining, and improving public personnel procedures that over time have proven beneficial in protecting and promoting the public interest
- Changing or removing public personnel policies that on balance hinder the protection and promotion of the public interest

Readers of the second edition of *Human Resource Management in Local Government* expressed an interest in a book that would serve not only as a reference but also as an educational and analytical tool. On the surface, providing such a book is not difficult to do since a seemingly solid body of knowledge has accumulated on personnel management in the public sector, often expressed as "best practices." But we are living in a time of transition, which leads to a questioning of well-established procedures. Together with the economy and society in general, government is going through a transformation of paradigmatic proportions, summarized as the shift from the modern to the postmodern epoch, which has profound implications for the workings of government in general and for human capital management in particular.[1]

The shift from an industrial to a high-tech economy is the most obvious indicator of the historical change. Public and private bureaucracies are asked to reengineer and reinvent themselves to make optimal use of high-tech capabilities. For cash-strapped jurisdictions this means finding money for the new investments; for human resource departments it means changing job descriptions, removing qualifications that are obsolete and adding new ones, revising testing procedures, and offering ongoing training opportunities to employees. Some jurisdictions are reviewing their merit systems to find ways to make them more flexible and adaptable to the new developments. However, it is important to remember the historical and theoretical reasons why certain personnel policies were adopted in the first place to retain the good ones in this time of change.

Another paradigm shift occurred as a result of fundamental changes in the view of human nature and in the value of human life. In premodern times, people were perceived as inherently different and unequal by nature, the aristocracy above the commoners, men superior to women, older people superior to younger people, and some racial or ethnic groups superior to other racial or ethnic groups. Work organizations and the division of labor reflected this belief in natural inequalities. The modern age argued in favor of equality, leading to the core values of equal rights and equal opportunities in politics, in education, and in employment. The postmodern age acknowledges human and cultural differences, but the differences do not imply superiority or inferiority. Historical and theoretical developments have tried to come to grips with these transformations.

The purpose of this introductory chapter is to provide some historical context for the rest of the book.

The historical development of professional personnel principles and practices

Public personnel management as both a professional practice and a systematic field of study is more than a hundred years old. The assassination of President James A. Garfield by an unhappy job seeker was a watershed event that set into motion changes in public employment procedures from haphazard judgments to decisions based on principles. The passage of the Civil Service Act of 1883, better known as the Pendleton Act, introduced the merit system at the federal level and became a model for state and local governments to follow.[2]

The Pendleton Act introduced four public personnel principles:

- *A competent workforce,* achieved by basing hiring decisions on merit and requiring competitive entrance exams
- *Job security* to ensure administrative continuity and stability despite changes and conflicts in the political ranks
- *Political neutrality* to ensure neutral competence and protection against political reprisals
- *Administration of personnel functions* by an independent Civil Service Commission to set the rules for a stable, neutral, and competent workforce; to implement the rules; and to adjudicate conflicts.

Originally, the act covered only about 10 percent of the federal workforce, but more and more job classes were included over time, and currently about 90 percent are in the classified services.[3] The inclusion of more ranks and job classes into the merit system was done not just to expand the meritocracy, but also to protect the jobs of loyal employees before a new president took office. Whatever the motive, competent public employees were a precondition for the Industrial Revolution to succeed.

Cities had to be rebuilt from the (under)ground up to meet the needs of the industrial age. Local governments built the infrastructure, including paved roads, pipes for water and sewers, and lines for electricity and gas. Large-scale assembly-line production required a sizeable number of workers to arrive at their work stations at the same time and to leave at a certain time. This, in turn, required efficient modes of mass transportation. The same efficiency requirement applied to the transport of raw materials to the factories and of finished products to the marketplace. States took on the tasks of making school education compulsory for the large number of workers and building state universities to train engineers and scientists.[4]

As pressure mounted to build the infrastructure, city officials and business leaders became frustrated with bureaucratic inefficiencies and outright corruption; searching for solutions, they were attracted by the idea of a merit system. Albany adopted one in 1884, Buffalo in 1885, New York in 1888, Chicago in 1895, and Seattle in 1896. But many cities originally limited meritorious hiring procedures to certain job classes, such as clerical workers, police, and firefighters, and for many years the patronage system dominated personnel functions in local government.

Franklin Roosevelt's administration promoted local governments to adopt the merit system in connection with its New Deal programs. County and city agencies were used to administer the programs established under the Social Security Act of 1935. When problems surfaced, Congress passed the Social Security Amendments Act of 1939, which required that local agencies in charge of dispensing federal funds adopt merit-based personnel principles. ICMA went further, promoting the adoption of merit principles in most municipal agencies, and using the *Municipal Year Book* and other outlets to record the progress.

In the 1960s, however, problems with the merit system surfaced, and criticism was leveled by both conservative and liberal writers. Conservatives charged that the principles of job security and the rigid job classifications created a disincentive for high performance,[5] and liberals observed that merit system practices led to the exclusion of minorities and women from the middle and upper ranks of government.[6] To deal with the issue of productivity, some cities introduced performance evaluations. The issue of discrimination received nationwide attention with the passage of the Civil Rights Act in 1964, the Equal Pay Act in 1963, and the Age Discrimination in Employment Act of 1967.

The federal government took comprehensive steps to help local governments implement the new equal opportunity requirements and generally improve the management capacity at the local level by passing the Intergovernmental Personnel Act (IPA) in 1970. The act provided grants-in-aid and technical assistance; it also encouraged cooperation in recruitment and examinations and the exchange of key employees between federal agencies and local governments. In addition, the new legislation spelled out updated merit personnel standards that highlighted the need for competitive recruitment and promotion procedures, fair and nondiscriminatory treatment of applicants and employees, adequate pay and training opportunities, and the dismissal of employees whose inadequate performance could not be corrected.[7] (See Exhibit 1 for an excerpt from the IPA.)

In the 1980s the Reagan administration cut much of the funding for IPA programs. This was apparently not very detrimental to city and county governments, perhaps because by that time a much larger number of universities offered MPA programs and many more local public administrators had a professional education. The growth of professional organizations such as ICMA, the National Civic League

Exhibit 1   Standards for a merit system of personnel administration

The quality of public service can be improved by the development of systems of personnel administration consistent with such merit principles as—

(a) Recruiting, selecting, and advancing employees on the basis of their relative ability, knowledge, and skills, including open consideration of qualified applicants for initial appointment.

(b) Providing equitable and adequate compensation.

(c) Training employees, as needed, to assure high quality performance.

(d) Retaining employees on the basis of the adequacy of their performance, correcting inadequate performance, and separating employees whose inadequate performance cannot be corrected.

(e) Assuring fair treatment of applicants and employees in all aspects of personnel administration without regard to political affiliation, race, color, national origin, sex, religious creed, age or handicap and with proper regard for their privacy and constitutional rights as citizens. This "fair treatment" principle includes compliance with the Federal equal employment opportunity and nondiscrimination laws.

(f) Assuring that employees are protected against coercion for partisan political purposes and are prohibited from using their official authority for the purpose of interfering with or affecting the result of an election or a nomination for office.

Source: 5 CFR 1 § 900.603, ucop.com/raohome/certs/5cfr900.html (accessed April 27, 2009).

(NCL), and the International Public Management Association for Human Resources (IPMA-HR) also contributed to capacity building.[8]

The first master's program in municipal administration was started by the University of Michigan in 1914. A more comprehensive undertaking was the Maxwell School of Citizenship and Public Affairs, established by Syracuse University in 1924. When the National Association of Schools of Public Affairs and Administration was established in 1970, 65 public administration, public policy, and public affairs programs were represented. By 1980, the number had grown to more than 200 programs, and the current number of accredited and nonaccredited programs is about 280.[9]

The NCL was originally founded in 1894 as the National Municipal League; its purpose was to create a national organization where local reform groups could exchange ideas and learn from each other on how to make city government "more honest, efficient, and effective." The organization currently sees its mission as fostering "collaboration between citizens, government, business, and nonprofit organizations in identifying and solving community problems."[10] ICMA also changed its focus and mission over time: originally established in 1914 as the City Managers' Association with the stated goal being "to promote the efficiency of City Managers and municipal work in general,"[11] over the years it broadened its mission "to create excellence in local governance by advocating and developing the professional management of local government worldwide."[12] IPMA-HR was established in 1973 by combining the Public Personnel Association, founded in 1906, and the Society for Personnel Administration, founded in 1937. It "represents the interests of human resource professionals at the federal, state, and local levels of government."[13]

The contents of this guide

The required or recommended principles and practices explained in this guide cover the whole range of goals and activities associated with human capital management:

- Linking human resource management to desired general governmental outcomes by taking stock of existing jobs, such as performing job analysis, planning the nature and number of new positions, and determining appropriate compensation levels.

- Attracting a high-performance workforce by recruiting, testing, and hiring the best possible applicants and properly orienting new employees.

- Retaining and developing an excellent workforce by nurturing a high-performance work culture and providing effective evaluations, training, educational opportunities, financial incentives, and promotions.

- Maintaining labor peace by working with unions during the certification process, in collective bargaining sessions, and in administering the union contract; in general, moving toward collaborative and interest-based bargaining strategies.

- Avoiding legal liabilities by maintaining up-to-date personnel policy documents and respecting the rights of job applicants and employees.

- Creating an environment for excellence by offering attractive pay and benefit plans.

- Strengthening a high-performance organizational culture by clearly communicating ethical standards, as well as employee and employer responsibilities.

- Limiting organizational damage by dealing with a problem economy, as well as with problem employees, in a timely manner.

- Applying the most effective human capital management practices despite limited resources by using technical assistance services offered by public and private entities around the country. Membership in a professional organization often includes access to an e-mail list where questions and answers about personnel matters can be shared.

All jurisdictions, irrespective of their size, are advised to adhere to legal and professional human resource management standards. Following proper personnel procedures when hiring, developing, and promoting a competent workforce not only provides a foundation for excellent public service but also serves as a form of risk management to protect the employer from debilitating lawsuits.

However, as the historical and theoretical reviews demonstrate, human capital management is in constant flux. The book acknowledges the uncertain future and controversial nature of major personnel practices in each chapter. For instance, Jonathan Tompkins, Aleksandra Stapczynski, and Siegrun Fox Freyss point out in Chapter 1 that the classical model of the merit system is being questioned. Merit systems imply standardization of personnel policies, and the benefits of that are weighed against the drawbacks in the form of rule-laden rigidities and an inability to provide the flexibility needed to manage the modern and, as some would say, postmodern workplace.

Affirmative action policies, covered by Stephanie Witt, W. David Patton, and Siegrun Fox Freyss in Chapter 2 and by John DiNome, Saundra Yaklin, David Rosenbloom, and Arlene Angelo in Chapter 5, are beset by uncertainties arising from legal and political challenges. Some opponents claim that affirmative action violates Title VII of the Civil Rights Act of 1964 by practicing reverse discrimination and creating illegal preferences for women and minorities. Cases that test various applications of affirmative action programs continue to occupy state and federal courts, creating an unstable legal climate nationwide.

Performance appraisals and pay for performance are other controversial personnel tools, as shown by Jenny L. Holland, Arthur H. McCurdy, and Nicholas P. Lovrich in Chapter 3. Introduced in the 1970s and 1980s to improve work output, performance evaluations were often poorly administered and brought disharmony to the workplace. More recently, proponents of team management have advocated abandoning individual performance evaluations and merit pay in favor of group rewards and constant attention to systemwide improvements. Other motivation experts argue that there is not one best way to motivate employees—that some employees respond better to individual rewards while others improve as attention is focused on team efforts and system shortcomings.[14]

In Chapter 4 Richard C. Kearney covers the important concepts and processes associated with traditional, adversarial union activities in local government; he also reports on an emerging trend called "interest-based bargaining," "getting to yes," or "win-win bargaining." This new approach acknowledge the interests of both sides—management and labor—in certain collective bargaining outcomes and seeks to turn the negotiations into a collaborative process.

In Chapter 5, the legal team of DiNome, Yaklin, Rosenbloom, and Angelo provide an inventory of the important laws regulating human resource management in local government. However, since statutory law and case law change constantly, they ask the public official to consult with legal counsel before making important personnel decisions. Likewise, Rosenbloom's analysis of the constitutional rights of public employees, as interpreted by the courts, clarifies day-to-day situations, but one can expect ongoing court tests over the public service model, which tries to reach a balance among the interests of the public employer, the government employee, and the public.

Cost pressures and the increasingly diverse needs of the workforce have affected pay and benefits, as described by N. Joseph Cayer and Will Volk in Chapter 6. Traditionally, governmental pay policies ensured predictable annual pay raises in the form of step increases or cost-of-living adjustments. A switch to pay for performance created morale problems, and some employers settled on a mix of pay raises that included both across-the-board pay increases and individual pay adjustments based on performance. To the traditional benefits of health insurance plans and pension plans, employers are adding wellness programs, employee assistance programs, and help with child and elder care; and to keep costs under control, employers are increasingly offering these benefits in the form of cafeteria plans and requiring employees to share in the cost.

While work organizations are being reinvented and reengineered, employers have to make it clear that certain boundaries should not be crossed. Chapter 7 presents findings from research conducted by Don A. Cozzetto, Theodore B. Pedeliski, Jonathan Tompkins, and Jonathan West, which indicate that incivility and even violence in the workplace are increasing. Accordingly, employers have to insist that threatening behavior on the job is unacceptable and have to communicate clear standards of conduct in word and deed.

Chapter 8, written by Charles Wise, Brian Clemow, Saranne Murray, Lisa Bingham, Arlene Angelo, and Siegrun Fox Freyss, shows that things can go wrong in two ways: a problem economy or a problem employee. When revenues decline drastically, employers have to cut costs or raise taxes. Cost cutting affects employees and is fraught with conflict. Concerning problem employees, the authors point out that the traditional method has been to punish the wrongdoer. Due process rights, however, circumscribe the disciplinary steps the employer can take, and the just cause doctrine requires the employer to have strong evidence before dismissing an employee. Case law is continually testing and balancing the rights of employers versus the rights of employees, making it impossible to provide clear guidance for users of this handbook. Regional preferences have created organizational and political traditions that require different personnel policies to improve performance. This handbook therefore avoids prescribing one-size-fits-all human resource management procedures. Instead, users are encouraged to assess the particular political and organizational culture of their jurisdictions and to adapt the personnel practices to local circumstances. For instance, an organization suffering from poorly performing patronage appointees might be advised to introduce the merit system or to strengthen it if it is legally in place. On the other hand, a jurisdiction suffering from rigidities caused by a formal merit system might consider reducing that system's influence.

In general, this guide provides access to essential human resource management techniques accumulated over the last one hundred years and currently considered the best practices in public personnel administration. In many instances, managers can use the tools to guide their personnel decisions. Where additional technical assistance is needed, the user is referred to the online supplement, which contains information on technical assistance and relevant consulting services—organizations that track trends and help public administrators stay current and make proactive human resource management decisions.

Notes

1 Siegrun Fox Freyss, "Local Government Operations and Human Resource Policies: Trends and Transformations," in *The Municipal Year Book 2004* (Washington, D.C.: ICMA, 2004), 17–25.

2 Siegrun F. Fox, "Professional Norms and Actual Practices in Local Personnel Administration: A Status Report," *Review of Public Personnel Administration* 13 (Spring 1993): 5–28.

3 The terms *merit system* and *civil service* are used interchangeably in this chapter. For a discussion of the historical development of the two terms, see Paul P. Van Riper, *History of the United States Civil Service* (Evanston, Ill.: Row, Peterson, 1958) 8, 99, 207; and Frederick C. Mosher, *Democracy and the Public Service*, 2nd ed. (New York: Oxford University Press, 1982), 145–150.

4 Freyss, "Local Government Operations."

5 Emanuel S. Savas and Sigmund G. Ginsburg, "The Civil Service: A Meritless System?" *The Public Interest* 32 (Summer 1973): 70–86.

6 Frances Gottfried, *The Merit System and Municipal Civil Service* (New York: Greenwood Press, 1988).

7 U.S. Civil Service Commission, Bureau of Intergovernmental Personnel Programs (BIPP), *The Intergovernmental Personnel Act: Improving Public Service Delivery*, BIPP 150-80 (Washington, D.C.: BIPP, Civil Service Commission, January 1978).

8 For more on the historical development of professional personnel standards in local government, see Fox, "Professional Norms and Actual Practices."

9 National Association of Schools of Public Affairs and Administration (NASPAA), "History," naspaa.org/about_naspaa/about/history.asp (accessed April 27, 2009).

10 National Civic League, "Our History," ncl.org/about/history.htm (accessed April 27, 2009).

11 David Arnold, *ICMA: A Chronicle of Service, July 7, 1986.*

12 ICMA, "Who We Are," icma.org/main/bc.asp?bcid = 656&hsid = 1&ssid1 = 17&ssid2 = 22 (accessed April 27, 2009).

13 International Public Management Association for Human Resources (IPMA-HR), ipma-hr.org (accessed April 27, 2009).

14 W. Edwards Deming, *Out of the Crisis* (Cambridge, Mass.: MIT Press, 1982), 110.

1

Planning and Paying for Work Done

Jonathan Tompkins, Aleksandra Stapczynski, and Siegrun Fox Freyss

Work positions are the basic building blocks of organizational life. As we explore new and better ways of organizing people to carry out the work of government, positions still provide the foundation. Teamwork is encouraged more today than in the past, duties are often defined more broadly, managers are increasingly given more discretion in assigning work, and yet all these changes take for granted the existence of relatively well-defined positions.

Once the duties and qualifications are determined, individuals with the required knowledge, skills, and abilities (KSAs) can be selected to fill vacant positions, new recruits can be oriented to their jobs, and their base pay can be set according to the demands that their jobs place on them. How to plan, define, classify, and evaluate positions, and how to compensate employees on the basis of work performed, are the subjects of Chapter 1.

Internal strategic planning

Guiding principle

- Operating departments must have a clear understanding of their strategic objectives.

Challenges

- Preventing political dissension, information overload, and simple inertia from reducing productivity
- In small jurisdictions where chief administrative officers (CAOs) and department heads may lack essential staff support, developing a results-oriented culture without using a formal planning process

Personnel management is most effective when policies, procedures, and daily decisions are linked systematically to the organization's mission. For this reason, our discussion of personnel management begins with strategic planning, a management tool for enhancing organizational performance by keeping everyone focused on mission-oriented goals and objectives.

Strategic planning is a systematic process undertaken by governments and their operating departments to establish why they exist, where they want to go, and how they will get there. It results in a strategic plan outlining future goals and objectives and the strategies for achieving them. There are two general types of strategic planning. *External* strategic planning aims at resolving political issues in the larger community. It involves representatives from a diverse range of community groups, as well as elected and appointed officials, and it addresses such issues as growth management, downtown renewal, waste disposal, and recycling programs. *Internal* strategic planning, by contrast, takes an inward look at local government programs and services. Its primary purpose is to improve organizational performance. For this reason, internal planning is more likely than external planning to address issues relating to personnel management. Such issues include developing human resources, purchasing a new management information system, and rewriting administrative procedures. Although input is solicited from many stakeholders, participation is usually limited to key line and staff officers. Elected officials should be included in the process or at least given the option to participate.

In practice, internal strategic planning can vary from a formal and institutionalized annual ritual to an informal and unscheduled set of discussions about organizational priorities. Whether formal or informal, internal strategic planning typically involves the following elements:

- Defining the organization's mission
- Conducting environmental analyses
- Identifying and prioritizing critical issues
- Establishing goals, objectives, and strategies
- Assigning responsibility and monitoring progress.

Exhibit 1–1 provides examples of a mission statement and goals, objectives, and strategies as typically set forth in a strategic plan.[1] Another approach is the SWOT (*s*trengths, *w*eaknesses, *o*pportunities, and *t*hreats) analysis developed by researchers at the Harvard Business School. As shown in Exhibit 1–2, the model includes

Exhibit 1-1 Elements of a strategic plan

Key element	Example
Mission statement	The mission of the city fire department is to ensure the safety of the community by responding to fires and other emergencies quickly, doing all it can to save lives and property, and educating the public about fire prevention.
Critical issue	Growing population; insufficient and aging firefighting equipment
Goal	Upgrade fire department equipment and operations to meet growing fire service demand
Objective	Obtain voter approval of bond issue in November election for new fire station in recently annexed area and for new firefighting equipment for all fire stations in the city
Strategies	Collect data on current capacity and response times to support argument that a new station and equipment is in the public's best interest
	Assess and prioritize future fire station locations; identify most cost-efficient equipment available for purchase

Exhibit 1-2   SWOT analysis: Following the Harvard model of strategic planning

		Internal	
		Strengths	*Weaknesses*
External	*Opportunities*	What are the strong points of the organization that enable it to make use of external opportunities?	What are the weak points of the organization that make it difficult to benefit from external opportunities?
	Threats	Does the internal strength make it possible for the organization to deal with external threats?	Do internal weaknesses make it difficult for the organization to deal with external threats?

an internal analysis of strengths and weaknesses, and an environmental scan to determine how the organization can make optimal use of opportunities and limit threats.[2]

As a management tool, internal strategic planning has much to recommend it. Personnel decisions are most effective when they are linked strategically to the organization's mission. A well-defined sense of mission, and the goals and objectives that flow from it, provide a point of departure for establishing personnel policies and practices and a baseline for judging their effectiveness. In addition, strategic planning provides opportunities to adapt successfully to changing external conditions. The environment in which agencies operate is a dynamic one. For example, the economic downturn in the early years of the new millennium produced a period of declining government revenues and a series of fiscal crises that, among other things, greatly constrained the ability of local governments to attract and retain the best available workers.[3] The more recent recession that began in late 2007 may have the opposite effect, at least among professionals and managers. Because the downturn is hitting private sector employees severely, those workers may be willing to accept lower governmental pay to obtain higher job security. Needless to say, the wise use of scarce resources is more important today than ever before. Similarly, increased globalization means that local governments require a more sophisticated, multicultural, and better educated workforce than ever before. In short, strategic planning provides both a means of establishing the essential linkages between administrative decisions and the attainment of institutional objectives, and a means of adapting successfully to a constantly changing environment.

Considerations relating to personnel management enter into the strategic planning process at two points.[4] First, current personnel capabilities must be taken into account when organizational goals and objectives and the strategies for achieving them are being identified. For example, employees may not possess the mix of KSAs required to achieve desired goals, or the state of morale may be so low that employees resist undertaking new strategic initiatives; KSAs may have to be enhanced and morale and motivation improved first. Consequently, human capacity building may emerge during deliberations as a critical issue in its own right. Strategies for building human capacity may include targeted recruitment efforts, more attractive benefit packages, job-specific training courses, employee development and internal promotion programs, and increased opportunities for employee involvement in decision making.

Second, once the strategic plan has been approved and communicated throughout the organization, personnel policies and practices must be adjusted so that they are consistent with and contribute to strategic objectives. Many areas of personnel management are likely to be affected by strategic planning. For example, an impending labor shortage may lead administrators to identify a 20 percent reduction in turnover as a strategic objective. Administrators at all levels must then review existing personnel policies and practices, and scrutinize their daily personnel decisions to ensure that they are contributing to reduced turnover. New personnel policies or programs may need to be developed; existing ones may need to be modified. Similarly, some jobs may need to be eliminated and others created or redesigned. Such changes must be adopted not because a neighboring jurisdiction is making them but because they clearly advance specific goals and objectives.

The city manager or county administrator has an important role to play at both of these points. In larger jurisdictions, the personnel director is generally responsible for offering advice during strategic deliberations, analyzing the gaps between current capabilities and projected needs, and adjusting personnel policies and practices as needed to implement the strategic plan. In smaller jurisdictions, however, the CAO and department heads have to undertake these responsibilities without the support of a personnel staff. How to do so successfully is one of the challenges of strategic planning.

Strategic planning is heavily process oriented and therefore difficult to sustain. Causes of system breakdown include political discord among participants, a sense of overload caused by tackling too many issues and collecting too much information, and the inertia that results when the process is perceived as a meaningless annual ritual. The remedy for each of these ills is sustained leadership. The CAO, department head, or someone designated as a "process champion" must have the time, energy, and will to keep the process on track. Administrators should not undertake strategic planning unless they are fully committed to its underlying purposes and prepared to exercise the necessary leadership. The latter includes a willingness to wade into the political fray to help participants reach agreement among competing priorities, restrict the goal-setting process to only a handful of issues each year, and hold designated individuals accountable for producing results.

Deciding whether to engage in strategic planning is neither easy nor simple. Strategic planning is deliberately designed to produce change, and change causes disruptions and generates resistance. Once the decision is made to proceed, the planning process must be carefully managed. If too much is attempted too quickly, or if there is insufficient leadership, the process will collapse of its own weight. Internal strategic planning is often easier to sustain at the department level, where there is more likely to be a unified sense of mission, fewer players, and less discord.

Another challenge is how to obtain the advantages of strategic planning in small jurisdictions where CAOs and department heads may lack the support staff required to undertake a time-consuming and labor-intensive process. In fact, strategic planning need not entail a formal and institutionalized process at all. A formal, sequential process of the kind described in textbooks can actually drive out strategic thinking. What is important is that administrators at all levels think and act strategically by linking what they do to the results they wish to achieve. Administrators can often obtain good results simply by encouraging strategic analysis at staff meetings, over lunch, and in the hallways. In short, they can develop a results-oriented culture by challenging each organizational unit to define its mission, identify the issues affecting it, establish strategic goals and objectives, and align personnel policies and practices with those goals and objectives.[5]

Succession planning

Guiding principles

- Succession planning should be an underlying theme in many personnel decisions, from hiring, developing, and promoting to encouraging or discouraging retirements.
- Good mentoring efforts should be acknowledged in performance evaluations.

Challenges

- Making succession planning a part of the organizational culture
- Not playing favorites; giving all potentially qualified employees a chance to move up into executive positions

A special form of workforce planning is succession planning. It acknowledges the aging and impending retirement of large numbers of midlevel and senior managers from the baby boom generation; it highlights the threat of a substantial brain drain and loss of institutional memory in the next few years; and it recognizes that the transition can be managed successfully. The following steps are recommended:

- Collecting data about the age of employees in key positions
- Conducting a job analysis of key positions (if not already done), including new competencies needed
- Identifying junior employees—perhaps as early as at the initial hiring—with the potential for promotion
- Providing developmental opportunities to build a pipeline of candidates who can move up into midlevel and senior positions as vacancies occur.

If there is no personnel department to do this work, the CAO or department heads may have to make succession planning a part of their assignments. Development opportunities can mean

- Giving special projects to junior employees to help them grow and gain more expertise
- Encouraging younger employees to seek more education and get an advanced degree. (Chapter 3 discusses developmental opportunities in greater detail.)

Employers can market their organizations as good places to work because of promotion opportunities. Strong candidates, who tend to have a longer time horizon and thus seek growth potential and career advancement opportunities, are likely to look at workplaces with this consideration in mind.

Research indicates that top executives need to take certain steps for succession planning to be effective: specifically, they should

- Embrace succession planning and make it part of the organizational culture
- Ensure that all key personnel receive training in how to mentor, coach, and create job shadowing opportunities
- Ensure that performance evaluation forms for middle and upper management include a section on successful mentoring and coaching
- Use a pay-for-performance system to reward a strong record on mentoring.

Although succession planning is primarily associated with the impending retirement of the baby boom generation,[6] vacancies in critical positions can occur for other reasons, such as a sudden illness or death. It is therefore recommended that institutional memory and unique KSAs be shared as they are acquired so as to broaden the pool of competent individuals who can assume the responsibilities in case of a sudden vacancy.[7]

The personnel function and the budget

Guiding principle

■ Adequate funding to attract, develop, motivate, and retain good employees is fundamental to organizational effectiveness.

Challenges

■ Giving personnel-related budget requests the time, attention, and level of priority they deserve in the budgeting process

■ Finding the optimal balance between economy and effectiveness

■ Providing managers with optimal flexibility in managing their budgets

The primary responsibility of personnel management is to attract, develop, motivate, and retain high-performing employees. How this responsibility is carried out changes continuously as administrators respond to internal needs and external opportunities and constraints. For instance, a labor shortage in a particular field may indicate the need both for more aggressive recruitment efforts to attract highly capable employees and for higher financial incentives to retain the best in the current workforce. Moreover, the growing complexity of employment law and labor relations increases the need to seek technical assistance from outside personnel specialists. When such demands cannot be accomplished with available resources, administrators must ask for budgetary enhancements.

Charged with balancing their budgets with limited revenues, city councils and county commissions tend to view requests for personnel-related enhancements with considerable skepticism. Since the budget allocates scarce resources to departments and programs, it is rarely possible to fund all budgetary requests. And since pay and benefits often represent more than 70 percent of the operating budget, proposed enhancements can have an enormous impact on the budget.[8] In the end, councils and commissions may opt for economy over promised gains in effectiveness. Nonetheless, because the ability to attract, develop, motivate, and retain good employees is a fundamental determinant of organizational effectiveness, local government administrators must see to it that strategic initiatives relating to personnel are given the time, attention, and level of priority they deserve during budgetary deliberations.

Three strategies are now being used by local governments to improve their ability to build an effective workforce. The greatest break from tradition is to allow managers to move funds between expense categories or line items as needed as long as their unit's overall budget allocation is not exceeded. Within that same constraint, ceilings on the number of full-time equivalent employees are also eliminated, allowing managers to spend payroll dollars as they wish. In a few jurisdictions, managers are also allowed to carry money saved into the next fiscal year. This strategy assumes that managers need greater flexibility in managing their budgets if they are to achieve their goals and that they can be trusted to use that authority responsibly. Advocates argue that the line-item budgets introduced in the early 1900s to tightly control expenditures are no longer needed because management is much more professionalized and because accounting and auditing procedures are much more sophisticated.[9] Nonetheless, delegating greater spending authority to line managers is likely to remain a tough sell.

A second strategy is to encourage performance budgeting by requiring department heads to tie their budgetary requests to their strategic plans. Several state and local jurisdictions have embraced this strategy since the Government Performance and Results Act of 1993 mandated it for federal agencies.[10] In general, this strategy requires departments to adopt strategic plans that specify clear goals and objectives and the indicators to be used to measure progress in achieving them. Departmental budget requests are then justified in terms of their respective contributions to attaining performance goals. If managers are also delegated greater spending authority, they can be held accountable not simply for staying within their budgets but for producing results as well. Being able to establish linkages between expenditures and strategic goals also improves the ability of administrators to obtain approval of their budgetary requests from economy-minded councils, boards, and commissions. This strategy is still in its experimental stages, however. Some administrators remain concerned that if their performance goals are not met, their budgets may be reduced.

A third, and more modest, strategy is to search for economies within traditional line-item budgets to free up funds for other purposes. If a department can reduce its payroll costs, it can then ask for authority to spend the funds for training, pay for performance, or other capacity-building uses. Many jurisdictions, for example, are economizing by reducing their core complement of full-time employees and relying more on temporary, part-time, and contract employees to handle seasonal or occasional work assignments. The challenge lies in reducing the size of the permanent workforce without overburdening employees, undermining morale, or harming service delivery.

In the final analysis, a jurisdiction's budget is the clearest indicator of the government's priorities and policy objectives. Administrators who understand the centrality of employees to organizational performance must be willing to wade into the political fray to support those personnel-related requests that clearly contribute to organizational performance. They should also explore the merits of allowing managers greater flexibility in managing their budgets. For elected and appointed officials alike, the search for an optimal balance between economy and effectiveness never ends.

Organization of the personnel function

Guiding principle

- Human resource policies should provide a solid organizational foundation but must also be open to new developments.

Challenges

- Establishing a proper degree of formalization and centralization while preserving needed flexibility
- Using merit systems to enhance personnel management without paralyzing it

The structure of the personnel system—whether it is organized on a merit or patronage basis, is highly centralized or decentralized, or is governed by detailed rules or general policies—clearly affects organizational performance. Highly rule-bound and centralized systems, for example, tend to reduce managerial flexibility, protect marginal employees, and rob the organization of the ability to adapt to changing circumstances. Conversely, a jurisdiction without any system at all—without a central personnel office or a uniform set of policies and procedures—may find it very difficult to ensure that all departments are complying with employment law and managing personnel effectively. Some degree of central policy direction and staff support is desirable to create stability and ensure fairness, but not so much that line managers lose the discretion and flexibility they need to carry out their missions. The challenge for administrators is to determine the level of formalization and centralization that is most appropriate to their circumstances and strategic objectives.

Organizational charts of the individual administrative units are useful in schematically placing positions and ranking them in job classes. When the organizational practice seems to defy the neat arrangement of functions and ranking of positions, however, the need for a more consistent classification scheme may become obvious. Sometimes it may be appropriate to revise the organizational chart of the whole administration to clarify alterations in the relationship between line and staff agencies.

Although personnel systems exist theoretically to support the attainment of organizational objectives, those objectives are constantly changing while the personnel systems are often fixed in statute, charter, or ordinance and are therefore slow to change. Personnel systems are also designed to achieve values other than organizational effectiveness. These values include due process, equal opportunity, and the elimination of patronage. In many locales, centralized merit systems continue to constrain managerial discretion long after the need for them has passed. Only recently have they begun to give way to organizational structures designed to empower managers rather than control them. While administrators in small cities and counties are probably not subject to the constraints of highly centralized merit systems, understanding their characteristics is useful for those wishing to design a personnel system that enhances performance while simultaneously protecting due process, equal opportunity, and merit.

The civil service system

A civil service system consists of a body of rules and regulations governing non-elected employees, including the methods of selecting, promoting, rewarding, and disciplining. Most of these rules and regulations pertain to the *career service*—those employees who competed for positions with the intent of making the civil service their career. A few rules and regulations pertain to other employees who may be dismissed at will.

The term *merit system* refers to any civil service system organized specifically to protect and promote merit principles. These principles include

- Competition for government jobs that is open to everyone
- Selection of civil servants based on their qualifications for office
- Protection of civil servants from partisan coercion
- Protection of civil servants from arbitrary treatment in all personnel actions.

These principles apply to employees in the career service but not to political appointees.

For nearly one hundred years the federal Civil Service Act of 1883 provided the model for state and local governments in establishing merit systems. The structural characteristics of the classic merit system are as follows:

A semi-independent commission with policy-making, administrative, and adjudicatory powers   The first merit systems placed control of the personnel system outside of the executive chain of command because reformers feared that CAOs would not be able to resist pressures to award jobs on the basis of patronage. Although the scope of a commission's authority varies from one jurisdiction to the next, commissions are generally responsible for establishing personnel policies, administering employment examinations, and enforcing and adjudicating merit rules.

Centralized testing   The primary task of traditional civil service commissions is to develop competitive exams for each major occupational category, administer and score exams, and rank eligible applicants in order of their scores. The purpose is to remove all but the final hiring decision from the hands of line managers so that civil servants cannot be appointed on the basis of patronage, nepotism, or other forms of favoritism. Although commissions today often share personnel duties with administrators, centralized testing remains a key feature of formal merit systems.

A high degree of formalization   Formalization refers to the written rules, regulations, and procedures that characterize organizational life. In traditional merit systems, personnel decisions are governed by highly detailed rules and regulations, complex administrative procedures, and seemingly endless paperwork. These are viewed as necessary to guard against every possible abuse of authority as well as to promote values such as pay equity, administrative efficiency, equal opportunity, and due process. Emphasis in formal merit systems is placed on regulating compliance with rules rather than on facilitating organizational performance.

Once viewed as a solution, formal merit systems are now viewed as the problem.[11] When combined with line-item budgets and rigid position classification systems, formal merit systems prevent managers from hiring employees in a timely manner and deny them the flexibility they need to reassign duties and pay employees on the basis of their level of performance. These constraints make it difficult to fulfill the essential personnel functions of attracting, developing, motivating, and retaining highly qualified employees.

The executive personnel office

The federal Civil Service Reform Act of 1978 introduced a model that had already been implemented by many local governments in the 1960s. An executive personnel office, directly accountable to the chief executive, was given the responsibility to administer personnel policies. In about half of local jurisdictions, civil service commissions have been retained in an advisory or adjudicatory capacity.[12]

Small jurisdictions do not need a separate personnel department. The CAO or department heads make most personnel decisions. Nevertheless, such jurisdictions are advised to have a centrally directed, merit-based personnel system. A uniform set of personnel policies helps to ensure that all department administrators are complying with merit principles and the requirements of employment law, that all employees are being treated fairly and consistently, and that all personnel decisions are contributing to the effective management of human resources.

Choosing the best approach

Because each government is unique in terms of its circumstances and strategic objectives, it is impossible to prescribe a single approach for organizing the personnel function. It is possible, however, to offer a few generalizations. First, if patronage and other forms of favoritism are clearly undermining the integrity and performance of civil servants, administrators should look for ways to institutionalize merit principles. Second, small jurisdictions without a professionally staffed personnel office and without uniform personnel policies should weigh the advantages of an organized personnel system against the costs. Third, if a decision is made to establish a personnel office, its primary mission should be defined in terms of service and technical assistance rather than administrative control. Fourth, the personnel office should seek to guide and direct line managers through broad policy statements rather than through detailed rules and regulations.

Generally speaking, it is better to hold managers accountable for their actions after the fact than to constrain their actions in advance through narrowly defined rules. Too often the rules and regulations imposed by a central office dictate courses of action that are not fully appropriate to situations at the department level. Being closer to the situation at hand, managers are better positioned to decide how to appraise, discipline, counsel, and reward employees. Finally, CAOs should explore the potential advantages of relaxing the constraints imposed by rigid line-item budgets, personnel ceilings, classification schemes, and pay systems.

Classification and compensation

Guiding principles

- Employees doing similar work should receive comparable pay.
- Variations in pay must be based on significant differences in responsibilities and required KSAs, and on the salaries paid by other employers in the marketplace.
- The process for classifying and evaluating the relative worth of positions must be fair.

Challenges

- Determining whether to contract with a consultant or to develop a comprehensive classification and pay plan in-house
- Complying with state and federal statutes concerning the design and implementation of classification and pay systems
- Educating employees about the process and purpose of a classification and compensation study
- Maintaining the integrity of a comprehensive classification and pay system

Employees are a local government's most important asset and one of its most significant expenditure items. Today, local governments need to develop aggressive pay policies to compete successfully for well-qualified employees. Compensation levels must be high enough to attract a strong applicant pool and retain the best among the current employees. Morale is enhanced when workers know that their pay is keeping up with or exceeding the prevailing market rate. The adoption of a classification and compensation system is thus an essential prerequisite for a well-managed, comprehensive personnel system.

A classification and compensation system is a process for reviewing job duties, classifying positions on the basis of uniform criteria, and allocating positions to salary grades that reflect their relative worth and market value. Such a system lays the foundation for many other parts of the larger personnel system: establishing qualifications for recruitment, testing, and selection; establishing lines of authority and areas of responsibility; and providing a basis for defining standards of work performed. A classification and pay plan that is continuously maintained results in

- Fewer requests for reclassifications
- Fewer grievances arising out of disputed job requirements
- Fewer pay inequities and morale problems
- Reduced subjectivity in pay determination
- A solid basis for evaluating work performance.

An effective classification and pay system will attract, reward, and retain qualified personnel.

One of the most fundamental and difficult tasks in the management of any personnel system is determining the comparative worth of each position. Employees are acutely aware of what they are paid, how much responsibility they are assigned, and the "status" of their positions in relation to most other positions. Perceived inequities in pay or status can be a source of intense dissatisfaction, which translates into declining morale, lost productivity, absenteeism, grievances, and chronic bickering.

Because individuals are unable to judge fairly the worth of their jobs compared with that of higher-paying jobs, and because measuring the relative worth of different jobs is not an exact science, it is impossible to eliminate all feelings among employees that inequities exist in the pay system. However, every effort must be made to achieve fair job groupings and an equitable pay level for all positions in the workforce. ICMA, the International Public Management Association for Human Resources (IPMA-HR), and other technical service providers, some of which are described in the online supplement to this text, conduct salary surveys to help governments determine appropriate pay levels. (The online supplement provides links to resources, including to the U.S. Office of Personnel Management [OPM]; for more on pay policies, see Chapter 6.)

Classification and pay studies are regularly commissioned by local governments to reexamine the responsibilities and work performed by the jurisdiction's workforce. Each position is classified and assigned a pay grade according to its relative economic worth in relation to the marketplace and all other similarly classified positions within the workforce. Finally, competitive compensation schedules are developed and proposed for the positions studied.

The local government should hire an outside consultant to conduct these studies for two important reasons. First, it is imperative that the entire process not only *be* objective but also *be perceived* as objective, and a consultant approaches the task with greater objectivity than can any member of the staff. A city manager or county administrator is inevitably perceived, especially by those not pleased with the results, as having a bias, no matter how professional the effort. Any staff member will have difficulty separating personalities from positions. But an experienced outside consultant specializing in this area comes in with little knowledge of the personalities and can better focus on the positions to be classified.

Second, developing a classification and pay system takes hundreds of hours. It is neither practical nor cost-effective for personnel directors or administrators to undertake such studies, given all their other responsibilities.

The initial implementation of the recommended classification and pay plan is not the final step in achieving pay equity and creating a motivated workforce. Rather, it establishes a uniform point of departure from which to regularly review classification and pay decisions, and to ensure that those decisions accurately reflect the jurisdiction's current service needs and the performance of employees. Each new position added and all subsequent adjustments made to the plan need to be consistent with the original plan to maintain its integrity and relevance.

Major public employers have their job classification and pay plans posted online, which provides a good starting point for comparison purposes. (See, for instance, the class specification list and salary list of Los Angeles County at dhrdcap.co.la .ca.us/classspec/index.cfm.) The federal government is a good source as well. It created the standard occupational classification, which federal agencies have to use and state and local governments "are strongly encouraged to use."[13]

Developing the classification and pay plan guiding principles

- A thorough job analysis provides the basis for valid job descriptions, testing procedures, and performance appraisals.
- Job descriptions must change as the specific requirements of the job change.
- Job classifications and pay scales must be updated regularly.

The following components represent the minimum scope of services that should be provided by a consultant hired to do a classification and pay plan.

Job analysis The initial step in the classification and pay study, job analysis is the process of systematically gathering and analyzing information about a job. Information is obtained about the nature of the work performed; the level of difficulty and complexity involved; the amount of responsibility inherent in the job; the physical and mental requirements; and the training, education, and/or experience needed to perform the job. Identifying the KSAs needed for a particular job is a critical element of job analysis. *Knowledge* refers to the information and concepts acquired through education and work experience. *Skills* are the manual and mental capabilities acquired through training and work experience. *Abilities* are the natural talents and aptitudes possessed by employees.

Various techniques may be used to collect the information for a job analysis. Desk audits can be conducted using questionnaires, interviews, work logs, or direct observation; the nature of the job determines which method to use. Direct observation, for instance, would be inappropriate for mostly mental work but has proven useful in assessing the amount of time employees claim to need for the completion of certain tasks.

Often, a combination of job analysis methods is used. For example, once the employee has completed a position analysis questionnaire (see Exhibit 1–3 for a sample excerpt), the immediate supervisor can review it and make appropriate comments. Next, interviews are conducted to clarify and augment the employee's questionnaire responses. New position descriptions are then drafted for each position. Employees and supervisors review the draft position descriptions and submit written comments. Final adjustments are then made.

Exhibit 1-3   Excerpt from a sample position analysis information sheet

POSITION ANALYSIS QUESTIONNAIRE

1.   **General Information**

Last Name: _____

First Name: _____

Official Job Title: _____

Usual Working Title _____

Department/Division: _____

Name & Title of your immediate supervisor _____

How many hours per week do you work (not including overtime)?   _____

What shift do you work (when do you begin and finish work)?   _____

How long have you held this position?   _____

How long have you worked for this municipality?   _____

2.   **Minimum Qualifications for Your Position**

A.   **Education**
What is the minimum level of education required for this position? (Check the level which applies.)

Elementary School Education   _____

High School Education (grades 9-12)   _____

Advanced Technical Education (which)   _____

College (indicate number of years)   _____

Bachelor's Degree required (which)   _____

Advanced Degree(s)   _____

B.   **Experience**
Please describe the type of experience needed to perform this job. Also indicate the minimum number of years and what type of experience is needed to perform this job.

C.   **Licenses/Certificates**
Are there any special licenses or certificates required to do this job?

© Human Resources Services, Inc. 2009

1

(continued)

Exhibit 1-3 Excerpt from a sample position analysis information sheet *(continued)*

D. **Special Knowledge/Abilities**
Please list any specialized knowledge or ability needed to perform this job.

3. **Communication/Contact with Others**

A. **The Public**
In a typical workday, how often do you deal with the public? (Check the one which applies.)

_____Constantly (the position is primarily one of public contact)

_____Frequently (more than half of the work is dealing with the public)

_____Seldom (usually do not deal directly with the public)

B. **Other Contacts**
In a typical workday, do you have contact with other individuals or outside organizations? Please list:

C. **Type of Contact**
Describe the type of contact you have with the public or others (by phone, in person, by writing, etc.)

4. **Supervision Received**

A. What kind of supervision do you receive regarding daily responsibilities? (i.e. oral, written, general suggestions, specific assignments, etc.)

Exhibit 1-3 Excerpt from a sample position analysis information sheet *(continued)*

B. Describe the level of supervision. (Check the appropriate answer.)

_____Hourly   _____Once per week
_____Twice per shift   _____Other (Please explain)
_____Once per shift   _____

[blank box]

5. **Errors**

If you make an error on the job, what are the *likely* consequences of that error? (Check all that apply.)

_____Personal injury/loss   _____Injuries to other employees

_____Delays or loss or service   _____Damages to buildings and/or equipment

_____Monetary loss   _____Legal ramifications

_____If necessary, please explain other consequences.

[blank box]

6. **Work Environment**

A. How much work time must you spend exposed to the following environmental conditions? (Show the amount of time by checking the appropriate box.)

	None	Up to 1/3	Up to 2/3	More than 2/3
Outdoor weather conditions				
Work in high, precarious places				
Work with toxic or caustic chemicals				
Fumes or airborne particles				
Extremes of heat/cold (not related to weather)				
Work near moving mechanical parts				
Risk of electrical shock				
Work with explosives				
Risk of radiation				
Vibration				

© Human Resources Services, Inc. 2009

3

Great care should be exercised in conducting a job analysis because it provides the foundation for many employment functions, such as

- Planning future personnel needs
- Restructuring positions
- Writing the job description and job announcement
- Designing the selection tests
- Determining compensation
- Evaluating performance
- Determining training needs
- Deciding on reassignments, demotions, or terminations.

To ensure their full cooperation with the job analysis, employees have to receive advance information about the techniques used and the purpose of the desk audit. Morale problems may arise if employees mistake the job evaluation for a performance evaluation.

Job descriptions The results of the job analysis are used to develop a job description, which is a written, summary statement of the job (see Exhibit 1–4). If job descriptions already exist, they should be reviewed and updated to ensure that they accurately describe the major tasks of the job, as well as the physical and mental requirements and the minimum qualifications needed to perform job duties. Updated job descriptions are essential to recruitment, selection, and work planning. Accurate documentation of the physical and mental requirements of the job also assists the jurisdiction in complying with the requirements of the Americans with Disabilities Act (ADA).

Job descriptions define the position, delineate levels of responsibility, and provide sufficient examples of major duties to establish the scope of the position. They are not intended to be either all-inclusive or restrictive. They do not provide a complete list of job tasks. It is neither necessary nor advisable to attempt to write an exhaustive position description; all that is necessary are enough examples of duties to present a clear picture of the essential work performed and the responsibilities of the position. Some jurisdictions use job descriptions that describe cross sections of responsibilities of several individuals holding similar positions and thus do not describe one position exactly. These general job descriptions can serve as the foundations for more specific descriptions.

The ADA requires job descriptions to identify the essential functions of a job. Exhibit 1–4 provides explanations of why job descriptions need to distinguish between essential and inessential duties and how to do it. First, the opening statement of purpose relates the job to the overall mission of government by underscoring the job's role in supporting the efforts of all other departments. Second, the description identifies the "essential functions" of the job, thereby communicating that these functions must be performed by all job incumbents with or without reasonable accommodation. Last, it includes legal disclaimers at the beginning of the "Essential Functions" section and again at the end of the description to discourage employees from arguing that related work assignments are "not in my job description." (For more on essential job functions, see Exhibit 1–5 on pages 19–20.)

Exhibit 1-4   Sample job description

ADMINISTRATIVE ASSISTANT

Position purpose

The purpose of this position is to perform moderately complex to complex secretarial, clerical, recordkeeping, and accounting and office duties under general direction of a municipal administrator, department/division head, program adviser, or other administrative employee. Work requires initiative and independent judgment in the application of prescribed policies, procedures, and methods. Performs all other related work as required.

Essential functions

(The essential functions or duties listed below and on attachments are intended only as illustrations of the various types of work that may be performed. The omission of specific statements of duties does not exclude them from the position if the work is similar, related, or a logical assignment to the position.)

Provides customer service by answering questions both in person or by telephone; provides information relative to departmental procedures; refers individuals to appropriate source as required.

Performs all general clerical duties including, but not limited to, word processing, making copies, filing, data entry, answering the telephone, and opening and delivering mail. Maintains records and files. Drafts correspondence. Schedules and maintains appointments.

Maintains department-related data, gathers information, and ensures the timely preparation and coordination of a variety of reports.

Prepares all necessary administrative documents to ensure the timely and accurate processing of the department's business functions including, but not limited, to requisitions, invoices, budget transfers, and supporting documentation. May maintain records and spreadsheets and documents related to purchases, payroll, budgets, checking, and other accounts and other miscellaneous administrative functions; prepares a variety of reports as directed.

Maintains internal control system for monitoring, ordering, and distributing materials and office supplies. Tracks the department budget.

May perform moderately complex accounting and bookkeeping tasks. May perform registrations and collect related fees.

Handles all office traffic; general public, employees, vendors, etc. Assists each with individual situation as needed.

Administrative assistant is cross-trained to assume the duties of another secretary when workload is heavy or the secretary is absent. Performs similar or related work as required.

Supervision

Complexity: Performs a variety of secretarial and clerical duties requiring the exercise of judgment in relation to problems, and the ability to work with numerous interruptions; is generally responsible for carrying through entire functions of considerable importance to the office.

(continued)

Independent action: Works under general direction generally setting own daily work plan and choosing between appropriate courses of action to achieve defined objectives; refers only unusual cases to supervisor.

Supervisory responsibility: May supervise interns or temporary help.

Work environment

Work is performed in an office environment. Majority of work is performed in a moderately noisy work environment, with frequent interruptions.

Operates computer, printer, telephone, copier, facsimile machine, and all other standard office equipment.

Makes frequent contact with department staff. Contacts are typically with the public, vendors, and outside agencies and organizations.

Maintains significant amount of department-oriented confidential information.

Errors could result in confusion and delay and adverse public relations.

Recommended minimum qualifications

Education, training, and experience
High school education and one to two years of experience in general clerical and secretarial work, with school experience preferred; or any equivalent combination of education, training, and experience.

Knowledge, ability, and skill
Knowledge: General knowledge of office procedures, practices, and terminology. Working knowledge of departmental operations. Knowledge of the operation of computer software applications. Knowledge of the operations of the pertinent municipal department/division/area helpful.

Ability: Ability to communicate effectively with staff, students, and the public. Ability to compose correspondence. Ability to follow oral and written instructions accurately. Ability to organize and prioritize multiple tasks. Must be able to operate a personal computer and display intermediate skill when using software programs for word processing, database, spreadsheets, and other software as required by the position. Ability to multitask.

Skill: Skill in using personal computers, popular word processing, database, accounting and spreadsheet applications. Good customer service skills. Skill in all of the above listed tools and equipment. Skill in typing and notetaking.

Physical requirements
(The physical demands described here are representative of those that must be met by an employee to successfully perform the essential functions of this job. Reasonable accommodations may be made to enable individuals with disabilities to perform the essential functions.)

While performing the duties of this job, the employee is frequently required to sit, communicate, or hear; occasionally required to walk, must be able to handle, or feel objects, tools, or controls; and reach with hands and arms. The employee must occasionally lift and/or move objects weighing up to 15 pounds. Vision and hearing at or correctable to normal ranges. This position requires the ability to operate a keyboard and calculator at efficient speed.

(This job description does not constitute an employment agreement between the employer and employee and is subject to change by the employer as the needs of the employer and requirements of the job change.)

Exhibit 1-5 Essential functions of a job

Overview

The Americans with Disabilities Act (ADA) prohibits employment discrimination against qualified individuals with disabilities. The ADA defines an "individual with a disability" as one who has a physical or mental impairment that substantially limits one or more major life activities; has a record of such an impairment; or is regarded as having such an impairment. A "qualified individual with a disability" is "an individual with a disability who meets the skill, experience, education, and other job-related requirements of a position held or desired, and who, with or without reasonable accommodation, can perform the essential functions of a job."

Many individuals with disabilities are qualified to perform all of the essential functions of jobs. However, if an individual with a disability who is otherwise qualified cannot perform one or more essential functions because of his/her disability, the supervisor must consider if there are modifications or adjustments (a "reasonable accommodation") that would help the individual to satisfactorily perform such functions.

Although it may be essential that a function be performed, it is often not essential that it be performed in a specific way. An individual with a disability may be able to satisfactorily perform an essential function if an accommodation enables him/her to use a different method and the accommodation does not impose an undue hardship for the organization. Consequently, supervisors should consider results or outcomes to be accomplished with respect to essential functions instead of the manner in which such functions are performed.

Definitions of essential and marginal functions

A. *Essential functions.* Job duties which a position incumbent must be able to satisfactorily perform, unaided or with the assistance of a reasonable accommodation.

B. *Marginal functions.* Job duties which may be reassigned to other employees without interfering with performance of the essential functions. These functions are marginal only to individuals who are unable to perform them with or without reasonable accommodations because of a covered disability.

Steps in identifying essential functions

A. Develop a preliminary list of job functions in order of importance, grouping related functions together whenever possible. Consider the following while developing this list:
- The results or outcomes to be accomplished instead of the manner in which functions are to be performed or have been performed in the past
- Avoid describing functions with verbs or adjectives which specify how they are performed.
- List processes or methods used only when critical to satisfactory job performance.
- The physical and mental demands which are required and any environmental factors which may have an impact on successful performance of the job
- List only those physical, mental, and environmental factors critical to satisfactory job performance.
- The knowledge, skills, and abilities (KSAs) critical to performance of the functions as well as specific education, training, and experience necessary for successful performance of the job

B. Review each job function with the following questions in mind. If "yes" can be answered to any of these questions, the function is essential; otherwise, the function is marginal.
- Does the position exist to perform the function?
- Would removing the function fundamentally change the job?
- Is the function critical to overall performance of the job?
- Is there a limited number of other employees available to perform the function or among whom the function may be distributed?
- Is the function highly specialized and is the position incumbent hired for special expertise or ability to perform the function?

(continued)

C. A small percentage of time spent performing a specific function does not necessarily make the function marginal.

D. If unsure whether or not a job function should be considered essential, categorize the function as marginal.

E. If a position description does not distinguish between essential and marginal functions, all functions listed are considered essential.

Essential functions checklist

☐ Develop a preliminary list of job functions in order of importance, grouping related functions together whenever possible.

☐ Review each job function with the following questions in mind:

- Does the position exist to perform the function?
- Would removing the function fundamentally change the job?
- Is the function critical to overall performance of the job?
- Is there a limited number of other employees available to perform the function or among whom the function may be distributed?
- Is the function highly specialized and is the position incumbent hired for special expertise or ability to perform the function?

☐ If "yes" can be answered to any of these questions, include the function in the Essential Functions section of the position description; otherwise, include the function in the Marginal Functions section.

☐ Categorize a function as marginal if unsure whether or not it can be considered essential.

Source: Human Resources Services, Inc.

Exhibit 1-6 Position rating summary sheet and sample grade determination chart

Position classification title: Assistant librarian

Factors	Final ratings	Final points
Physical environment	1	5
Knowledge, training, and education	5	75
Intellectual skills and effort	5	34
Physical skills and effort	2	20
Experience	4	40
Interactions with others	4	20
Confidentiality	2	10
Occupational risks	1	5
Complexity	3	15
Supervision received	4	30
Supervision given	2	10
Supervision scope	3	20
Judgment and initiative	4	60
Accountability	4	30
Total points		**374**

Score range	Grade
200–224	1
225–249	2
250–274	3
275–299	4
300–324	5
325–349	6
350–374	7
375–399	8
400–424	9
425–449	10

Source: Human Resources Services, Inc.

Position classification Positions, or groups of positions bearing the same job title, are next compared and contrasted with other positions in the workforce to determine their comparative worth. A standard method for evaluating job worth should be used. In point ranking, which is one of the most common methods, point values are assigned to key job factors. Below are some widely accepted compensable factors:

- Physical environment
- Basic knowledge, training, and education
- Intellectual skills and effort
- Physical skills and effort
- Experience
- Interaction with others
- Confidentiality
- Occupational risks
- Complexity
- Supervision received
- Supervision given
- Supervision scope
- Judgment and initiative
- Accountability

Rating scales are developed for each of these factors, and the position is assigned points according to the ratings given to it for each factor. The total accumulation of points for all fourteen factors determines how each position is ranked in contrast to all others within the study.

Exhibit 1–6 presents a rating sheet for the position of assistant librarian. The rating scale for knowledge, training, and education, for example, contains six possible levels (not shown). The assistant librarian position was rated at the fifth level for this factor—a level corresponding to 75 points. In total, the position received 374 points. Once the rating process is complete, positions can be assigned to specific pay grades according to their total scores, with higher-scoring jobs being placed in higher pay grades. With 374 points, the assistant librarian position would be assigned to Grade 7 and receive the corresponding salary. An example of a completed classification plan is shown in Exhibit 1–7. Note that this sample plan, with our assistant librarian at Grade 7, has a total of sixteen grades.

A job rating or job evaluation is not the same as a performance evaluation. The position, not the incumbent, is evaluated, assigned points, and slotted into an appropriate pay grade. While much of the work involved in evaluating job worth is subjective, the point ranking process increases the uniformity and objectivity in the application of judgment about positions and the grouping of positions.

Salary/wage survey The position classification process determines the relative worth of positions on the basis of job content, without regard to the marketplace. The next step, then, is to collect and analyze salary and wage data from comparable employers to ensure that employees are offered competitive salaries and wages.

In most cases, selections of "comparable" employers are based on

- Geographic location
- Population

Exhibit 1-7 Sample classification plan

Grades 1, 2, 3
No positions included in study

Grade 4
Council on Aging van driver

Grade 5
Animal control officer

Grade 6
Council on Aging outreach worker
Civilian communications officer

Grade 7
Assistant librarian

Grade 8
Finance commission administrator
Solid-waste coordinator/facilities manager

Grade 9
Assistant recreation director
Public health nurse
Youth services counselor

Grade 10
Assistant town treasurer

Grade 11
Computer systems analyst
Economic development officer
GIS specialist

Grade 12
Council on Aging director
Director of youth and family services
Health director
Recreation director
Library director
Superintendent of wastewater collection system
Human resource director
Town planner

Grade 13
Building commissioner
Superintendent of highways/cemeteries/trees
Town accountant

Grade 14
Deputy fire chief
Police lieutenant/administration
Police lieutenant/operations
Town engineer

Grade 15
Finance director
Chief information officer

Grade 16
Director of public works
Fire chief
Police chief

Source: Human Resources Services, Inc.

- Comparative wealth factors
- Form of government
- Number of employees
- Comparability of classifications.

For some positions, it may be desirable to survey other types of organizations, such as state government, a local university, or a private company. The data collected from these surveys are then used to ensure that the compensation plan as a whole, and the pay grades within it, provide pay that is fair relative to what other employers are paying. If competitive wages and salaries are not offered, recruitment and retention problems quickly arise.

Two examples of compensation plans are provided here. The plan shown in Exhibit 1–8 identifies ten fixed salary steps within each grade. Employees may be advanced through these salary steps on the basis of longevity, acquisition of additional knowledge and skills, job performance, or some combination of these factors. The plan shown in Exhibit 1–9 identifies only the salary range for each grade. This system allows greater flexibility in setting pay because employees are

Exhibit 1-8 Step-based compensation plan

The first three grades of a step-based compensation plan are shown here; the complete plan provides for fourteen grades. The percentage in the far left-hand column shows the increase in salary at Step 1 compared to Step 1 of the previous grade.

Proposed compensation plan, fiscal year

Base = 16,500.00
Hrs/Wk = 37.50

%	Grade		*Step 1*	*Step 2*	*Step 3*	*Step 4*	*Step 5*	*Step 6*	*Step 7*	*Step 8*	*Step 9*	*Step 10*
-	1	Hourly	8.43	8.77	9.12	9.48	9.86	10.26	10.67	11.09	11.54	12.00
		Weekly	316.09	328.74	341.89	355.56	369.78	384.57	399.96	415.96	432.59	449.90
		Annual	16,500.00	17,160.00	17,846.40	18,560.26	19,302.67	20,074.77	20,877.76	21,712.87	22,581.39	23,484.64
5	2	Hourly	8.85	9.20	9.57	9.96	10.35	10.77	11.20	11.65	12.11	12.60
		Weekly	331.90	345.17	358.98	373.34	388.27	403.80	419.96	436.75	454.22	472.39
		Annual	17,325.00	18,018.00	18,738.72	19,488.27	20,267.80	21,078.51	21,921.65	22,798.52	23,710.46	24,658.88
5	3	Hourly	9.29	9.66	10.05	10.45	10.87	11.31	11.76	12.23	12.72	13.23
		Weekly	348.49	362.43	376.93	392.01	407.69	423.99	440.95	458.59	476.93	496.01
		Annual	18,191.25	18,918.90	19,675.66	20,462.68	21,281.19	22,132.44	23,017.73	23,938.44	24,895.98	25,891.82

Exhibit 1-9 Salary range-based compensation plan

The first three grades of a salary range-based compensation plan are shown; the complete plan provides for ten grades. The percentage in the far left-hand column shows the increase in minimum salary compared to the minimum salary of the previous grade.

Proposed compensation plan, fiscal year

Base = 25,000.00

Percentage increase	Grade		Minimum	Midpoint	Maximum
8	1	Annual	25,000.00	30,291.00	35,582.80
8	2	Annual	27,000.00	32,715.00	38,429.42
11	3	Annual	29,160.00	35,332.00	41,503.77

not advanced through the same set of predetermined steps. One employee might be awarded a 2 percent pay increase and a second employee given a 4 percent increase, depending on their respective levels of performance or their acquisition of additional competencies.

A more sophisticated compensation plan seeks to achieve a "best fit" between the internal worth of the job, as determined through the point-ranking method, and the external worth of the job, as determined through salary and wage surveys. The pay range for each pay grade is established in a way that maximizes this best fit. Sometimes, however, it is necessary to place a job in a higher grade than is indicated by its internal worth. This occurs, for example, when there is a high demand for individuals trained in certain occupations, and applicants can therefore command higher salaries in the marketplace. While an occasional position may fall outside the grade range, a compensation plan that places too many positions outside the grade range means that the grade structure is inappropriate. Comparisons are made among the organization's current salaries to determine whether any positions have been incorrectly assigned. These positions are further reviewed to determine whether all job factors have been evaluated appropriately.

Plan administration   The final report provided by the consultant should include a methodology and rating manual enabling the city or county to maintain and update the classification and compensation plan. The consultant should also provide technical assistance for implementing the plan, showing, for example, how to negotiate with labor unions within the context of the study, how to develop a financial strategy for implementing the plan, and how to handle employee appeals regarding classification and reclassification decisions.

The classification plan should be reviewed as a whole every five years and continuously for individual positions or groups of positions when the job content changes dramatically. A position is reclassified only when there is a significant change in its requirements, in which case a new job description must be prepared. Reclassifications should not be used as a way to increase compensation when an employee has achieved the maximum step in the salary grade, nor should they be used as a way to reward an individual for special skills or for length of service to the community.

Alternative approaches to classification and pay

The traditional, standardized approach to classification and pay was developed in the early 1900s as a control mechanism to prevent managers from arbitrarily determining the pay received by individual employees. But while this method has proven highly successful in ensuring internal and external pay equity, it has three disadvantages.

First, it creates procedural hurdles that discourage managers from attempting to reclassify those positions that truly deserve to be reclassified. Second, it discourages managers from assigning tasks involving levels of difficulty and complexity greater than those represented by the job's current pay grade assignment; this in turn prevents employees from developing their talents to the fullest extent and robs the organization of the ability to benefit from those talents. Third, it precludes managers from rewarding employees for superior levels of performance, at least where a pay-for-performance system is not built on top of the traditional pay structure.

What these disadvantages amount to are the morale problems that are created when two individuals are given equal pay for equal work without regard to their level of performance. Where managers do not have the flexibility to reward individual performance, they are tempted to reclassify positions simply to secure a pay raise for a superior employee, something that undermines the integrity of the classification and pay plan. Consequently, a few jurisdictions are now experimenting with alternatives to the traditional approach. (For more on new compensation models, see *The New Compensation Model*, IQ Report, ICMA, December 1998.)

Broadbanding   Broadbanding replaces several pay grades with a few broad salary bands. The pay range for each band is much greater than that for a traditional pay grade. For example, if the federal government adopted the framework shown in Exhibit 1–10, the pay range for an engineering position could be as broad as ten traditional pay grades. No longer must the employee seek out a different line of work, possibly a managerial position, to secure economic advancement. Broad-

Exhibit 1-10 Framework for broadbanding

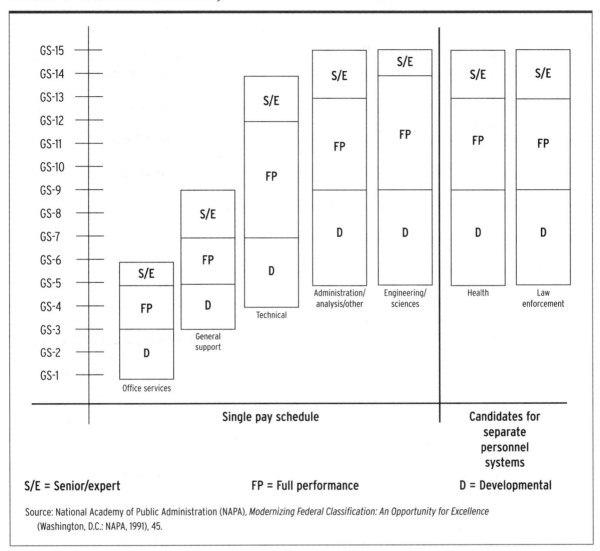

Source: National Academy of Public Administration (NAPA), *Modernizing Federal Classification: An Opportunity for Excellence* (Washington, D.C.: NAPA, 1991), 45.

banding allows employees to continue to move up in salary on the basis of higher levels of performance, competence, and training, and the supervisor is once again delegated responsibility for setting individual pay levels, at least within broad salary ranges. Emphasis is shifted from paying employees according to the jobs they hold to paying them according to their unique abilities and contributions. The success of such systems depends, however, on the use of an objective, widely accepted method for assessing individual performance and competence. (For more on broadbanding, see Chapters 3 and 6.)

Market-based pay A few jurisdictions, especially smaller ones, are now adopting market-based pay systems. Such a system skips the position classification step and assigns jobs to pay grades solely on the basis of marketplace comparisons. Its advantage is that the pay plan can be adjusted each year according to changes in labor supply and demand. Its disadvantage is that the pay plan may ignore significant differences in difficulty and complexity between jobs, paying them the same simply because they are paid the same in the marketplace. This system may also incorporate into the pay plan certain biases, such as race or sex, that might be inherent in external wage and salary structures.

Pay for performance If the traditional classification and pay process described above is used to determine each position's base pay, employers may construct a pay-for-performance system on top of this foundation. Such a system enables managers to compensate employees according to their individual levels of performance in addition to job content and labor market comparisons. (The issue of pay for performance is treated more fully in Chapter 3.)

Implementing the classification and pay plan

Once the classification and pay plan is complete, it is up to the city or county manager to see that it is properly implemented and maintained. Successful implementation will require equitable judgments made in a consistent and objective manner.

Initial step placements for current employees The placement of two or more positions (jobs) in a certain pay grade represents a judgment that those positions should be compensated comparably within the range provided for that grade. The organization can define steps or subranges within the grade in order to distinguish among employees (not positions) on the basis of established criteria. These criteria may include job performance, special abilities, experience, and other factors determined by the organization. For example, an applicant with several years of relevant work experience may be hired at a higher salary step than an applicant with very little experience, even though both hold positions in the same grade.

Red-circled positions and salaries Sometimes a pay exception is needed to recruit employees for positions where labor demand is high. An employee compensated at a level above the grade's maximum—known as a red-circled employee—can be held at that status in one of two ways until retirement or termination. First, a red-circled employee can be held at the current rate of pay until the pay plan is adjusted by cost-of-living increases to equal or exceed the employee's actual compensation. Alternatively, a red-circled employee may be treated like any other employee at the top of the grade. He or she may be eligible for cost-of-living adjustments (COLAs) but not step increases. It is recommended that a single administrative policy be adopted and subsequently applied in all cases.

Cost-of-living adjustments vs. step increases A COLA is different from a step increase. A COLA is intended to recognize a general rise in the costs for goods and services experienced by almost everyone. Each year the organization should determine an appropriate percentage COLA and apply that increase across the entire salary schedule. This raises the compensation rates for the entire salary schedule equal to changes in the cost of living. By contrast, a step increase and/or movement from minimum to maximum within the grade range recognizes factors worthy of compensation increases above the COLA. Such factors include superior performance and additional competence. This distinction between COLAs and step increases is crucial for the successful implementation of classification and compensation plans in the public sector.

Union issues Public organizations should consider the implications of a current or potential unionized workforce in developing classification and pay structures. As a representative of employees, the union has a legitimate interest in the introduction of new or revised salary structures. It can also influence the implementation of the new systems either positively or negatively, depending on the degree to which it supports them. Therefore, it is highly desirable that management work with the union in the development, introduction, and administration of salary structures. Agreement on management's rights, expectations about the process, and related issues must be made clear at the outset of the negotiations.

Legislation Construction and application of the classification and compensation plan are also affected by both federal and state legislation, particularly the Fair Labor Standards Act (FLSA). The act sets minimum wage, overtime pay, equal pay, child labor, and record-keeping requirements. The minimum wage provisions require employers to pay at least a minimum hourly rate regardless of the worth of the job. When the minimum is increased by law, the wages of those who already earn above the minimum may be adjusted accordingly.

Overtime pay is also regulated. For every nonexempt job, employers must pay one and a half times the employee's regular rate for all hours worked over 40 per week. Executive, professional, administrative, and other highly paid workers are exempt from the overtime provisions, although the burden falls on the employer to justify the exemption on the basis of the employee's actual duties, not just the job title.

FLSA requirements are highly complex and difficult to observe in practice. A thorough knowledge of the act is critically important to successful pay administration.

Complying with the requirements of Title VII of the Civil Rights Act (1964, amended in 1972) and the Equal Pay Act (1963) virtually requires a well-designed, clearly nondiscriminatory classification and compensation system. The haphazard pay arrangements adopted prior to the passage of these acts usually cannot withstand legal scrutiny today. Specific application of these statutes to the job review process means that jobs involving equal duties and responsibilities must be evaluated similarly and without discrimination based on race, color, age, sex, religion, national origin, handicap, or veteran status. Under the Equal Pay Act, for example, male and female dispatchers must be paid the same if their seniority and merit match, but a female dispatcher and male firefighter could be paid different rates. However, if a jurisdiction has committed itself to a comparable worth wage policy, a dispatcher and firefighter with the same number of points under a job evaluation point system must be paid comparably, with adjustments possible for differences in seniority and merit. (See Chapter 6 for more information on pay policies.)

Benefits There is another side to the compensation equation. Wages and salaries in most cases count for most of the compensation package, but without other benefits, government employers would find it very difficult to attract and retain qualified personnel. The benefit survey is usually part and parcel of the pay survey; in making marketplace comparisons, analysts must calculate the cost of the total wage and benefits package. However, benefits may also be viewed as a separate function to illustrate how the various pieces of the classification and compensation subsystems interrelate.

Benefits are generally spelled out in the personnel ordinance or bylaws or in any accompanying set of personnel rules and regulations. As is the case with salary adjustments, most determinations of benefits for union employees are made at the bargaining table for each unit, often resulting in a multiplicity of personnel policies.

Among the more common benefits are holidays, vacations, sick leave and sick leave "buy backs," personal and professional leave, educational incentive pay, medical and life insurance, workers' compensation or injury leave, pensions, unemployment compensation, shift differential pay, and skill pay. Some of these are required by state statute, but most are variable and hinge upon collective bargaining agreements. They can typically add 30 to 35 percent to the employee's base wage. (See Chapter 6 for more information on benefits.)

Interns and part-time, temporary, and contract employees

Employing civil servants on a full-time career basis allows the local government to attract and retain individuals who are highly skilled and committed. But the benefits of a large, full-time staff to cover every possible contingency must be balanced against the need to use personnel efficiently and economically.

It is especially difficult to staff a work unit efficiently where workloads vary significantly because of seasonal fluctuations or the infrequent need for special expertise. At times a department may have more employees than it actually needs, and at other times it may have too few. To allow for greater flexibility in staffing and to hold the line on payroll costs, private firms are relying increasingly on part-time, temporary, and contract employees. Although there are greater constraints on the use of such employees in the public sector, this strategy can nonetheless produce important cost savings, especially in smaller jurisdictions. Administrators initiate this strategy by distinguishing between core jobs that departments cannot do without and contingent jobs that can be filled using part-time, temporary, and contract employees. The challenge lies in reducing the size of the permanent workforce without overburdening the remaining full-time employees, undermining morale, or harming service delivery.

Interns Internship programs can be win-win situations in that the student gains needed work experience while the jurisdiction gets a temporary employee at relatively low cost. High school or undergraduate students often are expected to volunteer their time while graduate students usually receive a stipend. Interns can work part time during the academic year or full time during the summer break. They can be used successfully as management trainees and professional assistants or for short-term projects for which permanent staff is unavailable. However, staff time needs to be devoted to the intern's selection, supervision, and evaluation.

Part-time employees A part-time job is one in which the incumbent works fewer than thirty-five hours a week. It is generally viewed as a permanent position, but one in which the duties do not require a full-time worker. Part-time jobs not only reduce payroll costs but also allow departments to attract qualified workers who wish to devote more time to their families or to other personal needs. It is possible, although not always easy, to fill positions at any level and in any occupation on a part-time basis. State laws and local ordinances govern the conditions of employment for part-time employees, including their benefit levels. Those part-time employees who are employed at least half time often receive the same benefits as full-time workers, except that benefits such as sick leave and vacations are prorated. Where part-time employees are entitled to full benefits, the cost savings from employing them are somewhat reduced.

Caution

■ Be sure to ascertain what laws and ordinances govern the selection and employment of part-time, temporary, and contract employees in your jurisdiction.

■ Be careful not to reduce the permanent workforce to a point where the remaining employees are burdened with excessive workloads.

■ Develop expertise in contract administration before using the services of contract employees routinely.

Job sharing   Two half-time jobs may be created out of one full-time position. Job sharers perform all tasks jointly or divide them between themselves according to their skills, abilities, and interests. They also divide the workweek between themselves, choosing either to work half days or to work full days on an alternating basis. Because there are no cost savings inherent in job sharing (half-time workers, for example, are often entitled to full health insurance benefits), it is usually viewed as an alternative work schedule designed to attract qualified workers who for personal reasons do not wish to work full time.

Job sharing entails some potential difficulties. Although research has shown that job-sharing arrangements can increase job satisfaction and productivity, it has also shown that job sharers need to be highly compatible so that they can work well together with no loss in continuity.[14] Additionally, supervisors must determine how to evaluate work performance and what level of benefits to provide to job sharers.

A unique kind of job sharing often used by small cities and counties is to share employees between two or more jurisdictions through a contractual agreement that establishes the duties the employee is to perform for each jurisdiction, as well as the pay and benefits to be provided by each jurisdiction. For example, public health nurses, nutritionists, inspectors, and veterinarians are often shared among counties in rural areas. It is a useful means for securing the services of skilled individuals who wish to be employed full time but without incurring the full cost of employing them.

Temporary employees   A temporary worker is employed, generally on a full-time basis, for only a limited period of time. Substantial cost savings are possible by employing temporary employees to work on special, short-term projects or to handle workloads that are unusually high at certain times of year. Budgets often contain a line for such contingencies. Temporary employees are typically hired for low-paying, relatively unskilled positions because most people in technical, professional, and administrative career paths seek permanent positions. Although the use of temporary employees allows tax dollars to be used more efficiently, it tends to deny long-term employment opportunities to those with fewer skills. In addition, although temporary workers are easier to employ because they are not subject to the same competitive selection requirements as permanent employees, their use nonetheless entails considerable paperwork when waves of temps are constantly being hired and rehired.

A related cost-saving strategy is to hire temporary employees to fill vacant permanent positions for as long as the law allows. Money is saved because temporary employees are generally paid less, are denied COLAs, and are not entitled to insurance benefits. However, because this strategy is generally viewed as an abuse of employment authority, as well as an unjust practice from the employee's perspective, hiring temporary employees to fill permanent positions is usually regulated by state law. In many states, for example, temporaries can be hired only for a limited length of time and without the possibility of being continuously rehired.

Contract employees A contract employee is a temporary worker who contracts to provide a specific service or product by a specified date. It is an option used when individuals with specialized skills are needed for a relatively short period of time. It is often less expensive, for example, to hire consultants to accomplish special tasks than to maintain a permanent in-house staff to perform the same duties.

However, the use of contract employees is not without its difficulties. Controlling the performance of such individuals must be accomplished through contract compliance rather than direct supervision. There is the very real possibility of fraudulent claims for expenses, abuse of authority, or nonperformance that not only undermines mission attainment but also creates unneeded political shock waves. Unless contracts are carefully written and diligently enforced, the work performed may cost the agency more in the long run than if it were performed by in-house employees.

Some local governments contract out entire functions to a private employer. Money may be saved, for example, by hiring security guards who are paid lower salaries and benefits through a private employer. These savings may be offset, however, by a lower level of service and commitment.

Work teams

Guiding principles

- Work teams can improve performance when the work is complex and a variety of skills and experience is needed.
- The work to be done or the problem to be resolved determines the appropriate work team.
- Work team leaders and members need training before and during the change to team management.
- Hiring procedures should assess an applicant's ability to work in teams.

Challenges

- Making sure that the team approach is perceived by employees as a capacity-building innovation, not a temporary fad
- Identifying the work processes that will benefit from a team approach
- Encouraging executive and supervisory personnel to trust their employees and to switch from a top-down management approach to a mentoring and coaching role
- Helping employees accept the new organizational culture and increased responsibilities
- Adjusting personnel policies to reflect and reinforce the new organizational principles

Position-based personnel systems tend to discourage teamwork. Work is compartmentalized into sets of specialized tasks and assigned to individual workers. Each employee is held accountable for performing only those duties described in his or her position description. To early personnel theorists, this seemed highly efficient.

From their perspective, the idea of assigning broad responsibilities to groups of employees invited confusion, duplication of effort, and the abdication of individual responsibility. Today, however, there are compelling reasons to encourage team-work, and more flexible classification and pay systems may be needed to facilitate the shift toward team-based organizational structures.

Work teams are groups of employees who collaborate with one another to achieve common goals and objectives. When fully implemented, the team concept represents an alternative to the traditional top-down, hierarchical approach to decision making. In structural terms, decision making becomes much more horizontal as teams at all levels, composed of individuals from several levels and even from different units, bring their combined resources to bear on complex problems relating to core work processes. The synergy resulting from group collaboration has been shown to produce greater innovativeness, creativity, and risk taking.[15]

Establishing work teams is a deliberate strategy to increase employee involvement in decision making and problem solving. It is premised on the belief that those closest to work-related problems are best qualified and situated to analyze and resolve them. Advocates of team-based organizations believe that the tasks of government are now so complex, the amount of information to be assimilated so overwhelming, and the pace of change so great that decisions can no longer be made effectively by omniscient administrators at the top of the organizational pyramid. Nor can they be made effectively by specialists working in isolation. Ordinary employees are much better educated than in the past, and the use of teams, according to advocates, not only improves decision making and problem solving but also allows a fuller and wiser use of human potential. This occurs as individuals with unique talents and specialized knowledge are charged with working together to improve core work processes. Empowering workers in this way not only keeps everyone focused on their common mission but also increases motivation, morale, and commitment, and leads to a higher level of performance.

Teams and decision making

The kinds of teams now in use may be differentiated by their purpose, organizational structure, and the degree to which they hold decision-making authority.

Problem-solving teams A problem-solving team is a semipermanent group of five to twelve workers within a particular work unit who meet one to two hours each week to discuss their problems and make recommendations regarding needed changes. Problem-solving teams can be established in various functional areas and charged with continuously improving work processes and product or service quality. Experience with this type of team effort suggests that participation in decision making is not sufficient by itself to increase motivation, morale, and commitment. Managers must be willing to work closely with these teams and to implement recommended changes whenever possible. If recommendations are unwarranted or cannot be implemented, managers must be willing to offer team members full and frank explanations.

Special-purpose teams A special-purpose team is a temporary team of five to twelve members established for a specific purpose, such as redesigning a work process, introducing a new technology, investigating a work-related problem, or resolving labor-management difficulties. It is often called a cross-functional team when members are drawn from various units of the organization to resolve problems that cross departmental lines.

Self-directed teams   A self-directed team is a permanent team of workers that is fully responsible for a particular work function or process. The defining characteristic of this type of team is that workers manage themselves rather than receive direction and control from a work supervisor. The team is delegated an unusually broad scope of decision-making authority and is held accountable for producing positive results. Team members typically schedule their own work, set their own goals, select and train new members, appraise and reward their team's performance, and cross-train so that they can perform each other's tasks. As responsibility and decision-making authority are passed to self-directed teams, fewer middle managers and supervisors are needed. This type of team is based on the idea that those who do the work are the experts and that enormous gains in work performance and product quality can be had by empowering them to take charge of their own work situations.

Self-directed work teams are not widely used in the public sector. Unlike the other types, which can be adopted without changing the basic structure or culture of the organization, self-directed teams require fundamentally different structures and cultures. They aim to achieve a flatter organization in which operational decisions are no longer made by managers and first-line supervisors; those individuals must be willing to relinquish control, delegate authority, and take on new roles as facilitators and coaches. The success of this concept also requires the identification of concrete measures by which the group's performance, as well as each individual's contribution, can be evaluated and rewarded, something that is often difficult in the public sector.

Nonetheless, it is a concept worth investigating. Self-directed road maintenance teams, for example, might be given responsibility for the repair and maintenance of roads in specific geographical areas. The concept tends to work best where there is a distinct work process or geographical area over which a team can exercise meaningful control. Conversely, it works less well where stakes are high and decisions must be made quickly, such as in police, fire, and emergency units; where employees tend to work in isolation, such as accountants and building inspectors; and where employees see very little personal value in assuming additional responsibility, such as clerical workers performing highly routine duties.

Prerequisites for team success

Although research has documented the benefits of working in teams, these benefits do not come automatically. First, many employees are initially uncomfortable with assuming more responsibility, and supervisors are generally uncomfortable with relinquishing control. A high degree of trust must be built into the organizational culture if teamwork is to succeed. It then takes time for teams to trust that they will be allowed to make mistakes and for managers to trust that they will not be called on the carpet every time one of their teams makes unwanted headlines.

Second, moving toward a team-based organization requires considerable investment in training. Team members require training in interpersonal communication and problem-solving skills; team leaders require training in how to keep meetings on track; and managers require training in coaching and facilitating skills. Third, a team-oriented culture must be sustained by a clear set of norms that state, for example, that scapegoating or placing individual goals ahead of team goals is unacceptable. Fourth, information must be shared to a much greater degree than in position-based personnel systems. Full and complete information is needed for those at the bottom of the organizational pyramid to make informed decisions. The characteristics of effective and ineffective teams are summarized in Exhibit 1–11.

The team concept provides administrators with additional options for structuring work. Problem-solving and self-directed work teams are relatively permanent features, whereas the special-purpose teams are temporary and ad hoc in nature. All three involve the delegation of authority downward in the organization, with problem-solving teams requiring the least delegation and self-directed work teams the most. With the recent concern for quality, all three are typically charged with making continuous improvements to products or services and with satisfying the needs of customers or clients.

Although teamwork has been shown to produce greater innovation, risk taking, and productivity, team-based organizations require fundamental shifts in philosophy, attitude, and skills among managers and employees alike. Leadership practices, job descriptions, classification and pay systems, and career advancement policies may also have to be adjusted to support the team concept. Finally, upper management must be very strongly committed to the team concept if the inevitable resistance to change and fear of losing control is to be overcome.

Unions also have to be convinced that the team approach will benefit their members. This generally means that wages should be raised when rank-and-file employees increase their value to the organization through cross-training and

Exhibit 1-11   Effective and ineffective teams

Characteristics of effective teams	Characteristics of ineffective teams
Clearly defined, mutually set team goals	Unclear/unrealistic goals
Understanding and commitment to team goals	Low commitment
Atmosphere that encourages discussion by all members; free expression of feelings and ideas	Conformity; lack of disagreement
Prompt distribution of minutes of meetings to team members; informed members	Failure to share information
Good communication with each other and with other parts of the organization	Formal or structured communication; cautious or guarded communication
Efficient task-oriented meetings that focus on improvement	Poor meetings
Problem solving rather than blaming	Reliance on criticism
Frequent performance feedback	Lack of individual feedback; performance evaluation based on personal opinion
Cooperation and support of members	Competition among team members
Tolerance with emphasis on resolution	Failure to use team members' talents
Support of management	Low confidence in others
Decisions based on facts, not emotions or personalities	One-person decisions
Pride and spirit	Negative attitudes

Source: Adapted from Patricia A. Harris, *Total Quality Management: Strategies for Local Government* (Washington, D.C.: International City/County Management Association, 1993), 30.

by assuming management functions. Overall, traditionally adversarial labor-management relations have to be replaced with a more trusting work culture. Labor-management partnerships and interest-based bargaining are consensual methods of decision making promoted by the federal government through Executive Order 12871.[16]

Notes

1 For more information on strategic planning, see John M. Bryson, *Strategic Planning for Public and Nonprofit Organizations: A Guide to Strengthening and Sustaining Organizational Achievement* (San Francisco: Jossey-Bass, 1995); Gerald L. Gordon, *Strategic Planning for Local Government* (Washington, D.C.: ICMA, 1993).

2 Bryson, *Strategic Planning*, 30–31.

3 Penelope Lemov, "Deficit Deluge," *Governing* 15 (May 2002): 20–24.

4 Jonathan Tompkins, "Strategic Human Resources Management in Government," *Public Personnel Management* 31 (Spring 2002): 95–109.

5 For detailed information on workforce planning, see International Personnel Management Association (IPMA), *Workforce Planning Resource Guide for Public Sector Human Resource Professionals* (Washington, D.C.: IPMA, 2002); and U.S. Office of Personnel Management, Training and Management Assistance Web site at opm.gov/hrd/tma/.

6 U.S. General Accounting Office (GAO), *Senior Executive Service: Retirement Trends Underscore the Importance of Succession Planning* (Washington, D.C.: GAO, May 2000), 2–6, gao.gov/archive/2000/gg00113b.pdf (accessed April 8, 2009).

7 The how and why of succession planning have been extensively discussed in the professional literature. For instance, the entire winter 2004 issue of *Public Personnel Management* is devoted to workforce and succession planning. The online supplement to this book has links to governments and professional organizations that provide guidelines on how to do it and why it is essential for employers to do it.

8 Donald E. Klingner and John Nalbandian, *Public Personnel Management: Contexts and Strategies* (Upper Saddle River, N.J.: Prentice Hall, 1998), 70.

9 See David Osborne and Ted Gaebler, *Reinventing Government* (Reading, Mass.: Addison-Wesley, 1992).

10 Sunnyvale, California, was one of the first local governments to adopt performance budgeting.

11 National Commission on the State and Local Public Service, *Hard Truths/Tough Choices: An Agenda for State and Local Reform* (Albany, N.Y.: Nelson A. Rockefeller Institute of Government, 1993).

12 Siegrun F. Fox, "Professional Norms and Actual Practices in Local Personnel Administration: A Status Report," *Review of Public Personnel Administration* 13, no. 2 (Spring 1993): 5–28.

13 U.S. Office of Management and Budget, "Standard Occupational Classification (SOC)—Policy Committee's Recommendations for the 2010 SOC; Notice," *Federal Register* 73, no. 100 (May 22, 2008), 29930, bls.gov/soc/soc2010.pdf (accessed April 8, 2009).

14 Jon L. Pierce et al., *Alternative Work Schedules* (Boston: Allyn and Bacon, 1989).

15 Peter Mears, *Organization Teams* (Delray Beach, Fla.: St. Lucre Press, 1994), 3.

16 The National Performance Review (NPR), a project of the Clinton administration, provides information on ways to overcome an adversarial union culture and to implement teamwork. The NPR Web site has been archived at the University of North Texas and can be accessed at govinfo.library.unt.edu/npr/.

2

Recruiting for a High-Performance Workforce

Stephanie L. Witt, W. David Patton, and Siegrun Fox Freyss

The quality of any work organization depends on its people, and the best way to ensure excellence is to hire highly capable employees. The first step in hiring is to recruit well-qualified applicants, and the next step is to find the one person in the applicant pool who is the best match for the job. Careful selection procedures can help managers avoid personnel problems by weeding out applicants who are not capable or motivated. Yet the need for thoroughness in selection procedures must be balanced with the need for speed in hiring the most desirable candidate. This is because the favored candidate tends to be courted by several employers.

Standard procedures have been developed to select the best candidates for new or existing jobs. Federal and state laws, court rulings, local civil service ordinances,

---

Ethical standards of recruitment

The most important ethical standard to uphold in the process of recruitment is to maintain a fair and open hiring process. Your hiring process should be accessible to all qualified applicants, and the process should not be biased in favor of, or against, any particular candidates or types of candidates. In particular, it is critical that your hiring process be free of nepotism, which is defined as "favoritism shown or patronage granted to relatives, as in business."[1] Most jurisdictions have statutes or rules in place that limit the hiring of relatives. (These limitations are discussed more fully in Chapter 7.) Nepotism limitations can be complicated, especially in smaller jurisdictions where there is a smaller recruiting pool and familial relationships extend throughout the community. Some exceptions to a blanket nepotism rule may be appropriate; for example, a city employee whose employment precedes the election of a relative to the city council may be allowed to continue.[2] In general, however, most nepotism rules require that relatives not have immediate hiring, firing, or supervisory authority over other close relatives.[3]

1 *The American Heritage Dictionary of the English Language,* 4th ed. (Boston: Houghton Mifflin, 2000).
2 See, for example, Idaho's attorney general guidelines on application of the state nepotism statute: www2.state.id.us/ag/ops_guide_cert/1990/G101790.pdf.
3 See the Web site of Municipal Research and Services Center of Washington, mrsc.org/Subjects/Personnel/nepot.aspx, for a discussion of model nepotism ordinances in the state.

Equal employment opportunity and affirmative action

Equal employment opportunity (EEO)

Local governments with fifteen or more employees fall under Title VII of the 1964 Civil Rights Act, as amended in 1972, and Title I of the Americans with Disabilities Act (1990). All public employers are also included in the Age Discrimination in Employment Act (1967). Combined, these federal laws prohibit discrimination in all employment-related decisions, including recruiting, on the basis of race, color, religion, sex, national origin, physical disability, or age if the person is at least forty years old. Some states include sexual orientation. (See Chapter 5 for more on EEO compliance.)

Affirmative action

The conflict over affirmative action often fails to distinguish among three different legal foundations for affirmative action programs.

1. *Programs based on federal laws and regulations*
    1.1 Executive Order 11246, signed by President Lyndon Johnson in 1965, requires all federal contractors and subcontractors with fifty or more employees or with contracts worth $50,000 or more to maintain affirmative action plans.

    1.2 The Equal Employment Opportunity Act, passed by Congress in 1972, requires public employers to maintain records relevant to the determination of whether unlawful employment practices have been committed; in other words, governments have to collect data on the demographic composition of their workforce both up and down the ranks and horizontally across departments.

    1.3 In 1976 the Equal Employment Opportunity Commission issued a "Policy Statement on Affirmative Action Programs for State and Local Agencies" encouraging state and local jurisdictions to adopt affirmative action programs voluntarily. Two years later it issued the "Uniform Guidelines on Employee Selection Procedures."[1]

2. *Involuntary affirmative action programs*
    Some affirmative action programs have been imposed on employers by a consent decree or a court order. When courts have uncovered clearly unlawful employment practices and when the victims could be identified, judges have imposed affirmative action plans that may even contain mandatory hiring and promotion **quotas.** However, this remedy has to be of limited duration to keep "reverse discrimination" to a minimum. An important case is *U.S. v. Paradise* (1987). (See Chapter 5, p. 169 and fn 81.)

3. *Voluntary affirmative action programs*
    Most of the controversial affirmative action programs have been voluntary in nature. They may contain goals, but not quotas. On the surface, courts have not been consistent in their rulings. In *University of California Regents v. Bakke* (1978), the U.S. Supreme Court ruled that voluntary affirmative action programs could not result in **reverse discrimination.** In contrast, in *United Steelworkers of America v. Weber* (1979), the Court ruled in favor of a voluntary affirmative action training program. (See Chapter 5 for more on affirmative action compliance.)

Intended and unintended consequences of EEO and affirmative action

Equal employment opportunity is supposed to create a level playing field for all job applicants and employees.

Affirmative action programs are intended to speed up the process of achieving a level playing field in employment.

Reverse discrimination can happen when employers overshoot the aim of EEO and a level playing field. Supreme Court decisions have tried to clarify the tipping point when affirmative action policies become unlawful.

1   41 CFR 60-3; 60-3.13B; 60-3.17. The Equal Employment Opportunity Commission was created by the 1964 Civil Rights Act.

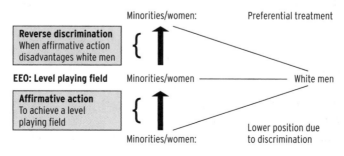

and collective bargaining agreements provide the legal protocol for many personnel decisions, including the hiring process. The most important principle to follow
throughout the hiring process is that all recruitment information, tests, and selection decisions must be based on the specific requirements of the job to be done.

The recruitment process ends with the employment contract (for executive-level
employees), employee orientation for the candidate selected, and notification of the
unsuccessful candidates. The purpose of the contract and orientation is to prevent
misunderstandings between the employer and the employee about job-related
expectations. Applicants not selected should be promptly notified about the decision not to hire them and thanked for applying.

A favorable public image can lighten the chore of filling vacant positions.
Careful and ongoing public relations efforts by the city or county can convey the
impression in the community that the government is a good place to work. However, word of mouth is also an important tool to attract talented job applicants, and
being a model employer is as important as image management.

Recruitment

Guiding principles

- All recruitment information, tests, and selection decisions must be based on the specific requirements of the job to be done.
- Communication with all applicants should be open and fair.
- Meticulous records should be kept of the application and selection documents.
- The confidentiality of the applicants' files should be safeguarded and access limited to employees with "a need to know."

Challenges

- Diversifying the workforce in all job classes and ranks
- Attracting highly qualified candidates

Recruitment is the process of finding the best people to fill vacancies in new or
existing jobs. Candidates can be recruited internally, from among eligible employees, or externally. The nature of the job determines the extent of the search. An
adequate recruitment effort is expensive: costs include money spent on advertising
and candidates' travel expenses, and staff time spent reviewing applicant files, and
interviewing and evaluating candidates. The more professional the job, the higher
the cost of recruiting and the longer it takes to fill the open position.

Who does what?

In the absence of a personnel director or personnel department, the chief executive
of the jurisdiction or the head of the department with the job opening will probably
handle recruitment. The person doing the recruitment should consult and work
with the direct supervisor of the available position since the supervisor is one of
the best sources for information about the knowledge, skills, and abilities (KSAs)
needed for the position. However, the supervisor's understanding of the opening
should be based on a carefully researched job analysis.

The chief administrative officer may wish to establish a search committee
including, if possible, the direct supervisor of the open position. The team can collaborate in writing the job description, reviewing applications, and interviewing the
finalists.

Recruitment may be handled either in-house by the city or outside by an external recruitment services agency. Many online recruitment services are available (e.g., usa.gov/Citizen/Topics/Work_for_the_Government.shtml), and many focus on recruiting diverse applicants. Search consultants can also be employed to help with national-level searches, although the price can be prohibitive for small communities.

Support staff is needed to handle the clerical aspects of the recruitment process. Recruitment files have to be compiled and stored securely to ensure their confidentiality and integrity. It is also appropriate to develop a recruitment information system so that applicants know where they stand in the selection process, and one person should be made responsible for communication with the candidates.

Regardless of who is in charge of the recruitment process, the equal employment opportunity (EEO)/affirmative action officer should be included in planning for the recruitment effort. If the city or county does not have such an officer, the legal counsel of the jurisdiction should review the process for compliance with legal requirements (also see Chapter 5).

The job announcement

The job announcement should include the essential job functions, qualifications for the job, location of the job, and pay range. The best tool with which to begin the recruitment process is a recently completed job analysis, since that describes the nature of the work, lists the essential job functions, states minimum education and experience required, indicates the physical demands of the job, and places the incumbent in the chain of command. (See Chapter 1 for more on job analysis.) From this analysis comes the job description, which is included in the announcement of the open position. The job description needs to be carefully thought through before its announcement because changes made during the selection phase may violate EEO principles. (Again, see Chapter 1 for more on the job description.)

It is important to ask for only those qualifications—KSAs, education, training, and experience—necessary for the successful performance of the job. For example, the employer should require a high school diploma only when it can be demonstrated that the duties of the job require such an education.[1] Basing the recruitment effort on the job analysis—that is, linking the selection criteria to the specific job tasks—avoids potential EEO/affirmative action problems later on.

The pay range for the new position should be based on several criteria, including the salary paid to the previous occupant, the qualifications needed for the job, and the relevant external labor market—local, regional, or national. (See Chapters 1 and 6 for more on determining the proper pay level.)

If the local government is doing an internal recruitment, the job announcement is posted for current employees to see. Many local governments also place job announcements on their Web sites.

Exhibit 2–1 shows a job announcement from the city of Santa Ana, California. Sample announcements can also be viewed at the Local Government Job Net site (govtjob.net) maintained by the Local Government Institute (lgi.org).

Internal vs. external recruiting

Early in the recruitment process, the hiring authority must decide whether to hire someone from inside or outside the organization. There are advantages and disadvantages to either strategy. Some positions are better suited to internal as opposed to external searches.

Exhibit 2-1 Sample job announcement

THE CITY OF SANTA ANA
Employment Opportunity

OUR PURPOSE: To provide quality service to enhance the safety, livability and prosperity of our community.

OUR VISION: To be the dynamic urban center of Orange County acclaimed for our: Investment in Children, Neighborhood Pride, Enriching Cultural Experiences, Appreciation of Diversity, Thriving Economic Climate, Quality Government Services and Leadership Among California's Cities.

POSITION: POLICE RECRUIT/BILINGUAL

SALARY: $4671 - $5678 Per Month**
Plus City-Paid Retirement
(5%/mo Bilingual Pay after completion of academy)

APPLY BY: OPEN UNTIL FURTHER NOTICE

OPEN COMPETITIVE EXAMINATION

ESSENTIAL FUNCTIONS INCLUDE BUT ARE NOT LIMITED TO:
Police Recruits are non-sworn (civilian) employees who attend a police academy to prepare for a career in law enforcement. Upon successful completion of this training, they are sworn in as Police Officers at a salary of $6470 - $9210 per month (includes base salary and pay additives). A comprehensive description of the essential functions of Police Officers is attached. Police Officers are key participants in a partnership of the City and community to identify and resolve crime problems affecting the quality of life of all residents. This community support and the diversity of cultures in Santa Ana make it an exciting and demanding place to work.

CHARACTERISTICS OF SUCCESSFUL PERFORMERS:
Successful Officers are characterized by the ability to make sound decisions which are based on fact, not emotion, quickly and repeatedly throughout the day. They demonstrate a strong sense of fairness and the ability to apply both the spirit and letter of the law within legal parameters of discretion. With a genuine concern for the safety of the community and the quality of life of its citizens, successful Police Officers are alert and ready to take action. They enjoy both working alone and as an integral part of a team effort. Ideal candidates are proficient in writing reports and handling paperwork and willingly work varying shifts, weekends and holidays.

REQUIREMENTS:
All applicants must meet all requirements defined by P.O.S.T. and those listed on the attached sheet. **Additionally, applicants must be fluent in both English and any one of the following languages: Spanish, Vietnamese, Samoan, Hmong, Korean, Cambodian or Farsi.**

NOTE: Individuals who have applied within the last six months and failed any testing component (excluding the physical agility examination and bilingual oral fluency examination) are not eligible to reapply for six months after the date on which they failed that component. For individuals who failed the psychological evaluation, the waiting period for reapplying is one year.

SELECTION:
A step-by-step description of the selection process is included in the "Application Instructions" sheet. In order to qualify for a position and be placed on the eligible list, an applicant must pass each of the following components:

1.   WRITTEN EXAMINATION: (qualifying) this P.O.S.T. multiple-choice examination is designed to measure four skills associated with reading and writing: clarity, vocabulary, spelling, and reading comprehension.

2.   PHYSICAL AGILITY EXAMINATION: (qualifying) will evaluate each applicant's physical strength, agility and endurance.

3.   BILINGUAL ORAL FLUENCY EXAMINATION: (qualifying) will evaluate ability to communicate effectively in both English and a second approved language.

4.   ORAL INTERVIEW EXAMINATION: (weight of 50%) will evaluate each applicant's communication, interpersonal and decision-making skills.

5.   BACKGROUND ORAL INTERVIEW EXAMINATION: (weight of 50%) will evaluate each applicant's background, experience, training and personal qualifications for the position.

Applicants must receive a passing score in every component of the selection process in order to be further considered. Those who are successful in all of the above will be placed on an eligible list and will be considered for appointment as vacancies occur.

NOTE: Prior to selection, a thorough police background investigation will be conducted. This review of suitability for employment will include an examination by a licensed psychologist, a polygraph examination, and a medical examination.

** Refer to the "Application Instructions" sheet for a comprehensive listing of the selection components, test dates, salary, and benefits.

01-09MC *(this bulletin supersedes the one posted 1/02/09)*
Bulletin Number

Additional Information on Reverse Side
Job Information Line: (714) 647-6500
Website: www.santa-ana.org/jobs
TTY User Relay Line 1 (800) 735-2929

04/03/09

Date Posted

Internal recruiting   Recruiting from the current workforce to fill an open position is most appropriately used for positions for which existing employees are likely to have the necessary skills. The job announcement can be placed in an employee newsletter, posted on bulletin boards, and, if appropriate, distributed to the collective bargaining unit. Employees can then nominate themselves for the opening. Internal recruiting needs to comply with EEO principles, existing civil service procedures, collective bargaining agreements, and other personnel rules under which the jurisdiction may be operating.

One advantage of internal recruitment is its lower demand on resources. It is less expensive and takes less time than an external search. A second advantage is that the candidates' strengths and weaknesses are known to the agency. Finally, internal recruitment may enhance employee morale by providing opportunities for advancement.

Internal recruiting has some possible disadvantages, however. In some jurisdictions, the employee with the most seniority has the first claim to an open position, even if he or she is only minimally qualified. Another drawback may be the ripple effect created when several people in the organization change jobs. Factions in the workforce may be aggravated when the internal promotion strengthens one faction. Employees left out of the promotion cycle may respond by reducing their work effort and causing dissent. To avoid negative repercussions, employers are advised to adhere to open and fair selection procedures and to keep all applicants informed about the selection process.

The advantages of both internal and external recruiting can be realized when local governments judiciously employ both strategies in their hiring decisions. If the recruitment policy is not rigid, managers can consider the needs of the organization for each position and decide whether to hire from the existing pool of employees or to look outside the organization. A policy statement outlining the criteria to use in deciding whether to recruit internally or externally should be established. Many local governments have policies describing recruitment procedures that begin with internal recruitment and proceed to external sources if no internal candidate is found.

External recruiting   If the local government is going to recruit from outside the organization, the administrator needs to determine the proper pool of candidates on the basis of the type of job to be filled. For example, it is not necessary to recruit nationally for a secretary-receptionist position, and an advertisement in the local newspaper will probably generate an adequate number of applicants. Other positions, however, such as engineer or information services director, will require a regional or nationwide search. The jurisdiction should allow for the increased cost and time associated with a national search. Generally, the higher the salary, the longer the time needed to fill the position. Costs include advertising the position, long-distance phone calls to check references, and travel expenses if candidates are invited for in-person interviews.

There are many resources available to assist with external recruiting. Technical assistance in conducting the search is available through professional organizations, some of which are listed at the end of this chapter and in the e-supplement. Online services bring employers and job seekers together. Employment services may also be available through state employment agencies.

Recruitment firms will assist in finding professional employees. In exchange for a fee, the human resource management consultant locates professionals meeting the job description. Care should be taken, however, in using this option. The recruiter should have worked with public sector agencies before and should understand the jurisdiction's commitment to affirmative action and any other priorities. The cost of a recruiter also needs to be carefully investigated, as it is likely to be high—often up to a third of the open position's salary.

On the other hand, the cost of a recruiter may be justified by the fact that most public organizations underestimate the indirect costs incurred when the in-house staff handles a search.[2] There is some evidence also that external recruiters can complete a search more quickly than an internal committee.

Advertising the job opening

The next steps in the recruitment process involve deciding where to post the announcement of a job opening and what to include.

Where to place the advertisement The decision about where and how to advertise should be based on the nature and size of the likely applicant pool. Placing an advertisement in a local or regional newspaper or in the local unemployment office can fill many entry-level positions. Other, more specialized positions will need to be advertised nationally. Most professions have their own journals, newsletters, and online services. (See the resource list at the end of this chapter and in the e-supplement.) Innovative methods include sending direct mail to professional associations and schools, contacting employers that have recently laid off large numbers of employees, and using outplacement firms. (Outplacement firms help organizations find jobs for displaced employees and can be an excellent resource for finding potential employees who have recently lost their jobs and are seeking work.) If the city or county wants to attract more minority applicants, it should consider placing advertisements in neighborhood weeklies that are based in ethnically diverse areas or at colleges and universities with large minority student populations.

Using job posting sites in professional associations, such as the Society for Women Engineers (see careers.swe.org/post.cfm) or the National Organization of Minority Architects, can also encourage applicants from a wider range of backgrounds and experiences to apply for the position you are advertising. It may also be feasible for your city to encourage applications from graduates of historically black colleges and universities (HBCUs) by contacting their placement offices. While HBCUs make up only 3 percent of the U.S. higher education system's institutions, they graduate nearly 25 percent of all African Americans earning baccalaureate degrees (see uncf.org/members/aboutHBCU.asp). There are also many commercial Web sites, such as Diversity.com or diversityjobs.com, that aim to connect employers and diverse applicants; for a fee, you can advertise your open position on such a site.

As more and more schools, libraries, and homes become connected to the Web, many people routinely look for work online. Posting jobs on a Web site allows the employer to use creative techniques in marketing its job openings. Newspaper ads, which are more expensive than announcements on an organization's home page, can be used as teasers to encourage job seekers to look at the full description online. For examples of local government job postings online, see Los Angeles County's site at dhr.lacounty.info.

The job ad

An effective ad should include the following components:

- A job title
- Minimum acceptable qualifications with respect to education or experience
- Essential job functions
- Typical duties and responsibilities
- Skills, certifications, or licenses required
- Forms and documents needed to apply for the job, as well as phone number or location for obtaining application forms
- Notice of whether successful applicants will have to undergo drug testing and pass a medical exam

- Nature of skills tests or other examinations and the approximate time and place for taking them
- Address of where to send the documents
- Deadline for application
- Date or time when those who meet minimum qualifications can expect notification about exams
- A statement confirming the jurisdiction's status as an EEO employer
- Whom to contact in case applicants wish to exercise their rights under the ADA and request reasonable accommodation during the application process.

The content of the advertisement The advertisement should attract applicants with the right qualifications. It should be specific enough to attract interest, but not so specific (e.g., with regard to compensation level if compensation is open) that it obligates the jurisdiction to contractual arrangements prematurely.

The advertisement should avoid any mention of sex, race, religion, age, ethnic origin, and physical capabilities unless those characteristics are considered bona fide occupational qualifications—in other words, requisites to the successful performance of the job. For example, it is illegal to advertise for "male lifeguards" for your city swimming pool or for a "female receptionist." If testing of any kind is involved, the advertisement should notify potential applicants of specific selection procedures to be used (e.g., pen and paper testing, physical agility testing) so that applicants who wish to ask for reasonable accommodation under the Americans with Disabilities Act (ADA) will be able to do so in a timely manner.[3]

Advertisements placed in periodicals outside of your geographical area may contain general information about your jurisdiction, including size, amenities, and other characteristics that you think might attract interested applicants.

Tips for successful recruiting

☐ Include the supervisor of the position in the hiring team.

☐ Use an up-to-date job analysis to determine the job requirements.

☐ Ensure that all advertising, application, testing, and selection procedures comply with EEO and affirmative action regulations, as well as with ADA requirements.

☐ Check the personnel manual and collective bargaining contracts for recruiting regulations.

☐ Tailor the scope of your search to the requirements of the position.

☐ Develop a recruitment information system so that applicants know where they stand in the selection process, and assign responsibility for communication with them.

Caution

■ Avoid any mention of sex, race, religion, age, ethnic origin, marital status, and physical capabilities in job ads unless those characteristics are considered bona fide occupational qualifications and essential for the job.

■ Be prepared to make reasonable accommodations for applicants who may request them under the ADA.

Selection

Guiding principles

■ All selection methods must be valid and reliable tests of the KSAs that candidates need to perform the job being filled.

■ The selection process should be open to anyone who feels qualified to apply.

■ Selection should follow principles of merit in choosing the best person for the job.

■ Friendships or family ties should not get in the way of selecting the best candidate.

■ Nepotism rules should be in place and enforced. (See also Chapter 7.)

Challenges

■ Ensuring that all selection criteria are job related

■ Ensuring that all selection criteria are applied consistently to all applicants

■ Balancing speed against thoroughness in selecting new employees

The first objective of the selection process is to find the individual who can perform most successfully in a specific position. To do this, the employer must understand the duties and responsibilities of the job and then test qualified candidates on the specific requirements of the job and the KSAs needed. Courts have determined that for selection criteria to be valid, they have to be job related as documented by the job analysis. Factors unrelated to the job, such as political affiliation or friendship, are not valid selection criteria. Employees hired on the basis of extraneous factors may not be capable of doing the jobs they are hired to do; more important, invalid selection procedures can lead to claims of illegal discrimination.

In fact, the second objective of the selection process is to provide a fair opportunity for all applicants to be hired. The selection process should be open to anyone who feels qualified to apply, and each test administered should provide each applicant who reaches that testing level with the same opportunity to demonstrate his or her abilities.

Who does what

In most organizations a number of people are involved in the selection process. A clerical employee may receive and review applications for completeness. If appropriate, that person may also be charged with protecting the confidentiality of the application files and limit access only to employees with "a need to know." The agency or department with the job opening may screen applications on the basis of minimum qualifications and prepare a list of qualified or eligible candidates. The department head, the chief administrator, or a committee can then test the candidates and interview the most promising ones.

Even though in most cases only one manager will have direct responsibility for the future employee, there are advantages to having more than one person involved in making a hiring decision. Having several people provide information about the job and input about each candidate's ability to perform in it allows for a variety of perspectives. Several people on a hiring panel can discuss the advantages and disadvantages of each candidate, and can make a decision based on a consensus of needs instead of the job requirements as interpreted by one person. Finally, with the potential for claims of discrimination, it is a good idea to have several people involved in the selection process to help keep the questioning job related and to provide documentation against false claims.

Minimum qualifications

Minimum qualifications describe the essential KSAs that an employee needs to actually perform the job. Applicants who do not meet the minimum qualifications need not be considered.

Usually, minimum qualifications include knowledge of the principles related to the work to be performed, experience doing similar work, and specific job skills needed to perform the job duties. Each qualification must be a valid indicator of performance. Quite often, employers specify qualifications that are not clearly job related. For example, many employers use a college degree as a minimum qualification for jobs without stopping to consider whether earning that degree is directly related to the performance of a specific job. It may be that the knowledge needed could be obtained through experience or a combination of education and experience.

Minimum qualifications are often established by law or public policy. Child labor laws apply to all government employment. Professional certifications are required or preferred for certain jobs in local governments—for example, teaching, nursing, and lifeguarding. In some cases, city attorneys, clerks, engineers, finance officers, and even human resource managers are required or requested to have professional certification. And some communities allow residency requirements as one of the minimum qualifications for a local government job.

If women and minorities are underrepresented in certain jobs and ranks, the affirmative action officer, chief executive, or other top staff member should keep a separate record of all applicants by sex and ethnicity, specifying the reasons why they were or were not retained for further consideration. (See Chapter 5 for more information on record keeping.)

Selection methods

Most organizations use several selection tools in sequence, such as application forms, performance tests, interviews, and reference checks. Each of these selection instruments must be designed to measure an applicant's abilities as they relate to actual job requirements, and should not be used to disqualify candidates because of factors not related to the job. However, candidates who at any step do not meet the qualifications identified in the job description can be disqualified and removed from further consideration.

Since not all jobs are the same, selection methods differ. The least costly selection method is the application form, which can be administered to many applicants and used to find those candidates who meet the minimum requirements of the job. Because of the time commitment, the most expensive approaches are performance tests administered at assessment centers or skill demonstration tests. Such tests should therefore be administered toward the end of the process, when a final choice is being made among a very small number of highly qualified candidates.

Actually, every step of the selection process, from the application form to the final interview, is a test and should be viewed as such by those making the hiring decision. Each testing component should specify minimum levels for the KSAs being evaluated and can also include a list of preferred or desired qualifications. Each component must also assign points for minimum and desired qualifications. Cutoff points can be designated to help in grouping candidates for further consideration—for example,

Minimal (candidate satisfies minimal qualifications)	70–79%
Good (candidate exceeds minimal qualifications by at least 10%)	80–89%
Excellent (candidate exceeds minimal qualifications by at least 20%)	90–100%

In addition, each test in the hiring process must be valid and reliable (see the sidebar on the next page). To be *valid*, tests must measure factors related to specific requirements of the job; to be *reliable*, tests must be applied consistently. The manager should also be certain to treat all applicants and eventual candidates in the same way. At every step of the hiring process, the manager should constantly ask whether the question is job related and whether he or she is being consistent with all candidates.

Application forms and résumés Application forms or résumés are used to screen out applicants who do not meet the minimum qualifications and to gather information for personnel records. In addition to an applicant's personal employment information such as name, address, social security number, and telephone number, these selection devices can provide information on the applicant's basic qualifications, such as level of education, employment experience, and job skills. Many cities now use an online application process (e.g., seattle.gov/jobs/newtosite .asp). Using some form of online submission may make it easier for applicants to apply (especially those applying from outside of the immediate area) and may make review of applications go more quickly. At a minimum, cities with well-functioning Web sites can easily post current openings and downloadable versions of their applications. If in-house expertise is available, an entirely electronic submission process can be created.

Exhibit 2–2 is an example of an application form from Boise, Idaho.

The information requested on applications must be related directly to the job to being filled. Questions that directly or indirectly lead to information about age, race, color, sex, religion, national origin, or physical disability or to personal information not related to required employment information or potential job performance should not be included. For example, many application forms include questions about age and marital status, but this information is usually irrelevant to the eventual performance of the job and could be used to make illegal hiring decisions. If such information is needed for determining benefits, it should be collected only after a hiring decision has been made.

Managers should exercise caution when reviewing application forms; there is evidence that nearly half of all applicants exaggerate their qualifications on application forms and résumés.[4] Factual information (e.g., places of employment, degrees earned, certifications) can be verified. Managers should ask for supporting

---

Validity and reliability

Validity

Validity refers to the appropriateness of the test instrument—whether it measures those attributes of a job that it is intended to measure. To be valid, the test must be job related. Three types of validity apply to testing: content validity, criterion validity, and construct validity.

To have *content validity*, the test has to be directly related to the KSAs needed to perform the duties and responsibilities of a job, and must cover the whole domain of the job and not exclude important KSAs. A recent job analysis should capture the job content.

To have *criterion validity*, the test has to measure a specific criterion of the job, such as the ability to make quick, accurate decisions in complex situations or to assume a leadership role in an unstructured setting. A test has criterion validity if its results have a strong relationship to required job behaviors and future performance. Examiners infer from the candidates' performance on the test how well they will perform in a similar situation on the job.

Construct validity applies to psychological tests, such as the Myers-Briggs personality test, for which theoretical constructs have been developed. Other test instruments can assess aptitudes or personality traits that research has identified as predictors for high or low performance in certain positions. Psychological profile tests have been developed for stressful jobs such as police officer or firefighter, in which little room for human error is tolerated. However, because these tests are grounded in psychological theory, they need to be administered by qualified psychologists.

The U.S. Supreme Court has ruled that selection criteria not directly related to job performance are not valid and are therefore prohibited.[1] The federal "Uniform Guidelines on Employee Selection Procedures" provide generally accepted rules for selection procedures and standards for validation of selection tests[2].

Two approaches to validate tests are concurrent validation and predictive validation. *Concurrent validation* uses a sample of current employees who take the proposed selection test while evaluators simultaneously collect information on their job performance. The test is considered valid when the range of low to high performance parallels the range of low to high test scores. In *predictive validation,* a job applicant's test results are compared against that individual's actual performance after being hired and on the job for a period of time. Regression analysis is the proper statistical procedure for both types of validation approaches. If the jurisdiction does not have the expertise in statistics or the necessary software, the resources of a nearby university could perhaps be used.

Reliability

Reliability refers to the consistent use and unambiguous nature of the test instrument. Tests are supposed to be applied consistently over time and across a variety of applicants. Reliability is also ensured when the test instrument is unambiguous and elicits consistent responses from test takers. In other words, a reliable testing method should consistently obtain similar scores from applicants with similar KSAs.

1 *Griggs v. Duke Power Company*, 28 L. Ed. 2d (1971); *Wards Cove Packing v. Atonio*, 104 L. Ed. 2d (1989).
2 41 CFR 60-3; 60-3.13B; 60-3.17, available from the U.S. Department of Labor at dol.gov/dol/allcfr/title_41/Part_60-3/toc.htm.

Exhibit 2-2 Sample job application form

APPLICATION FOR EMPLOYMENT

The City of Boise is an Equal Opportunity/Affirmative Action Employer. It is our policy to recruit, hire and promote qualified and qualifiable persons without regard to race, sex, religion, national origin, age or disability.

Give special attention to experience relative to the job in which you are applying. Be specific and thorough. Include all relevant temporary, part-time or volunteer work.

To: City of Boise Human Resources
601 W. Idaho St.
P.O. Box 500
Boise, ID 83701-0500

Phone: **(208) 384-3850**
Fax: **(208) 384-3868**
Web: **www.cityofboise.org**

Position Applied For: _____

Name: _____
Last   First   Middle

Present Address: _____
Street   City   State   Zip

Home Phone: _____   Work Phone: _____

Message Contact: _____
Name   Address   Phone

1. Are you willing to work: ☐ Full-Time ☐ Part-Time ☐ Temporary
2. Acceptable Salary: $ _____ per _____
3. If you are applying for a clerical position, you will be considered for openings in all departments unless you specify a particular department. _____
4. If considered for a position with the Police Department, are you willing to submit to a polygraph (lie detector)?
   ☐ yes ☐ no
5. When can you report for work? _____
6. Are you currently employed by the City of Boise? ☐ Yes ☐ No
7. Have you previously been employed by us? ☐ Yes ☐ No   If yes, when _____
8. Have you previously been employed under another name? ☐ Yes ☐ No   If yes, what name? _____
9. As required under the Immigration Reform and Control Act, any person working for the City of Boise, regardless of the nature of the job or the number of hours or months employed, will be required to show proof of identity and work eligibility.

   Do you legally have the right to work in the U.S.? ☐ Yes ☐ No

EDUCATION

Do you have a high school diploma or equivalent? (GED) ☐ Yes ☐ No

Circle the highest grade completed -- not including college.
1 2 3 4 5 6 7 8 9 10 11 12

Special Training or Education Beyond High School

Name of School/Location	Courses	Credit Hours Completed	Type of Degree/Date Received

EMPLOYMENT HISTORY

In the spaces below, list the specific tasks and responsibilities included in your work history, beginning with your present or last employment. If you have a long history of employment, **be sure to list those jobs which best relate to the position for which you are applying.** Employment verification may be made regarding all of your past experience. Please note if you do not want your present employer contacted. Use additional pages as necessary. **A resume will not be accepted in lieu of completing this portion of the application.**

Starting Date: _____   Ending Date: _____   Starting Salary: _____   Ending Salary: _____   Hours per Week: _____

Your Title: _____   May we contact your present employer? ☐ Yes ☐ No

Present or Last Employer - Name/Address & Phone: _____   Supervisor - Name & Title: _____

Reason for Leaving: _____

Duties (be specific): _____

Starting Date: _____   Ending Date: _____   Starting Salary: _____   Ending Salary: _____   Hours per Week: _____

Previous Employer - Name/Address & Phone: _____   Supervisor - Name & Title: _____   Your Title: _____

Reason for Leaving: _____

Duties (be specific): _____

Exhibit 2-2 Sample job application form *(continued)*

Starting Date:	Ending Date:	Starting Salary:	Ending Salary:	Hours per Week:
Previous Employer - Name/Address & Phone:			Supervisor - Name & Title:	Your Title:
Reason for Leaving:				
Duties (be specific):				

Starting Date:	Ending Date:	Starting Salary:	Ending Salary:	Hours per Week:
Previous Employer - Name/Address & Phone:			Supervisor - Name & Title:	Your Title:
Reason for Leaving:				
Duties (be specific):				

Starting Date:	Ending Date:	Starting Salary:	Ending Salary:	Hours per Week:
Previous Employer - Name/Address & Phone:			Supervisor - Name & Title:	Your Title:
Reason for Leaving:				
Duties (be specific):				

AFFIRMATIVE ACTION DATA REQUEST

To assist the City of Boise in its commitment to Equal Employment Opportunity, applicants are asked to voluntarily provide the following information. This questionnaire will be separated from the application and will not be used in any employment decisions.

Date: _____   Position applied for: _____

Name: _____   Age: _____

Sex: ☐ Female ☐ Male   Disabled: ☐ Yes ☐ No

Race: ☐ African American   ☐ Hispanic   ☐ Asian American/Pacific Islander
       ☐ American Indian/Alaskan Native   ☐ Caucasian

How were you informed of this opening?

☐ I am currently employed by the City of Boise   ☐ Walk-In   ☐ Private Placement Service
☐ Newspaper/Magazine Ad   ☐ College Placement Office   ☐ Job Interest Card
☐ Department of Employment   ☐ Internet Website   ☐ Other _____

WAR ERA VETERAN'S PREFERENCE STATEMENT

Idaho law provides veteran's preference for residents of Idaho who:

have been in active service in the armed forces of the United States during a recognized war period or other recognized conflict as defined by law; or,

are disabled veterans who served on active duty in the armed forces at any time; or,

are widowers of such individuals, who have not remarried; or, are a qualifying spouse of an eligible disabled veteran who is unable to perform the work in the position for which the spouse seeks to apply the preference.

If you are claiming eligibility for veteran's preference, please complete a Veteran's Preference Form and submit it with your application along with any required documentation. A copy of the Veteran's Preference Form may be obtained from the City of Boise Human Resources or by visiting our website at *www.cityofboise.org* .

CITY OF BOISE
Applicant Information

Introduction:

Thank you for your interest in employment with the City of Boise. The following information is provided to assist you in completing the application. Our goal is to find the best qualified applicant for the job.

If you have any questions, please call Human Resources at (208) 384-3850.

The City of Boise will provide reasonable accommodation to applicants applying for employment. If you wish such accommodation, please call Human Resources (208) 384-3850 or (208) 384-3760 (TDD & Voice).

Tips for Completing Your Application:

Review the qualifications listed in the job announcement. If you believe that you meet these qualifications, we invite you to complete the appropriate application material.

The job announcement identifies job duties as well as the knowledge and abilities needed to perform them. It is important that you describe your experience in detail in order to identify the knowledge and abilities that make you a good candidate for the job. *Some positions may require a resume or cover letter to be included with the application. For these specific instances, a notation on the job description will be made. **However, a resume will NOT be accepted in lieu of the City application.***

The information you provide will be used to determine your level of qualifications for the current recruitment opening(s). When completing application papers, be as thorough and complete as possible. Do not overstate or claim experience that you do not have. The following information may be helpful:

★ Read the entire job announcement. Consider the responsibilities of the position you're applying for and their relationship to your training and experience (paid or unpaid).
★ Organize your responses in draft form, then prepare your final response.
★ When identifying duties you performed for each employer, include your most pertinent experience.
★ Include your most complex or important accomplishments.
★ If you do not include important experience and abilities, Human Resources cannot properly assess your qualifications.
★ You must give specific, detailed accounts of your related education, training and experience. Once your application is submitted, no additional information will be accepted.
★ Make sure your statements clearly describe your experience and accomplishments. Avoid describing your experience with general words such as: coordinate, responsible, facilitate, etc. Avoid non-specific statements about experience such as: "I have done this for 10 years."
★ When describing education and training, identify specific course content, and special projects completed.
★ Avoid using words, phrases and acronyms that are common only to your profession or previous employer.
★ Be as clear, concise and legible as possible.
★ If you do not have enough space to identify your job duties, additional sheets may be attached.

It's a good idea to keep a copy of the application and job announcement to prepare for any test or interview that may be required. Copies will not be provided for you.

(OVER)

List any experiences and/or skills that you feel would especially qualify you for this position.

Typing	Licenses/Certificates	Seminars/Training	Association/Membership	Computer Software/Equipment
___ WPM				
Ten-Key by Touch: ☐ Yes ☐ No				

EMPLOYMENT REFERENCES
(Include individuals who are qualified to evaluate your capabilities.)

Name:	Address:	City:	State:	Phone:

SIGNATURE OF APPLICANT

I certify that all information given on this application is true, correct, and complete to the best of my knowledge. I also certify that I have accounted for all of my work, experience, and training on this application, and that I have not knowingly withheld any fact or circumstance which would, if disclosed, affect my application unfavorably.

The City of Boise is hereby authorized to make any investigation of my employment, educational or background history through investigative agencies or bureaus of its choice. I release all relevant parties from all liability of any damages resulting from furnishing such information.

If employed by the City of Boise, I agree to abide by its rules and regulations. I understand that discovery of misrepresentation or omission of facts herein will make me ineligible for employment or be cause for immediate dismissal. I agree to furnish additional information as may be required to complete my employment file. I understand that operating conditions may require me to temporarily and/or regularly work shifts other than the one for which I am applying and I agree to such scheduling change as directed by my supervisor.

I have read and reviewed the description of the job for which I am applying. I understand that I must be capable of performing the essential functions of the job effectively and safely, with or without reasonable accommodation.

I also understand that my employment may be subject to the successful completion of an employment physical examination, and that my continued employment may be conditioned upon satisfactorily continuing to meet job-related physical and mental requirements. If requested, I agree to submit to a job-related physical examination performed by a qualified medical person of the City of Boise's choice. Such exam shall be paid for by the City of Boise. I also agree that all information concerning said physical examination can be supplied to the City of Boise, or an authorized agent of this municipality, upon their request.

I further understand that the City of Boise is committed to providing a safe, productive, and efficient work environment and to employing a work force free from the use of illegal drugs, either on or off the job. The City of Boise has established a pre-employment drug and alcohol testing policy. Pre-employment testing of applicants: As a condition of hiring, applicants will be required to submit to a pre-employment drug and alcohol test conducted by the City of Boise's authorized representative. Applicants will provide a urine sample for drug testing. Breath alcohol testing will be performed by an evidential breath testing device. The test results will be maintained in a confidential file, and only released to the City of Boise, its representatives, or as otherwise authorized or required by law. The applicant releases the City of Boise and its representatives from all liabilities relating to the drug testing carried out under this policy, including, without limitation, the release of the test results. Any applicant who fails to report for a test, refuses to take a test, fails to provide a specimen, tampers with a test specimen or who is identified with verified positive test results will be denied employment at that time. Applicants identified with verified positive test results may reapply after one (1) year from the date of the initial test with proof of successful completion of a rehabilitation program through a state-licensed facility.

I understand that this is an application for employment and that no employment contract, either express or implied, is being offered. I also understand that if employed, such employment is for an indefinite period and can be terminated at will by either party, with or without notice, at any time, for any or no reason, and is subject to change in wages, conditions, benefits, and operating policies.

Date: _____   Signature of Applicant: _____

Source: City of Boise, cityofboise.org/departments/human_resources/ViewJobOpeningsAndApplyForAJob/recruit.aspx

documentation (e.g., education transcripts, certificates, degrees awarded) and contact former employers to confirm prior work experience.

Most organizations use a single application form for all applicants applying for any job within the organization. This practice may raise serious questions about job relatedness, and the information may not be sufficient to determine minimum qualifications for the specific job to be filled. A supplemental application form may be required for some jobs, asking for information specific to the job in question. Exhibit 2–3 is an example of a supplemental application form, also from Boise.

Eligibility lists   Following a review of application forms, many organizations establish an eligibility list, or a list of those who meet the minimum qualifications and are considered the most promising candidates for further evaluation. The most common number of candidates passed on to management for consideration is three, although the trend is toward including as many as five or ten. Other ideas for certifying eligible candidates are to use a percentage of those who meet minimum qualifications, or to establish categorical groupings such as satisfactory, good, and excellent and test everyone in the "excellent" category.

It is the policy of many public organizations to give extra consideration in the selection process to veterans, especially those with disabilities. This is often done by assigning these candidates extra points in a ranking system.

Written tests   Standardized methods of measuring knowledge or ability in specific job areas fell into disfavor with the courts and public employers in the 1960s and 1970s because many general tests at that time (such as intelligence and mechanical comprehension tests) were not clearly tied to performance in a specific job and had an adverse impact on minorities. However, more recently, tests have been carefully reconstructed to measure indicators related to job performance.

Standardized tests for specific jobs are available from various firms and organizations. ICMA and the International Public Management Association for Human Resources (IPMA-HR) offer tests for a variety of public sector jobs (see the e-supplement). Multiple-choice tests are easy to score, require little interpretation, and can be given to large numbers of applicants with little cost to the organization.

fyi

The selection sequence

Application forms and résumés: Evaluate candidate training and experience

Written tests: Measure and evaluate knowledge, analytical thinking abilities, and written communication skills

Performance tests: Measure and evaluate specialized abilities and skills

Oral examinations (interviews): Evaluate knowledge, verbal communication skills, and experience

Background investigations: Evaluate past performance and behavior

Probationary periods: Measure and evaluate performance on the job

Exhibit 2-3   Sample criminal history and driving record form

---

CRIMINAL HISTORY/DRIVING RECORD CHECK

All acceptable applicants for the position for which you have applied must successfully pass a criminal history and driving record check. In order to make the proper identification, the following information is necessary; Human Resources will not be responsible for omission of information needed to obtain an accurate record check. A conviction may or may not be grounds for disqualification. Each case will be considered individually.

Position applying for: _____

_____

| Last Name | First Name | Middle Name |

_____

Alias Names (Include Maiden/prior Married Names   Birth date   Sex   Social Security Number

Please list the name of any city or town in which you have lived during the last five (5) years:

| City, State | City, State | City, State |

| City, State | City, State | City, State |

****

In the space below, please list **ANY** misdemeanor and felony offenses, including D.U.I., for which you have been convicted or received a withheld judgment **within your lifetime**. Some juvenile offenses for which an individual is charged as an adult (tobacco, alcohol and drug charges) and traffic citations or moving violations such as inattentive driving **may** also fall into this category; it is the applicant's responsibility to verify the accuracy of the information contained within their record.

Approximate
   Date   City/State   Offense or Violation

****

Please list the approximate date and place of all traffic citations and moving violations received within the last **FIVE** (5) years including any driving related misdemeanor and felony offenses such as D.U.I., D.W.P., etc. Do not list parking tickets.

Approximate
   Date   City/State   Citation

****

I authorize Boise City to receive any and all information concerning myself related to my criminal records, and I understand that any of the above requested information not listed which appears on the security check will automatically disqualify me on the basis of falsification of the application.

_____   _____

Applicant's Signature   Date

Performance tests   Performance tests assess proficiency in or aptitude for executing essential job functions. These tests are given to applicants to measure their skill at performing some specific aspects of a job or their ability to be trained to do the work. The tests often simulate a major facet of the job and are therefore considered highly valid. However, they are also expensive to administer. For instance, when firefighters are tested for the job of engineer, they have to be individually observed demonstrating their ability to drive the engine, mentally calculate the engine pressure, pump water from a fire hydrant, and draft water from an open water source, all within a specified time period.

Physical tests are often given to candidates who will be required to perform physical tasks in their jobs. These tests must accurately reflect the common physical requirements of the job and cannot eliminate candidates for inability to perform in extreme cases. The ADA requires that written and physical tests allow for "reasonable accommodation" for applicants requesting it, and it prohibits employers from discriminating against employees who cannot perform tasks of a marginal, infrequent, or nonessential nature (see Chapter 5).

Interviews   Besides the application form, interviewing is probably the most common selection device used by employers. By itself the interview may also be the least valid and reliable method of selecting future employees.[5] Managers can use the interview to determine a candidate's ability to communicate verbally as well as to ask probing questions about performance and behavior in circumstances similar to potential job situations. Because of the personal interaction in an interview, managers can explore interests or concerns in greater detail than can be revealed in written tests or application forms. However, this characteristic of the interview also opens the door to questions that are not job related and could lead to information that might be used to make discriminatory or unfair decisions.

In other words, the validity of interviews becomes questionable when the interview strays into areas not related to the job. Personal interaction and human nature can combine in the interview to produce bias. Factors that can inappropriately influence the outcome of an interview include nonverbal behaviors such as body language, accent, friendliness, posture, and enthusiasm, as well as the clothing worn by candidates. Research indicates that nonverbal behavior in an interview situation tends to have a greater influence on a hiring decision than verbal responses.

Finally, administrators may not be well trained in conducting interviews properly and may have poor listening and communication skills. Much of the important information in an interview may never be heard or may be misinterpreted as a result of error and bias.

The reliability of interviews also tends to be poor. Interviews can be conducted by more than one person to gain the advantages of multiple perspectives and to protect the interviewers from any false claims from disgruntled candidates. Although agreement between interviewers on the facts and overall evaluations of candidates is fairly good, inter-rater reliability or consistency on subjective characteristics such as candidate leadership or honesty is often low. Another aspect of reliability deals with the consistency with which the interview is conducted among candidates. It is common to have an established list of questions that are asked of each candidate, but it is also common to see the line of questioning diverge from the plan.

The most common errors made by interviewers are not knowing the specific duties and responsibilities of the job to be performed, not planning questions (related to job duties) in advance of the interview, and straying into areas during the interview that are either not job related or unnecessary (and a waste of time). These errors can be avoided by taking the steps listed in the tips for successful interviews listed on page 54 before beginning the interview process.

Questions listed in the FYI sidebar on page 55 are usually prohibited because they lead to information that could be used to illegally discriminate against protected classes of applicants. Other questions provide information that is simply irrelevant to a candidate's future performance on the job. In rare cases there is a real and important job requirement—referred to as a bona fide occupational qualification—that may require interview questions related to otherwise illegal information. In most public sector job interviews, however, questions that call for illegal or unnecessary information are to be carefully avoided. If necessary for personnel records or employment benefits, some questions can be asked after the hiring decision has been made.

The best questions are those that provide the interview panel with information about the candidate's KSAs and attitudes necessary to perform successfully in the job. Questions that ask whether a candidate has a given skill or could perform a task rely on the candidate's own assessment of his or her abilities. More thoughtful questions would ask what the candidates would do in a hypothetical situation (related to the job to be performed) or, better yet, what they have actually done in other jobs similar to the one they would fill.

Behavioral and situational questions have been found to be both valid and reliable and good predictors of future performance. These kinds of questions are especially useful for assessing a candidate's temperament. Violence in the

---

fyi

Common interviewing errors

The following errors are easy to make in an interview:

- **Similarity error:** One candidate may appear similar to the interviewers themselves and therefore be favored.

- **Comparison error:** One candidate may stand out above the rest of the applicants by comparison and be favored even though he or she still does not meet the requirements of the job.

- **First impression error:** One candidate may become a favorite of the interviewers because of some information on the application form or some other bit of communication, and may therefore gain an advantage before any interviewing actually takes place. Research on interviewing has found that managers make up their minds about a candidate being interviewed in an average of four minutes.

- **Halo and horns effect:** One candidate may qualify in one aspect of a job, which influences the remainder of the interview, or interviewers may overreact to one unfavorable response. Unfortunately for the job candidate, one bad impression tends to influence those conducting the interview more than any of the positive impressions.

Tips for successful interviews

☐ Before beginning the interview process, conduct a careful job analysis of the position to determine the duties, responsibilities, and required KSAs.

☐ Assemble a panel of individuals with a strong interest in the selection outcome, and train them in proper interviewing techniques and ways to avoid common interviewing errors.

☐ Decide on the objectives you wish to accomplish during the interview. These should include obtaining information items that are not accessible through other selection methods.

☐ Plan past-behavior and hypothetical situation questions in advance of the meeting to enable the interviewers to gain an understanding of how each candidate will perform in the job.

☐ Use a standardized rating scale to evaluate each candidate on the same questions and then discuss these evaluations with the panel of interviewers after all the interviews have been held.

workplace has become a common concern; however, résumés do not reveal proclivity to disruptive behavior, former employers may not report incidents for fear of defamation suits, and direct questions can expose the hiring authority to a lawsuit for violation of privacy. Thus, one thing managers can do to avert problems in this area is to carefully screen job applicants for violent tendencies. One approach is to use role-playing to find out how the applicants handle stress and anger in typical job situations. Scenarios can be set up in which the candidates must handle a disgruntled client who is giving the public employee a hard time, respond to a citizen who doesn't understand a departmental decision, or deal with an employee who is insulting. The candidates are asked to think through each scenario and describe their responses. The objective of this "test" is to give the interviewer an idea of the candidates' ability to get along with difficult people and to deal with frustrating situations and challenges to authority.[6]

If your local government is an at-will employer, it is very important to instruct interviewers not to promise a job applicant job security in the course of an interview. (Neither should job security be promised at any stage of the recruitment process; see the sections in Chapter 5 on at-will employment and on oral and implied contracts, both of which are on page 124.)

Assessment centers   An assessment center is not a place but a process. It is a series of individual and group exercises used to appraise the abilities of candidates applying for managerial and other complex jobs.[7] Assessment centers may include tests measuring executive skills, such as leadership, management style, and intelligence. The set-up may also involve taking performance tests, writing memos, handling a poorly performing employee, using listening skills, preparing and delivering a speech, and dealing with sexual harassment problems. Group exercises or games can shed light on the candidates' abilities in areas such as delegation, team building, and conflict management. In simulations, a rather elaborate series of job-related situations is presented to a group of candidates, who behave in roles assigned by the assessors. The simulation allows for multiple responses and has preplanned, progressive steps for the candidates to act upon as the simulation unfolds.

Illegal questions

It is illegal to ask the following questions on an application form or in an employment interview:

Race, creed, national origin

What is your race?

What country does your family come from?

Where are you a citizen?

What is your previous foreign address?

What is your birthplace?

What is the name of a relative to be notified in case of emergency?

What is your native language?

Legal alternatives:

Are you legally able to work in the United States? Who would you like to be notified in the event of an emergency? What languages do you speak or write fluently (assuming foreign language skills are an essential job function)?

Sex, marital status

Are you male or female?

What is your maiden name?

Have you changed your name?

What is your sexual orientation?

Are you married?

Are you pregnant?

How many children do you have?

Do you have child care?

Do you plan on having any more children?

Legal alternative:

Do you have relevant work experience while using another name?

Age

What is your age?

When were you born?

Note: Information about age can be required, however, to ascertain whether the applicant meets minimal age requirement for the job.

Disability

Do you have any disabilities?

Have you had certain diseases?

Legal alternative:

Is there any reason you would not be able to perform the responsibilities and tasks of this position?

Height and weight

What is your height?

What is your weight?

Legal alternative:

Can you perform the essential job functions?

Religion

What is your religion?

What religious holidays do you celebrate?

To what organizations do you belong? In what groups are you a member?

Legal alternative:

Can you meet the work schedule for this job?

Military service

Have you been dishonorably discharged from the military?

Legal alternative:

What was your occupation while in military service? Did you receive training related to this job?

Criminal record

Have you ever been arrested?

Have you ever been convicted of any crime?

Legal alternative:

Have you been convicted of a crime related to the duties and responsibilities of this position?

Source: Paul Balbresky, "An Employment-Related Lawsuit May Put Your Local Government at Risk," *Public Management* 73 (November 1993): 13-15; see also James A. Buford Jr., *Personnel Management and Human Resources in Local Government* (Auburn, Ala.: Auburn University Press, 1991), 170-171.

The cone method

A popular technique for conducting employment interviews is known as the "cone method." The interviewers first determine their objectives for the interview and then examine each selected topic by using broad questions first, followed by more specific questions related to that topic. For example, if one of the objectives for the interview is to determine the amount of supervisory experience a candidate has had, the questions on this topic might move from the general to the specific as follows:

Opening question	Describe your experience supervising employees.
More specific questions	What were your responsibilities as a supervisor?
	What problems did you experience as a supervisor?
Probing questions	How did you handle that problem?
	Did you seek advice in responding to the problem?
More specific questions	How did you improve the performance of your employees?
	What were the duties of the employees you supervised?

Source: Thomas L. Moffatt, *Selection Interviewing for Managers* (New York: Harper and Row, 1979), 81-101.

Assessment centers commonly use an in-basket exercise. Each candidate is given an in-basket full of letters, memos, and telephone messages and is asked to deal with these items by first determining their importance and then deciding how to act on the information. Another test is the leaderless group problem. A small group of candidates is brought together and asked to solve a management problem. The solution is not as important as the process, and the candidates are observed and scored on their leadership traits and ability to work in groups. The assessment centers also usually include interviews in which the candidates are asked about their experiences handling work situations similar to those they can expect to encounter on the job.

Typically, a group of candidates for the same position is tested simultaneously in an assessment center. Watching the interaction of the candidates on the short list enables assessors to compare the highest-rated candidates against each other after they have passed a series of preliminary tests.

Assessment centers usually use a team of trained evaluators who conduct the tests and then discuss the results as a group. These assessors may include representatives from the department or area in which the candidate is to be employed, and they provide a wide range of perspectives for choosing the most acceptable candidate.

Caution

The following can ruin your selection process:

- Unclear job requirements
- Invalid or unreliable tests
- Untrained interviewers
- No reference check

The most important advantage of assessment centers is that the tests can be designed to focus on very specific aspects of the job and are therefore highly content valid. Assessment centers can also reliably test a number of candidates using very similar testing procedures.

The biggest problem with assessment centers is their cost. Their procedures can run from one to five days and can occupy the time of several assessors and candidates. Because of the cost, assessment centers are usually made available only to candidates applying for executive positions.

Assessment centers also carry the risk of bias related to measurement standards. The accepted characteristics of good managers or leaders are sometimes biased against women, who often display different management traits than men. Successful managers may display these male-oriented management traits, but female-oriented traits may be equally valid predictors of good leaders and managers. For example, when a candidate is doing the in-basket exercise described above, some evaluators might give high marks to participants who act independently and decisively, while others might favor a deliberative and consultative approach to decision making. The *right* response may exist only in the eye of the beholder.

Background investigations (reference checks)   As with any other selection method, the objectives of conducting background or reference checks should be decided on before the procedure is begun. The simplest objective is to verify information obtained from candidates on the application forms and in interviews. Another valuable use of reference checks is to determine past performance. One of the best indicators of future performance is how the employee performed in similar situations in the past. It is a must to develop a set of questions before beginning any reference interviews to ensure that the questions are job related.

It is a good idea to inform the candidate that you will be asking former employers and others who are familiar with the candidate's work for confidential personnel information. This can be accomplished with a notification and checkoff on the application form or a separate signed release.

The list of references can come from the candidate and from the candidate's list of former employers and instructors. Additional references not volunteered by the candidate can be obtained by asking the listed references for others who are familiar with the candidate's work history.

Reference checks are frequently conducted by telephone to save time and to hear spontaneous responses from those interviewed. Background checks by mail are slow, and the responses can be carefully crafted and uninformative. On the other hand, these responses can be more thoughtful than spontaneous answers, and the sources will include clues to the real performance history of the candidate. Reference checks can also be conducted in person, but this is typically done only for high-ranking, security-sensitive positions.

Reference checks are useful for weeding out candidates who have given false information in the selection process and for uncovering behavioral problems in the past. Employers are obligated to find any problems related to the candidate's ability to perform the job before hiring that individual, especially in the event of harm or injury to someone else. If the hired employee causes harm when a pattern of behavior in past employment indicated the danger, the employer can be sued for *negligent hiring*. (Similarly, former employers can be held liable for *negligent referral* if they hold back information that could have prevented a person from

Caution

■ To avoid violating privacy rights of job applicants, you must have their written consent before contacting high schools or colleges for transcripts, previous employers for references, or credit-reporting firms for credit reports.

causing harm to others in a future job situation. However, liability suits from former employees also threaten those employers who give poor references to prospective employers. Because of this possibility, many organizations do not allow their managers to give any more information than the job description and the former employee's dates of employment.)

For jobs requiring good financial management skills, the employer may want to review the finalists' credit history. However, the employer must have written permission to do so. If an applicant is denied employment because of information in the credit report, the Fair Credit Reporting Act requires the employer to inform the applicant of this in case the credit report is inaccurate.

A thorough Internet search may also be relevant. The search can start with the Web site of the previous employer. The candidate may also have his or her own Web site. Additional searches can include a review of the social networking sites, activities in professional organizations, and entries in newspaper stories.

The legality of inquiring into a finalist's criminal record varies among the states. Employers are advised to do an Internet search of the finalists—that is, a search of public records. To ensure transparency in the hiring processes, the hiring entity may wish to clarify in the job advertisement that background checks will be conducted. Many states have no statutes; some prohibit asking about arrest records. Questions about convictions, however, are lawful, but even then the refusal to hire a person because of a conviction has to be for job-related reasons. When a position involves the use of a government car, the driving record should be checked by contacting the state agency that issues driver's licenses.

Hiring

Guiding principle

■ A probationary period and careful orientation can help ensure strong performance in the future.

Challenges

■ Finding a proper balance between treating the new employee like a valued team member (with implied job security) and treating him or her like a probationer with no promise of continued employment

■ Finding a good mentor for the new employee and ensuring that proper guidance is provided

Even after the final selection is made, the process is not finished. First of all, the selected candidate may have to pass additional tests. Paperwork has to be completed, and the employee has to be oriented to the organization and the specific job responsibilities. Then it is wise to use a probationary period to find out whether the new employee can perform on the job.

The conditional job offer

Because of cost and privacy concerns, certain steps in the selection process are taken only after the preliminary job offer has been made and accepted. The job offer should be conditional on the new employee passing the final screening phases. These include verification of employment eligibility, a drug test, and medical screening.

Employment eligibility   To verify the employee's right to work in the United States, the employee and employer have to complete Form I-9 required by the U.S. Citizenship and Immigration Services, Department of Homeland Security. To prove identity and work eligibility, the employee has two options:

- Submit an original document from List A of the Lists of Acceptable Documents that establishes both identity and employment authorization—for example, (1) a U.S. passport or U.S. passport card or (2) a Permanent Resident Card or Alien Registration Receipt Card.

- Submit an original document from List B that establishes identity, such as a driver's license, state-issued I.D. card, or U.S. military card or draft record, *plus* an original document from List C that establishes employment authorization, such as a Social Security Account Number card or a U.S. birth certificate with official seal.

Employers are advised to keep photocopies of the documents that were examined, and they must retain the completed Form I-9 for three years after the date of hire or one year after the date that employment ends, whichever is later. Information about compliance with Citizenship and Immigration (CIS) rules can be found at uscis.gov/files/form/I-9_IFR_02-02-09.pdf.

Drug testing   From a legal standpoint it is less problematic to subject conditional hires to drug testing than to subject employees who are already on the payroll. Therefore, many jurisdictions routinely screen new recruits for the use of illegal drugs. However, the job announcement should list the drug test as a condition for employment so that applicants are forewarned, and testing procedures should be carefully controlled.

Public employers are, by definition, the government, which is held to a higher standard than private sector employers in respecting employee privacy. The U.S. Constitution prohibits the government from conducting unreasonable searches and committing other privacy infringements (see Chapter 5). The courts have attempted to balance this right to privacy with the public interest in safety, and have usually allowed drug testing for applicants and current employees who are involved in dangerous occupations (e.g., firefighters, public works employees), for jobs in which harm may come to others (e.g., drivers), and for jobs in which drug laws are enforced (e.g., police).

Drug testing is expensive, and evidence shows that some job candidates, whether drug users or not, say they are less likely to apply for jobs where drug testing is practiced. However, there are some good reasons to aim for a drug-free workplace. Research shows that drug and alcohol abuse is directly related to employee absenteeism and accidents on the job.[8] There may also be employer liability concerns when an employee who is under the influence of a drug causes an accident.

Medical examination   After the conditional job offer and before the new hire starts work, employers can require a full medical exam. Questions can be asked and tests can be conducted to ascertain whether the individual has the physical and mental capabilities needed to perform the job and does not pose a threat to him- or herself, to co-workers, to customers, or to property. However, all new employees in the same job class have to be subjected to the same medical exam. Under the ADA, the conditional job offer can be withdrawn after the medical exam if the employer demonstrates all of the following:

- The conditional hire could not perform an essential job function.
- No reasonable accommodation was possible, or the accommodation requested would mean an undue hardship for the employer.
- The withdrawal of the offer was solely for job-related reasons.

The conditional job offer can also be withdrawn if the employer can show that the new hire would pose a threat to him- or herself, to others, or to property.

The probationary period

Obviously, the most valid predictor of future performance is actual performance on the job. Most public organizations have a probationary period of three months to a year. The length of the probationary period is determined by the amount of time it takes to learn the responsibilities of the job and to accumulate a record that can be evaluated. The probationary period is an opportunity for managers to carefully evaluate the performance of the new employee. During probation, the worker is subject to termination at will and has fewer employment rights than permanent employees.

Many local governments do not consider the probationary period as part of the employee selection process. Instead, it is used as a learning period for new employees, during which they are trained, observed, counseled, and evaluated while actually performing the work they were hired to do.

Whatever the purpose of the probationary period, managers are responsible for properly training probationary employees and evaluating their performance. These evaluations should be regular and frequent, and should provide the employee with

> **Completing the hiring process**
>
> The following documents should be created or filed to complete the hiring process:
> - Letter offering the job to finalist
> - Letter from finalist accepting offer
> - CIS Form I-9
> - IRS Form W-4
> - Forms to sign up for employee benefits
> - Letters to applicants not selected

an assessment of performance and guidance on how to improve. At the end of the probationary period, a final evaluation should be scheduled with the employee to determine whether that individual has the potential to perform successfully in the job. If proper training and regular guidance have been conducted, the outcome of the final evaluation should come as no surprise to the employee.

Employee orientation

Employee orientation training sessions introduce recent hires to the requirements of their new jobs and to the general operation of the organization. Formal orientation can prevent misunderstandings and guard against informal orientation that may be inconsistent and misleading. Orientation training can also speed up the socialization process by introducing the new employees to co-workers, supervisors, mentors, and others who can help answer questions and make the newcomers feel comfortable in the new work environment.

All employees should get acquainted with the setting in which they will be working and be carefully prepared to perform their work assignments. They should understand the culture of the organization, including its history, the important people involved in the community, the structure of the local government, and the way in which each department is integrated into the overall mission of the jurisdiction. New recruits should be briefed on organization rules and regulations, introduced to those who will either affect the work product or receive the work of the employee, and trained so that they fully understand the demands of the work expected of them. A separate orientation can be scheduled with supervisors, who can explain the work product needed and the supervisory arrangements. An orientation session should also be scheduled to explain employee benefits and the method of paying the employee's salary.

An initial investment in time and orientation material can provide substantial benefits in terms of the speed with which the new employee achieves full productivity. An employee orientation checklist (see the FYI sidebar on page 62) can help supervisors ensure that all the topics needed for new employees are covered.

Many things cannot be taught in a formal employee orientation training session. The best source of information is often co-workers, who can explain facts and situations in the context of the organization's way of doing things. Mentoring or arranging for the opportunity to meet with several co-workers informally, such as in a lunch setting or after work, can help new employees feel comfortable asking questions and can provide them with an opportunity to learn many of the values, professional and ethical norms, and attitudes of important people within the organization.

Notes

1 Paul Balbresky, "An Employment-Related Lawsuit May Put Your Local Government at Risk," *Public Management* 73 (November 1993): 13–15.

2 Catherine Rush and Lizbeth Barclay, "Executive Search: Recruiting a Recruiter," *Public Management* 77 (July 1995): 20–22.

3 Balbresky, "An Employment-Related Lawsuit," 14.

4 Thomas E. Becker and Alan L. Colquitt, "Potential Versus Actual Faking of a Biodata Form: An Analysis along Several Dimensions of Item Type," *Personnel Psychology* 45 (1992): 389–406.

5 A. I. Huffcutt and W. Arthur Jr., "Hunter and Hunter (1984) Revisited: Interview Validity for Entry-Level Jobs," *Journal of Applied Psychology* 79 (1994): 184–190.

6 Michael Barrier, "When Laws Collide: Legally Screening out Potentially Violent Employees," *Nation's Business* 83 (February 1995): 23, findarticles.com/p/articles/mi_m1154/is_n2_v83/ai_16420283 (accessed March 22, 2009).

7 *Assessment Centers for Hiring and Development*, MIS Report 27 (ICMA, April 1990): 1.

8 Edward F. Etzel, Christopher D. Lantz, and Catherine A. Yura, "Alcohol and Drug Use, and Sources of Stress: A Survey of University Faculty, Staff, and Administrators," *Employee Assistance Quarterly* 11 (1995): 51–58.

Recruitment advertising outlets

American Planning Association, 1776 Massachusetts Avenue, NW, Washington, DC 20036; phone: (202) 872-0611; planning.org.

ASPA Recruiter Online, publicservicecareers.org.

ICMA Job Center, ICMA, 777 North Capitol Street, NE, Suite 500, Washington, DC 20002-4201; phone: (202) 962-3650; jobs.icma.org.

International Association of Chiefs of Police, 515 North Washington Street, Alexandria, VA 22314-2357; phone: (703) 836-6767, (800) THE IACP; fax: (703) 836-4543; theiacp.org.

International Association of Fire Chiefs, 4025 Fair Ridge Drive, Fairfax, VA 22033-2868; phone: (703) 273-0911; fax: (703) 273-9363; iafc.org.

International Code Council, 5203 Leesburg Pike, Suite 600, Falls Church, VA 22041; phone: (703) 931-4533; fax: (703) 379-1546; iccsafe.org.

International Public Management Association for Human Resources (IPMA-HR), 1617 Duke Street, Alexandria, VA 22314; phone: (703) 549-7100; fax: (703) 684-0948; Recruiter Service Employment Listings, ipma-hr.org/content.cfm?pageid=529.

Nation's Cities Weekly, 1301 Pennsylvania Ave SW, Suite 550, Washington, DC 2004; phone: (202) 626-3000; fax: (202) 626-3043; nlc.org/nlc_org/site/newsroom/nations_cities_weekly/index/cfm.

PORAC Law Enforcement News, 2495 Natomas Park Drive, Suite 555, Sacramento, CA 95833; phone: (800) 655-6397; porac.org/employment.html.

Public Works Online Edition, pwmag.com.

URISA Marketplace, Urban and Regional Information Systems Association, 1460 Renaissance Drive, Suite 305, Park Ridge, IL 60068; phone: (847) 824-6300; fax: (847) 824-6363; urisa.org/MarketplaceJobs.

3

Maintaining a High-Performance Workforce

Jenny L. Holland, Arthur H. McCurdy, and Nicholas P. Lovrich

Governments need a disproportionate number of knowledge workers. Attracting and retaining them, however, is an ongoing challenge, since compensation for strong performers tends to be higher in the corporate sector. Another pull factor is a general cultural decline in organizational commitment. Younger employees tend to be less loyal to employers and more likely to see themselves as "free agents." The competition for experienced workers is intensifying as Baby Boomers begin to exit the workforce and new generations of employees enter, many of whom have far different concepts of the employment relationship than the employees they replace. The success of local governments to compete for employees and maintain a high performance workforce is dependent on the jurisdiction's capacity to motivate employees and to keep them engaged in the noble act of providing services to the public.

This chapter discusses the predominant approaches to maintaining a high-performance workforce, including evaluating performance, setting goals, linking performance to compensation, linking performance to employee advancement and development, building teams and work groups, and managing special circumstances that can affect performance. These various approaches are interrelated with other personnel policies, such as recruitment (Chapter 2), pay and benefits (Chapter 6), expectations (Chapter 7), and disciplinary procedures (Chapter 8).

An assessment of the approaches taken to manage a high-performance workforce must also include a consideration of the labor relations environment and other laws, rules, and regulations governing the jurisdiction. These factors establish

The authors gratefully acknowledge the assistance of Carol Greene, the former director of the Association of Washington Cities Local Government Personnel Institute, in reviewing the first and second edition versions of this chapter from a practitioner's viewpoint and providing many useful insights. We also wish to acknowledge the support and assistance of numerous members of the Section on Personnel Administration and Labor Relations of the American Society for Public Administration for providing sources of information and research as well as serving as a sounding board for our observations on personnel issues. Steve Hays, Rick Kearney, Brent Steel, Jonathan West, and Meredith Newman all deserve special recognition in this regard.

the broad parameters for what a city, county, or special district can and cannot do in its personnel practices. The environments within which local governments exist vary considerably, but it is often possible to find similar jurisdictions to compare personnel policies.

A note of caution is due about adopting private sector practices. In one frequently cited discussion and review of the public administration literature, the authors observe that "a century of dialogue concludes that the public and private sectors are different."[1] Because they are indeed quite different, any private sector practices that would be adopted must first be scrutinized in the light of the unique legal and political contexts within which the public sector operates.

Evaluating employee performance

Guiding principles

- The organization's mission should determine important performance goals.
- Evaluation techniques must fit performance goals.
- Performance evaluation techniques must be valid and reliable.
- Cooperation between management and rank-and-file employees is as important as the evaluation technique selected.
- Performance evaluations should report both strengths and weaknesses.

Challenge

- Determining whether to develop in-house expertise or to contract out for the service

One of the primary means of maintaining a high-performance workforce is through the evaluation of employee performance. The aim of the periodic review is to ensure personal accountability to the goals of the organization. Thus, it is very important to select a performance evaluation technique that clearly supports achievement of the organization's goals and to connect expectations for employee performance to the mission of the organization.

Evaluations may be directed toward either individual or team performance. Their multiple applications fit broadly into one of two categories, depending largely on the outcomes desired from the performance appraisal system. First, there are *summative evaluations,* which are designed to assess an employee's overall strengths. These evaluations are developed primarily to review past performance, to recognize employee accomplishments or successes, and to distribute performance-based pay increases or bonuses. Second, there are *formative evaluations,* which are designed to diagnose an employee's weaknesses. These evaluations are developed primarily to either improve or redirect future performance; they set goals or objectives and identify employee training and development needs in order to broaden the organization's knowledge base or prepare individuals for promotion. When these two types of performance appraisal purposes are confused and combined, the process can be very stressful for the evaluated employee, and it may tempt that employee to hide weaknesses and avoid needed training—actions that are usually detrimental to organizational performance in the long run.[2]

It is important to ensure that all supervisors and employees understand the purposes of the performance appraisal system. Beyond associating the evaluation with the mission of the agency and the various applications mentioned above, the organization can also use the evaluation process to enhance employee motivation and communication between managers and employees. Finally, the formal appraisal document creates a paper trail in support of such important personnel decisions as performance-based pay increases, transfers, promotions, demotions, and terminations (see also Chapter 8).

Protecting the performance appraisal system from external and internal challenges

When an organization develops a performance evaluation system, several issues can arise in implementation that cause problems and therefore require careful attention.

Validity and reliability   The performance evaluation forms must meet the same standards of validity and reliability as do selection procedures for hiring (see the sidebar "Validity and Reliability" on page 46). Like the testing approaches, the appraisal forms need to be job related; that is, the rubrics used in the assessment must accurately measure the nature and quality of the employee's work. In other words, validity is concerned with measuring job-related behaviors and outcomes that are fair and do not discriminate. As noted in Chapters 1 and 2, it is very important to use systematic job analysis techniques to identify job-related criteria, which can then be used to design the performance evaluation document.

As is true for selection techniques, reliability refers to the level of consistency with which the evaluation techniques are applied. Discriminatory impacts must be avoided. Thus, training for supervisors is necessary to ensure that the evaluation system is understood and applied similarly by the different actors involved in the process—principally, employees, their supervisors, and managers.

Court challenges[3]   Legal challenges to performance evaluation systems are not uncommon. For example, employees have charged that personal traits were used for rating criteria, that rating standards were subjective, that the employer failed to inform them of rating standards, that rating standards were not job related, that standards had a disparate impact on particular groups of employees, and that raters were improperly trained. Amendments made in 1972 to Title VII of the Civil Rights Act of 1964 require public sector employers to validate any personnel evaluation technique that affects an employee's chances for promotion (see Chapter 5). Court decisions issued both prior and subsequent to the issuance of the long-standing "Uniform Guidelines on Employee Selection Procedures" (41 CFR 60) in 1978 show that performance evaluation instruments that were developed with the characteristics described in the sidebar on page 80 are best able to withstand judicial scrutiny.[4]

Tips for developing valid and reliable performance appraisal instruments

☐ Use a job analysis to develop the appraisal instrument.

☐ Develop a behavior-oriented or results-based rather than a personal trait-oriented instrument.

☐ Give those carrying out performance evaluations specific written instructions on how to use the performance appraisal instrument.

Clear, consistent top-level support If managers and employees are to take an evaluation system seriously, top-level management and the political leadership must give the system clear, consistent public support. Failure to present the evaluation process as a priority issue for management will lead to lax implementation, and the local government entity will not attain the full benefit that such a system is designed to produce. Lack of management support can also lead to morale issues. The seriousness of top management's support should be reinforced in the following ways.

Policies and procedures to ensure appropriate implementation of the system
The evaluation system must feature sufficient documentation to provide clear guidance for implementation. The documentation should include policies that reinforce the goals and objectives of the system. For example, it is increasingly recognized that managers and supervisors should have a performance standard and be evaluated for the timely completion of their subordinates' evaluations.

Employee participation in selecting and designing procedures Involving employees in the selection and design of an appraisal system can have a very positive impact. Employees may be selected for participation by the employer unilaterally or from nominations made by managers, supervisors, and employees—even those wishing to nominate themselves. Committees of employees may be fully empowered to select an appraisal system, or they may act in an advisory role. Additionally, participation can be encouraged by allowing employees sufficient on-the-job time to participate in the evaluation process, including release time for those who are involved in the development, assessment, and periodic redesign (i.e., fine tuning) of evaluation systems.

Training of managers, supervisors, and employees[5] Managers, supervisors, and employees must be provided with sufficient training and practice to understand and complete performance evaluations. They need adequate training on the following:

- *Subjectivity and bias.* Even the most objective performance evaluation systems call upon raters to make tough decisions. Unavoidably, subjective rater judgments can be influenced by biases irrelevant to actual performance. Supervisors must be made aware of the subjective elements of their ratings and receive training on avoiding biases in their assessments. Failure to be open about this subjectivity and potential for bias can lead to morale problems and undermine the acceptance of the process.
- *Cross-rater comparisons.* The subjective elements of most appraisals necessarily mean that one supervisor may interpret and implement an assessment system differently from another. In addition, the performance objectives of employees are often quite different, and so might not be directly comparable.
- *Periodic updating of evaluation instruments.* Most evaluation systems contain elements that are time bound; for example, key individuals or the technologies being used may change. New technologies come into place with increasing frequency. Consequently, the evaluation system should be reviewed periodically to keep it up-to-date.

The importance of continuous training and skill building cannot be overemphasized. It is absolutely necessary to develop and maintain a shared understanding and consistent administration of the evaluation system, and supervisors need support to do their best.

Unions and employee associations   Rights granted to union- or association-represented employees differ considerably across jurisdictions. It is therefore important to obtain legal advice with respect to those rights when creating a performance appraisal system. In addition, it is recommended that the union or employee association be involved in developing the appraisal system. Failure to do so will likely lead to troublesome resistance by the union or association, to employee grievances, and to subsequent negotiation problems. If an agreement cannot be reached, the employer should explore options with the assistance of labor relations or legal advisors. These options may include, but should not be limited to, exempting employees subject to the labor agreement from coverage under the evaluation system.

Choosing an evaluation method

One of the initial decisions that an employer must make is whether the development of a single ubiquitous evaluation system is appropriate for all employees and for all purposes; for instance, is the evaluation intended for summative or for formative purposes, or for both. If a single system is deemed to be inappropriate, the organization should consider the development of several parallel systems—systems that match the purposes for each agency and/or group of employees in the local government.

There are two methods commonly employed for drafting appraisal instruments. Both use job analysis techniques and meet the job-relatedness test. The first one uses the job descriptions (see Chapter 1) for singular positions or classes of positions. Job descriptions are written by supervisors (and perhaps involve the employee) and are analyzed and refined by personnel job analysts. The information they yield—for example, the list of tasks, responsibilities, level of supervision—provide the foundation for developing the performance appraisal instrument. Whoever creates the form, whether it be the chief administrator or a human resource consultant, then questions the job experts (i.e., the employees who perform the jobs and/or their supervisors) to identify desired work-related behaviors. These behaviors become the performance standards by which the employees will be evaluated. Scales ranging from exceeding to not meeting expectations are specified for each major behavior associated with the position or class of positions in question.

A second method uses job analysts and/or job experts who gather information about specific tasks (often called "critical incidents") that employees perform and the behaviors that are thought to contribute to the successful or unsuccessful completion of those tasks. Once these tasks and behaviors are identified, the personnel staff and/or job experts write a performance standard scale for the critical incidents representing the range of behaviors against which the employees will be evaluated. It should be noted that elements of these two methods can be mixed to create a hybrid method.

The techniques of performance appraisal

The techniques described here are categorized by their primary focus: comparison of employees against an "average" employee, comparison of employees against each other, evaluation by someone other than the supervisor, participatory techniques, upward and 360-degree techniques, and pass-fail techniques. Most of these techniques are best implemented with substantial employee participation.

Techniques that compare employees against an "average" employee

Several approaches have been created to evaluate the performance of an employee compared with that of an average employee. Which approach to use depends on the job contents and on the internal or external resources available to develop a technique and administer it appropriately.

Narrative essays   The rater writes substantial comments about the employee's job-related behaviors (see Exhibit 3–1 for an example). This technique is sometimes combined with employee ranking techniques described in the next section, "Techniques That Compare Employees against Each Other" (but see the Caution box on page 82).

Narrative essays provide substantially more information as to why particular ratings were given than do simple numerical rating systems, but they have several disadvantages:

- They are time-consuming.
- They require substantial training of raters.
- They create a bias in favor of employees blessed with supervisors who have strong writing skills.
- They are subject to rating inflation over time as raters try to find new superlatives to describe their more able employees.
- It is extremely difficult to make comparisons between ratings since different raters describe their employees differently.
- Raters tend to focus mostly on either the positive or the negative aspects of an employee's performance rather than providing a balanced assessment.

Objective (preestablished) standards   This technique uses preestablished standards for such indicators as quality of work, quantity of work, timeliness, etc., and

Exhibit 3-1   Example of appraisal technique with narrative

Employee name: _____   Rating period: _____

Rating criteria	*Narrative description of performance*
1. Delegating work to subordinates	1.
2. Meeting deadlines	2.
3. Keeping current with applicable regulations	3.

Overall rating of employee (circle the most appropriate):

| Outstanding | Exceeds expectations | Meets expectations | Needs improvement | Not acceptable |

Rating instructions: Write a paragraph to describe how the employee performed in each of the rating criteria. Include examples of the employee's work in the description. Then select the performance rating that best describes the employee's overall performance.

Exhibit 3-2   Example of appraisal technique with objective (preestablished) standards

Employee name: _____   Rating period: _____

Primary duties or responsibilities	*Performance standards*	*Rating*	*Comments*
1. Assesses if clients meet requirements for benefit eligibility	A. Contacts clients by phone once per month to reapprove benefit receipt	Outstanding Exceeds standard Meets standard Needs improvement Not acceptable	
	B. Meets client in client's home once per quarter to review client needs for types of benefits	Outstanding Exceeds standard Meets standard Needs improvement Not acceptable	

Rating instructions: Mark the performance level that best describes the performance of the employee for each primary responsibility and note the reason(s) for the choice in the comments column.

Note: The evaluator must also have definitions for each of the rating levels.

for related indicators such as the number or percentage of total claims processed in a month by an employee (see Exhibit 3–2).

Forced-choice rating   This technique identifies positive behaviors that are related to successful job performance. From among multiple behaviors, supervisors choose those that best describe the employee's performance (see Exhibit 3–3). There is no apparent right or best answer known to the rater. In larger jurisdictions the personnel office uses a weighted scale to score the rater's choices. Smaller communities can contract with an outside human resource consultant.

This technique reduces rater bias since the rater does not know the weighting scheme for scoring the ratings. Supervisors tend to dislike the technique, however, because they do not know how they are rating each employee. Moreover, the technique grants the personnel office or human resource consultant ultimate control since the job evaluation is used to develop the rating instrument. This technique also requires the maintenance of confidentiality regarding the weighting methodology. However, the need for confidentiality may result in suspicion and distrust of the methodology among those displeased by outcomes of the process.

The weighted checklist   This technique is similar to the forced-choice rating technique but features some noteworthy differences (see Exhibit 3–4). The first step in developing the weighted checklist involves obtaining a "laundry list" of statements from supervisors describing effective and ineffective behaviors that contribute to or detract from successful job performance. The second step is for a smaller group of experienced "judges" to rank the statements in order of importance. Those statements that most of the judges agree on and rank similarly are included in the rating checklist given to the supervisor, to whom the weighting values of the statements remain unknown. This technique has the same advantages and disadvantages as the forced-choice rating.

Exhibit 3-3 Example of forced-choice appraisal technique

Employee name: _____		Rating period: _____	
Item			
1	MOST		LEAST
	A	Does not anticipate problems	A
	B	Grasps explanations quickly	B
	C	Rarely wastes time on the job	C
	D	Easy to talk to	D
2	MOST		LEAST
	A	Leader in group activities at work	A
	B	Wastes time on unimportant things	B
	C	Cool and calm under stress	C
	D	Hard worker and good example to others	D
3	MOST		LEAST
	A	Polite with clients	A
	B	Avoids taking on new responsibilities	B
	C	Takes advantage of training programs	C
	D	Able to delegate responsibilities	D

Rating instructions: In each item the rater circles the letter of the phrase that is *most* like the subject being evaluated *and* the letter of the phrase that is *least* like the subject being evaluated.

Note on scoring: If one of the positive (favorable) items is checked as most characteristic, the employee receives credit; similarly, one of the negative items marked as least descriptive also merits a positive credit.

The critical incident assessment This approach is recommended in the evaluation of professionals. The technique lists job-related behaviors or agreed-upon objectives. The rater records examples of noteworthy critical incidents (examples of past work) and assesses the employee's performance—good and bad—against the list (see Exhibit 3–5).

This technique focuses the supervisor's attention on high-priority behaviors and goals. The supervisor is trusted to record truly representative critical incidents of the employees' work, while the employees feel trusted to do a good job using their own discretion on lower-priority goals. However, to the extent that the critical incident examples selected for attention in the evaluation process are not representative, the technique is subject to rater bias. This system is relatively more time-consuming than others since supervisors need to write up and maintain systematic notes of employee work examples.

Behaviorally anchored rating scales (BARS) This technique, like the weighted checklist, begins with supervisors providing descriptions of effective and ineffective behaviors that contribute to or detract from successful job performance. Personnel specialists use job analysis techniques to ensure that these behaviors are job

Exhibit 3-4   Example of weighted checklist appraisal technique

Employee name: _____ Rating period: _____	
Item	*Weighting*
☐ Employees enjoy working with him or her.	(+)
☐ Takes a long-range viewpoint.	(+)
☐ Expects too much of subordinates.	(−)
☐ Schedules his or her work well.	(+)
☐ Wastes much time preparing for meetings.	(−)
☐ Works well with managers from other agencies.	(+)
☐ Knows where important questions can be directed.	(+)
☐ Is unable to delegate responsibilities.	(−)
☐ Makes all efforts to involve subordinates in work decisions.	(+)
☐ Can be expected to maintain work schedules and deadlines.	(+)

Rating instructions: Check all items that apply to the employee's work behavior.

Exhibit 3-5   Example of critical incident assessment technique

Employee name: _____   Position: _____

Rating period: _____   to _____

Objectives	*Representative examples of performance (successful and unsuccessful)*
1. Train field workers well	1.
	2.
	3.
	4.
2. Improve quality of services to walk-in clients	1.
	2.
	3.
	4.
3. Achieve better cost control over long-distance telephone use	1.
	2.
	3.
	4.

Rating instructions: Note both successful (good) and unsuccessful (poor) examples of the employee's work efforts to meet the objectives as they occur throughout the rating period.

related. A group of experienced judges then evaluates and ranks the statements on a performance scale ranging from excellent to poor. Those descriptions upon which most of the judges agree and rank similarly are included in the BARS instrument (see Exhibit 3–6). Supervisors then compare the employee's performance against the descriptive statements and choose the statements that most closely characterize the *typical behaviors* of the employee. The chosen statements for each behavior correspond to points on the BARS rating scale.

This technique reduces rater bias and has withstood the scrutiny of the courts. It is an advanced form of performance appraisal and requires substantial effort and expertise to develop. If the jurisdiction lacks the personnel specialists in-house, it may be advisable to contract with a human resource consulting firm.

Exhibit 3–6   Example of behaviorally anchored rating scale (BARS) item

Willingness and ability of employee to meet deadlines:

5 — Could be expected to meet deadlines, no matter how unusual the circumstances, by increasing efforts until the work is done.

Could be expected to meet deadlines comfortably by delegating the less important duties to others

4 — Could be expected always to meet deadlines on time by delegating most of the work to others

Could be expected to meet deadlines within a reasonable length of time

3 — Could be expected to offer to work at home after failing to get work out on the deadline day once in a while

Could be expected to fail to meet deadlines on a regular basis, but be ready to devote personal time to catching up

2 — Could be expected to be behind schedule all the time, but appear to work hard to catch up

Could be expected to be behind schedule and display little effort to catch up

1 — Could be expected to ignore deadlines and get work in on time only infrequently

Rating instructions: Select the statement that best reflects the work behavior of the employee.

Note: This is an example of one of the possible items that could be used on a BARS rating instrument. In addition to selecting the statement that best identifies the employee's typical behavior, the rater could also be asked to write examples of the employee's work to support the selection made.

Techniques that compare employees against each other   When the employer needs to know about the different levels of performance among a class of employees, a ranking approach may be applied that compares employees against each other. The ranking then can be used to determine merit pay or bonus pay, promotions, mentoring assignments, and similar personnel decisions.

Paired employee comparisons   This technique requires the rater to rank each employee against other employees for a number of work behaviors (see Exhibit 3–7). A summary score is tallied for each employee to determine the employee's rank in comparison with other employees the rater supervises.

This technique reduces rater bias by eliminating the ability to rate employees similarly on all behaviors, and it is relatively easy to develop and implement. However, the technique makes it difficult for supervisors to rank more than a handful of employees. Moreover, employees and supervisors alike tend to dislike these comparisons, and the method can create discord if the rankings are leaked.

Forced distribution of employees   This technique may be appropriate for a relatively large number of employees in the same class. It requires the supervisor to sort employees on a percentage scale, such as the top 20 percent, lowest 20 percent, etc. Employees are ranked in distributions for several categories of merit that are considered important for the organization (see Exhibit 3–8).

Forced distribution has the same pros and cons as paired employee comparisons. Research indicates that employees prefer to work in settings where "all pull their weight"—where no stars and no slackers threaten team cohesion and an overall strong performance.

Techniques that use evaluators other than the supervisor   The techniques described in this section could use any of the rating formats for which examples have already been provided. The wording of the questions may need to be modified, however, to reflect the change in who completes the employees' performance evaluations.

Exhibit 3-7   Example of paired employee comparisons appraisal technique

Supervisor name: _____	Comparisons of employee pairs	
Department/unit: _____	1. Employee A	Employee B
	2. Employee A	Employee C
Rating period: _____	3. Employee A	Employee D
Employees supervised: Employee A	4. Employee A	Employee E
Employee B	5. Employee B	Employee C
Employee C	6. Employee B	Employee D
Employee D	7. Employee B	Employee E
Employee E	8. Employee C	Employee D
	9. Employee C	Employee E
	10. Employee D	Employee E

Rating instructions: Circle the employee whose overall performance is better between each pair of employees.

Note on scoring: Add the number of times each employee is circled and then rank the employees in descending order by the total number of times each is chosen.

Exhibit 3-8   Example of forced distribution of employees' ratings appraisal technique

Supervisor name: _____   Rating period: _____

Department/unit: _____

10% Highest	Next 20%	Middle 40%	Next 20%	10% Lowest
	_____	_____	_____	
		_____	_____	
		_____		
_____	_____	_____		

Rating instructions: Place the names of your ten employees in the appropriate categories according to their overall performance.

Self-ratings   The self-rating technique is based on the employee's participation in establishing objectives, and then rating his or her own performance in having worked toward those objectives.

Self-rating establishes clearer patterns of communication of expectations between supervisor and employees and often generates genuine employee commitment. Its disadvantages, however, are that it can be subject to bias and rating inflation (self-ratings tend to be higher than supervisory ratings among poor performers), and it requires substantial supervisor and employee time and effort to complete.

Peer ratings   The underlying concept is that co-workers are in the best position to know how well or how poorly fellow employees do their job.

Anonymous ratings by co-workers tend to be more accurate than either self-ratings or supervisory ratings, and they can encourage more of a group commitment to work. However, there are several noteworthy disadvantages to peer ratings:

- Anonymity is very difficult to maintain in smaller groups.
- Reliability is lower if the co-workers do not work closely with the evaluated employee or do not perform similar kinds of work.
- Peer ratings are disliked by employees.
- Differences in co-worker ratings can cause persisting workplace conflict.
- Co-workers can easily conspire—consciously or subconsciously—to inflate each other's ratings or to scapegoat productive but socially unpopular employees.

Field review   This technique uses the services of a "neutral" outsider to perform the evaluation. The outsider should be unquestionably knowledgeable about the work.

Field review is well suited to situations in which interpersonal relationships between supervisors and employees are poor, or in which the organization detects the presence of biased supervisory reviews. However, both employees and supervisors tend to dislike the use of outside raters, perhaps because there is no guarantee that field reviews will be free of the same kinds of bias that are found in supervisory evaluations. Moreover, field reviews may incur significant additional costs and disrupt the flow of work.

Participatory techniques   In participatory reviews, the employee is drawn into the process of setting performance objectives. Management by objectives (MBO) and work planning and review (WPR) are examples of participatory techniques. Goal setting establishes standards against which the employee is evaluated, so the focus of evaluation is on outcomes or results. Exhibit 3–9 provides an example of the MBO-type format. WPR, which is less comprehensive than MBO, stresses periodic supervisor-employee reviews of work plans and employee progress in meeting plans, midcourse plan revisions, and the identification of employee training needs.

Participatory techniques improve communication, clarify work expectations, and increase the employee's commitment to goal attainment. But they can also have disadvantages, such as

- When results become the focus of the evaluation, the organization must guard against overzealous individual competitiveness, a "results by any means" mentality, and, where quantity or timeliness is the objective, a potential drop in work quality.
- Participatory techniques require a time commitment by supervisors and employees to discuss and set goals, review progress, and complete the appraisal.
- Evaluative decisions must be made even though factors beyond the control of the employee can influence attainment of results.
- Participatory techniques tend to be less successful for positions that are not executive, managerial, or professional.

Exhibit 3-9   Example of MBO goal-setting approach (a participatory technique)

Employee name: _____   Rating period: _____

In the coming six months, the following objectives will be pursued and success will be determined by these associated results.

Objectives	*Results sought*
1. Train field workers well	Preparation of five staff members to assume supervisory duties at field offices in rural areas
2. Improve quality of services to walk-in clients	Conduct search for and locate the most willing/able employee to take on receptionist duties as required
3. Achieve better cost control over long-distance telephone use	Hold a staff meeting to discuss the problem of telephone charges and appoint a committee to formulate a plan to achieve a 15 percent reduction in charges

Agreed to on: _____
(Date)

Agreed to by: _____
(Evaluatee)

_____
(Evaluator)

Upward and 360-degree feedback techniques   These techniques use evaluators other than the supervisor to rate employee performance. But otherwise they can make use of any of the rating formats previously discussed, provided that the wording of the questions is modified to reflect the change in who completes the performance evaluation report.

Upward feedback   The technique of soliciting supervisor ratings from subordinates represents an effort to underscore the importance of feedback in an organization. Managers need to know how supervisors are viewed by employees.

Maintaining the anonymity of raters produces more accurate evaluations, but it makes reconciling differences in ratings by individual employees difficult. Another problem is the difficulty of maintaining anonymity. Moreover, a clear potential exists among employees for conspiring to inflate or deflate ratings to make their boss look good or bad, depending on their personal feelings.

360-degree feedback   The 360-degree technique, also known as multisource performance evaluation, obtains simultaneous evaluations from a combination of sources such as superiors, subordinates, and peers, as well as people outside the organization, such as agency clients. All the sources in question are people with whom the employee works or interacts. This technique uses observable work behaviors that are considered important for the successful accomplishment of the work and that personnel specialists usually validate as being performance based. The employee's behaviors are ranked against a scale by those asked to complete the evaluation. The resultant product is a report to the employee based on the various responses obtained on the evaluation instrument. Commonly, the evaluations are submitted anonymously.

Self-rating may also be used in conjunction with this technique. The accuracy of the employee's self-perception of performance can be gauged by the feedback received from persons inside and outside the employee's work unit. When the gap between self- and other ratings is relatively wide, the employee's work output can be addressed with appropriate training and development programs.[6] In general, through 360-degree feedback, employees can be made aware of how essential they are to the organization and how they stand with their peers and their customers. Most employees consider this kind of evaluation to be fair, which makes it more effective than many other forms of performance appraisal. However, the 360-degree feedback is quite time-consuming and administratively burdensome.

Another problem involves the issue of anonymity or confidentiality. Experience with the technique indicates that anonymity tends to be difficult to maintain, especially in small workgroups or where the employee has a limited number of outside contacts. Moreover, reconciling differences in ratings from the various sources can be problematic, and report writing can be difficult. Finally, in jobs where the employee has to enforce the law (e.g., police officer, animal control agent, building code inspector), citizens cited for violations may give poor ratings to employees who do an excellent job.

Pass-fail techniques   Because most evaluation approaches are time-consuming and supervisors tend to dislike the process, designers of evaluation instruments have been seeking methods that "keep it simple" and require less time and effort to complete. A recent innovation has been the pass-fail evaluation in which there are only two performance categories: one either passes (meets or exceeds stated expectations) or fails (does not meet stated expectations). In a now classic article on performance appraisal, John Nalbandian noted in 1991 that supervisors believe they know how their employees perform based on an informal assessment and that formal reviews duplicate assessments that have already been made.[7]

Another problem noted with many evaluation systems is that many evaluators find it difficult to distinguish between various levels of job performance and thus tend to avoid the extreme values—for example, outstanding or unsatisfactory—in favor of those in the middle of the scale. As a result, few employees fail, and so both employees and supervisors often consider the performance appraisal process to be meaningless.[8] Additionally, there is a failure to complete evaluations on a timely basis. This delay is especially tempting when supervisory performance plans do not include a performance standard for the completion of appraisals. Since the vast majority of employee evaluations are favorable, eliminating a substantial amount of the paperwork should improve the rate of timely completion.

Pass-fail evaluation simplifies the process by documenting the informal evaluations of supervisors, and limiting the choice in performance ratings to two global categories. In so doing, the technique focuses attention on employees who are not performing to expectations. For those employees who *are* performing to expectations, supervisors are freed from the time-consuming formal process so they can devote more time and effort to their poorly performing employees. It is important to note that for those employees judged to be performing poorly, formal documentation of failure to meet expectations is necessary. The pass-fail technique may be used in conjunction with any of the previously discussed techniques for the required documentation.

While the fundamental advantage of the pass-fail technique is the reliance on informal assessments of employees and the diminished time commitment, there are some disadvantages:

- The pass-fail focus may be perceived as more negative since written documentation is produced only for those who "fail" in the evaluation. To avoid this pitfall, the organization needs to ensure that the evaluation and disciplinary processes are separate so the evaluation process can concentrate on the development of the employee.
- Pass-fail may place more pressure on both formal and informal methods of employee recognition. The majority of employees doing well cannot be ignored; they need ongoing positive reinforcement of their performance.
- The absence of formal evaluations on "passing" performance may not provide documentation to support compensation, promotion, or other human resource decisions.
- Pass-fail assessment does not eliminate the need for the training of employees, supervisors, and managers or for consistent standards against which employee performance is judged, both informally and formally.

Evaluation techniques to avoid   An evaluation instrument that uses personal traits, such as neatness, honesty, or friendliness, without drawing linkages to particular job tasks seldom, if ever, withstands court scrutiny and should therefore not be implemented. Exhibit 3–10 is an example of a trait-based system that uses a graphic rating scale format.

Exhibit 3-10   Trait-based example (using a graphic rating scale format)

	Outstanding	Good	Satisfactory	Fair	Unsatisfactory
Employee name: _____ Agency: _____ Review period: _____					
1. Job knowledge	☐	☐	☐	☐	☐
2. Interpersonal relationships	☐	☐	☐	☐	☐
3. Quantity of work	☐	☐	☐	☐	☐
4. Quality of work	☐	☐	☐	☐	☐
5. Dependability	☐	☐	☐	☐	☐
6. Initiative	☐	☐	☐	☐	☐
7. Supervisory skills (if applicable)	☐	☐	☐	☐	☐

Supervisor: _____   Date: _____

Comments: _____

Implementing the program

To reinforce the organization's commitment to its mission, managers and supervisors should be subject to the same kind of evaluation as are rank-and-file employees. To ensure their timely compliance and commitment to the evaluation system, top management should include in their evaluations specific performance objectives that support the implementation and the maintenance of the performance evaluation system under which the supervisors and their managers are being rated.

Training   The proper training of employees, supervisors, and managers in the creation and use of the performance evaluation system is essential to ensure that the evaluation program is perceived as fair—that is, that the instrument is applied consistently by different raters and that rater error and biases are kept to a minimum.

Elements of a good appraisal

- The objectives of the evaluation are established before the start of the appraisal period.
- Specific competencies or skills to be measured are listed with examples of successful behaviors.
- The rating scale being used fits the organization's culture and objectives.
- Space is included for the employee's self-appraisal.
- Space is included for specific comments from the supervisor about the employee's performance.
- Suggestions are provided for employee development.
- Objectives are established for the next appraisal date.

Source: Adapted from Carla Joinson, "Making Sure Employees Measure Up," *HR Magazine* 46, no. 3 (March 2001).

This will help to ensure buy-in from everyone involved. Training should include how to write performance objectives. Additionally, supervisors need to understand how the evaluation solidifies power relationships and how to manage those relationships sensitively.

It will be necessary for training purposes to prepare manuals and worksheets that explain the performance appraisal system and provide answers to commonly encountered problems. A "pilot agency" can be used to test out a new performance appraisal instrument, and supportive materials can be developed if necessary after the pilot test is debriefed. A new performance appraisal system can also be phased in by implementing the system for a "pilot group" of employees, such as the top-echelon management group. This technique has the advantage of familiarizing (training) top management with the system before managers administer it to their subordinates, and it helps support a perception of a fair system since the system would be known to apply to all employees—even top management.

Timing   Performance appraisals may be administered either on an individual employee's employment anniversary or on an established time schedule for all employees. Each option has advantages and disadvantages. In a nutshell, a universal evaluation date may align performance reviews with the budget cycle and organizational goals and objectives. Universal evaluation dates also mean that the supervisor is evaluating all employees under the same environmental conditions. However, a universal evaluation date may cause a time crunch on supervisors since they must review all employees simultaneously. Anniversary date evaluations avoid the time crunch problem, but very likely mean that the supervisor is producing evaluations for employees under different circumstances. For example, one employee may be evaluated when the supervisor is under very tight time constraints for completing other tasks while another employee may be appraised when the supervisor is not under such pressures and can devote sufficient time to the task.

Periodic employee-supervisor performance status reviews   Supervisors' periodic reviews of employees' progress toward the accomplishment of performance objectives are important to communication efforts. Periodic reviews allow the supervisor and employee to exchange ideas on options for continued progress, and also allow for discussion and negotiation of any changes that may need to be made in the established performance objectives. The length of time between periodic reviews may vary depending on the type of work involved, but as a general rule these reviews should be conducted quarterly. Three months usually allow enough time between reviews for the employee to demonstrate additional accomplishment of performance objectives and is not overly burdensome for supervisors who must complete the reviews.

Criticism in performance reviews must be handled very carefully.[9] When supervisors use reviews as a vehicle for criticism, they risk intensifying the conflicts that may be at the root of the negatives that emerge from the evaluation. Criticism is rarely a motivator; even well-placed and modulated criticism is very often seen as a personal attack on the employee.[10] If the supervisor conveys sarcasm or contempt, the employee may feel humiliated, defensive, and angry, and these feelings lead to evasion of responsibility, passive resistance, and other noncompliant behaviors. The sidebar on page 82 offers some tips for keeping performance reviews positive.

Tips on communicating performance appraisals effectively

☐ Do not delay providing feedback to employees about performance.

☐ Balance criticism with praise and appreciation for the positive.

☐ Focus on the results of a person's performance. Avoid any criticism that focuses on character or a person's innate deficiencies.

☐ Be specific, focusing on incidents or problems.

☐ Offer solutions.

☐ Be empathetic. As an appraiser, put yourself in the place of the person being evaluated.

☐ Operate on the assumption that even an objective and dispassionate appraisal may be interpreted as a deprecation causing embarrassment and hurt feelings.

Source: Daniel Goleman, *Emotional Intelligence* (New York: Bantam Books, 1994), chap. 10.

Employee response and appeals   Employees must be provided with the results of their evaluations and the evaluator's report in a timely manner. They have a right to inspect and review their performance evaluation records. They should also be informed that they have a right to respond to and rebut negative entries.

Employees may also have a right to ask for arbitration or submit a formal grievance over their evaluations. Because of the due process rights of public employees and the potential for using performance evaluations in disciplinary proceedings, a formal procedure for appeal of adverse actions needs to be established. However, if the employer makes a procedural mistake in the performance appraisal, an employee is not entitled to any relief unless he or she would otherwise have been retained, promoted, or rewarded.[11] (See Chapter 5 for further discussion of employee rights in this context.)

Caution

■ Federal law requires public sector employers to validate any personnel technique that affects an employee's chances for promotion. Consequently, if performance evaluations are used in determining employee promotions, the appraisal system must not discriminate against protected employees (as defined under Title VII).

■ Evaluation techniques that make use of personal traits in the abstract, such as dependability or initiative, should be avoided.

■ Too little employee and supervisory involvement in the process of selecting and designing the procedures or too few resources for supporting a performance evaluation system (money and time for training, time for supervision and monitoring) can cause failure.

■ Using the performance evaluation system as an alternate disciplinary process will undermine its purposes and erode employee support for it.

■ An appraisal system cannot violate provisions of a negotiated labor agreement.

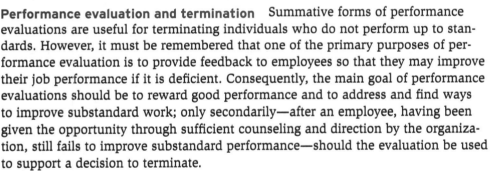

Tips for evaluating employee performance

☐ Take the time to thoroughly determine why the organization desires to implement a performance appraisal system, and then identify the appraisal techniques that most closely fit these purposes.

☐ Identify goals that are associated with the agency's mission. This process moves from the top down, with each level of the organization selecting goals that assist the next level up to achieve its goals.

☐ Begin communication about the evaluation system early and continue through the development process.

☐ Develop a comprehensive training plan for managers and supervisors as well as for all employees.

☐ Ensure that the performance appraisal instrument elicits a balanced account of the employee's performance.

☐ Review appraisal results with employees, identifying both strengths and weaknesses.

☐ Reinforce management's commitment to the evaluation system by including accurate and timely completion of employees' evaluations in the managers' and supervisors' appraisal criteria.

Performance evaluation and termination   Summative forms of performance evaluations are useful for terminating individuals who do not perform up to standards. However, it must be remembered that one of the primary purposes of performance evaluation is to provide feedback to employees so that they may improve their job performance if it is deficient. Consequently, the main goal of performance evaluations should be to reward good performance and to address and find ways to improve substandard work; only secondarily—after an employee, having been given the opportunity through sufficient counseling and direction by the organization, still fails to improve substandard performance—should the evaluation be used to support a decision to terminate.

When employees are terminated for performance-related reasons, a written record of the organization's efforts to correct performance deficiencies is invaluable. Certainly, there may be occasions when an employee does something so egregious that immediate termination is warranted. In most cases, however, deficient performance is a longer-term problem. Performance evaluations, properly done, officially document the employee's job behavior deficiencies, record the organization's efforts to correct them, and establish that the employee was given sufficient time to make the corrections. Such documentation is often critical for withstanding adverse action appeals, employee grievances, or court challenges to termination decisions. (Chapter 8 provides detailed information about problem employees and due process procedures.)

Generational differences and sustainability-related topics

Guiding principles

- Generational transitions need to be anticipated and consciously planned.
- Conflicts due to generational differences should be dampened and positive synergies cultivated.
- Personnel policies should be revised to promote environmental sustainability goals.

Challenges

- Planning for replacement of the "greatest generation"
- Building bridges across generational divides
- Creating better understanding of potential synergies of multigenerational teams
- Creating policies and options for sustainability-promoting work arrangements, such as telework

The twenty-first-century workplace consists of employees from various generations: "Radio Babies" (born 1930–1945), Baby Boomers (born 1946–1964), Generation Xers (born 1965–1976), Generation Ys (born 1977–1990), and Millenials (born 1991 or later).[12] Employees across these cohorts have varied work styles and preferences, as well as "unique work ethics, different perspectives on work, distinct and preferred ways of managing and being managed, idiosyncratic styles, and unique ways of viewing such work-world issues as quality, service, and... showing up for work."[13] For instance, members of younger generations typically consider work conditions, such as hours and methods, to be negotiable, while members of older generations do not. This is considered to be the primary source of contention across generations —younger generations want more work-related flexibility than their parents had, while older generations firmly believe in working within the established structure and "paying your dues."[14]

Consideration of these cross-generational differences by managers and supervisors can be introduced when examining how and when the various tools available to maintain an effective and highly motivated workforce should be implemented. Tools that may work well for one group may not be as effective for another and therefore may need to be adapted to fit the preferences of the alternate group. For example, Generation Xers prefer a certain amount of autonomy in the workplace. They want the freedom and flexibility to use their own work methods to "get the job done," whether by telecommuting or choosing nontraditional work hours, etc. On the contrary, Radio Babies may be uncomfortable with such freedom because the environments in which they have worked throughout their lives have typically been hierarchically structured, promoting a "command-and-control" style of leadership.[15] Differences in work preferences and routines will therefore require different methods and tools on the part of supervisors to manage and evaluate employees effectively.

An effective manager or supervisor will be aware of the various generations present in the workplace, will understand the preferences and work styles unique to each cohort, and will be flexible to accommodate these varied preferences.[16] Generational preferences can be considered, for instance, when collaborating with employees on the development of goals and the evaluation of strengths and weaknesses. Allowing individuals from different cohorts to work according to their generational styles will contribute to a work environment and evaluation process that enables employees to maximize their full potential. To manage work style diversity, supervisory personnel may want to seek training to understand the characteristics of each generation so as to become more "generational friendly,"[17] understand their own generational placement, and learn how to best communicate and interact with subordinates from different cohorts.

Organizations need to recognize that the various generations may bring different skill sets to the workplace. Millennials tend to be technologically savvy, which can provide a tremendous advantage for employers. However, this ability also presents new challenges. One of the noteworthy concerns associated with various technologies such as Internet-related tools is security of agency property. For instance, the use of instant messaging between employees on agency computers creates opportunities for firewall breaches.[18] Thus, new technology may bring into the workplace not only improved methods of communication but also potential problems that require the attention of management.

Among other work-related changes are efforts to reduce environmental impacts and promote sustainability. For example, in 1991 the Washington State Legislature enacted a Commute Trip Reduction (CTR) law, which was incorporated into the Washington Clean Air Act.[19] The law is intended to reduce traffic congestion, air pollution, and petroleum consumption through the use of employer-based programs that decrease the number of single-occupancy commute trips to work. Other methods of compliance include increased use of high-occupancy vehicles for ride sharing, walking or bicycling, and avoiding commutes during peak travel periods.[20] Additionally, many employers are making available the option to telecommute, which allows employees to work from home through the use of telecommunication tools (e.g., phone, fax, computer) and thus avoid the commute to work entirely. Many public agencies and Washington-based businesses have made this option available, which may have particular appeal for Generations X and Y, as it allows them more job flexibility and, for Generation X in particular, more family time at home.[21]

Understanding and managing generational differences will be a key to successfully maintaining a high-performance workforce in the years ahead. The tools and techniques discussed in this chapter will assist managers in their tasks. Regardless of generation, however, managers need to use the approaches discussed and master three basic sets of skills: (1) helping employees understand how their skills and talents will have an impact on the mission and goals of the organization; (2) developing communication systems to provide employees with the information they need when they need it; and (3) customizing incentives in accordance with what motivates each individual employee.[22]

Improving performance through goal setting

Guiding principles

■ Goals should be specific, clear, and realistic statements of potential attainment.

■ Goals should be set jointly with the employee.

■ Goals may be changed when circumstances change.

Challenges

- Developing and maintaining communication between employees and management
- Clearly identifying how goals help to attain the organization's mission
- Scheduling periodic progress checks
- Providing appropriate opportunities for employee development
- Creating realistic expectations regarding pay adjustments, job advancement and other rewards

A distinction must be made between goals and performance standards; the terms are often used interchangeably but then define different things. *Performance standards* are the general expectations established by the employer for performance and are identified by terms such as "exceeds expectations," "meets expectations," etc. In contrast, *goals* may be understood as target levels toward which the employee is to work. In principle, goals should stretch the employee's capabilities—that is, be high enough to challenge the employee to perform at an increased capacity but not so high that they are impossible to attain. The employee may not fully attain the goals that have been set in a performance contract (see below), but in the process of pursuing the goals, he or she may very well meet or exceed the standards established for measuring satisfactory performance.

In addition to generational differences in how employees approach work, all employees within an organization have strengths and weaknesses that are reflected in how they approach their work. Performance evaluation provides the opportunity to work with employees to identify the types of knowledge, skills, and abilities (KSAs) that could be developed to improve performance in their current work, enable them to perform work that they may be assigned to take on in the future, or prepare them for promotions. These KSAs can be referred to as the employee's development needs.

Performance evaluation systems can thus use goal setting for three distinct purposes: to improve performance deficiencies, to develop employees' capabilities to increase productivity, and to challenge employees to perform at higher levels.

Requirements for effective goal setting

To improve performance through goal setting, the employee should be consulted in establishing performance standards, made aware of ongoing progress checks, and given opportunities to improve through on-the-job training or other learning approaches.

Communication and employee participation　The identification of development needs for the employee to improve performance can create stress because such needs are unavoidably personal. The supervisor is in a position of power over the subordinate employee, which often leaves the employee feeling vulnerable. Thus, supervisors and managers need to be trained in how to build and maintain positive communications with employees. If the local government does not have in-house expertise to develop such comprehensive training, it may be able to enter into a contract with a local government association, a university-based institute, or a for-profit service provider.

Employees likely will be more committed to attaining goals if they are allowed to participate in establishing the standards that will be used in appraising their performance. Meaningful participation is multifaceted and includes having input in developing performance standards and the rating form, providing for self-evaluation, and establishing two-way communication.[23] Such participation facilitates communication between the employee and the supervisor, thereby promoting a clearer understanding between the two of what is expected. In turn, the enhanced communication allows an exchange of ideas on how to approach goals most effectively, often enlightening the supervisor about the employee's interests and career plans.

A performance evaluation system that includes goal setting can create an expectation that the employee should receive increased compensation for acquiring higher KSA levels. The organization must be open and very clear about its intentions with respect to this issue. Employees must know whether they will receive development pay, and if they do not, they must understand what the long-term value of increasing their KSAs will be to themselves, the agency, and the local government employing them. (See the section below on "Linking Performance to Compensation.")

Progress checks   It is necessary to establish a pattern—and an expectation on the part of supervisors and employees—of periodic checks on the employee's progress in pursuing and completing development assignments or training. This goal will require a concerted effort by supervisors, reinforced by management, to allot the time necessary for having follow-up meetings with the employee. Progress checks are not only an accountability measure but also an opportunity for coaching and mentoring in order to improve employee success and keep employees engaged in the organization.

Employee development opportunities   Once development needs are identified by the supervisor and employee, the organization must make a commitment to provide the employee with the opportunities required to fulfill them. Depending on the course of action identified, these opportunities may involve periodic on-the-job training, workshops, continuing education, distance and online learning, or other avenues. Providing these career development opportunities can be quite beneficial for the organization; Linda Gravett and Robin Throckmorton find that Generations X and Y are inclined to stay with organizations that provide such opportunities.[24] Therefore, it is important to recognize that the identification of development needs creates an ongoing expectation on the part of the employee to have development opportunities provided. Failure to provide such opportunities will likely result in morale problems and a general loss of trust in management and the evaluation system.

Tips for improving performance through goal setting

☐ Provide comprehensive training on goal setting for managers and supervisors.

☐ Fund employee development and make sure that managers release employees for development opportunities.

☐ Clearly communicate the local government's policies regarding pay adjustments and career advancement.

Caution

■ Ignoring the distinction between "performance contract" goals (stretch goals) and performance standards will increase supervisor-employee conflict as employees press for lower goal levels and weaken support for the evaluation system.

■ Any appearance of favoritism should be avoided because the development of trust is essential in goal setting.

Elements of a goal-setting system

To be effective, a goal-setting system should include performance contracts, an individual development plan, and an employee assistance program.

Performance contracts   Goal setting that establishes challenging or stretch performance levels tends to foster higher levels of productivity. The commitment that the employee makes to achieve the goals represents a performance contract. The contract identifies targets for the employee to achieve—targets that are higher than "satisfactory" performance levels but are not the standards against which the employee will be evaluated. Stretch goals are meant to challenge the capabilities of the employee, not to establish ever-higher levels for performance evaluation.

The stretch goals need to have two particular characteristics. First, they must be specific goals written in concrete terms. For example, "I will process the payroll in five hours," *not* "I will process the payroll as fast as I can." Second, they must be high enough to challenge the capabilities of the employee to perform at an increased capacity, but not so high that they are beyond the realistic reach of the employee. For instance, if it is widely known that an employee can process the payroll in seven hours, establishing a stretch goal of six hours may be realistic, whereas setting a goal of three hours is not. If goals are not realizable by the employee, they will not improve the employee's motivation or productivity and may, in fact, dampen motivation.

The individual development plan   An individual development plan provides a means of confronting any deficiencies of the employee in a constructive way, especially if the employee is involved in the planning. The focus should be on providing the employee with opportunities to expand his or her KSAs, not only to meet current performance standards but also to prepare for future advancement. The supervisor and employee should work together to determine specific KSAs that the employee could develop and then jointly identify the means to do so.

Employee assistance programs   Another means of redressing performance deficiencies is to refer employees to an employee assistance program (EAP) (if the organization has one) or to a certified counselor under contract with the jurisdiction. While this is usually a delicate matter psychologically and legally, discussion with the employee as well as the referral must be made in the context of performance deficiencies in the employee's work; any focus on personality or on perceived addiction problems should be avoided. (See Chapters 5, 7, and 8 for additional pertinent information.)

Linking compensation to performance

Guiding principles

- Performance evaluations should be linked to compensation decisions. Pay policies should be monitored to ensure that they contribute to high performance.

- Performance-based and developmental pay decisions need to be transparent, fair, and equitable.

Challenges

- Achieving a proper balance between pay and other forms of work incentives—that is, between intrinsic and extrinsic motivators

- Getting enough money appropriated in the budget so that incentive pay is meaningful and effective in raising performance, skills, and competencies

- Developing performance appraisals that clearly establish similarities or differences in employees' performance and justify any or no differences in pay raises

- Determining how to structure incentive pay to promote teamwork and group cohesion

Employees are spurred to greater performance by different motivators, roughly identified as either intrinsic or extrinsic in nature.[25] Linking pay to performance falls in the extrinsic category. New employees may receive a base pay determined by a job classification system or labor market conditions. But subsequent pay raises may be based on performance appraisals or a mix of pay raise policies. (See Chapter 6 for details on pay policies.) Performance-based pay is especially recommended in competitive labor markets where retention is a problem.

Pay that is linked to an individual's contributions is categorized as either *performance* or *development* pay. But the two pay policies are not mutually exclusive, and elements of both may be used in a pay system. Performance pay is further subdivided into *merit* pay or *bonus* pay. Merit pay is added to the employee's base pay and permanently increases the employee's compensation level. The alternative is a one-time bonus. The advantage of one-time payments for the organization is that they hold down increases in compensation budgets. However, David Carnevale notes that the effectiveness of bonus pay is predicated on acceptable levels of base pay.[26] If base pay levels in conjunction with one-time bonuses are not perceived as adequate, employees may feel that the system does not reward them enough for adding value to the organization and thus may not be sufficiently motivated to increase their skill or competency levels permanently. One way to resolve this issue is to provide, whenever possible, a combination of a base pay increase and a one-time bonus payment.

Research indicates, however, that rewards must be more than minimal for the benefits of an assessment-based pay system to work well.[27] Consequently, development of merit, skill-based, or competency-based pay systems requires a long-term commitment to fund the pay structure adequately. Failure to do so will weaken the link between performance evaluation and pay. Similarly, when employees are evenly skilled or possess different but equally valuable skills or competencies, the link between job performance and pay expectations is weakened if fixed limits are placed on the proportion of employees that can be rated within each level of performance.

Tips for linking performance and compensation

☐ Establish a funding source for performance-based pay and a long-term commitment to continued funding.

☐ Develop comprehensive training for managers and supervisors in linking compensation to performance, or contract for such services if in-house expertise is not available.

As with other aspects of performance evaluation, job analysis plays an important role no matter which assessment-based compensation system is used. (See Chapter 1 for more information about job analysis.) Once again, managers, supervisors, and employees must be trained on the nature and purposes of the evaluation system to understand how such elements as performance standards, skill sets, or competencies are determined. Managers and supervisors must also be thoroughly trained to explain the system to their employees, and to describe its relationship to the organization's mission. Training in this area should emphasize the principle that employees are to be treated equitably.

Finally, because of the due process rights of public employees and the potential for pay increases to be denied as a result of adverse performance evaluations, some form of appeal to adverse actions needs to be established. (See Chapters 5 and 8 for further discussion.)

Pay for performance (merit or bonus pay)

Performance pay is designed to reward employees according to their level of performance. Employees demonstrating higher levels of qualitative and quantitative output are eligible for larger salary adjustments; unsatisfactory levels of performance may receive smaller or no pay adjustments.

Performance pay programs require that the organization develop clear standards for evaluating employees. This is important so that employees are treated equitably; that is, employees who are rated the same with respect to work standards should be rewarded similarly. In addition, similar jobs should have similar performance objectives and pay levels to avoid the perception of favoritism among employees. Clear guidelines and training of supervisors and managers is essential to ensure that such consistency is maintained. Clear standards are also needed to ensure that the organization rewards the right behaviors—that is, those activities that contribute to the success of the organization's mission.

Other potential pitfalls have been noted; for instance, tying compensation to certain performance measures tends to cause employees to focus their work only on those areas for which they will be rewarded. Neglect of noncompensated areas may mean that some important work will not be performed, or at least not performed with enthusiasm. Additionally, employees may not pursue potential areas of innovation because there is no clear perception that such work will be fairly compensated. Since these outcomes could be detrimental to the organization, it is important to establish a clear understanding of expectations at the outset and to revisit the expectations periodically.

Skill-based and competency-based pay (development pay)

Skill-based and competency-based pay systems are similar, and both differ from merit-based pay systems in that they focus on the qualifications that the employee

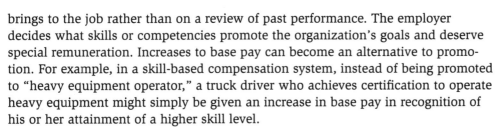

Caution

- Abandonment of a performance-based pay program will almost certainly alienate employees and depress performance.
- An evaluation and compensation system cannot violate any provisions of a labor agreement.
- Inequities will create the perception of favoritism.
- Using performance evaluations to determine pay can raise due process issues.

brings to the job rather than on a review of past performance. The employer decides what skills or competencies promote the organization's goals and deserve special remuneration. Increases to base pay can become an alternative to promotion. For example, in a skill-based compensation system, instead of being promoted to "heavy equipment operator," a truck driver who achieves certification to operate heavy equipment might simply be given an increase in base pay in recognition of his or her attainment of a higher skill level.

The difference between skills and competencies is that skills are typically associated with manual functions, such as truck driving, whereas competencies are more broadly defined. Competencies may include such attributes as an advanced educational degree, special certification, (e.g., as CPA), or fluency in a second language. Consequently, competency-based pay systems are viewed as being applicable to all types of work within the organization, including management positions.

The skills or competencies for which an employee is compensated do not have to be limited to those necessary for performance in the employee's current job. The focus is not on the minimum qualifications necessary to do certain work. Instead, employees are rewarded for developing skills or competencies that can enhance their ability to perform in their current jobs, skills that can boost their eligibility for potential future jobs, or skills that will provide them with a broader understanding of the functions of government. It should be noted that skill- and competency-based pay arrangements may tend to increase compensation budgets as they mature. However, the underlying theory for rewarding employee development is that employees who have a wider range of skills or competencies are more valuable to the organization as a fungible asset that can be moved to wherever the skill or competency is needed, enabling the organization to readily adjust to demands from its environment.

Linking performance to advancement or special assignments
Guiding principles

- Selection criteria for advancement must be job related.
- Classification and pay grades must be flexible enough to support the link between job performance and advancement or special assignments.

Challenge

- Ensuring that advancement criteria and procedures are clear and fair

Advancement opportunities are a scarce commodity: usually there are fewer opportunities than there are people who want them. The employer must decide whether advancement will be awarded strictly on the basis of merit—that is, to the best qualified—or whether other considerations, including affirmative action (either voluntary or court ordered), diversity, retention, or seniority should play a role. Merit system rules and labor contracts may also be constraints in this regard.

Any selection criteria for advancement must be job related for two reasons. First, if such criteria discriminate against employees in a protected class under Title VII of the Civil Rights Act, the employer must be able to prove that such discrimination was the result of a compelling business necessity and that no less discriminatory alternative personnel practice is available. (See the section on court challenges earlier in this chapter.)

Second, not basing advancement decisions on job-related behaviors can lead to the perception that favoritism is the determining factor. To avoid creating such a perception, it is also good practice to have several parties with an active stake in the agency's work share in the decisions on advancement.

Past performance is not an infallible indicator of future performance—either in the same position or in a promotional slot.[28] For example, a top performer as an individual contributor (nonsupervisor) simply may not have the required KSAs, such as people skills, to be a successful supervisor or manager. Even if the employee has demonstrated possession of the required expertise, he or she may simply not wish to take on the social and interpersonal consequences of being a supervisor. Many newer-generation employees eschew the responsibilities of leadership, for example, and prefer to work in temporary work group settings wherein the leadership responsibilities are shared.

Steps in the creation of an effective advancement system

A well-managed promotion system includes job analysis, the creation of career tracks, union support, clear and fair procedures, identification of likely candidates, and training in preparation for advancement.

Base the system on job analysis   To ensure that employee advancement is based on job-related criteria, job analysis should be used to identify essential job-related KSAs, which in turn should be used as the basis for developing career tracks or ladders.

Establish career tracks   Various positions within the organization that have common or related KSAs can be identified for career tracks—natural progressions from position to position that employees may choose to follow, either in the same job or in related jobs. Career tracks show employees that a currently held job—and previously held jobs—can prepare them for higher-level positions of the same or a related type.

Negotiate with unions/employee associations   The organization's labor relations and/or legal advisors should be consulted with respect to the necessity or desirability of negotiating with the unions/employee associations over the selection of employees for promotion, special work assignments, and developmental opportunities. If the unions/employee associations are unwilling to subject represented employees to the same rules for advancement that apply to nonrepresented employees, different procedures for employees covered by labor agreements may be necessary.

Develop clear, consistent, and equitable procedures   Employee advancement and development procedures must be perceived by employees as equitable so that no one feels unfairly excluded from opportunities. Part of ensuring that a local government's procedures are clear and equitable is to apply them carefully and consistently over time. Also important are clear and consistent announcements and training for employees, supervisors, and managers.

Do succession planning As described in Chapter 1, succession planning helps the organization identify and develop a pool of employees who can fill vacancies for managerial and executive positions as they occur. Through this process, the organization helps to ensure that there is a ready supply of employees who have the requisite KSAs for successfully achieving the organization's mission. In most cases succession planning entails identifying and maintaining records of the KSAs of individual employees. It may also be used to identify career paths that provide the essential KSAs for employees. Given the large-scale generational replacement taking place at all levels of government because of the retirement of the Baby Boomers, succession planning has taken on a particular importance in recent years.

Provide opportunities for development Development opportunities may be provided either within or outside of the employee's career track. Using job analysis techniques, the organization can identify a range of KSAs that are considered strategic—that is, those that the organization requires in order to accomplish its mission. Once the strategic qualifications are known, the positions requiring them also may be identified. For example, if managing contracts is a critical part of the organization's mission, then essential KSAs associated with contracting need to be developed in employees.

Developmental assignments outside the employee's normal career path necessarily mean that the employee (and the organization) is taking a risk to learn new KSAs. However, both the employee and the organization can gain in the process: the employee acquires new capabilities, and the organization gains by having an employee who has a broadened understanding of the organization and additional KSAs that it considers to be strategically important.

Legal guidelines for linking performance to advancement

Union contracts, civil service rules, and consent decrees may contain provisions that regulate how the employer offers developmental and promotional opportunities.

Union/employee association contractual provisions Many labor agreements contain provisions governing promotion, lateral assignments, temporary assignments, training opportunities, and other areas that may affect employee advancement decisions. It should be noted that court reviews have found bona fide seniority systems established by such provisions to be valid under most circumstances. The organization's labor relations and/or legal advisors should be consulted when the jurisdiction is developing its career track and promotional policies.

Civil service rules and procedures If the jurisdiction has a civil service system, it must comply with the system's rules and procedures. The provisions may have to be amended and the job classification system may have to be reformed to allow for increased flexibility in job assignments (broadbanding) or for the promotion of diversity.

Equal employment opportunity and affirmative action Although the law is continuing to evolve with respect to affirmative action, making it less of a

Broadbanding

As described in Chapter 1, broadbanding is an alternative to traditional job classification and pay-grading programs; it combines multiple grade levels into a smaller number of job and pay bands. Changing to broadbanding originally requires a large investment in development, training, and communication with managers, supervisors, and employees alike. The advantage of broadbanding is that greater latitude is gained in assigning work to employees. Their responsibilities may be expanded or substantially changed without the necessity of reclassifying their jobs. Consequently, the organization spends much less effort on activities that are not directly related to its mission, such as attempting to get employees reclassified.

Even with the increased latitude for assignment of work possible with broadbanding, it is important that the selection of employees for development opportunities be made within the guidelines established by the courts and the "Uniform Guidelines for Employee Selection Procedures" (U.S. Department of Labor, dol.gov/dol/allcfr/title_41/Part_60-3/toc.htm.)

Broadbanding vs. traditional classification and grade-level example

Classification	Grade	Banding title	Band level
Department director	18	Senior executive	9
Deputy director	17	Executive	8
Assistant director	16	Executive	8
Division administrator 2	15	Senior administrator	7
Lawyer 2	14	Senior advisor	7
Division administrator 1	14	Senior administrator	7
Bureau chief 2	13	Administrator	6
Lawyer 1	12	Advisor	6
Bureau chief 1	12	Administrator	6
Supervisor 2	11	Supervisor	5
Supervisor 1	10	Supervisor	5
Lead worker	9	Senior professional	4
Professional 3	9	Senior professional	4
Professional 2	8	Professional	3
Specialist 3	8	Senior specialist	3
Professional 1	7	Professional	3
Technician 4	7	Senior technician	3
Specialist 2	6	Senior specialist	3
Technician 3	6	Senior technician	3
Specialist 1	5	Specialist	2
Administrative assistant 4	5	Senior administrative support	2
Technician 2	5	Technician	2
Administrative assistant 3	4	Senior administrative support	2
Technician 1	4	Technician	2
Clerical worker 4	4	Senior administrative support	2
Administrative assistant 2	3	Administrative support	1
Clerical worker 3	3	Administrative support	1
Administrative assistant 1	2	Administrative support	1
Clerical worker 2	2	Administrative support	1
Clerical worker 1	1	Administrative support	1

Tips for employee advancement

☐ Establish career tracks.

☐ Establish clear, consistent, fair procedures for advancement.

☐ Involve parties with a stake in the agency's work in decisions on advancement.

☐ Do succession planning for supervisory, midmanagement, and executive positions, as well as for employees in key professional positions.

☐ Provide opportunities for employee development.

Caution

■ An employee's past success may not predict future performance in a higher position.

■ Public employers that rely on performance evaluations to make career track or developmental assignment decisions affecting the chances for promotion of a protected class of employees must be able to show either that the evaluation system does not discriminate against protected employees or that its discriminatory results reflect a compelling business necessity and that no less discriminatory alternative is available.

■ Techniques developed for employee advancement cannot violate provisions of a labor agreement.

consideration than in the past, the equal employment opportunity (EEO) principle has been accepted as a core value of employment in the United States. In recent years some states, such as California and Washington, have enacted restrictions on affirmative action in public employment and university enrollment via either ballot initiatives or legislation, but these states remain the exception rather than the rule. If a local government agency is subject to a consent decree regarding employee advancement, procedures must be carefully scrutinized and enforced to ensure compliance. Even organizations that are not subject to a consent decree or court order should avoid the possibility of future court involvement by ensuring that advancement procedures do not discriminate and are properly enforced. (See Chapters 2 and 5 for more on EEO and affirmative action.)

Other motivators for high performance

Guiding principles

■ Pay is not the only motivator for high performance.

■ Employee motivation is significantly influenced by the quality of supervisory skills.

Challenges

■ Determining which motivators are most effective in your organization

■ Determining which motivators are most important to each subordinate

■ Adapting the reward system to a team-based environment

Unquestionably, pay is a powerful motivator of employee behavior. However, it has long been recognized that other factors also affect the level of employee motivation to a major extent. The recent literature on generational differences notes that motivators differ for each generation and vary from individual to individual. As a result, managers must try to identify the motivators that are important to each employee. In addition, it is essential that the rewards, whatever they are, motivate the behaviors that the organization needs the most. Job-related criteria must be used to identify the desired behaviors to be rewarded. However, reward structures should be monitored to ensure that they do not encourage counterproductive behavior, such as employees selecting easy cases to improve their output rates.

The skills with which a supervisor is able to coach employees, coax their best efforts, resolve conflicts among them, mediate between work groups and outsiders, and otherwise maintain a productive work environment are vital to the effective motivation of employees individually and in work groups. Supervisors should also understand how to adjust their style to obtain the best results from each employee. Thus, the recognition, rewarding, and development of "people skills" in supervisors and managers is very important to the success of any motivational system and especially one within the setting of a multigenerational workforce.

Finally, the legal rights of represented employees vary greatly across jurisdictions, so it is important for an organization to consult with its labor relations and/or legal advisors and to involve the union/employee association when designing a reward system.

Rewarding teams and work groups

Historically, organizations have rewarded individual employees for their solitary accomplishments. More recently, however, considerable attention has been focused on the organizational contributions made by groups of employees. Consequently, employers now must determine to what extent collaborative efforts should be encouraged and rewarded. This issue is particularly important when employees are expected to actively participate in team problem solving to improve services to their customers (internal and external). If "employee empowerment" is a significant part of a jurisdiction's activities, some attention to group awards is advisable.

This, too, is an area that merits special attention with a multigenerational workforce. Younger generations are likely to prefer working in temporary project groups that come into being and disappear so that new combinations of skills and insights can be assembled. Local governments throughout the country are undertaking internal work groups, interagency collaborative processes, and outreach efforts to citizens, and the human resource management practices of those organizations must meet the challenge of rewarding employees who make important contributions to these types of efforts.[29]

Development of trust and respect between managers, supervisors, and employees is also essential. While there is a natural tendency for people to like some individuals more than others, perceptions of favoritism must be avoided so that trust and respect are not eroded. Employees must have the confidence that rewards will be distributed equitably and on the basis of contribution to a common effort rather than on the basis of favoritism.

As is true for individual rewards, the organization must make sure that the behaviors being encouraged are central to its mission: the more clearly behaviors are central to the mission, the more effective the offer of rewards for group accomplishment will be. The performance evaluation techniques discussed previously can be designed to include team-oriented standards for evaluation. Such standards can then be systematically tied to a team reward structure.

Unions/employee associations historically have been suspicious of employer proposals for group reward systems, and this issue will most likely present a substantial obstacle to effective implementation of such systems for represented employees. Failure to allow the employee unions/associations to participate in the development of a group reward system will likely lead to their resistance, grievance claims, and negotiation problems.

Monetary rewards other than salary adjustments

Monetary rewards may take several forms other than salary adjustments or bonuses. In addition to those discussed below, monetary rewards may be granted in the form of employee benefits such as child care, flexible work hours, or paid parking. (See Chapter 6 for further discussion.)

Training opportunities   Local governments can pay for training opportunities of the employee's choice, including workshops and classes offered through accredited universities and professional schools. These opportunities should be related, however, to the needs of the organization. For on-site training in particular, course curricula should accommodate the different learning styles that are characteristic of each generation. For instance, Radio Babies are comfortable with lecture-based learning while Baby Boomers prefer the opportunity to talk and share ideas with one another. Generation Xers prefer to work independently and report back to the group, while Generation Yers respond well to training that incorporates technology-related tools and promotes a relaxed, conversational environment.[30] Overall, training in a multigenerational workplace must accommodate these different learning styles to maximize effectiveness across generational cohorts.

Development opportunities   In addition to, or as an alternative to, formal training, opportunities for acquiring new KSAs can be provided through mentoring, on-the-job training, and challenging temporary assignments. The successful completion of special projects, under the guidance of an experienced senior advisor, may improve the employee's chance of being promoted. Developmental assignments may include some additional compensation to reward the employee for the risk involved in taking on the new assignment.

Extra time off   Depending on the amount of paid time off currently offered by the organization, many employees consider extra time off to be a highly desirable feature of employment. This is a particularly important area to explore for jurisdictions seeking to become more "family friendly," a feature that younger generational cohorts and older cohorts alike tend to value.

Gifts   Gifts can range from inexpensive to expensive. They can be prespecified (such as computer equipment) and may include monetary gift certificates at local stores or area restaurants.

Nonmonetary rewards

Since the importance of any specific type of reward will vary among generational cohorts and individual employees, administrators should attempt to determine the kinds of nonmonetary rewards that are considered most desirable. (See Chapter 6 for additional pertinent information and possible alternative rewards, such as preferred parking spaces.)

Tips for motivating employees

☐ Provide training to supervisors regarding the impact of their supervisory style on employee motivation.

☐ Use job analysis to ensure that rewarded behaviors help the organization accomplish its mission.

☐ Informally solicit ideas from employees about monetary and nonmonetary rewards they consider valuable.

☐ Select an array of monetary and nonmonetary rewards for potential distribution, and develop clear guidelines for making awards.

Flexible work arrangements   Allowing employees to arrange their workdays to meet family or other obligations can be a valuable motivator. Examples of flexible work arrangements include job sharing and telecommuting. Advances in technology and improvements in technology infrastructure make telecommuting far less daunting than it once was. However, accountability for performance continues to be a challenge with flexible work arrangements, which highlights the importance of effective goal setting with employees to establish measurable expectations for performance.

Participation   The opportunity to provide their talent and input on special projects or in a routine decision-making setting (most particularly in budget development) can be a motivator for some employees.

Awards/recognition   Awards such as certificates of achievement should be accompanied by public recognition from the supervisor and by special publicity, such as being featured in an employee newsletter or in news releases to the local media.

Managing organizational change

Guiding principles

■ Performance objectives for employees must change as the organization's mission changes.

■ The purpose of the change needs to be made apparent and supported by all levels of management.

Challenges

■ Adapting human resource practices and principles to the new organizational mission

■ Updating important human resource documents, such as job descriptions, testing instruments, and performance appraisal forms

■ Helping supervisors and employees adapt to new procedures and work structures

Managing organizational change is an important function of chief administrators. In the area of human resource management it means assisting employees to adapt to new procedures and work structures.

It is important for the organization to keep employees informed about changes that it is planning or that are in process. Communication requires a commitment of time, effort, and money to provide information to employees on a continuous basis. If employees understand what the organization is doing and why, they are less likely to lose motivation and more likely to maintain trust in the organization.

Performance evaluation in the midst of change

Organizational changes may alter the mission of the organization and thus require the organization to review whether its current performance evaluation system supports the accomplishment of its new mission. Even without a major change in agency mission, it is worthwhile to evaluate a performance evaluation system periodically to ensure that it encourages productive behaviors. It is highly useful to have a diverse group conduct the review and formulate recommendations for improvements; this group can be composed of employees, supervisors, and managers from different agencies. The relevant union/employee association must also be involved.

Similarly, the performance objectives established for each employee should not be considered "cast in concrete." Previously identified performance objectives may no longer contribute to the accomplishment of the organization's newly defined mission. Managers and supervisors must thus be willing to amend the performance objectives of their employees, and employees must be encouraged to renegotiate those performance objectives that are no longer priorities for the organization or that may not be attainable as initially constructed. For example, if a performance standard is set to improve outreach activities, budget reductions may have an impact on full attainment of the standard, and the supervisor and employee should discuss revisions. As noted earlier, periodic reviews by the employee and supervisor of both applicable performance objectives and the employee's progress are advisable.

When objectives change   When performance objectives are abandoned, updated, or completely replaced, the supervisor and employee should be given sufficient time to change the performance appraisal instrument and specified work behaviors. If adequate time cannot be provided, either some interim level of accomplishment should be agreed upon or the new objectives should not be included during the performance rating period in question. The employee can still be assigned to work on the new task, but it must be recognized that the employee will naturally focus on those work assignments for which he or she will be evaluated.

When the supervisor changes   Procedures for evaluating employees whose supervisor has changed should be fair to both the employee and the new supervisor. The new supervisor must have sufficient time to observe and work with the employee. The employee must have sufficient time to work on the performance objectives during the new supervisor's tenure. In addition to fairness, the organization must consider two other issues that will affect how it deals with changes in supervisors: first, the date that the organization has established for completing performance ratings—that is, timing for ratings (see the first section of this chapter for more on this issue); and second, whether the organization prefers to have new supervisors establish new performance objectives with their employees.

If the performance rating period is not a universal, established period for all agency employees, the new supervisors could work with the employees to establish performance objectives for a new rating period. However, two considerations should be addressed if this approach is taken. First, new supervisors must have sufficient

Tips for managing organizational change

☐ Develop and stick to a communication plan regarding any organizational change.

☐ Make sure that clear guidelines are in place and that training is provided for managers and supervisors regarding changes to performance objectives.

☐ Establish a periodic review schedule to ensure that the performance evaluation system continues to support the organization's mission and organizational objectives.

time to understand the mission and tasks of the work unit for which they are responsible before they attempt to negotiate performance objectives with employees. Consequently, there will likely be periods during which employees receive too little guidance for whatever work they will be held responsible. Second, if a new rating period is duly established, the date on which the employee is rated shifts—perhaps from the employee's anniversary date to a new rating cycle date—which can complicate record keeping. And if the performance evaluation is tied to pay, some provision needs to be made for granting pay adjustments under this circumstance.

One way to deal with these issues is to have the vacating supervisor complete a "close out" performance evaluation for the portion of the rating period during which the employee worked under his or her supervision. The new supervisor can then evaluate the employee for the remainder of the rating period using the performance objectives that the employee established with the previous supervisor—subject to any changes that the new supervisor may have negotiated with the employee. Ideally, both the vacating and incoming supervisors will have sufficient time to observe the employee, and the employee will have sufficient time to achieve some progress on the performance objectives for each supervisor. If the new supervisor does not have enough time to observe and evaluate, the vacating supervisor may be required to complete the evaluation in consultation with the new supervisor. Alternatively, both supervisors may jointly complete the performance evaluation. This approach does not necessitate changing the evaluation period, so it is suitable in systems that use either a universal rating date or the employment anniversary date. However, there may be circumstances in which it may not be desirable or possible to have the vacating supervisor participate in the evaluation.

Downsizing the workforce

Guiding principles

■ Downsizing decisions should be based on job-related criteria.

■ Performance evaluations should be only one of many considerations in making layoff decisions.

■ Appropriate documentation must be maintained for all employees, including those who are terminated for poor performance.

■ Union contracts should be reviewed concerning provisions for furlough and bumping rights.

■ Unions may have to be involved in reduction-in-force (RIF) situations under meet-and-confer provisions.

Challenges

- Retaining employees whose positions and competencies are central to the organization's mission while protecting seniority rights of employees
- Making certain that employees will be evaluated and layoff decisions will be made fairly and consistently
- Maintaining morale among employees

Downsizing decisions should *not* be seen as an opportunity to get rid of employees who are viewed as troublesome or undesirable for one reason or another. Rather, the focus of a downsizing program should be on retaining employees whose positions and competencies are central to agency survival and service function accomplishment. Failure to base downsizing decisions on performance criteria and centrality to mission will likely lead to legal challenges and a lesser likelihood of the organization prevailing in those challenges.

It is just as important to keep employees informed about what the organization is planning in downsizing situations as it is in other, more desirable agency expansion situations. Although downsizing inevitably affects employee morale and productivity, employees who understand what the organization is doing and why are less likely to lose motivation and trust in the organization than are employees who are kept in the dark.

Determining whom to lay off   Performance evaluation is only one tool to use when layoff decisions must be made. Moreover, it should be one of the last options to consider since there are many other decisions that must precede the identification of specific employees for termination.

One of the first decisions that the organization must make is what functions or agency responsibilities need to be downsized. It must then decide how many positions must be eliminated, and at what levels within the organization, to meet downsizing targets. Another decision to be made is whether to provide for bumping or transfer rights for the employees affected. Such rights may enable the organization to retain employees who have attained higher levels of KSAs, as well as higher performance evaluation results; however, they can also be disruptive. Bumping—a practice in which a junior worker may be displaced by a senior worker whose job has been abolished—adds an element of uncertainty for the organization and employees, and transfer rights require a great deal of administrative effort both to document and to implement. Other decisions may include issues such as what assistance, if any, to provide employees who will be laid off and how much notice the employees should be given.

Only after all the planning decisions have been made should performance evaluations be used to compare employees and determine whom to lay off. Again, the performance evaluations should not be the sole decision criterion since other work-related attributes of the employee might be important. For example, an employee with a higher attainment of important KSAs may be the appropriate choice for retention even if his or her recent evaluations have not been as good as those of other employees. A related concern is whether other employees are available to perform the work of the ones being laid off. Additionally, EEO, workplace diversity, and seniority rights, as well as consent decrees or court orders, may be issues for consideration when determining the specific employees to be laid off.

Tips for downsizing the workforce

☐ Develop a communication plan for dealing with downsizing.

☐ Provide guidelines and training to managers and supervisors on the criteria for selecting employees for layoff.

☐ Establish a position or committee to coordinate layoff decisions made by the various units affected by the downsizing to ensure that the agency's mission is not compromised, to ensure consistency in making layoff decisions, to lessen bumping or transfer problems, etc.

☐ In a union environment, coordinate downsizing with labor representatives.

Cross-rater comparability   One of the challenges in a downsizing environment is making certain that employees will be evaluated, and layoff decisions made, on the basis of the same criteria. Inequities create the perception of favoritism among employees. Consequently, it is important that downsizing criteria and decisions are consistent among jobs and employees, whether or not the employees have the same supervisor. Clear guidelines and consistent themes in the training of supervisors and managers are therefore essential to maximize the likelihood that equity is maintained.

Union/employee association agreement provisions   If employees subject to the evaluation system are covered by a labor agreement, it is essential that downsizing and termination procedures comply with relevant provisions of the contract. Seniority rights tend to be included in union contracts and thus are typically protected in the case of a RIF. As with other issues, the organization's labor relations and/or legal advisors should be consulted when policy is being created in this area.

The union/employee association may not be willing to become involved in planning a layoff. However, informing the union/employee association about downsizing plans and offering it the opportunity to contribute ideas will reduce the likelihood of grievances, unfair labor practice charges, or even court challenges. The union/association may have specific rights under its labor agreement or under federal and state law governing labor relations. Furthermore, employee organizations may have alternative ideas of how to meet the goals of the downsizing, or they may be willing to amend procedures in their labor agreement in helpful ways in exchange for other considerations.

Additionally, employees have specific rights—often called *Weingarten* rights (see Chapter 8)—to representation for actions reasonably expected to lead to a disciplinary process. Therefore, the agency should involve the union/employee association early on for cases in which a local government may terminate an employee for cause (see Chapter 4 for specifics).

Civil service rules/regulations/procedures   If the jurisdiction has a civil service system, it must comply with the rules and procedures of that system. These rules may limit the options available to the organization with respect to downsizing. They may also give employees bumping and transfer rights that must be taken into account.

Consent decrees and court orders   If the organization is subject to a consent decree or court order regarding employee advancement, it should seek legal advice to ensure that downsizing decisions do not violate that decree or order. Procedures must be carefully scrutinized and enforced to ensure compliance. Organizations that are not subject to a consent decree or court order should still ensure that their downsizing procedures do not unfairly discriminate. Recent decisions in the adjudication of affirmative action indicate that the granting of preference to protected groups in layoff situations in adherence to affirmative action goals generally is not permitted, and may be viewed as reverse discrimination—particularly where bona fide seniority rights come into play.

Appeal to adverse action   Because of the due process rights of public employees and the perception that termination is the workplace equivalent of capital punishment, some form of appeal to adverse actions must be established. In some cases, the appeal procedure will be specified in a labor agreement or in civil service rules, but employees who are not covered by such agreements or rules should also be afforded an appropriate appeal process. (See Chapter 5 for further discussion.)

Notes

1 Marc Holzer and Kathe Callahan, *Government at Work: Best Practices and Model Programs* (Thousand Oaks, Calif.: Sage, 1998), 6.

2 Janet L. Barnes-Farrell and Angela M. Lynch, "Performance Appraisal and Feedback Programs," *The Human Resources Program-Evaluation Handbook*, ed. Jack E. Edwards, John C. Scott and Nambury S. Raju (Thousand Oaks, Calif.: Sage, 2003), 155–176; and Herbert H. Meyer, Emanuel Kay, and John R. P. French, "Split Roles in Performance Appraisal," *Harvard Business Review* (January–February 1965): 123–129.

3 This section is based on Donald E. Klingner and John Nalbandian, *Public Personnel Management: Contexts and Strategies*, 5th ed. (Upper Saddle River, N.J.: Prentice Hall, 1998), 262–268, 317–326; and Jonathan Tompkins, *Human Resource Management in Government: Hitting the Ground Running* (New York: HarperCollins College Publishers, 1995), 249–252.

4 *Albemarle Paper Company v. Moody* (1975), 422 U.S. 405; *Rowe v. General Motors Corporation* (1972), 457 F. 2d 248; *Wade v. Mississippi Cooperative Extension Service* (1974), 372 F. Supp. 126; *Watson v. Fort Worth Bank and Trust* (1988), 487 U.S. 977; *Zell v. U.S.* (1979), 472 F. Supp. 356. The "Uniform Guidelines for Employee Selection Procedures" is available at the U.S. Department of Labor, dol.gov/dol/allcfr/title_41/Part_60-3/toc.htm.

5 ICMA produces materials for supervisory skills training, such as the training manual *Effective Supervisory Practices: Better Results through Teamwork*, 4th ed., ed. Scot Wrighton (2005).

6 Francis J. Yammarino and Leanne E. Atwater, "Implications of Self-Other Rating Agreement for Human Resources Management," *Organizational Dynamics* 25 (Spring 1997): 35–44.

7 John Nalbandian, "Performance Appraisal: If Only People Were Not Involved," in *Classics of Public Personnel Policy*, 2nd ed., ed. Frank J. Thompson (Belmont, Calif.: Wadsworth, 1991), reprinted from *Public Administration Review* 41 (May–June 1981): 392–396.

8 Dennis Daley, "The Trials and Tribulations of Performance Appraisal: Problems and Prospects on Entering the Twenty-First Century," in *Public Personnel Administration: Problems and Prospects*, 4th ed., ed. Steven W. Hays and Richard C. Kearney (Upper Saddle River, N.J.: Prentice Hall, Inc., 2003), 154–166.

9 See Robert A. Baron, "Countering the Effects of Destructive Criticism: The Relative Efficacy of Four Interventions," *Journal of Applied Psychology* 75, no. 3 (1990): 234–245.

10 Daniel Goleman, *Emotional Intelligence* (New York: Bantam Books, 1994), chap. 10.

11 See W. H. Holley Jr. and H. S. Feild, "Performance Appraisal and the Law," *Labor Law Journal* 7, no. 523 (July 1975).

12 Linda Gravett and Robin Throckmorton, *Bridging the Generation Gap: How to Get Radio Babies, Boomers, Gen Xers, and Gen Yers to Work Together and Achieve More* (Franklin Lakes, N.J.: Career Press, 2007). See also Ron Zemke, Claire Raines, and Bob Filipczak, *Generations at Work: Managing the Clash of Veterans, Boomers, Xers, and Nexters in Your Workplace* (New York: American Management Association, 2000), who define the generations as follows: Veterans (born 1922–1943), Baby Boomers (born 1943–1960), Generation Xers (born 1960–1980), and Generation Nexters (born 1980–2000).

13 Zemke, Rainers, and Filipczak, *Generations at Work*, 25.

14 Gravett and Throckmorton, *Bridging the Generation Gap*.

15 Zemke, Rainers, and Filipczak, *Generations at Work*.

16 Ibid.; Gravett and Throckmorton, *Bridging the Generation Gap*.

17 Zemke, Rainers, and Filipczak, *Generations at Work*, 157.

18 Hilton Collins, "Generation 2.0 at Work," *Government Technology* 21, no. 7 (2008), 16–20.

19 *Revised Code of Washington* § 70.94.521–551 (1991).

20 For the Washington state law, see wsdot. wa.gov/TDM/CTR. Other states, including Oregon (deq.state.or.us/nwr/ECO/eco.htm) and Arizona (maricopa.gov/aq/divisions/trip_ reduction/default.aspx), have passed commute trip reduction laws with similar goals.

21 Gravett and Throckmorton, *Bridging the Generation Gap*.

22 Carolyn A. Martin and Bruce Tulgan, *Managing the Generation Mix: From Urgency to Opportunity* (Amherst, Mass.: HRD Press, 2006), 95–96.

23 Gary E. Roberts, "Employee Performance Appraisal System Participation: A Technique That Works," *Public Personnel Management* 32, no. 1 (2003): 89–97.

24 Gravett and Throckmorton, *Bridging the Generation Gap*.

25 Edward L. Deci and Richard M. Ryan, *Intrinsic Motivation and Self-Determination in Human Behavior* (New York: Plenum Press, 1985).

26 David G. Carnevale, *Trustworthy Government: Leadership and Management Strategies for Building Trust and High Performance* (San Francisco: Jossey-Bass, 1995), 111–115.

27 James L. Perry, "Compensation, Merit Pay, and Motivation," in Hays and Kearney, eds., *Public Personnel Administration*, 143–153.

28 On the question of predicting future performance through test validation, see Barnes-Farrell and Lynch, "Performance Appraisal and Feedback Programs"; also see Jay M. Shafritz et al., *Personnel Management in Government: Politics and Process*, 5th ed. (New York: Marcel Dekker, 2001), 246–251; and Klingner and Nalbandian, *Public Personnel Management*, 193.

29 Beth J. Asch, "The Economic Complexities of Incentive Reforms," in *High-Performance Government*, ed. Robert Klitgaard and Paul C. Light (Santa Monica, Calif.: Rand Corporation, 2005), 318.

30 Gravett and Throckmorton, *Bridging the Generation Gap*.

4

Labor-Management Relations and Collective Bargaining

Richard C. Kearney

In stark contrast to unions in the private sector, whose membership had declined precipitously to around 9 percent of the nonagricultural workforce by 2008, public employee unions remain robust. The overall rate of unionization for public workers was 41 percent in 2008. Labor organizations represented about 33 percent of federal employees, 35 percent of state employees, and an impressive 46 percent of local government workers.[1] The unionization percentage is highest at the municipal level, particularly for teachers, police officers, and firefighters.

A union environment presents special challenges to local government managers. Following brief historical and legal overviews of public sector unionization and collective bargaining, this chapter notes the major labor organizations and examines the current policy environment. It sets out the fundamental elements of the collective bargaining process and concludes with contemporary challenges in local government labor-management relations. Throughout, it gives special attention to emerging and best practices.

Historical and legal framework

Guiding principle

■ Collective bargaining for local government employees is not federally mandated.

From their early roots in skilled craft technologies such as shoemaking and carpentry, through the widespread organization of industrial workers during the 1930s and 1940s, to the recent decline in membership and political clout, labor unions have been a controversial component of human resource management in the private sector. Their best days were in the years immediately following passage of the 1935 National Labor Relations Act (NLRA) (also known as the Wagner Act). But broad changes in national, regional, and global economic factors; increasingly unfavorable legal and political environments; and intense management opposition conspired to cut union membership from one-third of the private labor force in the mid-1950s to its low point of 9 percent today.

Unions in government have had a quite different experience. Although they had an early presence in federal defense facilities and the postal service, unions did not enjoy significant growth in federal employment until the 1960s. Similarly, police officers, firefighters, teachers, and state workers began organizing during the late nineteenth and early twentieth centuries, but organizational prosperity awaited important changes in their legal environment in the 1960s and 1970s.

The right to organize and join unions received constitutional protection through the First Amendment by a string of federal court decisions (e.g., *McLaughlin v. Tilendis* [1967]; *Atkins v. Charlotte* [1969]). But these decisions did not require public employers to bargain collectively with unions. While the NLRA, as amended by the Landrum-Griffin and Taft-Hartley acts, grants the right to bargain collectively to virtually all nonsupervisory employees in the private and nonprofit sectors, public employees can do so only when that right has been granted by the employing jurisdiction. Regulation of public employee labor relations is the responsibility of the respective government jurisdictions. Federal employee collective bargaining rights are embodied in the Civil Service Reform Act of 1978 and various agency-specific legislation. Collective bargaining for state and local workers is governed primarily by state law and, in some cases, local ordinances. However, many federal laws apply to the workplace no matter where it is situated (see Exhibit 4–1).

Thus, a key difference between private and public sector labor relations and collective bargaining is that no national law mandates bargaining rights for state and local employees and their unions. For now, state and local collective bargaining remains a patchwork of state statutes, attorney general opinions, gubernatorial executive orders, court decisions,[2] and local ordinances. Sun Belt states are generally unsympathetic to organized labor in any venue. North Carolina, South Carolina, and Virginia explicitly prohibit state agencies and local governments from recognizing unions and negotiating with them. Unhappy state and local workers in these three states may organize and join a union, but their collective voice will not be heard through collective bargaining.

Some states permit certain categories of public employees to bargain collectively but not others. For instance, teachers may bargain in Tennessee, but, with some exceptions, municipal and county employees may not. Idaho and Oklahoma grant bargaining rights to teachers and firefighters. Forty three states grant bargaining rights to one or more categories of local government workers. Twenty-seven states, mostly across the northern tier of the country, give negotiating rights to virtually *all* categories of state and local employees. Exhibit 4–2 shows the bargaining status for

Exhibit 4-1   Major federal laws affecting public sector labor relations

Social Security Act of 1935	Equal Employment Opportunity Act of 1972
Fair Labor Standards Act (1938) (as amended)	Employee Retirement Income Security Act (1974)
Civil Rights Act of 1964	Americans with Disabilities Act (1990)
Urban Mass Transportation Act (1964)	Civil Rights Act of 1991
Age Discrimination in Employment Act (1967)	Family and Medical Leave Act (1993)
Occupational Safety and Health Act (1970)	

major state and local government functions across the United States; Exhibit 4–3 shows the geographical distribution of state and local collective bargaining rights across the country.

Bills are regularly introduced in Congress to grant bargaining rights to state and local employees throughout the country. Such a bill (H.R. 4137, S. 1642) passed the House and was approaching passage in the Senate in 2008 when a prime champion of the legislation, Sen. Edward Kennedy, was diagnosed with a serious health problem. The bill stalled. If passed, it would have extended collective bargaining rights to all state and local public safety workers, including local government police and firefighters.

State bargaining laws cover expansive territory. In general, they

- Establish employee and management rights
- Create or identify an existing agency to administer labor relations, often called the public employee relations board (PERB)

Exhibit 4-2   State bargaining status, 2007

(X: collective bargaining provisions; Y: meet and confer provisions)

State	State	Local	Police	Firefighters	K–12 teachers
Alabama	–	Y	–	Y	–
Alaska	X	X	X	X	X
Arizona	–	–	–	–	–
Arkansas	–	–	–	–	–
California	Y	Y[1]	Y[1]	Y[1]	X
Colorado	X[3]	–	–	–	–
Connecticut	X	X	X	X	X
Delaware	X	X[1]	X	X	X
Florida	X	X[1]	X	X	X
Georgia	–	–	–	X	–
Hawaii	X	X	X	X	X
Idaho	–	–	–	X	X
Illinois	X	X	X	X	X
Indiana	–	–	–	–	X
Iowa	X	X	X	X	X
Kansas	Y	Y[1]	Y[1]	Y[1]	X
Kentucky	–	–	X	X	–
Louisiana	–	–	–	–	–
Maine	X	X	X	X	X
Maryland	X	X[2]	–	–	X
Massachusetts	X	X	X	X	X
Michigan	X	X	X	X	X
Minnesota	X	X	X	X	X
Mississippi	–	–	–	–	–
Missouri	X[4]	X	X	X	X
Montana	X	X	X	X	X
Nebraska	X	X	X	X	Y
Nevada	–	X	X	X	X
New Hampshire	X	X	X	X	X

(continued)

Exhibit 4-2   State bargaining status, 2007 *(continued)*

State	State	Local	Police	Firefighters	K–12 teachers
New Jersey	X	X	X	X	X
New Mexico	X[3]	X	X	X	X
New York	X	X	X	X	X
North Carolina	–	–	–	–	–
North Dakota	Y[2]	Y[2]	Y[2]	Y[2]	X
Ohio	X	X	X	X	X
Oklahoma	–	X	X	X	X
Oregon	X	X[1]	X	X	X
Pennsylvania	X	X	X	X	X
Rhode Island	X	X	X	X	X
South Carolina	–	–	–	–	–
South Dakota	X	X	X	X	X
Tennessee	–	–	–	–	X
Texas	–	–	X[1]	X[1]	–
Utah	–	–	–	–	X
Vermont	X	X	X	X	X
Virginia	–	–	–	–	–
Washington	X	X	X	X	X
West Virginia	Y[2]	Y[2]	Y[2]	Y[2]	Y[2]
Wisconsin	X	X	X	X	X
Wyoming	–	–	–	X	–

Source: Compiled from various sources, including John Lund and Cheryl L. Maranto, "Public Sector Laws: An Update," in *Public Sector Employment in a Time of Transition,* ed. Dale Belman, Morley Gunderson, and Douglas Hyatt (Ithaca, N.Y.: Cornell University Press, 1997), 21-58.

1 Local opinion permitted.   2 Meet and confer established by attorney general opinion.
3 Collective bargaining established through executive order.   4 Court ordered collective bargaining.

Exhibit 4-3   Geographical representation of state and local collective bargaining

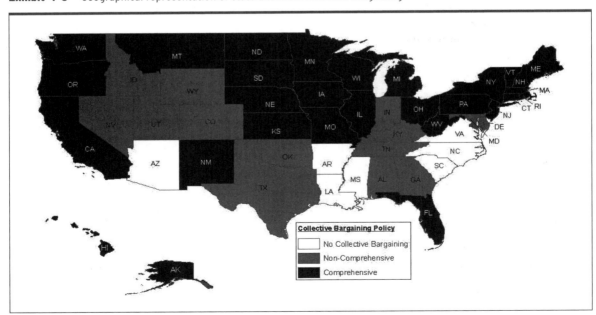

Collective Bargaining Policy
- No Collective Bargaining
- Non-Comprehensive
- Comprehensive

- Determine which employees will be included in a bargaining unit and how a union will be recognized
- Identify which compensation, human resource, and policy issues are appropriate for bargaining
- Specify unfair labor practices
- Establish procedures for resolving negotiating impasses
- Specify how the union will be treated as the exclusive representative of the bargaining unit (union security provisions).

Employee organizations in state and local government

A distinction can be made between employee associations and unions. Associations exist primarily to provide professional benefits and services to their members. Most, including the South Carolina State Employees Association and the Texas Public Employees Association, are also engaged in lobbying and advocacy activities to win favorable treatment for their members by the legislative and executive branches of government. Over time, some associations, such as the National Education Association (NEA), have morphed into unions that use collective bargaining as the chief means for winning improved wages, benefits, and working conditions from government employers.

Some unions, such as the American Federation of State, County, and Municipal Employees, the NEA, the International Association of Fire Fighters, and the Fraternal Order of Police, concentrate their efforts on organizing and representing public sector employees. Others, such as the Service Employees International Union (SEIU), the American Nurses Association, and the International Brotherhood of Teamsters, are general-purpose organizations that operate across public, private, and nonprofit sectors. (See Exhibit 4–4 for membership figures for the largest organizations of public employees.)

Conflict over strategies split the national labor movement in 2005. The SEIU, the Teamsters, and five other unions left the American Federation of Labor–Congress of Industrial Organizations (AFL-CIO) and created the Change to Win Federation. The AFL-CIO was criticized for spending too much energy on lobbying and elections and not enough time on membership drives, a trend that the new federation wants to reverse. It argues that electoral and legislative successes fail to materialize when union membership is in decline.

Exhibit 4-4   Membership of largest state and local government employee organizations (January 1, 2008)

National Education Association	3,200,000
American Federation of State, County, and Municipal Employees	1,400,000
American Federation of Teachers	1,300,000
Service Employees International Union	1,800,000
Fraternal Order of Police	324,000
International Association of Fire Fighters	280,000

Source: Organization Web sites.

Collective bargaining process

Guiding principles

- Preparation is the key to effective bargaining.
- Bargaining in good faith is critical to successful negotiation.

Challenge

- Replacing adversarial bargaining with interest-based bargaining that results in a win-win outcome

Why do public workers join unions? For the same reasons as their counterparts in industry and nonprofit organizations: they are dissatisfied with one or more aspects of their jobs and consequently seek improvement through collective action. They may be discontented with pay, health care benefits, job security, hazardous working conditions, unfair or arbitrary management actions, or any number of annoyances.

Collective bargaining is a continuous process in which representatives of government employers (management) meet with employee representatives (the union) to jointly establish the terms and conditions of employment for members of a bargaining unit. Decision-making authority is shared by the parties, who sign a legal and binding contract. In *meet and confer,* union and management representatives meet to discuss terms and conditions of employment, but only management has final decision-making authority. In practice, meet and confer has developed into collective bargaining in most jurisdictions. The principal elements of the collective bargaining process are outlined below. The principal steps in collective bargaining are shown in Exhibit 4–5.

Determining the bargaining unit

Which group of employees will a union represent? This group may be initially identified by the employees themselves, by a union seeking to represent them, by the

Exhibit 4-5   The collective bargaining process

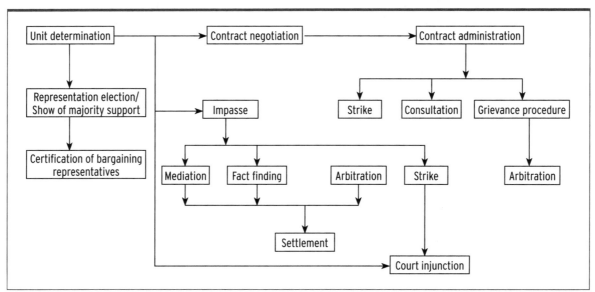

state administrative agency, by management, or by a court. Criteria for determining the bargaining unit vary, but they usually take into account a "community of interest" among members, the history and prior extent of collective bargaining in the jurisdiction, and the efficiency of agency operations, among other considerations. Most jurisdictions, but not all, follow the NLRA in excluding bona fide supervisors and confidential employees from the bargaining unit. However, some states and localities combine supervisors and subordinates in the same unit, whereas others permit separate bargaining units for supervisors. The general trend is toward consolidating bargaining units into large groups of represented workers, but to segregate bona fide supervisors from other employees.

Deciding the bargaining unit representative

Which union will represent the members in the unit? An employer may voluntarily recognize a union as the official representative of the bargaining unit upon a showing of majority support by its members. In some cases a representation election must be held in which members are given a choice between two or more unions, along with an option to vote "no union." Voting is by secret ballot, and a runoff election is held if none of the choices receives majority support. The winning union is certified as the bargaining representative by the PERB or other labor relations agency. This arrangement grants the union the right of exclusive representation of the unit for a minimum period of time; during this time, management must not deal with any other union or group of employees purporting to represent all or a portion of the unit. The union may be decertified if it loses majority support of unit members.

Negotiating the contract

Union and management representatives negotiate the terms of a contract. The union team typically includes the local union president, his or her aides, selected union members, and, increasingly, a labor lawyer and a representative from the national union. Members of the local government management team may include the city or county manager or an assistant manager, the human resource director, the finance director, relevant department heads, the city or county attorney, the mayor's representative, or other officials, although elected officials rarely sit on the management bargaining team. Each team designates a chief negotiator to serve as team leader and spokesperson.

The general public may also participate in negotiations in some jurisdictions, as determined by state law or local ordinance. Sunshine laws may permit media access, freedom of information concerning documents and data, public hearings or negotiations, and even a public representative at the bargaining table. Under Florida's sunshine law, all negotiations must be held in public. Sunshine bargaining is optional in Iowa, Massachusetts, Nevada, and New Jersey.

Preparation is the key to effective bargaining. Both teams should be intimately familiar with the provisions of the previous contract and their experience with its implementation. Wage and benefit data need to be analyzed, particularly data from other local bargaining units and neighboring jurisdictions. National, state, and local legal developments should also be examined, including relevant court cases. Both parties must identify their bargaining goals and proposals, amass supporting data, and anticipate the other side's reactions, objectives, and proposals. Finally, dates, times, and places for the negotiations must be agreed to.

Bargaining laws require both parties to negotiate in good faith over all issues properly within the scope of bargaining. Such bargaining in good faith is critical to negotiating a successful contract. (See the sidebar outlining the basic principles of good-faith bargaining below.)

Collective bargaining is a political process with high stakes. Future wages, benefits, working conditions, organizational performance, and the overall quality of work life are in play. The union leader's reputation and survival are on the line. The mayor and council's reelection chances may be hinging on the public's reaction to the outcomes of the negotiations. The union wants "more," and management seeks to hold the line or perhaps wring concessions out of the union. A single strategic error or miscalculation can be very costly. Meanwhile, the media, voters, and other stakeholders are watching. Under these stressful conditions, astute negotiators will attempt to draw lessons from others' experiences.

Conventionally, collective bargaining has been adversarial, with each side predetermining fixed "positions" and trying to force the other side to make concessions by applying negotiating skills, clever tactics, and political power. Personal attacks or implied and overt threats may be employed. This traditional "us versus them" approach is about power and winning at the expense of the other party. It tends to leave behind a reservoir of distrust, ill will, and hurt feelings, along with a gloating winner and a resentful loser.

As labor-management relations change, so does the philosophy of collective bargaining. Today, a growing number of local jurisdictions are using interest-based bargaining, also known as "Getting to Yes," "mutual gains," and "win-win bargaining" approaches. As popularized by Roger Fisher and William Ury in *Getting to Yes: Negotiating Agreement without Giving In,* this approach begins with very different

fyi

The duty to bargain in good faith: Basic principles

- Time limits for commencing negotiations. Parties must furnish notice of the intent to modify or terminate an existing or expiring agreement.

- Obligation to provide timely information. The public employer is required to provide relevant information on any matter within the mandatory scope of bargaining that the employee organization requests.

- Prohibitions against bypassing the bargaining representatives. To avoid the "end run," some jurisdictions prohibit communications between the union representatives and any other official who is not a designated management bargaining representative.

- Requirement that the employer make no unilateral changes in existing wages, hours, and working conditions while negotiations are under way.

- Prohibition against work stoppages during negotiations.

- Formal procedures to resolve impasses.

- Duty to reduce the bargaining agreement to writing and to execute it.

- Prohibition against bad-faith bargaining, which exists when one or both of the parties simply go through the motions without any real intention of reaching agreement. Indications of bad-faith bargaining include dilatory tactics, failure to offer proposals or counterproposals, and refusal to make concessions on any issue.

Elected officials and the bargaining process

The relationship between the council and the local government manager can, at times, be filled with tension. Small fissures can periodically threaten to separate the complex web of trust and support that binds legislators and the executive together, especially in reformed local governments. The collective bargaining process can cause those small fissures to become large rifts if the local government manager is not careful and thoughtful when dealing with the elected officials. Although there are no perfect techniques to avoid the pitfalls, there are strategies managers can employ prior to and during collective bargaining to maintain and perhaps enhance their relationships with local elected officials.

- **Meet early in the process.** Seventy-five to ninety days before the start of collective bargaining, meet with the council. The local government manager's primary purpose is to listen to the elected officials' opinions and positions regarding wages, benefits, and other topics that are collectively bargained. The manager needs to determine if there is a consensus regarding wages and benefits, and if the legislative body is unified or divided on collective bargaining issues.

- **Offer good analysis quickly.** Within seven days of the first meeting, meet again to (1) present an analysis of the costs of the various issues raised in the first meeting, (2) give the legislative body feedback as to the practicality of the issues, and (3) identify unrealistic positions that would be nonstarters at the table. This second meeting should help both the legislative body and the local government manager begin to sharpen their positions on the various issues.

- **Meet again.** At this third meeting, held within a week of the second, the local government manager should outline negotiating positions to be taken on the issues raised at the two earlier meetings. While the positions may be further refined, the outline represents the local government's bargaining agenda. It is critical that the legislative body sign off on the agenda and affirm its agreement on the issues and points to be negotiated on the municipality's behalf by the local government manager.

- **Share the union's issues and positions.** Early in the collective bargaining process, both sides exchange positions on issues. Even though the initial list (agenda) of positions will be modified through the collective bargaining process, the elected officials should see the union's opening proposal. Sharing the opening positions may give a sense as to how far apart the parties are and how difficult the process may be.

- **Meet again, and again, and again.** For many local governments, the collective bargaining team includes senior managers but not elected officials. While this model has advantages, one of its biggest disadvantages is that elected officials are often the last to know. Don't let that happen. Meet often and regularly with the elected officials to keep them informed.

- **If in doubt, wait.** The manager's ability to verbally agree to settle an issue at the collective bargaining table is a function of the authority that members of the legislative body give to the manager to settle issues without first checking with them. Local government managers who are not sure how strong their support is or how divided their legislative body is over collective bargaining issues need to practice patience. When in doubt about settling an issue, check with the legislative body first.

assumptions from those found in traditional bargaining. The parties identify their major issues and "interests" instead of taking hard, unyielding positions. Thus, "people are separated from the problem."[3] They develop options for themselves and the other side to consider, basing these alternatives on objective criteria and the perceived interests of the other party. If it works out as intended, win-win bargaining results in a contract acceptable to both the union and management and does no harm to the long-term relationship between the parties. One permutation of interest-based bargaining is gain sharing, in which dollar savings are shared.

Gain sharing

Gain-sharing programs have received far more support in the private sector than in the public sector, although several high-profile municipalities have made gain sharing a part of their labor-management relations.

Gain sharing (also known as productivity bargaining) is the sharing with municipal employees of any dollar savings generated by productivity improvements or changes in work procedures. Gain sharing has also been used to retain jobs that might have been cut because of budget problems. It is a way to make municipal costs of providing a public service comparable with private costs and to avoid contracting out a service.

The notion of gain sharing has far more support with municipal union leaders than with public officials. Public officials, for the most part, view any savings generated by workplace reforms as belonging to the taxpayers, not to the employees. This belief, coupled with the difficulty of accurately measuring dollar savings, means that some public officials view gain-sharing programs with caution.

Notwithstanding the problems, gain sharing can be an element in creating a different relationship between labor and management, as exemplified by the following:

- The City of New Rochelle, New York, and the American Federation of State, County, and Municipal Employees (AFSCME) Council 66 and Local 663 developed a gain-sharing program in which productivity gains were used to help fund wage increases. Through attrition, the sanitation department reduced its crew size from four employees to three employees per truck.

- In what has become one of the more notable experiments in gain sharing, the City of Indianapolis, Indiana, and AFSCME Council 62 launched gain-sharing initiatives in the public works department.

- Wisconsin state employees helped create a cost-savings commission to discuss ways to reduce costs, with savings to be distributed through employee salaries.

Source: See the American Federation of State, County, and Municipal Employees Web site at afscme.org for up-to-date examples of gain-sharing programs.

Interest-based bargaining has attained success in numerous local government arenas, from public schools to sanitation. But it is not appropriate as a "gateway" change that is intended to propel other fundamental changes in the organization. Rather, a certain level of trust and good faith is required or must first be built. The most positive results of interest-based bargaining tend to occur when both parties go through joint training prior to negotiations and use a facilitator during collective bargaining.

Tips for managers: Maintaining good labor-management relations

- ☐ Know the legal environment and the provisions of contracts.
- ☐ Prepare carefully for collective bargaining. Gather all relevant wage and benefit data, identify bargaining goals, and anticipate the union's issues, objectives, and reactions.
- ☐ Communicate early and often with elected officials about the bargaining process.
- ☐ Negotiate in good faith.
- ☐ Practice patience and control your emotions.
- ☐ Move toward a collaborative approach to bargaining.
- ☐ Look for the underlying causes of grievances.
- ☐ Involve employees in problem solving and decision making.
- ☐ Develop a backup plan you can live with.

Handwritten margin notes:
- Get in writing
- Not personal
- Respect everyone
- Bring understanding

In jurisdictions where management, the union, or both are committed to traditional tactics and not genuinely willing to embrace—or at least entertain—the principles of interest-based bargaining, the process is destined to fail. It must also be understood that there are places and times in which traditional, adversarial bargaining is called for because of the nature of the dispute, the comfort zone of the parties, an ugly history of labor-management relations, intense constituent pressures on the union team, or political problems for management.[4]

Resolving bargaining impasses

Guiding principles

- Strikes can—and do—occur in government.
- Contingency planning and good communication can shorten work stoppages.
- Arbitration focuses on equity, the public interest, acceptability to the parties, comparability with similar jurisdictions, and the ability of the jurisdiction to pay.
- The availability of arbitration lessens pressure for a voluntary settlement.

Negotiation impasses are common, but several proven means exist for settling them, including the strike, mediation, fact finding, and arbitration.

The strike

The NLRA permits strikes as a legitimate means for settling private and nonprofit sector differences when those differences cannot be resolved at the negotiating table. As recently as the late 1970s, strikes were common. Since then the strike rate has declined significantly owing to structural changes in the economy, global competition, a growing willingness of employers to hire permanent replacements for striking workers, and other reasons.

In government, federal employee work stoppages are categorically prohibited. Thirty-five states also outlaw public employee strikes, and the vast majority of labor contracts contain no-strike clauses to preclude work stoppages during the life of the contract. An illegal strike is typically met with an injunction and imposition of fines or other penalties on the union and the strikers themselves.

But some states permit certain local government employees to strike legally. Beginning with Vermont in 1967, ten states have enacted laws granting some categories of employees a limited right to strike. Additionally, courts in another three states have upheld the right of some categories of public employees to strike. In virtually all instances, strikes are forbidden for essential employees (e.g., police, firefighters, correctional employees, hospital workers). Most permissive legislation requires the union to comply with specific provisions—including mediation, fact finding, arbitration, and prior notice—before executing a strike.

The record on strike legislation is mixed. Permissive strike policies are associated with high strike frequency in some states (e.g., Pennsylvania) but low frequency in others (e.g., Vermont). Strike incidence actually declined in several states (e.g., Ohio and Illinois) after they decided to authorize work stoppages. A prohibition against work stoppages discourages but does not prevent them. Evidence does show, however, that the compulsory use of arbitration in contract disputes diminishes the incidence of strikes.

Generally, management today does a much more thorough and effective job of contingency planning for work stoppages than it did in the past. Strikes—legal or not—are anticipated, and arrangements are made to continue the delivery of basic and essential services by management employees and others. When public management executes its strike contingency plan effectively and also garners public support for the management point of view on the dispute, the duration of the strike can be shortened significantly.

Fortunately, most impasses are resolved through means other than a work stoppage. The most common techniques for resolving disputes over contracts are mediation, fact finding, and arbitration.

Mediation

Once an impasse is declared by either party or the labor relations agency, the next step is usually to call in a mediator. A mediator is a nonbiased third party whose purpose is to help the other two parties attain a voluntary settlement. Mediators may be dispatched by the Federal Mediation and Conciliation Service, the state labor relations agency, or other sources. Successful mediators meet individually and jointly with the parties, help them to understand the other's interests, facilitate a climate that is conducive to settlement, and steer them to the terms of a final contract. The mediator cannot impose a solution, but he or she may suggest possibilities for resolving the impasse.

Fact finding

If mediation fails, fact finding begins. Fact finding may also be used as a first step. A fact finder or fact-finding panel, usually composed of three members, is obtained from the same sources that are tapped for mediators. In some jurisdictions, a mediator's role may be transformed into that of a fact finder. Procedurally more formal than mediation, fact finding consists of a quasi-judicial process with evidence, a written transcript, and, in most cases, written, nonbinding recommendations for settlement. Fact finding is something of a misnomer because all labor disagree-

---

fyi

Best practices for collaborative labor-management relations

The new municipal workplace has incorporated elements of a different philosophy of labor-management relations. The elements of this new philosophy include the following:

- Giving employees enhanced training, knowledge, and information about their jobs and the municipal organization

- Encouraging and training managers and supervisors to be coaches and mentors

- Designing municipal workplace policies to be supportive rather than restrictive, enabling employees to be positive contributors to the team

- Using measurement tools such as benchmarking, citizen surveys, and outcome measures to improve public services

- Encouraging municipal managers, supervisors, and employees to collaborate when providing public services

- Incorporating technology to enhance employee skills and knowledge; new technology coupled with greater flexibility in work rules leads to productivity gains, which can mean maintaining and enhancing public services

- Teaching frontline municipal workers problem-solving skills to facilitate a quick response to citizens' concerns

- Offering compensation based on skill building, knowledge acquired, and seniority rather than relying on rigid classification plans that fail to recognize employee achievements

- Finding common goals for labor and management to achieve

- Supporting ongoing innovation and collaboration through such efforts as labor-management committees.

ments start with at least two sets of "facts." The principal task of the fact finder is to derive from the evidence the most objective facts and bring them to the attention of the parties and the various stakeholders. Like mediation, fact finding cannot impose terms on the parties.

Arbitration

Arbitration resembles fact finding in that it involves each party formally presenting supportive evidence to one or more neutrals. Unlike fact finding, however, arbitration is final and binding on the parties. Its purpose is to produce a fair settlement that protects the parties and the public interest and to avoid work stoppages. Arbitration may be mandated by law or by the administrative agency when negotiations fail, or the union and management may agree voluntarily to use the technique to resolve a negotiation impasse.

The parties may select an arbitrator from a list provided by the American Arbitration Association, the state PERB, or other sources, or arbitrators may be designated by the PERB or a court. When a three-person (tripartite) panel is used, a truly neutral arbitrator typically works with other "neutrals" who are known to favor one side or the other. Thus, tripartite arbitration is, in this sense, a continuation of collective bargaining.

The decision-making criteria that arbitrators consider usually include equity, the public interest, acceptability to the parties, comparative data from similar or nearby jurisdictions, and, increasingly, the jurisdiction's ability to pay.

There are two types of arbitration: conventional and final offer. Conventional arbitration maximizes the neutral person's authority, permitting him or her to favor the interests of one side or the other or to split the difference. Final-offer arbitration requires each party to submit its "last best offer" to the arbitrator, who is bound to accept the terms of one or the other as presented. "Final offer by package" means that the arbitrator must accept the best offer in its entirety, even if multiple issues are involved. "Final offer by issue" permits separate decisions on each item in dispute.

Arbitration peacefully and effectively resolves interest impasses without the strike and accompanying service disruptions. However, it is controversial for three major reasons. First, it delegates important decision-making authority to an individual or panel of individuals who cannot be held accountable by the voters or elected officials. Arbitrators' decisions can significantly affect the jurisdiction's budget and even precipitate a subsequent tax or fee hike, but such decisions are subject only to limited review by courts and elected officials. For this reason, arbitration has been ruled unconstitutional by courts in five states: Colorado, Maryland, Nebraska, South Dakota, and Utah.

A second criticism of arbitration comes from management, which, in most local governments, is convinced that the arbitration outcomes favor the unions—a conclusion supported implicitly by unions' general enthusiasm for the process. Empirical evidence indicates that arbitration decisions do not significantly favor one party or the other. Nonetheless, the mere availability of arbitration does appear to boost salary and benefits, presumably by encouraging management to settle on known terms rather than assume the risk of the unknown. Finally, it is argued that arbitration "chills" collective bargaining by holding open the possibility that one or both parties may obtain more from the arbitrator than from a negotiated agreement. Thus, the availability of arbitration tends to lessen the pressure for a voluntary settlement.

Administering the contract

Guiding principles

- Successful contract administration is the joint responsibility of the union and management.
- Grievances may be symptomatic of an underlying workplace problem.
- The new, collaborative workplace gives employees more opportunities to participate in problem solving and decision making.

Negotiating contracts and resolving disputes over them capture the labor relations spotlight, but the day-to-day problems of living with the contract define—and test—the labor-management relationship. Conflicts over issues unresolved at the bargaining table often continue after the contract is formally signed. Vague language or legalese, confusing clauses, hurt personal feelings, and other problems must be worked out through side meetings or the grievance process.

The contract serves as the law of the workplace. It has legal standing superior to that of a commercial contract. Its provisions address, often in exquisite detail, obvious issues such as union and management rights, wages, hours of work, benefits, union security, antidiscrimination and affirmative action, residency requirements, layoffs, reductions in force (RIFs), union political activities, and employee discipline and dismissal. Hundreds of other, less obvious issues may be covered as well, including washup time, laundry expenses, and teacher lunchroom duty.

Administrative oversight for implementing the terms of the contract during its specified life is the responsibility of the PERB, another administrative agency, or, occasionally, the courts. At the end of the day, however, successful contract administration is the responsibility of the union and management.

Grievances

A variety of vehicles exist for addressing conflicts arising from contract interpretation. As a rule, work stoppages over a disagreement concerning an existing contract are impermissible. A party can file an unfair labor practice charge with the appropriate administrative or judicial body, or can register an informal complaint. Litigation may be an option. But usually, allegations of a violation of contract language or other disputes under the contract are resolved through formal grievance procedures.

Exhibit 4–6 illustrates a typical grievance procedure. The most common grievances are over disciplinary actions, absenteeism, health and safety issues, vacation assignments, work assignments, promotions, overtime, RIFs, and allegations of discrimination. Note that when the parties cannot settle a grievance voluntarily, grievance arbitration serves as the final step. As is the case with interest disputes, a neutral arbitrator hears the evidence presented by the parties and renders a final and binding judgment. Among the factors considered by the grievance arbitrator are past practice, the prior bargaining record of the parties, and previous arbitration awards.

Grievances may be symptomatic of an underlying workplace problem, such as difficult, arbitrary, or insensitive supervisors; a hostile or unsafe working environment; introduction of new technology; or personality conflicts between a union steward and supervisor. Sometimes grievances result from intentional violations of contract language. For example, during a flood or other natural disaster, management may be forced to take preemptive action regardless of contract language.

Unions should be expected to investigate all allegations of contract violations made against management by a member of the bargaining unit, and to proceed with most of them. Grievance representation is a key responsibility of the union and one through which it demonstrates its value to members. Management should also take seriously its responsibility to defend itself and, when appropriate, take up its own grievances against the union.

Tensions between the union and management resulting from grievances may escalate and be difficult and frustrating to handle. Grievance procedures demand valuable management time and energy. An excessive number of grievances, even trivial ones, can seriously disrupt the workplace. But, as in a marriage, some disagreements are to be expected and, when properly and maturely handled, can help identify and resolve systemic problems and even strengthen the relationship.

Exhibit 4-6   A typical grievance procedure

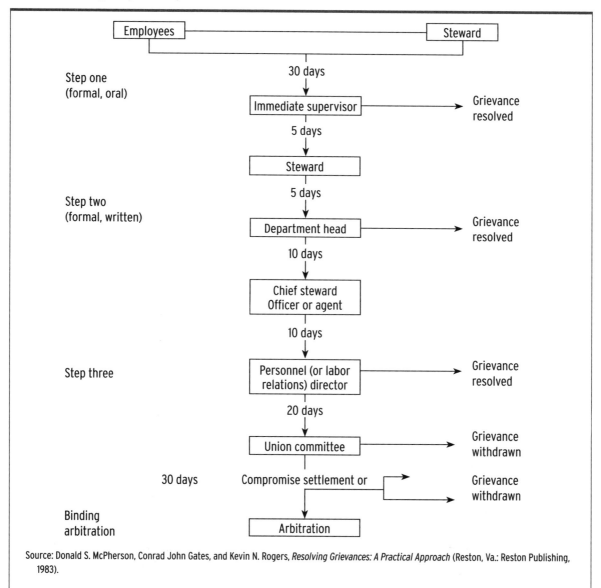

Source: Donald S. McPherson, Conrad John Gates, and Kevin N. Rogers, *Resolving Grievances: A Practical Approach* (Reston, Va.: Reston Publishing, 1983).

Employee participation initiatives

Other techniques for encouraging and organizing constructive dialogue between unions and management take place outside the bargaining and grievance processes. The new, collaborative workplace for improving government gives employees opportunities to participate in problem solving and decision making as never before. Examples of several such employee participation techniques follow.

Quality of Work Life (QWL) programs   QWL programs have been used for more than two decades to improve employee workplaces and working conditions, leading to better quality of public services and enhanced productivity. A QWL program is guided by a steering committee of labor and management employees who discuss and implement changes involving service delivery and employee empowerment.

Total Quality Management (TQM) programs   TQM, as first developed by W. Edwards Deming, focuses on how a service or program is delivered, and emphasizes the quality of the product. Management and union work cooperatively to meet the expectations of citizens and empower first-line employees to be problem solvers in order to improve the delivery of public services. TQM programs are not as popular today as they were in the early 1990s, but similar initiatives based on involving employees in continuous improvement of work processes have survived under other names.

Labor-management committees   Labor-management committees reflect the most far-reaching efforts to change labor-management relations. Called by a variety of names, all labor-management committees share a common element: the creation of a partnership committed to improving the relationship between employees and management and to resolving workplace issues of mutual concern. Underscoring the relationship is the idea that employees are the foundation of the organization and that the organization will be no stronger than the relationship that exists between labor and management. On the national level, the International Association of Fire Chiefs and the International Association of Fire Fighters encourage local fire chiefs and local union leaders to participate in labor-management committees aimed at improving relations.

Challenges in local government labor-management relations

Some of the challenges confronting labor-management relations in local government—such as overcoming a historically poisonous labor-management environment, finding and using alternatives to adversarial processes, and coping with persistent taxing and spending constraints—are long-standing. Other challenges are of more recent vintage, such as the mortgage loan and credit crises of 2008 that depleted local property and sales tax revenues.

Taxing and spending limitations have always plagued local governments. At the bottom of the fiscal food chain, municipalities, counties, towns, and townships are highly dependent on their respective state governments and, to a much lesser extent, on the federal government. Tax-resistant citizens aggressively attack tax and fee increases. Thus, local governments are at the mercy of economic forces that they cannot meaningfully influence. For unions and management, this means that

Caution

The following missteps can get a local government manager in serious trouble:

■ Failing to prepare properly for collective bargaining

■ Using delaying tactics or refusing to make concessions

■ Leaving elected officials "in the dark" about labor negotiations

■ Neglecting training for collaborative bargaining

■ Ignoring grievances.

RIFs must be considered from time to time and that pay hikes and benefit contributions are constrained. Collective bargaining is much more difficult when the size of the financial pie is shrinking.

Positive union-management relations are critical to performance-based government. The development of new techniques for delivering services, the adoption of labor-saving technologies, the contracting out for services and jobs, and the implementation of human resource management innovations, such as broadbanding position classifications and performance- or competency-based pay, are among the many reforms that call for union participation and cooperation. Union resistance has doomed many a reinventing-government initiative.

The old saying "necessity is the mother of invention" is particularly fitting given the approach local governments have taken to deal with financial crises, cutbacks in federal and state aid, perceptions of inefficiency, the lack of public support for higher taxes, and citizens' demands for increased public service. Local government leaders realize that maintaining the status quo will not make government work better and cost less. What is needed to initiate reforms is, in part, to change the relationship between management and unions.

Although changing employee relationships built over decades will not be accomplished by quick fixes, a growing number of local governments are seeking ways to create an environment that empowers workers to solve problems and improve the delivery of public services. But unions have opposed any "empowerment" that increases employees' responsibilities without a concomitant boost in pay. Changing adversarial relationships requires elected officials, local government managers, unions, and employees to find better ways to work together.[5]

Notes

1 Bureau of Labor Statistics, "Economic News Release," bls.gov/news.release/union2.t03.htm (accessed April 15, 2009).

2 In November 2007, the governor of Colorado issued an executive order authorizing collective bargaining for state employees. A May 2007 ruling of the Missouri Supreme Court held that all public employees in that state have a right to bargaining.

3 Roger Fisher, William Ury, and Bruce Patton, *Getting to Yes: Negotiating Agreement without Giving In,* 2nd ed. (New York: Penguin Books, 1991), 17.

4 Richard C. Kearney, *Labor Relations in the Public Sector,* 4th ed. (New York: CRC Press, 2009).

5 Barry Rubin and Richard Rubin, "Labor-Management Relations: Conditions for Collaboration," *Public Personnel Management* 35, no. 4 (2006): 283–298.

5

Employee Rights: Avoiding Legal Liability

John A. DiNome, Saundra M. Yaklin, David H. Rosenbloom, and Arlene J. Angelo

An important responsibility of public managers is to balance the citizens' right to receive efficient, effective, equitable, and responsive service from government with the public employees' right to be treated with equity and dignity. The U.S. Constitution, state constitutions, codified law, and common-law practices set the legal framework for the rights and responsibilities in the public employer-employee relationship.

Other chapters in this book address many of these rights and responsibilities in the context of specific personnel procedures. This chapter summarizes the major federal laws and court rulings affecting human resources. It also describes important documents used to communicate employment-related rights and duties, provides practical tips, and offers sample language. Employers may not be able to completely avoid lawsuits filed by unhappy job applicants or employees, but they can at least protect themselves and the jurisdiction from liability claims by not violating the rights of job seekers and employees.

Employee contracts

Guiding principle

- The legal foundation for employment needs to be made clear, whether it is based on civil service statutes, a union contract, an individual contract, or the "at-will" principle.

Challenge

- Avoiding changing at-will employment situations through implied or oral contracts

Editor's Note: Most of this chapter was written by John A. DiNome and Saundra M. Yaklin, with assistance from Caroline A. O'Connell. Alexander E. Gallin, Samuel Veytsman, Sara S. Kennedy, and Jarrod J. Malone assisted with updating the chapter for the second edition. The last section, which addresses constitutional rights, was written by David H. Rosenbloom. The sections on oaths and whistle-blower protection were contributed by Charles R. Wise. Arlene J. Angelo updated and revised the chapter to reflect current legislation for the third edition.

Employment at will

The doctrine of employment at will provides that an employer may discharge an employee for any reason not prohibited by law, or for no reason at all. However, when an employee has an employment contract or there is a statutory restriction, an employer does not have this freedom.

Most public employees are covered by civil service statutes or collective bargaining agreements and are, therefore, not employees at will. Rather, the requirements of the statute or collective bargaining agreement must be met before the employee may be terminated. However, some municipal employees are at-will employees. For example, in many states, city managers, chiefs of police, and department heads are at-will employees.

Employers should be aware that their written or oral statements, including employee policy manuals, may create an employment contract with their at-will employees or create additional rights for employees protected by civil service statutes and collective bargaining agreements.

Oral and implied contracts

In many states, oral statements made by an employer—for example, "you will be employed as long as you do your job"—may create an oral employment contract and rebut the presumption of employment at will. Most states require objective evidence of intent between the parties to create an oral contract and to dispel the at-will employment rule. Examples of objective evidence include statements and documents that indicate an intent to create an employment contract. Ultimately, the employee may have the burden to prove that the employment relationship is not at will.

Many state courts have found that an implied contract also exists where an employee supplies "additional consideration" to the employer. Sufficient additional consideration is found when an employee gives an employer a substantial benefit or undergoes a substantial hardship. For example, courts commonly find that an employment contract has been created when an employee relocates to take a job that he or she believes has been offered. If the court deems this to be adequate consideration, the employee is not at will and must be employed for a reasonable amount of time.

Personnel policy manual

Guiding principles

- The personnel policy manual should include an employment contract disclaimer.
- The personnel policy manual should use clear, concise language.

Challenge

- Keeping the personnel policy manual up-to-date, and informing employees of any changes that might affect them

Many employers, particularly nonunionized ones, publish personnel policy manuals for their workforce. As a general rule, employers should use these manuals as a means of communicating with their employees, setting forth standards for workplace performance and conduct, and describing employee benefits. The manual should be written in clear, concise language, and it should be kept up-to-date; changes made to the manual should be publicized.

Caution
An at-will employer should not use language in the personnel policy manual that implies that employees can be fired only for just cause.

However, employers must also carefully design their personnel manuals to avoid making unintended contractual guarantees to their employees. This and other legal issues surrounding personnel policy manuals are discussed in the paragraphs below.

Personnel policies as contracts

In many jurisdictions, statements and policies contained in an employee handbook can create contractual obligations. For example, if an employee handbook states that an employee will be fired only for just cause, an employee terminated without cause may have a breach-of-contract claim. A few states, such as Pennsylvania, have held that handbooks are generally not employment contracts. Thus, an employer should check state law to see whether and how its personnel handbook may give rise to contractual liability.

Employee handbooks should contain a disclaimer stating clearly that the handbook is not a contract and is subject to change; otherwise, an employer may be contractually bound by any statements contained in the handbook. Disclaimers must also be conspicuous; for example, a disclaimer that appears in the middle of a paragraph on page 25 may be insufficient. Therefore, an employer must carefully draft a disclaimer and place it within the first few pages of the handbook. Such a disclaimer might read:

> Your employment relationship with *[employer]* is considered "at will." This means that your employment with *[employer]* has no defined or definite duration. Either you or *[employer]* may terminate the employment relationship with or without cause, with or without notice, for any reason that is not prohibited by law. This handbook is not a contract and is subject to change without notice.

Employee handbooks should also include an acknowledgment form to document that the employee has received the handbook and understands its contents. Further, by signing the form, employees acknowledge that their employment is at will and that the handbook creates no contractual obligations between them and the employer. The acknowledgment might be worded as follows:

> I have this day received a copy of *[employer]* employee handbook. I understand that the handbook contains management guidelines only and that the *[employer]* may, from time to time and at its discretion, change, modify, or delete rules, policies, or benefits contained in the handbook.

> I understand that neither the handbook nor any other communication by a management representative, whether oral or written, is in any way intended to and does not create a contract of employment. I understand that my employment relationship with *[employer]* is, as described in this handbook, an employment-at-will relationship. As such, my employment with *[employer]* is voluntarily entered into, and I am free to resign at any time. Similarly, *[employer]* may terminate the employment relationship whenever it believes it is appropriate, with or without cause, with or without notice.

Political patronage

A public employer may not make decisions regarding lower-level public employees on the basis of political affiliation.[1] This includes hiring decisions, promotions, transfers, discharges, and other job actions. "Lower-level" public employees include all nonconfidential and non-policy-making employees. Further, an employer may not recommend that an employee support a particular political candidate. It is important to include this information in the employee handbook.

Equal employment opportunity and harassment policies

All employee handbooks should contain a statement of policy on equal employment opportunity (EEO). For example:

> The *[employer]* strictly follows a policy of nondiscrimination in all employment policies and practices. Our employment policies and practices treat everyone equally. We hire and develop the best people available on the basis of job-related qualifications. No distinctions are made in rates of pay or employment opportunities, including recruiting, hiring, training, benefits, promotions, transfers, or treatment on the job, on the basis of color, religious belief, sex, age, race, national origin, disability, handicap, or other prohibited criteria as these terms are used under applicable law.

In some jurisdictions, discrimination on the basis of sexual orientation is prohibited, and the employer's policy must include "sexual orientation" in the list of prohibited criteria. It is also very important that an employee handbook set forth the jurisdiction's policy on sexual and other types of harassment (see Exhibit 5–1). An established policy may discourage employees from committing any illegal activity. And in the event that there is a claim of harassment, a policy can provide the basis for defense. (See the section on sexual harassment on pages 142–145 and the section on other types of harassment on page 145.)

First Amendment rights of public employees

Public employees enjoy certain First Amendment protections against speech restrictions in the workplace. There are, however, certain limitations on those free speech rights. The Supreme Court has established that only speech that involves "a matter of public concern" and does not interfere with the effective functioning of the workplace is protected under the First Amendment.

As a result of the First Amendment protection given to public employees, a government employer may impose restrictions on speech in the workplace only if it can demonstrate that the restriction is vital to the efficient operation of the workplace. An employer may require professional conduct by its employees and may prohibit profanity in the workplace. A public employer may not, however, restrict its employees from possessing particular types of magazines (for example) at work, because the mere possession of these magazines does not compromise workplace efficiency.[2] Public employers should consider these First Amendment issues before including rules in the employee handbook that restrict employee speech and expression. (See the last section of this chapter for more on public employees' constitutional rights.)

Leaves of absence and the Family and Medical Leave Act

Employers should clearly outline in the employee handbook their policy on leaves of absence. Further, the handbook should describe the employer's Family and

Exhibit 5-1 Sample harassment policy

All employees have a duty to report sexual and other types of harassment whether they feel that they have been a victim of it or believe that they have observed it.

It is the policy of the *[employer]* to maintain a working environment for employees free from sexual harassment and harassment because of an employee's color, religious belief, sex, age, race, national origin, disability, sexual orientation, or other prohibited criteria. Harassment in any form or manner is expressly prohibited, and all reported or suspected occurrences of it will be promptly and thoroughly investigated. If harassment in violation of this policy has occurred, this municipality will take appropriate corrective action, including discipline or discharge of the offending employee.

Sexual harassment defined

Sexual harassment includes unwelcome sexual advances, requests for sexual favors, or other verbal or physical conduct of a sexual nature when

- Submission to the conduct is an explicit or implicit condition of employment.
- Submission to or rejection of the conduct is used as the basis for an employment decision.
- The conduct has the purpose or effect of unreasonably interfering with an individual's work performance or creating an intimidating, hostile work environment.
- Slurs, jokes, or derogatory comments are based on an individual's sex. This includes verbal comments as well as written comments in e-mails, posters, memoranda, or other documents.

Reporting harassment

Any incident of prohibited harassment from a co-worker or others who deal with the *[employer]* should be reported immediately to the supervisor or to the personnel office. Complaints of harassment from a supervisor should be reported immediately by the employee to the department head or to the personnel office. *[List title and telephone number of individual to receive report]*.

To the extent practicable, all complaints of harassment will remain confidential. It may be necessary, however, to disclose the nature or the origin of the complaint in order to investigate it properly or to take corrective action. The *[employer]* will take all necessary steps to ensure that a person who makes a good faith complaint, or any witness who comes forward in an investigation, will not be retaliated against in any way.

Corrective action

If the municipality concludes that harassment has occurred, it will take immediate steps to ensure that the harassment is stopped and does not recur. This may include suspension or termination of the individual(s) responsible for the harassment.

Medical Leave Act (FMLA) policy. It should explain that although the FMLA allows certain employees to take twelve weeks off for reasons defined by the act, if an employer has its own leave-of-absence policy, an employee is not entitled to both the leave of absence and the FMLA time. The policies themselves should also make this clear. An employer may also include in the handbook a statement that employees are required to substitute accrued paid leave time for unpaid FMLA time. If an employee chooses—or if the employer requires—the substitution of paid leave, the

Exhibit 5-2   Sample policy on workplace violence

It is *[employer]*'s policy to promote a safe environment for its employees. *[Employer]* is committed to working with its employees to maintain a work environment free of violence, threats of violence, harassment, intimidation, and other disruptive behavior. While this kind of conduct is not pervasive at our facilities, no workplace is immune. Every workplace is affected by disruptive behavior at one time or another.

Violence, threats, harassment, intimidation, and other disruptive behavior in our workplace will not be tolerated; that is, all reports of incidents will be taken seriously and will be dealt with appropriately. Unacceptable behavior can include oral or written statements, gestures, or expressions that communicate a direct or indirect threat of physical harm. Individuals who commit such acts will be removed from the premises and will be subject to disciplinary action (up to and including termination), criminal penalties, or both.

We need your cooperation to implement this policy effectively and maintain a safe working environment. Do not ignore violent, threatening, harassing, intimidating, or other disruptive behavior. If you observe or experience such behavior by anyone on *[employer]*'s premises, whether he or she is an employee of *[employer]* or not, report it immediately to *[title and telephone number of individual to receive report]*. Individuals who receive such reports should seek advice from *[title of person primarily responsible for investigating workplace violence]* regarding investigating the incident and initiating appropriate action.

employer must inform the employee that any procedural requirements of the paid leave policy must be satisfied. Compensatory time may be substituted by public employees for unpaid FMLA leave. (See the sections on the FMLA on pages 139 and 146–153.)

Workplace violence

As discussed further on, government employers have a duty to maintain a safe work environment and, therefore, should also include a policy prohibiting workplace violence in the employee handbook. (See Exhibit 5–2 above and the section on workplace violence beginning on page 156.)

Other policies

These are just a few of the policies that should be included in an employer's policy manual. In particular, many states have laws regarding employee pay and break requirements. Employers are encouraged to consult their counsel regarding state, local, and other legal requirements that affect policy manuals.

Personnel records

Guiding principle

■ Personnel records should be kept in accordance with federal, state, and local laws.

Challenge

■ Maintaining a complete, up-to-date personnel file for each employee

Employers should maintain a complete and up-to-date personnel file for each employee. This is simply a good management practice, but it is also required in case of an adverse personnel decision. Employers are tempted to create a paper trail only for poorly performing employees. However, in case of a lawsuit, judges want to see evidence of how the problem employee's performance differed from that of co-workers, and therefore, for the purpose of comparison, proper records need to be kept for all employees.

Record retention

Most employment laws require employers to maintain records. The chart in Exhibit 5–3 on pages 130–131 lists the records that must be kept and the time period for retention. To prevent tampering and to maintain their confidentiality, personnel files must be kept in a secure place. Government employers should contact their legal counsel to find out about state and local record-keeping requirements.

Confidentiality of personnel files

Personnel files of public employees may or may not enjoy protection, depending on the state and political culture in which the public employees operate. Some states, such as New York, exempt from disclosure the personnel files of police, firefighters, and paramedics to ensure that these employees are not the object of opportunistic civil suits.[3] Other states exempt material from the personnel files of public employees and teachers, as well as files of applicants for public positions.[4]

fyi

Confidential records

- Medical and mental health histories and personal records on client or patient treatment in medical facilities
- Genetic information, including results of genetic tests on the employee or the employee's family members and family medical history
- Information on human immunodeficiency virus (HIV) or acquired immune deficiency syndrome (AIDS) conditions
- Adoption records, child protection services files
- Correctional files
- Credit or loan histories, tax returns
- Information that, if disclosed, would result in economic or personal hardship to the subject party
- Information of a personal nature reported in confidence to an agency and not relevant to the ordinary work of such agency
- Lists of names and addresses (including public employees) that could be used for commercial or fund-raising purposes
- Employment records or personal references of applicants for employment
- Test results (employment and educational)

   Personal information may not be regarded as confidential information when identifying details are deleted or when the person to whom the record pertains consents in writing to the disclosure.

Source: Theodore Pedeliski.

Exhibit 5-3 Records that must be kept

Statute	Records to be kept	Time period
Title VII of the Civil Rights Act of 1964 (Title VII); Americans with Disabilities Act (ADA)	All personnel or employment records, including application forms; job advertisements; documentation concerning hiring, firing, promotion, demotion, transfer, or layoff decisions; payroll records; job descriptions; employment handbooks; documentation referencing training programs, employee evaluations, and requests for reasonable accommodation	For one year from when the record was made or the personnel action was taken
	Records relating to bias or discrimination, including but not limited to appraisals, job description, payroll, and other records relating to charging party and all similarly situated employees	Until the Equal Employment Opportunity Commission charge and suits are resolved
	EEO-1 Forms (for employers with 100 or more employees)	A copy of the most recently filed report must be available
Fair Labor Standards Act (FLSA) (including the Equal Pay Act of 1963)	Payroll records with the following information: employee's full name, address including zip code, date of birth, sex, and occupation; the time of day and day of the week on which the employee's workweek begins; the regular hourly rate of pay for any workweek in which overtime compensation is due and an explanation for the basis of the pay rate as well as a notation of any payment excluded from the employee's regular rate, the hours worked each workday and the total hours worked each workweek; the total daily or weekly straight time earnings; the total premium pay for overtime hours; the total additions to or deductions from wages paid each pay period; and the date of payment and pay period covered by payment	For three years
	Collective and individual employment contracts	
	Records of sales or business	
	For administrating executive or professional employees, documents regarding the basis on which wages are paid	
	Employees' time sheets or time cards	
	Wage rate tables used to calculate wages, salaries, or overtime	
	Records of deductions or additions to the individual's pay (and any records used to determine the deductions or additions)	
	Order, shipping, and billing records, including customer orders and invoices, shipping records, and delivery records that the employer makes or retains in the normal course of business	
	Certificates of age for employees who are minors	

Exhibit 5-3   Records that must be kept *(continued)*

Statute	Records to be kept	Time period
Age Discrimination in Employment Act of 1967 (ADEA)	Payroll records with each individual employee's name, address, date of birth, occupation, rate of pay, and compensation weekly computation	For three years
	Employee benefit plans	For one year after the termination of plan
	All employment and personnel records that relate to promotion, demotion, layoff, job applications, résumés, recall or discharge; job orders submitted to either a labor organization or employment agency for the recruitment of personnel; test papers of employer-administered aptitude test and physical examination test results; and advertisements	For one year
	Application forms for positions known to be of a temporary nature	For 90 days
Family and Medical Leave Act of 1993 (FMLA)	Same records as FLSA	For three years
	In addition, employers must maintain all documentation related to FMLA leave, including but not limited to dates and hours of FMLA leave taken, employee handbook provisions outlining employer policies and referencing leave benefits, copies of employee's notices of leave to employer, and records of disputes with employees over FMLA benefits	For three years
State Occupational Safety and Health Administration (OSHA) laws	Employers may be required to maintain medical records and exposure information on each employee. Check your state's OSHA law for exact requirements.	Varies for each state
Immigration Reform and Control Act	U.S. Citizenship and Immigration Services (CIS) Form I-9 and Employment Eligibility Verification Form	For three years from hiring or one year after employee's termination
Employee Retirement Income Security Act (ERISA)	Records regarding employee's health and/or welfare benefit plan, including but not limited to • Benefit plans • Summary plan descriptions • Employee notices	For six years
Department of Labor requirements	Records reflecting the benefits that are, or may become, due to any employee, and the name and address of each such employee	As long as any possibility exists that they might be relevant to a determination of benefits entitlement

Contents of personnel file

(also see Exhibit 5-3)

- Job description (see Chapter 1)
- Application form and related documents, such as test results (see Chapter 2)
- Letters with conditional job offer and final job offer, including pay rate (see Chapter 2)
- CIS Form I-9 and copies of documents presented to affirm identity and work eligibility (see Chapter 2)
- Requests for reasonable accommodation
- Internal Revenue Service Form W-4
- Employee benefits forms (see Chapter 6)
- Form acknowledging receipt of employee handbook (see this chapter)
- Regularly scheduled performance appraisals (see Chapter 3)
- Participation in training and educational programs
- Promotions, special recognitions, and awards
- Written reprimands and other disciplinary decisions (see Chapter 7)

This list is based on a similar list published in Fred S. Steingold, *The Employer's Legal Handbook* (Berkeley, Calif.: Nolo Press, 1996), chap. 2, p. 3.

Personnel files may be open to disclosure under a state's open-records statutes, or disclosure may turn on a balancing of the employee's privacy interests against the public's "right to know," and where the balance is equal, the judgment is tilted in favor of disclosure. Schoolteachers are particularly vulnerable to disclosure of their personnel records in this context as there is a public interest in the revelation of any behaviors that would be harmful to children or of any lack of fitness to teach. Some states preserve confidentiality of records for the period of the administrative hearings and permit disclosure only once proceedings are complete.

The Americans with Disabilities Act (ADA) requires that information from physical or medical exams be kept in separate, locked files and that access to them be restricted. According to the ADA, an employee's need for reasonable accommodation can be disclosed to supervisors, or the need for special attention in case of an emergency evacuation can be shared with security staff.

Tips for success in maintaining personnel records

- ☐ Adhere to federal, state, and local laws in retaining personnel records.
- ☐ Maintain a complete personnel file for each employee, and keep the files in a secure place.
- ☐ Abide by state and local laws in allowing employees access to their personnel files.
- ☐ Keep medical files separate from regular personnel files, and restrict access to them to a need-to-know basis.

Right to inspect records (state law)

Many states have laws that require employers to let employees access their own personnel records at least once a year. Again, an employer should contact its legal counsel regarding state and local laws. Some states may have online information on record keeping and open records.

Discrimination

Guiding principles

- All employees and all candidates for employment must be treated equally—that is, without regard to their race, sex, religion, national origin, age, disability, or other protected category.
- The local government's legal counsel, the state equal employment agency, and the Equal Employment Opportunity Commission (EEOC) can provide guidance in case of EEO and affirmative action questions.
- EEO principles should be applied to all aspects of human resource management, including planning future jobs; determining pay; advertising job openings; and hiring, developing, promoting, and disciplining employees.

Challenge

- Keeping up with nondiscrimination laws and amendments, and properly interpreting respective court decisions

Many laws regulate discrimination by local government employers. To help public administrators spot problems before they spiral into lawsuits, this section identifies and briefly explains the major discrimination laws and describes how the EEOC enforces many of them. When municipal employers suspect a problem, they should contact legal counsel. The EEOC provides useful information online, accessible through its home page at eeoc.gov.

Major discrimination laws

The chart in Exhibit 5–4 on pages 136–137 gives a condensed summary of some of the major laws governing discrimination by employers.

Title VII of the Civil Rights Act of 1964 (42 U.S.C. § 2000e et seq) Employers (but not individual supervisors or managers) may be sued under Title VII if they (1) are engaged in an industry affecting commerce and (2) have fifteen or more employees for each working day in twenty or more calendar weeks in the current or preceding calendar year. In 1972, Title VII was amended to include state and local governments, agencies, and political subdivisions.[5] Title VII protects both employees and applicants.

What it prohibits This statute, including its amendments, prohibits discrimination in employment on the basis of race, color, religion, sex (including pregnancy), and national origin. It also prohibits sexual harassment and harassment based on the other categories protected by Title VII, which is explained in detail in the next section of this chapter (see pages 142–145). Title VII's nondiscrimination provision applies to all aspects of the employment relationship, including recruitment, hiring, compensation, promotion, discipline, and discharge. Employees may bring discrimination suits under Title VII for several reasons:

- *Disparate treatment.* Often employees sue because they feel that they have been treated differently from other employees who are not in their protected class.
- *Disparate impact.* Employees may sue because they believe that a test or employment policy unfairly excludes their protected class.
- *Harassment or hostile work environment.* Employees may sue because they feel that they have been harassed because of their protected class or that their work environment is abusive toward their protected class.
- *Reasonable accommodation.* Employees may sue because they feel that their religious needs are not being accommodated.

How it is enforced   Individuals who feel that they have been discriminated against in employment must file a charge with either the local EEOC office or a local or state discrimination agency that the EEOC has certified. (See pages 140–142 for an explanation of what happens when an EEOC charge is filed.) Employers who have violated the employment provisions of Title VII may be required to hire applicants or reinstate their former employees with or without back pay. In 1991, Congress enacted the Civil Rights Act of 1991 (42 U.S.C. § 1981a), which provides that employers who violate Title VII may also be required to pay up to $300,000 in compensatory damages, such as damages for pain and suffering, and punitive damages. Political subdivisions cannot be required to pay punitive damages but can be required to pay compensatory damages.

Civil Rights Act of 1871 (42 U.S.C. § 1983)   This act covers local governments and individual public officials who are acting in their official capacities.[6] Government officials may be immune from liability if they are carrying out an official legislative or judicial function, such as enacting an ordinance. However, in most employment situations, public managers are immune from liability only if "their conduct does not violate clearly established statutory or constitutional rights of which a reasonable person would have known."[7] The jurisdiction itself is not immune from suits by its employees.[8]

What it prohibits   Section 1983 prohibits "state actors" from depriving a person of rights, privileges, and immunities secured by the Constitution or laws of the United States. Claims under Section 1983 in the public employment context usually involve alleged violations of the equal protection, free speech, and due process clauses of the Constitution. In the discrimination context, employees generally claim that they have not been treated equally or have been discriminated against on the basis of race, color, sex, religion, national origin, age, disability, or some other distinction.

How it is enforced   Employees often bring Section 1983 suits instead of Title VII suits because they do not have to follow any of the administrative procedures required to bring suit under Title VII. They may file directly with either a federal or a state court. The relief available to employees under Section 1983 is now similar to the relief available under Title VII. Employers may be ordered to reinstate or hire an employee; they may also be required to pay back wages, emotional damages, and attorneys' fees. While local officials may be required to pay punitive damages,[9] the jurisdiction itself cannot be required to pay punitive damages.[10] However, unlike under Title VII, compensatory and punitive damages are not capped at $300,000.

Civil Rights Act of 1866 (42 U.S.C. § 1981) This act covers local government employers who have an employment contract with an employee. Section 1981 provides that "all persons...shall have the same right to make and enforce contracts...as...white citizens." The Civil Rights Act of 1991 defines "make and enforce contracts" in Section 1981 to include the "making, performance, modification, and termination of contracts, and the enjoyment of all benefits, privileges, terms, and conditions of the contractual relationship." There is no minimum number of employees. Both local government entities and officials may be sued under this act, either directly or indirectly through Section 1983 described above.[11]

What it prohibits Courts have found that Section 1981 prohibits discrimination based on race, color, and ethnic characteristics.

How it is enforced Employees often bring Section 1981 suits instead of Title VII suits because they do not have to follow any of the administrative procedures required to bring suit under Title VII. They may file directly with either a federal or a state court. The relief available to employees under Section 1981 is now similar to the relief available under Title VII. Employers may be ordered to reinstate or hire an employee; they may also be required to pay back wages, emotional damages, and attorneys' fees. While local officials may be required to pay punitive damages,[12] the jurisdiction itself cannot be required to pay punitive damages.[13] Like suits under Section 1983 above, there is no cap on compensatory and punitive damages.

Title I of the Americans with Disabilities Act of 1990 (42 U.S.C. § 12101 et seq) Employers generally (but not individual supervisors or managers) are covered if they (1) engage in an industry affecting commerce and (2) have fifteen or more employees for each working day in twenty or more calendar weeks in the current or preceding calendar year (42 U.S.C. §§ 2000e[a], 12111[5]). Most local governmental employers are covered by this act.[14]

What it prohibits Title I of the ADA prohibits employment discrimination against a qualified individual with a disability because of the disability. A person with a "disability" is an individual who (1) has a physical or mental impairment that substantially limits one or more major life activities, (2) has a record of such an impairment, or (3) is regarded as having such an impairment.

The ADA Amendments Act of 2008 expanded the protections afforded under the ADA in a number of ways. One such expansion relates to the determination of whether an individual is "substantially limited" by an impairment. This determination must now be made without considering mitigating measures, such as medications taken by the individual to control a medical condition. The ADA covers job application procedures; testing; hiring; advancement; discharge; compensation; job training; and other terms, conditions, and privileges of employment.

To enable "otherwise qualified" individuals with disabilities to perform the essential functions of the job, employers must also make "reasonable accommodations" for those individuals unless doing so would impose an "undue hardship" on the organization. Under the ADA, "undue hardship" requires a showing of significant difficulty or expense by the employer. Employers who are trying to accommodate an employee's disability can call the Job Accommodation Network at (800) 526-7234 for reasonable suggestions.

Exhibit 5-4 Laws regarding discrimination

Discrimination law	Who is covered?	What is prohibited?
Title VII of the Civil Rights Act of 1964 (42 U.S.C. § 2000e et seq)	Employers who are (1) engaged in an industry affecting commerce with (2) 15 or more employees for each working day in 20 or more calendar weeks in the current or preceding calendar year. In 1972, Title VII was amended to include state and local governments, agencies, and political subdivisions.	Discrimination against employees with respect to their "compensation, terms, conditions or privileges of employment, because of [their] race, color, religion, sex or national origin" (42 U.S.C. § 2000e-2).
Civil Rights Act of 1871 (42 U.S.C. § 1983)	Persons acting "under the color of state law." Local governments are generally covered by this act as well. (There is no minimum number of employees.)	Deprivation of employees' constitutional and legal rights, privileges, and immunities because of their race, color, religion, sex, or national origin.
Civil Rights Act of 1866 (42 U.S.C. § 1981)	Local government employers who have an employment contract with an employee. (There is no minimum number of employees.)	Discrimination against employees in the "making, performance, modification, and termination of contracts, and the enjoyment of all benefits, privileges, terms, and conditions of the contractual relationship" because of their race, color, or ethnicity (42 U.S.C. § 1981b).
Title I of the Americans with Disabilities Act of 1990 (42 U.S.C. § 12101 et seq)	Local government employers who are (1) engaged in an industry affecting commerce with (2) 15 or more employees for each working day in 20 or more calendar weeks in the current or preceding calendar year (42 U.S.C. § 12111 [5]).	Discrimination against qualified individuals with a disability with respect to job application procedures, compensation, terms, conditions, and privileges of employment because of their disability.
Sections 504 and 503 of the Rehabilitation Act of 1973 (29 U.S.C. § 794 et seq)	Any department, agency, or instrumentality of a state or local government that receives or distributes federal financial assistance. Section 503 applies to local government employers who enter into contracts in excess of $10,000 with the federal government to provide nonpersonal services.	Discrimination against an otherwise qualified individual with a disability because of the disability.
Age Discrimination in Employment Act of 1967 (20 U.S.C. § 621 et seq)	Employers who are (1) engaged in an industry affecting commerce with (2) 20 or more employees for each working day in 20 or more calendar weeks in the current or preceding calendar year (29 U.S.C. § 630). Since 1991, local government employees generally have been protected by this act; however, law enforcement officers and firefighters are partially exempt.	Discriminating against employees "with respect to [their] compensation, terms, conditions, or privileges of employment" because of age.

Exhibit 5-4   Laws regarding discrimination *(continued)*

Discrimination law	Who is covered?	What is prohibited?
Equal Pay Act of 1963 (29 U.S.C. § 206)	Most public employees.	Prohibits employers from paying their employees different wages on the basis of sex.
Family and Medical Leave Act of 1993 (29 U.S.C. § 2601 et seq)	State and local governments are covered by this act regardless of the number of employees (29 C.F.R. 825.108). An employee is covered if the employee (1) has worked for 12 months for the employer, (2) has worked at least 1,250 hours during the previous 12 months, and (3) works at a work site where the public agency employs 50 or more employees within 75 miles (29 U.S.C. § 2611 [2]).	Under the FMLA, employees are entitled to leave time. It is unlawful for employers to (1) interfere with an employee's right to request or take leave or (2) discriminate against an employee for opposing actions that are illegal under this act (29 U.S.C. § 2815).
Uniform Services Employment and Reemployment Rights Act of 1994 (38 U.S.C. § 43) (USERRA)	All employers in the public and private sectors.	Prohibits discrimination against veterans and grants reemployment rights to those serving in the military.

How it is enforced   The ADA is enforced by the EEOC under the same administrative scheme as Title VII discussed above. The Title VII remedies are available to employees who sue under the ADA. In reasonable accommodation cases, however, an employer is not liable for emotional pain and suffering or punitive damages if it can show that it consulted with the employee and made a good-faith effort to provide reasonable accommodation.

Sections 504 and 503 of the Rehabilitation Act of 1973 (29 U.S.C. § 794 et seq)   Any department, agency, or instrumentality of a local government that receives or distributes federal financial assistance is covered by Section 504 of the Rehabilitation Act (29 U.S.C. § 794). Section 503 (29 U.S.C. § 793) applies to local government employers who enter into contracts in excess of $10,000 with the federal government to provide nonpersonal services, such as construction.[15]

What it prohibits   Section 504 prohibits recipients of federal funding from discriminating on the basis of non-job-related disabilities and requires employers to make reasonable accommodation for their employees. The requirements and cases under this law are very similar to those under the ADA. Section 503 also requires government contractors to take affirmative action to employ and advance qualified persons with disabilities.

How it is enforced   The Civil Rights Division of the Department of Justice coordinates enforcement of Section 504. Section 503 is enforced by the Office of Federal Contract Compliance Programs in the U.S. Department of Labor (DOL).

Age Discrimination in Employment Act of 1967 (29 U.S.C. § 621 et seq)

According to the Age Discrimination in Employment Act (ADEA), employers are generally covered if they (1) are engaged in an industry affecting commerce, and (2) have twenty or more employees for each working day in twenty or more calendar weeks in the current or preceding calendar year (29 U.S.C. § 630).

In 1991, Congress extended the ADEA to cover local and state government employers. More recently, in 2000, the U.S. Supreme Court held that Congress had overstepped its authority and found that the ADEA did not validly abrogate the states' Eleventh Amendment immunity from suit. Therefore, the ADEA does not apply to state governmental employers.[16] Local governmental employers are still generally covered by the ADEA, however, with only a few governmental employers who are considered "arms of the state" exempt from the ADEA.[17] Individual governmental employers should contact their local counsel to determine whether they are covered by the ADEA and other federal discrimination laws. As a practical matter, even if a governmental employer is exempt from the ADEA, it will still be subject to a similar state law.

Police officers and firefighters are partially exempt from the requirements of the ADEA. Although this exemption expired on December 31, 1993,[18] Congress restored it on September 30, 1996. Under the restored exemption, a governmental employer does not violate the ADEA when discharging its firefighters or police officers on the basis of age if the following three criteria are met:

- The employer has complied with any EEOC regulations allowing police officers and firefighters to take mental and physical fitness tests.

- The employee has either (1) attained the age of retirement under a state or local law in effect on March 3, 1983, or (2) attained the age of retirement specified in a state or local law enacted after September 30, 1996, that provides for retirement at age fifty-five or after.

- The retirement is taken "pursuant to a bona fide...retirement plan that is not a subterfuge to evade the purposes of [the ADEA]."

What it prohibits The ADEA protects individuals aged forty and over from discrimination based on age. Like Title VII, the ADEA's protection extends to hiring, discharge, promotions, compensation, benefits, and all other conditions or privileges of employment. Under the 1990 amendments to the ADEA, known as the Older Workers' Benefit and Protection Act (26 U.S.C. § 626), employees cannot waive their ADEA claims unless employers strictly comply with the following requirements:

- The employee must receive something of value in addition to his or her normal salary and benefits.

- The release must be in plain English and specifically mention the ADEA.

- The employee must be notified in writing of his or her right to consult an attorney.

- The employee must be given at least twenty-one days to consider the offer.

- The agreement must provide the employee with the right to revoke the agreement for up to seven days after signing the agreement. Employers should not pay any release amount until after the seven-day waiting period.

- When a severance agreement or release is made in connection with an exit incentive plan offered to a group of employees, the employer must meet more imposing requirements. The employer must provide written notice of (1) the plan's eligibility factors, (2) the groups of employees eligible for the plan, (3) the job titles and ages of employees eligible for the program, (4) the ages of all employees in those same job classifications or organizational units who are not eligible, and (5) any time limits for accepting. After providing this notice, the employer must give the employees forty-five days to consider the offer (as opposed to twenty-one days for individual employees).

How it is enforced   The ADEA is enforced by the EEOC but under a slightly different administrative scheme than Title VII. Employees must file with the EEOC but may then file suit directly with a court within sixty days. Employers may be ordered to reinstate or hire employees; they may also be required to pay back and front wages and attorneys' fees. Although punitive damages are not available, employers may have to pay double damages if a violation was "willful."

Equal Pay Act of 1963 (29 U.S.C. § 206)   The Equal Pay Act stipulates no minimum number of employees and applies to most public employees.[19] Local government employees are exempt if they (1) are not subject to civil service laws and (2) hold an elected office or are appointed by an elected official to be a member of the official's personal staff or to make policy.[20]

What it prohibits   The Equal Pay Act prohibits employers from paying their employees different wages on the basis of sex. "Wages" refers to any form of compensation, including benefits and retirement plans.

How it is enforced   The EEOC is in charge of enforcing the Equal Pay Act, and employees may file with the EEOC. Employees may also file suit directly with a court as long as they bring their claims within two years. Employees may recover back pay, double damages, and attorneys' fees.

Family and Medical Leave Act of 1993 (29 U.S.C. § 2601 et seq)   Both state and local governments are covered by this act.[21] The FMLA mandates that employers provide eligible employees with up to twelve workweeks of leave time in each leave year for certain qualifying conditions. Those conditions are

- The serious health condition of the employee or a qualifying family member
- The birth, adoption, or placement of a new child with the employee
- A qualifying exigency arising out of a military service member's active duty in support of a contingency operation.

Employers are also required to provide up to twenty-six workweeks of leave time in a twelve-month period to eligible employees who are caring for a covered military service member wounded in the line of duty.

What it prohibits   It is unlawful for employers to (1) interfere with an employee's right to request or take leave, or (2) discriminate against an employee for opposing actions that are illegal under this act (29 U.S.C. §2815).

How it is enforced   The FMLA is enforced by the Wage and Hour Division of the DOL. Employees may file complaints with the department and may also sue in either state or federal court. Employees may be reinstated or promoted and receive back pay, attorneys' fees, and double damages.

**Uniform Services Employment and Reemployment Rights Act of 1994
(38 U.S.C. § 4311) (USERRA)**   USERRA is intended to minimize the disadvantages to an individual that occur when that person needs to be absent from his or her civilian employment to serve in this country's uniformed services. The act defines the cumulative length of time that an individual may be absent from work for uniformed services duty and retain reemployment rights. Covering employees who serve or have served in the uniformed services, USERRA seeks to ensure that those who serve their country will retain their civilian employment and benefits, and can seek employment free from discrimination because of their service. The discrimination provisions of USERRA address problems regarding initial employment, reemployment, retention in employment, promotion, or any other benefit of employment. USERRA provides enhanced protection for disabled veterans, requiring employers to make reasonable efforts to accommodate the disability.

What it prohibits   USERRA prohibits discrimination in employment based on past, present, or future military service.

How it is enforced   USERRA is administered by the DOL through the Veterans' Employment and Training Service (VETS). VETS assists those persons who are experiencing problems with their civilian employment that are related to their military service and provides information about the act to employers.

State and local discrimination acts   Most states and many local governments have laws prohibiting discrimination that are very similar to the federal acts outlined above. In addition, some state and local governments have laws prohibiting discrimination on the basis of sexual orientation. These jurisdictions usually have a special agency that enforces these laws and coordinates efforts with the EEOC. Public managers should contact legal counsel to find out about their state and local laws.

Retaliation claims   Most discrimination laws also contain provisions prohibiting employers from retaliating against employees who complain about discrimination or bring actions to enforce their rights. The U.S. Supreme Court has held that the antiretaliation provision of Title VII also extends to employees who speak out about discrimination by answering questions in an employer's internal investigation of alleged discrimination.[22]

EEOC charges

EEOC regulations specify who can file charges and what procedures to follow.

Who files   Individual employees may file a charge of discrimination with the EEOC under Title VII, the ADA, the ADEA, or the Equal Pay Act. In some cases, associations such as unions may also file discrimination charges against an employer. Additionally, the EEOC may file its own charges against an employer.

The charge and notice   Generally, a charge contains the name of the employee, the name of the employer, and a statement of the facts constituting the alleged discrimination. The EEOC usually accepts employee statements that are vague and allows employees to amend their charges if the new charges are related to or grow out of the original charges. Once a charge is filed, the EEOC sends a copy to the employer.

Timing   Charges must generally be filed with the EEOC within 180 days after the alleged discrimination occurred. In some cases, the deadline is "tolled" or stopped. For example, if an employer maintains a policy that is discriminatory or that repeatedly subjects an employee to the same type of harassment, the violation is continuous and an employee may file within 180 days of the last violation. Employees may also file after 180 days if they did not know that an employer action, such as termination, was taken for discriminatory reasons. The Lilly Ledbetter Fair Pay Act, which was signed into law on January 29, 2009, and is retroactive to May 28, 2007, changed the time limits for bringing a compensation-related charge with the EEOC. Now, the 180-day filing period begins to run with each paycheck an employee receives instead of on the date that a discriminatory pay decision is first made. The act supersedes the Supreme Court decision in *Ledbetter v. Goodyear Tire & Rubber Co., Inc.,* 550 U.S. 618 (2007).

If an employee files in a state that has an authorized state discrimination agency, the employee has 300 days from when the discrimination occurred to file with the EEOC. The EEOC has various arrangements with state agencies, many of which allow an employee to file with both agencies by simply filing with one. However, only one agency will investigate at a time.

Document requests and the employer position statement   The EEOC will generally send employers a list of the documents that it seeks. Employers should also file a letter with the assigned EEOC investigator stating their position on the charge; this is known as a position statement. If an employer does not provide the requested documents, the EEOC has the authority to issue subpoenas that will be enforced by the federal courts provided that the charge is valid, the description of the relevant documents is clear, and the subpoena is issued for a legitimate purpose.[23]

Fact-finding conference   The EEOC may require a fact-finding conference, at which the investigator questions both the employee and an employer representative. The conference, usually held at the EEOC field office, is used to define the issues, resolve issues that can be resolved, and determine whether settlement may be possible.

Interviews and on-site investigations   The EEOC also has the power to interview witnesses and conduct on-site investigations of an employer's premises and documents. The employer has the right to have an attorney present during interviews of management employees only. The employer also has the right to have a company representative accompany an investigator who comes on site.

EEOC determinations/right to sue   Employees may withdraw their charges only if the EEOC consents to the withdrawal. However, should the EEOC determine that a charge was not filed in time or that, based on the evidence before it, it cannot conclude that discrimination occurred, it must dismiss the charge. The EEOC may also dismiss the charge if the employee is uncooperative, cannot be found, or refuses a settlement offer made by the employer that provides full relief for the discrimination.

After the EEOC concludes its investigation, it issues a letter of determination to the employee and employer. The letter states whether, on the basis of the information obtained in the investigation, the EEOC has concluded that discrimination

Tips for avoiding discrimination suits

☐ Review hiring practices to ensure that the jurisdiction is reaching out to a diverse applicant pool.

☐ Ensure that employees have the opportunity to discuss and seek redress of grievances before going to an outside agency (such as the EEOC).

☐ Conduct workplace training on racial sensitivity and sexual harassment.

occurred. The letter also informs the employee that he or she has 90 days in which to sue in federal court. The EEOC is supposed to issue its determination within 120 days after the charge is filed, but this requirement is not mandatory and is seldom observed. If an investigation is ongoing, an employee may request, in writing, a right-to-sue letter at any time after 180 days from the date the charge is filed. Employees have the right to sue regardless of the EEOC's finding.

Dispute resolution duties   If the EEOC finds reasonable cause to believe that discrimination has occurred, it must make an attempt for thirty days to have the parties reach a conciliation agreement. Employees are not required to sign a conciliation agreement, however, and may bring an individual suit after receiving the right-to-sue letter.[24] On July 17, 1995, the EEOC issued an alternative dispute resolution policy indicating that it intended to begin using alternative dispute resolution procedures such as mediation. The commission has now instituted mediation programs in all its district offices. The EEOC mediation program encourages parties to resolve their disputes voluntarily through the use of a neutral mediator and is not binding unless the parties reach a settlement agreement.

Suits   Both the EEOC and individuals have the power to bring suit or intervene in a suit in a federal court on discrimination charges. Employers may be required to hire or reinstate their employees with or without back pay. Under the Civil Rights Act of 1991 (42 U.S.C. § 1981a), governmental employers may also be required to pay up to $300,000 in compensatory damages for pain and suffering. In reasonable accommodation cases under the ADA, compensatory damages are not awarded if the employer shows that it has consulted with the person with a disability who asked for an accommodation and that it made a good-faith effort to provide a reasonable accommodation. (See pages 133–140 for a discussion on the relief available under each law enforced by the EEOC.)

Sexual harassment

Guiding principles

■ Employees who feel that their concerns have been addressed may be less likely to sue.

■ Employers must conduct sexual harassment investigations fairly and discreetly to avoid suits by wrongly accused employees.

Challenges

- Drawing a line between acceptable office romance and unacceptable sexual harassment
- Stopping clumsy or boorish behavior before it becomes sexual harassment
- Protecting the privacy rights of the alleged victim and the alleged perpetrator while gathering evidence concerning the charges

Title VII of the Civil Rights Act of 1964 (42 U.S.C. § 2000e et seq) and many state and local laws prohibit both sexual discrimination and sexual harassment. This section is designed to help local government employers identify and deal with sexual harassment.

The law

Title VII explicitly prohibits sexual discrimination. Sexual discrimination occurs when an employer treats an employee, male or female, differently because of the employee's sex. Examples of sexual discrimination include paying a woman a lower salary than a man who performs the same job and has the same experience, refusing to promote women, or providing lower benefits for male employees.

Courts have broadened Title VII by finding that sexual harassment is a form of sex discrimination. Sexual harassment involves unwelcome sexual advances, requests for sexual favors, or other contacts of a sexual nature, as illustrated in Exhibit 5–5. Courts have ruled that Title VII covers sexual harassment claims not only between persons of the opposite sex but also between people of the same sex, whether heterosexual or homosexual.

There are two types of sexual harassment: quid pro quo and hostile work environment. Quid pro quo harassment is usually easy to spot. It involves sex in exchange for hiring, promotion, job security, or other employment benefits or detriments. Hostile work environment harassment is more subtle. It involves sexual advances, requests for sexual favors, or other verbal or sexual conduct that interferes with an employee's work or creates an intimidating, hostile, or offensive workplace.

Under two Supreme Courts cases decided in 1998,[25] employers are strictly liable for either type of sexual harassment committed by their supervisors if the employee suffers a tangible job detriment. If the employee has not suffered a tangible job

Exhibit 5-5   What is sexual harassment?

Sexual discrimination = different or unfair treatment of an employee because of his or her sex

Examples: limits on an employee's job opportunities or different levels of pay, bonuses, or benefits

Sexual harassment = unwelcome sexual advances, requests for sexual favors, or other contact that is sexual

There are two types of sexual harassment:

- Quid pro quo—when submission to or rejection of sexual harassment is used for employment decisions
  Examples: demotion, discipline, or discharge for refusing to have sex
- Hostile work environment—sexual harassment that unreasonably interferes with an employee's work or creates an intimidating, hostile, or offensive workplace
  Examples: sexual comments, jokes, repeated sexual advances, pornographic displays

Caution

■ Employees today are suing for discrimination and receiving multimillion-dollar awards.

■ Employees who are wrongly disciplined for harassment may sue for discrimination or defamation.

detriment, an employer may be able to defend itself successfully against a sexual harassment claim if it can show that (1) it exercised reasonable care to prevent and promptly correct any sexually harassing behavior and (2) the plaintiff employee unreasonably failed to take preventive opportunities provided by the employer.[26] To avoid liability, it is essential that an employer take all necessary steps to prevent sexual harassment (see the following section). Further, if an employee does claim sexual harassment, the employer must promptly investigate and take action as appropriate.

Many states and local jurisdictions also have laws that prohibit sexual harassment. Public administrators should ask their legal counsel about the laws in their state. Often employees sue under a state or local law in order to receive large monetary awards because many state discrimination laws do not have the cap on punitive damages contained in Title VII. Employees may also sue under a state or local law in order to sue the individual accused of harassment because individual employees are not liable under Title VII.

Solutions and approaches

To minimize liability for sexual harassment, employers must take steps before harassment occurs, investigate employee complaints of harassment, and take appropriate measures to correct the problem. Prompt investigation and disciplinary action aids in the defense of a lawsuit involving a hostile work environment claim. In addition, employees who feel that their concerns have been addressed may be less likely to sue. Employers must conduct their investigations fairly and discreetly to avoid suits by a wrongly accused employee.

To protect themselves against potential sexual harassment claims, employers may want to adopt a policy prohibiting relationships between supervisors and subordinates. There are some concerns about an employee's right of privacy and freedom of association, and some state statutes prohibit employers from regulating off-hours activities, which protects all legal recreational activities. In general, however, courts allow public employers significant leeway in regulating an employee's conduct because these employers have a significant interest in providing government services effectively, and employers may adopt a clear policy prohibiting romance while in the workplace.[27]

Several steps can be taken before harassment occurs.

Carefully recruit employees   Employees should be asked in their interviews why they left their prior jobs. They should also be asked if they have ever been accused of sexual harassment or of violating an employment discrimination law. Employers should check potential employees' references.

Adopt a written policy against sexual harassment   This policy should give examples of sexual harassment. It should then clearly state that the employer does not tolerate sexual harassment and will discipline offenders up to and including discharge. The policy should require employees to report harassment immediately and

Tips for avoiding sexual harassment problems

☐ Make sure that all employees, both management and rank and file, understand that sexual harassment is sex discrimination and prohibited under Title VII of the Civil Rights Act.

☐ Develop a sexual harassment policy, including steps that alleged victims should take to deal with the problem.

☐ Post the sexual harassment policy on bulletin boards devoted to personnel issues.

☐ Train all employees to recognize and avoid the two types of sexual harassment—quid pro quo and hostile work environment.

should also set forth a clear procedure for doing so. Assurances that there will be no retaliation against an employee for making a good-faith report of sexual harassment or participating in a sexual harassment investigation should be included in the policy. (See Exhibit 5–1 on page 127 for a sample harassment policy.)

Set up a procedure for addressing sexual harassment   The employer should designate the person or persons to whom employees should bring their harassment concerns. There should also be an alternate person for employees to contact in case the person doing the harassing is precisely the person to whom the employee has been instructed to report such behavior. Large employers often provide a phone number where employees may complain and get advice anonymously.

Train managers, supervisory employees, and human resource employees   An employer should conduct a sexual harassment awareness seminar for its supervisory employees in which the supervisors are given problems and examples and asked to identify sexual harassment. Courts have dismissed some sexual harassment claims partly because the employer had a good prevention program.

Train all employees   All employees should be taught how to recognize sexual harassment. They should be told that sexual harassment will not be tolerated. They should also be told what to do if sexual harassment occurs. Every employee should be given a copy of the sexual harassment policy and required to sign a form acknowledging its receipt. Unfortunately, employers and employees can also be falsely accused of sexual harassment. A worker threatened with an adverse personnel decision—demotion or firing—may try to deflect the action by claiming sexual harassment. Managers can take a few steps to avoid the appearance of wrongdoing:

• Keep the door open when meeting with a problem employee.

• If confidentiality and a closed door are required, a staff member (e.g., a secretary) should be present at the meeting and should take notes.

Other types of harassment

Courts have found that employees can also bring suits for harassment based on other types of prohibited criteria, including race, color, national origin, religion, age, and disability. Therefore, employers must broaden their sexual harassment policies to prohibit other types of harassment, and the discussion above regarding preventing, investigating, and promptly correcting sexual harassment applies with equal force to these other types of harassment. (See Exhibit 5–1 for a sample harassment policy.)

Family and Medical Leave Act

Guiding principles

- Employers should notify the employee that requested leave qualifies as FMLA leave and designate it as such.

- Employers may require that the employee produce a medical certification for a serious health condition.

Challenge

- Properly identifying which employees are covered, what types of leave fall under FMLA, and where to post notifications

Employers must pay special attention to the notice requirements under the FMLA.

Who and what are covered?

The FMLA generally covers state and local government employers regardless of the number of employees (see note 21). However, an employee is covered only if he or she (1) has worked for the employer for twelve months, (2) has at least 1,250 hours of service within the previous twelve months, and (3) works at a work site where the public agency employs fifty or more employees within seventy-five miles of that site. To be eligible for FMLA leave, employees must need the leave

- To care for a newborn, newly adopted child, or new foster child
- To care for a spouse, child, or parent who has a serious health condition
- Because a serious health condition makes the employee unable to perform the functions of his or her position. A "serious health condition" is defined as an "illness, injury, impairment, or physical or mental condition that involves: (a) inpatient care in a hospital, hospice, or residential medical care facility; or (b) continuing treatment by a health care provider" (29 U.S.C. § 2611 [11]). An employer may require that the employee produce a medical certification of the serious health condition. The DOL has published a form to be used for medical certification (see Exhibit 5–6a).

Employees are also entitled to take FMLA leave because of any "qualifying exigency" arising out of the fact that the employee's spouse, son, daughter, or parent is a covered military member on active duty or has been notified of an impending call to active-duty status in support of a contingency operation. A qualifying exigency may include short-notice deployment, military events, child care and school activities, rest and recuperation, and other specified activities related to active-duty status. Further, an eligible employee may take up to twenty-six weeks of unpaid leave during a twelve-month period to care for a covered military service member with a serious injury or illness incurred in the line of duty on active duty if the employee is the spouse, son, daughter, parent, or next of kin of the service member.

Checklist of basic employer requirements

The following are requirements that employers must adhere to under the FMLA.

- Employers must provide eligible employees with up to twelve weeks of unpaid leave during a twelve-month period (and up to twenty-six weeks for the care of a covered military service member with a serious illness or injury incurred in the line of duty on active duty).

Exhibit 5-6a Department of Labor form for certification of health care provider

Certification of Health Care Provider
(Family and Medical Leave Act of 1993)

U.S. Department of Labor
Employment Standards Administration
Wage and Hour Division

OMB No.: 1215-0181
Expires: 09-30-2010

*(When completed, this form goes to the employee, **Not to the Department of Labor**.)*

1. Employee's Name

2. Patient's Name *(If different from employee)*

3. Page 4 describes what is meant by a **"serious health condition"** under the Family and Medical Leave Act. Does the patient's condition[1] qualify under any of the categories described? If so, please check the applicable category.

(1) _____ (2) _____ (3) _____ (4) _____ (5) _____ (6) _____ , or None of the above _____

4. Describe the **medical facts** which support your certification, including a brief statement as to how the medical facts meet the criteria of one of these categories:

5. a. State the approximate **date** the condition commenced, and the probable duration of the condition (and also the probable duration of the patient's present **incapacity**[2] if different):

   b. Will it be necessary for the employee to take work only **intermittently or to work on a less than full schedule** as a result of the condition (including for treatment described in Item 6 below)?

   If yes, give the probable duration:

   c. If the condition is a **chronic condition** (condition #4) or **pregnancy**, state whether the patient is presently incapacitated[2] and the **likely duration and frequency of episodes of incapacity**[2]:

[1] Here and elsewhere on this form, the information sought relates **only** to the condition for which the employee is taking FMLA leave.

[2] "Incapacity," for purposes of FMLA, is defined to mean inability to work, attend school or perform other regular daily activities due to the serious health condition, treatment therefor, or recovery therefrom.

Page 1 of 4

Form WH-380
Revised December 1999

6. a. If additional **treatments** will be required for the condition, provide an estimate of the probable number of such treatments.

   If the patient will be absent from work or other daily activities because of **treatment** on an **intermittent** or **part-time** basis, also provide an estimate of the probable number of and interval between such treatments, actual or estimated dates of treatment if known, and period required for recovery if any:

   b. If any of these treatments will be provided by **another provider of health services** (e.g., physical therapist), please state the nature of the treatments:

   c. **If a regimen of continuing treatment** by the patient is required under your supervision, provide a general description of such regimen (e.g., prescription drugs, physical therapy requiring special equipment):

7. a. If medical leave is required for the employee's **absence from work** because of the **employee's own condition** (including absences due to pregnancy or a chronic condition), is the employee **unable to perform work** of any kind?

   b. If able to perform some work, is the employee **unable to perform any one or more of the essential functions of the employee's job** (the employee or the employer should supply you with information about the essential job functions)? If yes, please list the essential functions the employee is unable to perform:

   c. If neither a. nor b. applies, is it necessary for the employee to be **absent from work for treatment?**

Page 2 of 4

Exhibit 5-6a Department of Labor form for certification of health care provider *(continued)*

---

8. a. If leave is required to **care for a family member** of the employee with a serious health condition, **does the patient require assistance** for basic medical or personal needs or safety, or for transportation?

b. If no, would the employee's presence to provide **psychological comfort** be beneficial to the patient or assist in the patient's recovery?

c. If the patient will need care only **intermittently** or on a part-time basis, please indicate the probable **duration** of this need:

_____   _____
Signature of Health Care Provider   Type of Practice

_____   _____
Address   Telephone Number

_____
                                                                                                 Date

To be completed by the employee needing family leave to care for a family member:

State the care you will provide and an estimate of the period during which care will be provided, including a schedule if leave is to be taken intermittently or if it will be necessary for you to work less than a full schedule:

_____   _____
Employee Signature   Date

Page 3 of 4

A **"Serious Health Condition"** means an illness, injury impairment, or physical or mental condition that involves one of the following:

1. Hospital Care

   Inpatient care (*i.e.*, an overnight stay) in a hospital, hospice, or residential medical care facility, including any period of incapacity[2] or subsequent treatment in connection with or consequent to such inpatient care.

2. Absence Plus Treatment

   (a) A period of incapacity[2] of **more than three consecutive calendar days** (including any subsequent treatment or period of incapacity[2] relating to the same condition), that also involves:

   (1) **Treatment[3] two or more times** by a health care provider, by a nurse or physician's assistant under direct supervision of a health care provider, or by a provider of health care services (*e.g.*, physical therapist) under orders of, or on referral by, a health care provider; or

   (2) **Treatment** by a health care provider on **at least one occasion** which results in a **regimen of continuing treatment[4]** under the supervision of the health care provider.

3. Pregnancy

   Any period of incapacity due to **pregnancy**, or for **prenatal care.**

4. Chronic Conditions Requiring Treatments

   A **chronic** condition which:

   (1) Requires **periodic visits** for treatment by a health care provider, or by a nurse or physician's assistant under direct supervision of a health care provider;

   (2) Continues over an **extended period of time** (including recurring episodes of a single underlying condition); and

   (3) May cause **episodic** rather than a continuing period of incapacity[2] (*e.g.*, asthma, diabetes, epilepsy, etc.).

5. Permanent/Long-term Conditions Requiring Supervision

   A period of **Incapacity[2]** which is **permanent or long-term** due to a condition for which treatment may not be effective. The employee or family member must be **under the continuing supervision of, but need not be receiving active treatment by, a health care provider.** Examples include Alzheimer's, a severe stroke, or the terminal stages of a disease.

6. Multiple Treatments (Non-Chronic Conditions)

   Any period of absence to receive **multiple treatments** (including any period of recovery therefrom) by a health care provider or by a provider of health care services under orders of, or on referral by, a health care provider, either for **restorative surgery** after an accident or other injury, **or** for a condition that **would likely result in a period of Incapacity[2] of more than three consecutive calendar days in the absence of medical intervention or treatment**, such as cancer (chemotherapy, radiation, etc.), severe arthritis (physical therapy), and kidney disease (dialysis).

This optional form may be used by employees to satisfy a mandatory requirement to furnish a medical certification (when requested) from a health care provider, including second or third opinions and recertification (29 CFR 825.306).

Note: Persons are not required to respond to this collection of information unless it displays a currently valid OMB control number.

[3] Treatment includes examinations to determine if a serious health condition exists and evaluations of the condition. Treatment does not include routine physical examinations, eye examinations, or dental examinations.

[4] A regimen of continuing treatment includes, for example, a course of prescription medication (*e.g.*, an antibiotic) or therapy requiring special equipment to resolve or alleviate the health condition. A regimen of treatment does not include the taking of over-the-counter medications such as aspirin, antihistamines, or salves; or bed-rest, drinking fluids, exercise, and other similar activities that can be initiated without a visit to a health care provider.

Public Burden Statement

We estimate that it will take an average of 20 minutes to complete this collection of information, including the time for reviewing instructions, searching existing data sources, gathering and maintaining the data needed, and completing and reviewing the collection of information. If you have any comments regarding this burden estimate or any other aspect of this collection of information, including suggestions for reducing this burden, send them to the Administrator, Wage and Hour Division, Department of Labor, Room S-3502, 200 Constitution Avenue, N.W., Washington, D.C. 20210.

DO NOT SEND THE COMPLETED FORM TO THIS OFFICE; IT GOES TO THE EMPLOYEE.

*U.S. GPO: 2000-461-954/25505

Page 4 of 4

- Employers must provide the notices described below.
- Employers must continue to provide health benefits that the employee would normally be entitled to during the leave.
- Unless the employee is a "key employee"—one who is paid on a salary basis and is among the highest-paid 10 percent of employees within seventy-five miles of the work site—the employer must return the employee either to his or her previous position or to "an equivalent position" that has equivalent pay, benefits, and other terms of employment. Key employees may be denied a position if "denial is necessary to prevent substantial and grievous economic injury to the operations of the employer" (29 U.S.C. § 2614b) (see Exhibit 5–6b).

Designation of FMLA leave

Employees must give thirty days' prior notice when leave is foreseeable. When leave is not foreseeable thirty days in advance, employees must generally notify the employer as soon as practicable, which means either the same day or the next business day after the need for FMLA leave has become apparent. They must also explain the reasons that thirty days' advance notice was not practicable. Employees do not have to say they want FMLA leave. They must merely provide sufficient information for the employer to reasonably determine whether the FMLA may apply to the leave request.

Exhibit 5-6b   Sample FMLA notices for key employees

Notification of "key employee" status

This will serve as notice that you, _____, are considered a "key employee" of the Township. As one of the most highly compensated employees of the Township, it is anticipated that it may cause substantial and grievous economic injury to restore you to your prior position or an equivalent one at the conclusion of your FMLA leave period. If, during the period of your FMLA leave, it becomes apparent that restoration would cause the Township substantial and grievous economic injury, we will notify you at that point and provide you with an opportunity to return to work immediately. If you choose to remain on leave, you may request reinstatement at the conclusion of your leave period, and the Township will restore you to your prior position or an equivalent one if no substantial and grievous economic injury would result. In the event that the Township cannot restore you to employment, you will have incurred no liability for the cost of your health care premiums during the period of leave.

Notification of anticipated substantial and grievous economic injury

This will serve as official notice that the Township faces substantial and grievous economic injury if it were to reinstate you at the end of your Family and Medical Leave. Consequently, unless you return to work immediately, it may be necessary to deny you restoration to employment at the conclusion of your leave. If you elect to remain on leave, the Township will nevertheless consider if it is possible to reinstate you, at the conclusion of your leave period. However, if it is determined that to do so would cause substantial and grievous economic injury at that time, restoration to employment will be denied. If you choose to remain on leave and the Township is unable to reinstate you at the conclusion of your leave, you will not be obligated for the cost of the health care coverage which the Township will have maintained on your behalf.

Under federal DOL regulations, it is the employer's duty to designate the leave as FMLA qualifying. In general, the employer may do so only after it has notified the employee that the absence will be FMLA leave, and such notification should be given within five business days after the employer discovers that the leave qualifies as FMLA leave. DOL regulations put the burden on the employer to designate leave as FMLA qualifying and penalize the employer who fails to do so by requiring the employer to grant up to an additional twelve weeks of leave (29 C.F.R. § 825.700[a]). For example, under DOL regulations, if an employee goes out on leave for surgery and receives twelve weeks of leave but the employer does not tell the employee that the leave is FMLA leave until the thirteenth week, the employer may be viewed as interfering, restraining, or denying the employee's protected rights, which can give rise to employer liability. Therefore, to avoid lawsuits, discord, and confusion, it is strongly recommended that employers promptly designate in writing whether an employee's leave qualifies as FMLA leave.

Notices required

The following items identify the various notices that employers must post with regard to the FLMA.

- The employer must post in the workplace an FMLA notice approved by the DOL (see Exhibit 5–6c).

- The employer must also have an FMLA policy in the employee handbook if it has a handbook. If the employer does not have a handbook, it must give the employee a document summarizing the FMLA. Electronic distribution of all required notices is permissible, provided that the distribution is accessible to all employees and applicants. The policy should stipulate any medical certification requirement that the employer intends to enforce.

- When an employee requests leave or an employer designates leave as FMLA leave, the employer must give the employee written notice of the employee's rights and obligations (see Exhibit 5–6d on pages 152–153).

- The employer must notify the employee that the leave has been designated as FMLA leave. The notice must be in writing and must generally occur within five business days after the employer learns of the need for leave. If the employer requires paid leave to be substituted for unpaid FMLA leave, or a fitness-for-duty certification to be presented before the employee can be restored to employment, the employer must inform the employee at the time of designating the FMLA leave. The employer must also notify the employee of the amount of leave counted against the employee's FMLA entitlement. If such notice is oral, it must be confirmed in writing no later than the following payday.

- The employer must notify the employee verbally whenever medical certification is required. The employer must also either (1) notify the employee in writing every time medical certification is required or (2) provide notice of the medical certification requirements in both the employee handbook and the employer response notice (see Exhibit 5–6e on page 153).

Exhibit 5-6c   Department of Labor notification of rights under FMLA

EMPLOYEE RIGHTS AND RESPONSIBILITIES
UNDER THE FAMILY AND MEDICAL LEAVE ACT

Basic Leave Entitlement

FMLA requires covered employers to provide up to 12 weeks of unpaid, job-protected leave to eligible employees for the following reasons:

- For incapacity due to pregnancy, prenatal medical care or child birth;
- To care for the employee's child after birth, or placement for adoption or foster care;
- To care for the employee's spouse, son or daughter, or parent, who has a serious health condition; or
- For a serious health condition that makes the employee unable to perform the employee's job.

Military Family Leave Entitlements

Eligible employees with a spouse, son, daughter, or parent on active duty or call to active duty status in the National Guard or Reserves in support of a contingency operation may use their 12-week leave entitlement to address certain qualifying exigencies. Qualifying exigencies may include attending certain military events, arranging for alternative childcare, addressing certain financial and legal arrangements, attending certain counseling sessions, and attending post-deployment reintegration briefings.

FMLA also includes a special leave entitlement that permits eligible employees to take up to 26 weeks of leave to care for a covered servicemember during a single 12-month period. A covered servicemember is a current member of the Armed Forces, including a member of the National Guard or Reserves, who has a serious injury or illness incurred in the line of duty on active duty that may render the servicemember medically unfit to perform his or her duties for which the servicemember is undergoing medical treatment, recuperation, or therapy; or is in outpatient status; or is on the temporary disability retired list.

Benefits and Protections

During FMLA leave, the employer must maintain the employee's health coverage under any "group health plan" on the same terms as if the employee had continued to work. Upon return from FMLA leave, most employees must be restored to their original or equivalent positions with equivalent pay, benefits, and other employment terms.

Use of FMLA leave cannot result in the loss of any employment benefit that accrued prior to the start of an employee's leave.

Eligibility Requirements

Employees are eligible if they have worked for a covered employer for at least one year, for 1,250 hours over the previous 12 months, and if at least 50 employees are employed by the employer within 75 miles.

Definition of Serious Health Condition

A serious health condition is an illness, injury, impairment, or physical or mental condition that involves either an overnight stay in a medical care facility, or continuing treatment by a health care provider for a condition that either prevents the employee from performing the functions of the employee's job, or prevents the qualified family member from participating in school or other daily activities.

Subject to certain conditions, the continuing treatment requirement may be met by a period of incapacity of more than 3 consecutive calendar days combined with at least two visits to a health care provider or one visit and a regimen of continuing treatment, or incapacity due to pregnancy, or incapacity due to a chronic condition. Other conditions may meet the definition of continuing treatment.

Use of Leave

An employee does not need to use this leave entitlement in one block. Leave can be taken intermittently or on a reduced leave schedule when medically necessary. Employees must make reasonable efforts to schedule leave for planned medical treatment so as not to unduly disrupt the employer's operations. Leave due to qualifying exigencies may also be taken on an intermittent basis.

Substitution of Paid Leave for Unpaid Leave

Employees may choose or employers may require use of accrued paid leave while taking FMLA leave. In order to use paid leave for FMLA leave, employees must comply with the employer's normal paid leave policies.

Employee Responsibilities

Employees must provide 30 days advance notice of the need to take FMLA leave when the need is foreseeable. When 30 days notice is not possible, the employee must provide notice as soon as practicable and generally must comply with an employer's normal call-in procedures.

Employees must provide sufficient information for the employer to determine if the leave may qualify for FMLA protection and the anticipated timing and duration of the leave. Sufficient information may include that the employee is unable to perform job functions, the family member is unable to perform daily activities, the need for hospitalization or continuing treatment by a health care provider, or circumstances supporting the need for military family leave. Employees also must inform the employer if the requested leave is for a reason for which FMLA leave was previously taken or certified. Employees also may be required to provide a certification and periodic recertification supporting the need for leave.

Employer Responsibilities

Covered employers must inform employees requesting leave whether they are eligible under FMLA. If they are, the notice must specify any additional information required as well as the employees' rights and responsibilities. If they are not eligible, the employer must provide a reason for the ineligibility.

Covered employers must inform employees if leave will be designated as FMLA-protected and the amount of leave counted against the employee's leave entitlement. If the employer determines that the leave is not FMLA-protected, the employer must notify the employee.

Unlawful Acts by Employers

FMLA makes it unlawful for any employer to:

- Interfere with, restrain, or deny the exercise of any right provided under FMLA;
- Discharge or discriminate against any person for opposing any practice made unlawful by FMLA or for involvement in any proceeding under or relating to FMLA.

Enforcement

An employee may file a complaint with the U.S. Department of Labor or may bring a private lawsuit against an employer.

FMLA does not affect any Federal or State law prohibiting discrimination, or supersede any State or local law or collective bargaining agreement which provides greater family or medical leave rights.

FMLA section 109 (29 U.S.C. § 2619) requires FMLA covered employers to post the text of this notice. Regulations 29 C.F.R. § 825.300(a) may require additional disclosures.

For additional information:
1-866-4US-WAGE (1-866-487-9243) TTY: 1-877-889-5627
WWW.WAGEHOUR.DOL.GOV

U.S. Wage and Hour Division

U.S. Department of Labor | Employment Standards Administration | Wage and Hour Division   WHD Publication 1420 Revised January 2009

Exhibit 5-6d   Sample notice to be given at time of leave request

---

Employee rights, obligations, and responsibilities when exercising family and medical leave

As an employee requesting Family and Medical Leave, you should already have been provided with a summary of your rights. This notice is to serve as a reminder of your corresponding obligations and what we at the Township expect of you when you exercise Family and Medical Leave. Specifically, the Township expects and requires that you comply with the following requirements:

1. The leave you have requested will be counted against your annual leave entitlement. This entitlement allows you to exercise up to twelve (12) weeks of qualifying leave in a 12-month period. This 12-month period is calculated on a rolling basis by counting backwards from the date of your leave. For Military Caregiver leave, you are entitled to up to 26 work weeks of unpaid leave during a 12-month period beginning on the first day that you take leave to care for a covered service member. When requesting leave, you must give 30 days advance notice for foreseeable leave events; otherwise, leave will be denied until the expiration of the applicable notice period. If thirty days' advance notice is not practicable, you must give notice as soon as practicable and explain why 30 days' advance notice was not practicable.

2. The Township requires that when you exercise FMLA leave because of a personal illness or the illness of a family member, the health care provider must provide us with medical certification of the need for leave, and additional recertifications of the need for leave every thirty (30) days or at the expiration of the period of incapacity as indicated in the prior certification form. The Township will provide medical certification forms for you to submit to the health care provider. Failure to obtain requested medical certification within fifteen (15) days may result in the denial of FMLA leave.

3. An employee may substitute accrued paid leave for unpaid Family and Medical Leave. Unless written authorization is granted from the Township, accrued sick leave may be used only for purposes specified in the sick leave policy. (In accordance with our policy, employees must substitute accrued paid vacation and personal days before unpaid leave is permitted.) Employees must satisfy all procedural requirements of the applicable paid leave policy.

4. During any period of Family and Medical Leave, the Township will continue to make premium payments to maintain an employee's health care coverage. However, this does not eliminate the requirement of employee co-payments for those employees who normally have co-payments toward their insurance coverage. As part of your leave information package, you will be provided with information on how to make your co-payments while on leave. If any co-payment is more than thirty (30) days past due, the Township will terminate your health care coverage for the duration of the leave period after 15 days' notice. Health care coverage will be restored upon return to work.

5. In accordance with our policy, all employees who are absent from work on a leave of absence for personal illness or injury must present a medical certification indicating that he or she is fit for duty and is able to return to employment. No one will be reinstated to work until his or her fitness-for-duty certification has been received.

6. Included in your FMLA information package will be notification if you are considered a "key employee." If you have received "key employee" notification, it means that under appropriate circumstances, you may be denied restoration to employment. If it is determined that restoring a key employee from a leave period would cause substantial and

Exhibit 5-6d Sample notice to be given at time of leave request *(continued)*

---

grievous economic injury, the Township will be forced to deny that employee restoration to employment. If the Township becomes concerned that a key employee may have to be denied restoration, it will provide that employee with written notice and an opportunity to return to work. Once notified, that employee may return to work or may remain on leave. An employee who remains on leave will be entitled to a continuation of health care benefits and will be considered for restoration of employment at the conclusion of his or her leave period if to do so will not cause substantial and grievous economic injury at that time.

7. At the conclusion of a Family and Medical Leave period, an employee will be returned to his or her prior job whenever possible. If that is impossible, the employee will be placed in an equivalent position with equal benefits, pay, and other terms and conditions of employment. The Township is not obligated to reinstate any employee whose job position is eliminated while on leave.

8. The Township will be entitled to recoup the costs of providing health care coverage for an employee during the leave period if that employee fails to return to work at the conclusion of his or her Family and Medical Leave period. This obligation does not apply in certain situations where the Township grants an additional leave of absence and the employee subsequently returns to work, or where the employee is unable to return to work for reasons beyond his or her control.

9. Falsification of any leave request, medical certification, or other form or document will be punishable by termination.

10. The Township has always had an open door policy. If you should ever have questions or concerns about your rights or obligations with regard to Family and Medical Leave, management is always willing to assist you.

Exhibit 5-6e Sample notices of requirement of medical certification

---

Notice of requirement of medical certification for personal illness

The Township hereby notifies you that since you have requested leave for the care and treatment of a personal medical condition, the Township will require the attached medical certification form to be filled out by your health care provider prior to the granting of any leave, unless circumstances make this impracticable. You have fifteen (15) days to provide this certification. In addition, the Township will require that your physician submit continuing medical certifications of the need for leave every thirty (30) days or at the expiration of the period of incapacity as indicated on the prior medical certification form. Failure to submit this certification within fifteen (15) days may result in the denial of FMLA leave. In accordance with our uniform policy, no employee exercising leave for a medical condition may return to work without certification from his or her health care provider that the employee is fit to return to work.

Notice of requirement of medical certification for family member

The Township hereby notifies you that since you have requested leave to care for the medical condition of a qualifying family member, you must submit the attached medical certification form to be completed by the treating physician. Additional medical certification of the continuing need for leave will be required every thirty (30) days or at the expiration of the period of incapacity as indicated on the prior medical certification form. Leave will not be granted until the appropriate medical certification form is submitted, unless it is impracticable to do so, and the failure to provide subsequent certifications within fifteen (15) days may result in the denial of FMLA leave.

Workers' compensation

Guiding principles

■ Every workers' compensation claim should be routinely investigated.

■ Injured workers should be encouraged to come back to work as soon as they have recovered.

■ Safety training programs prevent injuries.

Challenges

■ Minimizing workplace-related accidents

■ Minimizing fraudulent compensation claims

Workers' compensation is a state program created by statute. Employers should check their particular state laws because workers' compensation laws vary from state to state. Workers' compensation acts are designed to compensate workers for injuries or death arising out of employment. It is important that all employers educate their employees about their workers' compensation policies and procedures before an employee is injured. When an employee is injured, an employer should (1) evaluate the injury, (2) determine if the injury arose in the course of employment, and (3) investigate the injury.

Antifraud measures and investigation of workers' compensation claims

Approximately 20 percent of all filed workers' compensation claims are fraudulent. To discourage fraudulent claims, employers should routinely investigate all workers' compensation claims filed. An employer should begin by taking a written statement from the injured worker. Some states have particular requirements regarding statements, so employers should check state laws first. An employer may also want to interview witnesses to the accident and obtain written statements from them.

The employer should also make use of return-to-work programs, which are designed to motivate employees to return to work promptly, as soon as their injuries are healed. Without this type of program, employees often stay out of work longer than is necessary while still collecting workers' compensation. Note that return-to-work accommodations (e.g., light duty) must be temporary in nature and not "guaranteed" positions. In addition, to minimize liability under the ADA, these positions should be limited to workers' compensation cases and not include all classes of off-duty injuries.

Cost control

An employer can take other steps to lower workers' compensation costs. First, it is important that employers have safety training programs to teach employees how to handle themselves in dangerous situations. Employees who are trained to use equipment safely will be less likely to injure themselves.

Second, an employer can create voluntary wellness programs for employees. These programs should be designed to educate employees about healthy lifestyles and should offer screenings for the early detection of high blood pressure, lung disease, and other ailments. Wellness programs generally encourage employees to exercise, maintain a proper diet, and not smoke. If employees are healthy, their chances of being injured are greatly reduced. Some employer health maintenance organizations offer wellness incentives such as reimbursement for health club expenses. Under the Genetic Information Nondiscrimination Act, enacted May 21, 2008, employers may not request genetic information regarding an employee or the employee's family except in very limited circumstances, and may not discriminate against employees on the basis of their genetic information. While voluntary wellness programs that seek family medical history are permitted, the information obtained must be kept completely confidential.

Access to physicians

In some states an employer has a statutory right to have the injured worker examined by the employer's physician, or may permit the injured employee to choose the examining physician. A few states require that an impartial physician be appointed for the evaluation. Employers should check their state's workers' compensation statute to determine who has the right to choose the physician to examine the injured employee. More often than not, the initial evaluation is the most critical element of a claim for benefits.

Other disability statutes

Workers' compensation may not be the only aspect to be investigated when an employee is injured. Some states have created specific funds that offer broad protection for uniformed public sector employees with temporary disabilities. In Pennsylvania, for example, the Heart and Lung Act (53 Pa. Stat. Ann. § 637 [1974]) specifically applies to police officers and firefighters injured during the performance of their job duties and provides full benefits to injured individuals who are temporarily disabled as a result of work-related injury. An employer should check its particular state's law to determine whether a statute other than workers' compensation applies.

Reforming trends

Dramatic legislative reforms instituted by many states in the early to mid-1990s to reduce workers' compensation costs shifted the balance from an extremely employee-oriented slant to one that attempts to address long-neglected employer concerns. The beginning of the new millennium brought even more economic hardship to struggling employers and workers' compensation programs. In response, states enacted a flurry of legislation. Such legislation includes the following:

- Investments in technology and software to enhance efficiency and streamline services by digitizing case files and automatically cross-checking employees on disability with employees also reported working
- Creation of special antifraud investigation units combined with tougher penalties for workers' compensation fraud
- Attempts to reduce the massive litigation backlog, including creation of many informal resolution methods outside the traditional hearing process and reduction of attorneys' fees
- Revision of medical fee schedules in an attempt to control costs and improve services.[28]

Workplace violence

Guiding principles

- Local government employers should not permit even the slightest threat or indication of violence in the workplace to go unchecked.
- Employers should avoid negligent hiring by conducting an appropriate background check.
- Employers need to let applicants know that a background check will be conducted.
- When asked to provide references about a past or current violent employee, employers should avoid negligent referral by giving only positive information about the applicant; comments should be limited to factual information, such as dates of employment.
- Employers should consult with their employment lawyers as to whether the state has passed a job references immunity law.

Challenge

- Balancing the rights of employees to a safe workplace and the rights of the public to have an efficient and effective government against the rights of other employees to have their privacy protected, to be free from defamation, and, if applicable, to receive protection under the ADA

Workplace violence is a problem that any employer may face. Some states have adopted legislation that protects state employees from workplace violence. For example, in 1996, the governor of New Jersey signed an executive order stating that the state of New Jersey will not tolerate threats of violence by or against its employees.[29] Government employers should contact legal counsel to determine whether their states have enacted workplace violence laws. In addition, although local governmental employers are exempt from the federal Occupational Safety and Health Act, they may be subject to state safety and health laws that deal with violence in the workplace.

Prevention of workplace violence

To prevent workplace violence, employers should have a written workplace violence prevention plan. This plan should include a policy that forbids workplace violence, threats, and related actions. The Occupational Safety and Health Administration (OSHA) has recently reissued voluntary guidelines for health care and social service workers that detail how an employer can implement a workplace violence prevention program. There are four elements to such a program: management commitment and employee involvement, work site analysis, hazard prevention and control, and safety and health training.[30]

Management commitment and employee involvement   Management commitment refers to management's support for and aid in implementing a workplace violence prevention program. Employee involvement means that employees have the opportunity to express their own commitment to the prevention of workplace violence by providing suggestions and their own evaluations of the program.

Work site analysis   An examination of the workplace for any potential workplace hazards may include a review of security procedures and an analysis of any prior incidents of violence.

Hazard prevention and control Once potential hazards are discovered through the work site analysis, the next stage is to develop measures through different work practices to prevent or control these hazards.

Safety and health training Through proper training, employees can learn how to avoid a violent situation and how to protect themselves when faced with one.

Discipline of violent employees

Once an employer has identified a violent or potentially violent employee, it must carefully balance the rights of the identified employee against the rights of other employees. Before terminating an employee for violent tendencies, the employer should consider referring the employee to psychological counseling. If the employer decides to terminate an employee, it should make sure that police or other security personnel are available to escort the employee off the premises and to monitor the workplace.

If an employer terminates an employee for being violent, it must be aware of potential ADA and defamation claims. Employees may fall under the ADA if they suffer from a mental impairment that substantially limits them in a major life activity. Although courts generally reject such claims when an employee has exhibited violent behavior, defense of even an unwarranted suit is expensive.

An employee may also have a defamation claim if an employer tells other persons about the employee's violent acts. For example, when an employer gives a negative reference regarding an employee who has been fired for a violent act, that employee may have a cause of action for defamation against the employer. To avoid such a claim, an employer should give only the relevant employment history of the employee, such as his or her dates of employment. On the other hand, some public entities have been sued by subsequent employers of terminated employees because when they called for references, they were given only positive information and were not warned, for example, about the employee's history of violence. This then is another situation in which it would be wise to get input from an employment lawyer.

To deal with the legal ambiguity, at least thirty-four states have passed job reference immunity laws, which protect employers who provide information about current or previous employees to a new employer. Usually these laws stipulate that the reference must be provided at the request of the employee or the prospective employer, and that the information has to be job related and truthful.[31] However, even in states that have job reference immunity laws, a public employer may still be subject to a defamation lawsuit when a former employee alleges that the information provided was not "truthful." Therefore, even where there are immunity statutes, public employers must be careful concerning the type and quantity of information they disclose.

Victims of workplace violence

In addition to suits by violent former employees, employers are subject to suits by employees who are victims of workplace violence. Government employers have a duty to maintain a safe work environment for their employees. They may be liable to an employee or a third party for the violent acts of their employees under state OSHA statutes, as landowners, and under common-law negligence actions.

Tips for avoiding workplace violence

☐ Assess the potential for workplace violence in your organization.

☐ Implement a workplace violence prevention program.

☐ Act with prudence, balancing your duty to protect your employees from harm with your duty not to defame an employee.

An employer may be vicariously liable for actions of its employees if the actions occurred on the job. An employer also has a duty to warn its employees of any foreseeable risks of harm that may be caused by another employee. For example, if an employer is aware that an employee poses a particular risk, it may be required to alert its employees of the potential danger. But before an employer discloses such information, it must consider that it may be subject to a defamation claim or an ADA claim by that employee if it discloses false, medical, or private information.

A victim of workplace violence may also have a cause of action against an employer for the negligent hiring or retention of the violent employee. An employer may be liable in this regard if it knew or had reason to know of dangerous characteristics of an employee. Negligent hiring is found when the employer knew or should have known of the employee's unfitness before the employee was actually hired. The focus of negligent hiring is on whether the employer used reasonable care during the recruitment process. To avoid potential liability, employers should check all references given to them by job applicants. Further, employers whose employees regularly deal with customers may consider conducting a criminal background investigation, although criminal background checks may require notice to the employee who is the subject of the investigation, and the employer may be prohibited from requesting certain information, such as arrest records or convictions that are not related to an employee's job.

Negligent retention occurs when an employer becomes aware of problems with an employee that indicate the employee's unfitness but fails to take any action. If an employer becomes aware of any unusual conduct of an employee that suggests that the employee is potentially dangerous, it should investigate and evaluate the situation and then choose an appropriate course of action. For more on avoiding violence in the workplace and handling potentially violent employees, see Chapters 7 and 8.

Healthy workplace

Guiding principle

■ Many local governments are responsible under state law for protecting employees against hazardous conditions and materials in the workplace.

Challenge

■ Protecting employees' right to privacy against the right of other employees to a healthy workplace and the right of the public to safe government services

Smoking

Smoking in the workplace is generally regulated by state law. Most states require that employers have at least a written policy on smoking. Some states require

fyi

Sample "no smoking" policy

The state of [_____] does not permit smoking in places of public accommodation except in designated areas. In accordance with this law, it is the policy of this department that smoking is permitted only in designated areas. Employees who violate his policy will be subject to disciplinary procedures, which may include dismissal.

employers to implement a policy designating smoking and nonsmoking areas in the workplace. Government workplaces are often covered by statutes that ban smoking in public buildings (except in designated areas), and some states, such as New York, have nearly banned smoking in the workplace altogether. On the flip side, many states have enacted "smokers' rights" laws, which prevent employers from discriminating against employees who smoke while off-duty or outside the workplace.

Employers who implement "no smoking" policies often include in their policies an allowance for smoking breaks. This break time is usually taken from an employee's lunch period. For example, an employer who generally gives employees forty-five minutes for lunch may instead give two ten-minute smoking breaks and reduce the lunch period to twenty-five minutes. However, before implementing such a policy, employers must check the break requirement for their state to make sure that the lunch break meets state requirements. In New York, for example, employers must give employees a thirty-minute lunch break (N.Y. Lab. L. § 162[2]).

Several states have statutes stipulating that government employers may be liable for injuries suffered by their employees from fumes and smoke. In Pennsylvania, for example, the Heart and Lung Act (53 Pa. Stat. Ann § 637[a]) provides that municipal employees engaged as police officers, corrections officers, or firefighters will receive their full salary for temporary disabilities, including diseases of the heart and respiratory failure, caused by such things as fumes and smoke. Therefore, employers who are considering implementing a "no smoking" policy should consider their states' particular laws. An employer whose workforce is unionized must first negotiate with union representatives before implementing a "no smoking" policy.

Infectious diseases

Policies and procedures to prevent and control infections are key elements in providing a healthy and safe work environment. Because emergency and public safety workers are at risk of exposure to bloodborne pathogens such as HIV and hepatitis B, such procedures may also be required for government employers under state safety and health laws.

Bloodborne pathogens   The risk of infection with bloodborne pathogens depends on the employee's likelihood of exposure to blood and other possibly infectious materials. The Centers for Disease Control and Prevention (CDC) has recommended hepatitis B vaccinations for occupational groups who are frequently exposed to blood, such as emergency medical technicians, police officers, and firefighters.

The CDC has also updated its guidelines for protection of emergency and public safety workers who may be exposed to HIV, hepatitis B, and hepatitis C.[32] The updated guidelines still emphasize exposure prevention as the primary means of reducing bloodborne pathogen infections, but they also require that employers have exposure control plans in place for prompt reporting and treatment when exposure occurs. The guidelines discuss when pre-exposure hepatitis B vaccinations are required and the effectiveness of post-exposure treatment for hepatitis B and HIV, including HBIG (hepatitis B immune globulin), hepatitis B vaccine, and HIV PEP (post-exposure prophylaxis), all of which are most effective when administered as soon after the exposure as possible.

Tuberculosis   The spread of tuberculosis increased in the 1990s. As a result, the CDC published a model for tuberculosis control programs in 1994, which generally applies to health care facilities,[33] and updated that model in 2003.[34] OSHA has withdrawn its proposed guidelines, but occupations in which the spread of tuberculosis is high have taken their own precautions. For example, almost all states require teachers and other school officials to be tested for tuberculosis upon employment. To the extent that they have not already done so, local governments should implement their own tuberculosis control program to combat the spread of this deadly disease.

Constitutional rights

Guiding principle

■ Efficiency, economy, discipline, harmony, and other administrative values do not trump employees' constitutional rights.

Challenge

■ Balancing the constitutional rights of employees against the right of the public to an efficient and effective government service and the responsibility of the government employer to provide such a service

Public employees have broad constitutional rights in addition to the job protections they may enjoy under civil service laws and regulations. These rights are not abrogated by the need to serve the public with efficiency, economy, discipline, and harmony. Rather, the judiciary assesses these rights by balancing the interests of the employer, the employees, and the public. Understanding the logical structure of public employees' constitutional rights will help managers and supervisors avoid violating them.

Ambiguous law, high stakes

Upon hearing of an assassination attempt on President Ronald Reagan, a deputized employee in a constable's office said, "Shoot, if they go for him again, I hope they get him."[35] A public school security guard failed to note on his application that he had been convicted of a felony.[36] At a dinner break, a nurse told a trainee about problems in a public hospital's cross-training program and, allegedly, in its obstetrics department.[37] A public school teacher wrote a letter to a local newspaper criticizing the school board, opposing greater funding for the schools, and apparently mistakenly suggesting that money earmarked for education previously had been diverted to sports.[38] All four employees were fired.

Caution

■ "Insubordination" may turn out to be constitutionally protected speech. Even comments made only to a supervisor or manager may be protected if they deal with matters of public concern.

■ Never compel or pressure an employee to join any organization, no matter how civic-minded it may be.

■ Be very careful when taking any personnel action based on partisanship. Because the constitutional law has changed drastically since the mid-1970s, past practices may no longer be constitutional.

■ Where an employee has a reasonable expectation of privacy, a search of his or her work space, files, desk, and so forth must be reasonable in both inception and scope. No fishing expeditions; the objects of the search should be identified beforehand.

■ Avoid implicitly classifying employees, whether on the basis of age, sex, ethnicity, creed, or race, in ways that reinforce social stereotypes.

In one way or another, each dismissal was constitutionally defective. Because public employees have a broad array of constitutional rights,[39] constitutional law is a significant concern of public human resource management. This differentiates the public sector substantially from the private sector, where the employer's sole *constitutional* responsibility is compliance with the Thirteenth Amendment's proscription of slavery and involuntary servitude. The concept of employment at the will of the employer, which still prevails in much of the private sector, does not fully apply to local governments because of constitutional constraints as well as civil service protection, union rules, and state laws.

Contemporary constitutional law poses significant problems for public managers. Caution is required in adopting private sector models and techniques, so often popular with reformers and the media and, apparently, in the public culture.[40] Constitutional law is "what the courts say it is," which is sometimes opaque or counterintuitive.[41] Key standards may be vague, or subjective, or may require the complicated balancing of a number of factors. Yet the stakes are high. Violating a public employee's constitutional rights can trigger substantial liability damages, both compensatory and punitive.

Public managers need not become constitutional lawyers to do their jobs, but they should understand the logical structure of employees' constitutional rights. Even though Supreme Court justices, circuit courts, and lawyers may disagree over the appropriate outcome of specific cases, knowledge of these structures will prevent many violations and much liability. It will also increase productive thinking about how to integrate employees' constitutional rights with core human resource management values. It is toward this end that this section provides a general guide to the current constitutional law of public personnel management.

The "public service model": A framework for analyzing public employees' constitutional rights

The current model for analyzing public employees' constitutional rights crystallized in the mid-1980s. Called the "public service model," it seeks to promote the

Caution

■ Common sense and constitutional law don't always mix. When in doubt, consult an attorney who is familiar with public employment law and practices.

■ Don't confuse administrative convenience and standard managerial values, such as efficiency and economy, with the public interest. The courts respect these concerns but typically subordinate them to individual rights.

public interest by balancing three sets of concerns: the interests of the government as employer, the interests of the employees in exercising their constitutional rights, and the public's concern with the way its affairs are run by administrative agencies.[42]

The model's fundamental premise is that "the government's interest in achieving its goals as effectively and efficiently as possible is elevated from a relatively subordinate interest when it acts as a sovereign [dealing with ordinary citizens] to a significant one when it acts as employer."[43] This enables governments to require their employees to sacrifice some constitutional rights as a condition of joining and remaining in the public service. However, to be constitutional, such conditions must on balance serve the public interest. The public interest generally includes open government, accountability, safety, customer service, honesty, and political responsiveness.

In applying this balancing model, the courts may side with either the government or the employee. For instance, the Supreme Court has supported restrictions on the partisan political activities of public employees[44] but has opposed governmental efforts to suppress employees' whistle-blowing.[45] In terms of the public service model, there is no inconsistency in these opinions even though they have disparate impacts on the scope of public employees' First Amendment rights. Context becomes all-important. Restrictions on political activity serve the public interest by reducing the likelihood that partisanship will interfere with office operations and service to the public. Protecting whistle-blowers, on the other hand, promotes the public's interest in learning of governmental mismanagement, waste, fraud, abuse of power, and specific dangers to community health or safety.

The public service model determines the general structure of public employees' First Amendment, Fourth Amendment, procedural and substantive due process, and equal protection rights. Each of these structures, in turn, requires additional balancing of one kind or another.

First Amendment rights

Government employees' First Amendment rights, as interpreted by the courts, are complex and constantly evolving.

Restrictions on partisan speech and activity   Restrictions on public employees' partisan speech, electioneering, or campaign management are generally constitutional.[46] However, care should be taken to avoid vagueness in drafting or applying such regulations. It is also important that they not be overly broad—that is, not prohibit more than is necessary to achieve the governmental objectives of efficiency, the appearance of partisan neutrality, and protection of employees from partisan coercion.

General speech on matters of public concern   Public employees' general speech on matters of public concern enjoys considerable constitutional protection. It is valued by the public service model precisely because it can inform the citizenry about government and public affairs. Remarks on matters of public concern made privately "will rarely, if ever, justify the discharge of a public employee"[47] because they have little potential to harm legitimate governmental objectives. If such remarks are made publicly, however, it is necessary to "arrive at a balance between the interests of the [employee], as a citizen, in commenting upon matters of public concern and the interests of the State, as an employer, in promoting the efficiency of the public services it performs through its employees."[48]

On the basis of such a balancing, the deputized employee's comments regarding the assassination attempt on President Reagan were constitutionally protected because (1) she had a strong interest in making them during a general discussion with a co-worker as a means of underscoring her opposition to Reagan's civil rights policies, and (2) the remarks posed no threat to the constable's mission as her position was purely clerical and involved no law enforcement activity.

Adverse action based on an employee's speech on matters of public concern is more likely to be constitutional when the remarks impair discipline or harmony in the workplace, interfere with close working relationships or normal operations, or cast doubt on the employee's ability to do his or her job. Situational factors, including the time, place, manner, and context of the remarks, must also be taken into account in determining their likely impact. For instance, an offhand statement to a co-worker by a low-level employee may be treated more favorably than a similar one made to a large public crowd by a high-level career executive.

Inaccuracy is potentially a basis for discipline only if the government can show that the employee knew the remarks were incorrect or acted with disregard for their truth or falsity.[49] Consequently, the public employer faces a very heavy—indeed, almost impossible—burden of persuasion when trying to discipline an employee such as the teacher whose newspaper letter allegedly contained damaging falsehoods. Finally, non-work-related expressive activity by public employees, such as publishing novels, cannot constitutionally be treated differently than similar activity by any member of the public unless the government can show a "nexus" to a significant governmental interest as an employer.[50]

The application of these rules and balances is sometimes complicated by dispute over what the employee actually said. In such cases, whoever is acting on behalf of the governmental employer must take "reasonable steps" to ascertain the content of the remarks. This requirement gives public employees some procedural protection against being disciplined for comments they may not have made. However, the current standard for what is reasonable is exceptionally vague: "only procedures outside the range of what a reasonable manager would use may be condemned as unreasonable."[51] To be on the safe side, public managers should at least interview the employee involved and any witnesses to the remarks at issue.

Because they are of no particular interest to the public, employees' publicly made remarks on matters of *private* concern do not enjoy constitutional protection when they impede legitimate governmental interests.[52] For example, a public comment about a co-worker's annoying habits is not of public concern and can be the basis for discipline if it harms the governmental employer's efficiency or public image. In some instances, it can be difficult to determine whether a remark is of private or public concern. Generally, matters of office politics and personalities are considered of private concern only, unless they can be construed as legitimate whistle-blowing.

Although the Supreme Court has not yet dealt with public employees' speech via voice or e-mail, use of these channels should not affect the constitutional analysis with respect to whether the *content* of the remarks is of public or private concern. However, they may present some thorny issues regarding whether their *context* is private or public. Either channel can be used to communicate with one, a few, or many individuals, any of whom may reveal the remarks to the employer. Direct monitoring of voice or e-mail by the public employer is potentially constrained by the Fourth Amendment (see the section on Fourth Amendment privacy).

Freedom of association   Under the public service balancing model, public employees are generally free to join organizations insofar as their membership does not create a conflict of interest with their jobs. Membership in unsavory or even subversive organizations is not per se grounds for dismissal because "those who join an organization but do not share its unlawful purposes and . . . activities, surely pose no threat, either as citizens or as public employees."[53] By contrast, membership can be off-limits to employees when it conflicts with their official responsibilities or appears to invite impropriety.[54] For example, managers are commonly banned from joining unions representing rank-and-file employees.

Public employees also have broad protections against being forced to join organizations. With limited exceptions, partisan patronage is now an unconstitutional basis for public personnel decisions to hire, fire, train, transfer, promote, discipline, or undertake similar actions. In a series of three cases beginning in 1976, the Supreme Court reasoned that, on balance, the contributions that patronage makes to the government's interests in loyalty, accountability, and party competition are outweighed by its infringement on public employees' freedom of association and belief.[55]

Nor can public employees be compelled to join labor unions. Nonmembers even have constitutional protections against the assessment of unreasonable "counterpart" or "fair share" fees by the unions representing the bargaining units in which they work. "[T]he constitutional requirements for the Union's collection of agency fees include an adequate explanation of the basis for the fee, a reasonably prompt opportunity to challenge the amount of the fee before an impartial decision maker, and an escrow for amounts reasonably in dispute while such challenges are pending."[56]

Religion   The Constitution's dual guarantees that government will neither establish religion nor abridge individuals' religious freedom present complex issues, but limited guidance, for public human resource management. The "establishment clause" is read to mean that government cannot require, encourage, or foster any religious behavior at all. The clause is not satisfied merely by nondenominationalism or nonsectarianism. Under the leading test, to survive a challenge based on the establishment clause, government regulations or practices must meet three criteria: (1) they must have a secular purpose, (2) their principal effect must neither advance nor inhibit religion, and (3) they cannot excessively entangle government in religion.[57] In public employment, these restrictions are bolstered by the specific constitutional provision that "no religious Test shall ever be required as a Qualification to any Office or public Trust under the United States" (Article VI, clause 3).[58] Clearly, the public employer cannot put pressure on employees to engage in religious activity, such as prayer breakfasts, or to discuss their religious beliefs.

The extent to which governments can constitutionally abridge the exercise of religious freedom in the workplace is less certain. When ordinary citizens are involved, religious expression is currently treated like expression generally. If a public space is open for any type of public speech or display, there is a strong presumption that religious speech and displays must be permitted as well. The fact that public property is used by private parties to express or encourage religion does not violate the establishment clause.[59]

However, transferring this general model to public employment presents problems. As noted above, public employees' workplace speech on matters of private concern is not constitutionally protected when it is detrimental to an agency's mission. Does this mean that an employee can be disciplined for private religious expression that causes disharmony? No doubt that proselytizing at work, like partisan speech, can be prohibited, but what about displaying religious symbols, headgear, or jewelry; putting "I Love Jesus"(or the pope or Louis Farrakhan) on a screen saver; or hanging the picture of a religious leader on one's cubicle wall? The Supreme Court has given little guidance, and there are no definitive answers.[60]

Reasonably accommodating employees' religious practices is generally favored by civil rights law, but exceptions to workplace rules should be made with caution. When a practice is prohibited if motivated by secular concerns but permitted as religious activity, such as deviation from uniform dress or dress codes, accommodation can be in tension with the establishment clause.[61] Again, the parameters are uncertain, and reasonableness may be the only guide.

Oaths   Governments sometimes try to limit an employee's freedom of association by having the employee swear an oath of allegiance. So long as the scope of the oath does not exceed a statement of allegiance, it is constitutional. Courts have struck down oaths because of vague language or for requiring employees to give up constitutional rights of speech and belief.[62]

Oaths come in positive and negative form. Positive oaths that are struck down usually are too vague. Far more common are negative, disclaimer-type oaths that require applicants or employees to forswear membership in certain kinds of organizations. Courts have been skeptical of such disclaimer oaths, especially when they have been so specific as to name forbidden organizations.[63]

Whistle-blower protection   The Supreme Court has substantially ensured First Amendment protection of public employees who criticize government policy.[64] A whole new set of procedural safeguards is necessary to protect the rights of individuals who uncover waste or wrongdoing within government. In recent decades, courts have increasingly ruled in favor of whistle-blowers, and there are many specific provisions in federal and state law that seek to protect employees who reveal corruption.

But these antiretaliation clauses are limited to protecting employees who report violations of the particular law in which they are found. The Whistle Blower Protection Act of 1989 introduced some important innovations in safeguarding outspoken federal employees from retribution. This legislation makes it much easier for whistle-blowers to prove their cases; it increases the burden on the government to defend against these claims; it allows whistle-blowers to appeal their own cases; it enhances confidentiality safeguards; and it puts the federal Office of the Special Counsel more surely in the corner of the whistle-blower.

One important difference between whistle-blower protection and free speech protection is that whistle-blower retribution cannot even be one of the factors leading to an adverse action. Courts have ruled that an adverse action cannot be based even partly on reprisal because of the "chilling" effect it would have on other employees.[65] Although this act applies only to federal employees, some state legislators have used it as a model. County and municipal managers should consult legal counsel about laws protecting whistle-blowers at their level of government.[66]

Fourth Amendment privacy

It is firmly established that "individuals do not lose Fourth Amendment rights" against unreasonable searches or seizures "merely because they work for the government instead of a private employer."[67] Their Fourth Amendment rights are structured as follows:

First, in order to enjoy any protection at all, the employee must have a "reasonable expectation of privacy" under the circumstances. For instance, an employee who has a private office to which only he or she and a janitor have a key will have a reasonable expectation of privacy in it. In a building in which briefcases, handbags, suitcases, and so forth are not screened, employees will have a reasonable expectation of privacy in their contents even if work spaces are open or shared.

Second, any governmental search must be reasonable in both inception and scope.[68] That is, the purpose must be sound and defined in such a way that it limits the search's scope. The ambiguity of this standard invites litigation, but the standard is intended to be flexible. The governmental interests in efficiency and effectiveness preclude requiring warrants or findings of probable cause for undertaking workplace searches of public employees' desks, files, and other work-related spaces that are not prompted by law enforcement.

Third, searches may be reasonable even when they are not based on a suspicion that any particular employee has violated a workplace rule. They may be used in administrative (noncriminal) drug-testing schemes for personnel in law enforcement, public safety, or other positions where, on balance, the employees have a reduced expectation of privacy, and the government and public interests outweigh their privacy interests.[69] However, drug testing for human resource management purposes must be reasonable and avoid entanglement with criminal actions.

As noted earlier, applying these principles to voice and e-mail may raise some difficult questions. Technologically, e-mail is a relatively open communication channel so it may be difficult to demonstrate a reasonable expectation of privacy in its use at work. Voice mail, of course, is more akin to a telephone conversation, in which one does have a reasonable expectation of privacy. But the employer may be able to reduce this expectation by not providing private passwords or by informing employees that voice mail (or even telephone conversations) will be monitored for business reasons (e.g., efficient and appropriate communication with customers). Nevertheless, Fourth Amendment protection may be applied to communications that are clearly private in content, such as between spouses about family matters.

Procedural due process

The Fifth and Fourteenth Amendments protect individuals against the deprivation of life, liberty, or property without due process of law. Procedural due process requires fundamental fairness. It is a check on incorrect, arbitrary, capricious, and discriminatory decisions in individual cases. However, it does not involve a specific

Tips for constitutional practice

☐ Think in terms of the "public service model." Remember that the employer's interests may differ from the public's interest.

☐ Each of the constitutional rights discussed in this section has a logical structure. By understanding these structures, you will be able to ask the right questions and better analyze situations. It is especially important to know threshold questions. For instance, was the employee's remark on a matter of public concern? Did the employee have a reasonable expectation of privacy under the circumstances?

☐ When balancing claims according to the public service model or procedural due process, do not overestimate the importance of administrative values and concerns.

☐ Whenever possible, before disciplining an employee, give him or her notice of the reasons and at least an informal opportunity to respond.

formula, and it ranges from a minimal give and take (notice and opportunity to respond) to elaborate hearings with courtroom-like procedures (oral presentation of evidence and arguments, confrontation and cross-examination of adverse witnesses, right to counsel, disclosure of opposing evidence, impartial decision maker, determination on the record of the proceedings, and written explanation of the decision).

The structure of procedural due process is based on the premise that there is often a tension between the government's interest in using less elaborate procedures for the sake of speed, efficiency, and economy on the one hand, and the individual's desire for maximum procedural protection on the other. Consequently, determining when procedural due process applies and what it mandates requires a balance among the following concerns: (1) the private interests affected by the government action; (2) the risk that the procedure used will result in error, and the probable value of alternative procedures in reducing the error rate; and (3) the government's interest in using the procedure afforded, including the administrative and financial burdens of alternatives.[70]

In the context of public human resource management, procedural due process is most commonly triggered by civil service statutes that establish an employee's property right or interest in his or her job. Once a regulation establishes an expectation of continuing employment, termination depends on constitutional due process rather than on civil service rules and procedures.[71] Prior to termination, "the tenured public employee is entitled to oral or written notice of the charges against him, an explanation of the employer's evidence, and an opportunity to present his side of the story."[72] Depending on the circumstances, the employee will often be entitled to a more elaborate post-termination hearing as well.

Additional employee interests that may trigger a right to procedural due process include abridgment of liberty and harm to reputation or future employability.[73] When any of these interests are involved, hearings may be required even if the employee has no civil service status or tenure, as in the case of probationary employees.[74] The timing and scope of the hearings will vary with the balancing of the other two factors.

The higher the probability that the procedures in place will yield correct decisions, the less likely that they will require augmentation or elaboration. All else being equal (i.e., rules are valid and applied uniformly), if there is no factual dispute, there is no need for a hearing at all.[75] However, caution is necessary as the courts may be prone to hairsplitting. An employee who is dismissed for "lying" on his or her application is entitled to due process since the false information may have been the result of a mistake rather than an intent to deceive: such was the case of the public school security guard who thought his conviction was for a misdemeanor rather than a felony.[76]

Finally, the Supreme Court has recognized that the government has a strong interest in removing or disciplining unsatisfactory employees without having to go through burdensome or prolonged procedures. Thus, hearings need not be held before tenured employees are suspended, without pay, for disciplinary reasons. Post-suspension hearings, held within a reasonable time, satisfy constitutional due process.[77]

Substantive due process

The Fifth and Fourteenth Amendments protect individuals against the deprivation of liberty without due process of law. But they do not define *liberty*. "Substantive due process" is the label applied to judicial decisions that give substance to the term *liberty*. It is a hotly contested area of constitutional law because it allows the courts great discretion in determining what is protected. However, in terms of public human resource management, the Supreme Court has thus far limited the concept of substantive due process to "freedom of personal choice in matters of marriage and family life."[78] Thus, it has held that highly restrictive mandatory maternity leaves for schoolteachers are unconstitutional. Taking any action against an employee or applicant because she had an abortion or a child would also trigger substantive due process protection, as filtered through the public service model.

By contrast, the Court has specifically upheld grooming standards for male police officers (length of hair, beards, moustaches) and residency requirements for urban employees in the face of substantive due process challenges.[79] Substantive due process is inherently open-ended and subjective, but the more fundamental the courts consider a right to be, the more likely it is to enjoy protection in the context of public employment.

Equal protection

The constitutional guarantee of equal protection under the laws, contained in the Fourteenth Amendment (and applied to the federal government through the Fifth), is currently of great importance to public affirmative action and related efforts to achieve socially diverse workforces. It has an elaborate structure.

The threshold question for the application of equal protection analysis is whether a policy, law, regulation, practice, or other governmental action classifies people in order to treat them differently. If there is such a classification, the courts use a three-tiered approach to determining its constitutionality:

Suspect classifications Classifications based on race, ethnicity, and, for state and local governments, alienage (noncitizenship) are called "suspect."[80] This is because, in view of the nation's history, it is reasonable to suspect that they will be used to discriminate, thereby defeating the guarantee of equal protection. Suspect classifications are subject to "strict judicial scrutiny." The burden of persuasion is on the government, and the courts are not deferential to government claims of policy or administrative expertise. Such classifications can be sustained only if they serve a compelling governmental interest and are "narrowly tailored." One possible example of a compelling governmental interest in this context is to remedy past, proven racial discrimination against identifiable individuals.[81] The Supreme Court has never held that diversity in the public service is a compelling governmental interest. However, while discussing affirmative action in higher public education, the Court said:

> Effective participation by members of all racial and ethnic groups in the civic life of our Nation is essential if the dream of one Nation, indivisible, is to be realized.... In order to cultivate a set of leaders with legitimacy in the eyes of the citizenry, it is necessary that the path to leadership be visibly open to talented and qualified individuals of every race and ethnicity.[82]

Narrow tailoring requires that the intrusion of suspect classifications on the principle of equal protection be limited. For instance, in terms of remedial racial quotas for hiring and promotion, it requires (1) an assessment of the efficacy of alternative remedies; (2) a fixed duration, in terms of either time or achievement of the policy objectives; (3) hiring and promotion targets that closely reflect the availability of members of the minority group(s) in the relevant workforce; (4) waiver provisions so that it is never necessary to hire or promote an unqualified individual; (5) limited harmful impact on innocent third parties; and (6) an individualized consideration of each candidate.[83]

In the context of today's affirmative action, it should be noted that all race- or ethnicity based classifications are suspect even if their purpose is to further equal opportunity or workforce diversity. In this context, the purpose does not have to be discriminatory.

Nonsuspect classifications   Classifications based on age, residency, income, and similar factors are "nonsuspect," or ordinary. There is no particular reason to believe that these classifications threaten the purposes of the equal protection clause. They are subject to "rational basis" judicial review. Ordinary judicial scrutiny is exercised: the burden of persuasion is generally on the challenger to show that such classifications are not rationally related to the achievement of a legitimate governmental purpose.[84]

In terms of public human resource management, this means that qualifications based on age,[85] residency,[86] education, and perhaps low income for certain positions[87] are not likely to be deemed unconstitutional unless they are wholly irrational or interfere with the exercise of a fundamental constitutional right (see the following section on sex-based classifications). Use of these classifications can also be regulated by statute, as in the case of age discrimination. Federal classifications based on alienage are treated as nonsuspect because the national government has broad constitutional authority regarding immigration and naturalization.[88]

Sex-based classifications   Sex-based classifications fall in between the suspect and nonsuspect tiers. At an earlier time, such classifications received only rational basis review because their putative purpose was to protect women—from long working hours, unsavory workplaces (such as bars), the corruption of electoral politics (by restrictions on suffrage), and the depravity that might be revealed in criminal trials (by exclusion from jury service).

Since the 1970s, as the society and courts became more sensitive to sex-based inequalities, male/female classifications have been subject to "intermediate" judicial scrutiny. They must be substantially related to the achievement of important governmental objectives, and they require an "exceedingly persuasive justification."[89]

Practices that promote occupational segregation or pay differentials based on sex are vulnerable to constitutional challenge. As the constitutional law now stands, the status of affirmative action for women differs from that for racial and ethnic minorities. The Supreme Court has not decided whether or when promoting sex-based diversity in traditionally male (or female) occupations is constitutionally acceptable under intermediate scrutiny.

Sometimes nonsuspect or sex-based classifications interfere with the exercise of a fundamental constitutional right or liberty. For example, in the late 1960s, the Supreme Court held that one-year durational residency requirements for eligibility for state welfare benefits violated indigents' fundamental constitutional right to travel interstate.[90] In such cases, the classification will be subject to strict scrutiny and will need to serve a compelling governmental interest in a way that is least invasive of the protected constitutional right.

Conclusion

Although this section may raise more specific questions than it answers, it provides public managers with the conceptual tools to identify personnel practices that may violate public employees' constitutional rights. Constitutional law is vague and amorphous in some respects, but it also has logical structures. Understanding these structures tells us how to think about human resource management problems and issues in a constitutional context. It will help public managers to build systems and procedures that harmonize governmental interests with constitutional requirements. And that, in turn, will help reduce lawsuits with all their attendant expense in terms of money, time, anxiety, and animosity.

Notes

1 *Rutan v. Republican Party of Illinois*, 497 U.S. 62 (1990).

2 See *Johnson v. County of Los Angeles Fire Dept.*, 865 F. Supp. 1430 (1994).

3 See N.Y. Civ. Rts. L. § 50-a.

4 See, for example, in North Dakota, *Hovet v. Hebron Public School District*, 419 N.W.2nd 189 (N.D., 1988), *City of Grand Forks v. Grand Forks Herald*, 307 N.W.2nd 572 (N.D., 1981), and *Forum Publishing Company v. City of Fargo*, 391 N.W.2nd 169 (N.D., 1986).

5 The United States Supreme Court has long held that Congress had the power to and did abrogate the states' Eleventh Amendment immunity for the purposes of Title VII; see *Fitzpatrick v. Blitzer*, 427 U.S. 445 (1976). Therefore, Title VII covers both state and local governmental employers.

6 *Monell v. Department of Social Services*, 436 U.S. 658, 663 (1978). Local municipalities are subject to suits under Section 1983, *Monell*,

supra, but state governmental entities are not, *Will v. Michigan Dep't. of State Police*, 491 U.S. 58 (1989).

7 *Harlow v. Fitzgerald*, 457 U.S. 800, 818 (1982).

8 *Owen v. City of Independence*, 445 U.S. 622 (1980).

9 *Smith v. Wade*, 461 U.S. 30, 56 (1983).

10 *City of Newport v. Fact Concerts*, 453 U.S. 247, 263–71 (1981).

11 The federal courts of appeals differ in their opinion as to whether a plaintiff may sue governmental employers directly under Section 1981 or must also simultaneously bring an action under Section 1983: compare *Federation of African-American Contractors v. City of Oakland*, 96 F.3d 1204 (9th Cir. 1996) with *Dennis v. County of Fairfax*, 55 F.3d 151 (4th Cir. 1995). In practice, plaintiffs often bring employment discrimination claims against local governments under both sections.

12 *Smith*, 461 U.S. 30, 56.

13 *City of Newport*, 453 U.S. 247, 263–71. See, for example, *Ransom Funches v. City of Dallas*, 1999 U.S. Dist. LEXIS 6269 (N.D. Texas, April 28, 1999).

14 In 2001, the United States Supreme Court ruled in *Board of Trustees of the Univ. of Alabama*, 531 U.S. 356, that states are not required to make reasonable accommodations under the ADA for their employees so long as their actions toward disabled individuals have a rational basis. However, generally local governmental employers are still subject to the ADA. Some governmental employers may be exempt if they are considered to be an "arm of the state." Governmental employers should consult with their local counsel to determine whether they may be exempt from the ADA, but as a practical matter, most governmental employers are subject to similar state disability acts.

15 Local governments that contract with the federal government are covered by this act. See, for example, *Board of Gov. of Univ. of North Carolina v. Dept. of Labor*, 917 F.2d 812 (4th Cir. 1990).

16 *Kimel v. Florida Board of Regents*, 528 U.S. 62 (2000).

17 See *Narin v. Lower Merion School Dist.*, 206 F.3d 323 (3d Cir. 2000) (school district covered by ADEA); *Gavin v. Clarkstown Central School Dist.*, 84 F. Supp. 2d 540 (S.D.N.Y. 2000) (school district covered by ADEA); *Sapienza v. Cook County Office of Public Defender*, 128 F. Supp. 2d (N.D. Ill. 2001) (Illinois counties and public defender's office that was arm of county covered by ADEA). Compare *Adams v. Calvert County Public Schools*, 201 F. Supp. 2d 516 (D. Md. 2002) (county board of education not covered by ADEA where it was arm of state under Maryland law).

18 Age Discrimination in Employment Amendments of 1996, Pub. L. No. 104-208, Subsec. 2(c) & (d), 110 Stat. 3009-25 (codified at 29 U.S.C. § 623j).

19 Most courts that have considered the issue find that all governmental employers (state and local) may be sued under the Equal Pay Act. See, for example, *Varner v. Illinois State Univ.*, 226 F.3d 927 (7th Cir. 2000).

20 29 U.S.C. § 203(e).

21 The U.S. Supreme Court affirmed in *Nevada Dept. of Human Resources v. Hibbs*, 123 S. Ct. 1972 (2003), that state governmental employers are not immune from suits under the FMLA. Therefore, both state and local governmental employers are covered by this act.

22 *Crawford v. Metropolitan Government of Nashville*, 129 S.Ct. 846 (2009).

23 *EEOC v. Shell Oil Co.*, 466 U.S. 54 (1984); 29 C.F.R. § 1601.16(a)(2).

24 *Sedlacek v. Hach*, 752 F.2d 333 (8th Cir. 1985).

25 *Burlington Indus., Inc. v. Ellerth*, No. 97-569 (June 26, 1998), and *Faragher v. City of Boca Raton*, No. 97-282 (June 26, 1998).

26 *Burlington Indus.*, No. 97-569, and *Faragher*, No. 97-282.

27 *Kukla v. Village of Antioch*, 647 F. Supp 799 (N.D. Ill. 1986).

28 N.Y. State Workers' Compensation Board press release, June 27, 2003; N.Y. State Insurance Department press release, September 21, 2000; N.Y. State Workers' Compensation Board press release, January 24, 2000.

29 N.J. Admin. Code, Executive Order No. 49 (1996).

30 "Guidelines for Preventing Workplace Violence for Health Care and Social Service Workers," OSHA 3148 (revised 2003). These guidelines may be obtained by contacting OSHA or by visiting OSHA's Web site at OSHA.gov, where OSHA also has other helpful publications and information regarding workplace violence.

31 *Individual Emp. Rts. Manual* (BNA) 515:122 (2003).

32 The Centers for Disease Control and Prevention (CDC), "Updated U.S. Public Health Guidelines for the Management of Occupational Exposures to HBV, HCV and HIV and Recommendations for Postexposure Prophylaxis" (2001), cdc.gov.

33 CDC, "Guidelines for Preventing the Transmission of Mycobacterium Tuberculosis in Health-Care Facilities" (1994).

34 CDC, "Guidelines for Environmental Infection Control in Health-Care Facilities" (2003).

35 *Rankin v. McPherson*, 483 U.S. 378 (1987).

36 *Cleveland Board of Education v. Loudermill*, 470 U.S. 532 (1985).

37 *Waters v. Churchill*, 511 U.S. 661 (1994).

38 *Pickering v. Board of Education*, 391 U.S. 563 (1968).

39 See David Rosenbloom and Rosemary O'Leary, *Public Administration and Law*, 2nd ed. (New York: Marcel Dekker, 1997), chapter 6, for a more detailed discussion; see also David Rosenbloom and James Carroll, "Public Personnel Administration and Law," in *Handbook of Public Personnel Administration*, ed. Jack Rabin et al. (New York: Marcel Dekker, 1994), 71–113.

40 The federal National Performance Review, headed by Vice President Al Gore, sought to make the federal government operate in a more businesslike fashion. See Al Gore, *From Red Tape to Results: Creating a Government That Works Better and Costs Less* (Washington, D.C.: U.S. Government Printing Office, 1993), and Al Gore, *Businesslike Government: Lessons Learned from American's Best Companies*

(Washington, D.C.: U.S. Government Printing Office, 1997). For a review of some of the constitutional problems involved in such reforms, see David Rosenbloom, "Constitutional Problems for the New Public Management in the United States," in *Current Public Policy Issues: The 1998 Annals*, ed. Khi Thai and Rosalyn Carter (Boca Raton, Fla.: Academics Press, 1998).

41 Justice Lewis Powell in *Owen v. City of Independence*, 445 U.S. 622, 669 (1980).

42 See "Developments in the Law—Public Employment," *Harvard Law Review* 97 (1984): 1611–1800, for a comprehensive analysis.

43 *Waters*, 511 U.S. 661, 675.

44 *U.S. Civil Service Commission v. National Association of Letter Carriers*, 413 U.S. 548 (1973).

45 *Pickering*, 391 U.S. 563. See *Connick v. Meyers*, 461 U.S. 138 (1983), for the Supreme Court's effort to distinguish between employee speech of public versus private concern.

46 *U.S. Civil Service Commission v. National Association of Letter Carriers*, 548.

47 *Rankin*, 378, 327, note 13.

48 *Id.* at 384.

49 *Pickering*, 391 U.S. 563.

50 *U.S. v. National Treasury Employees Union*, 513 U.S. 454 (1995).

51 *Waters*, 511 U.S. at 661, 678.

52 *Connick*, 461 U.S. 138.

53 *Elfbrandt v. Russell*, 384 U.S. 11, 17 (1966).

54 See Robert Roberts, *White House Ethics: The History of the Politics of Conflict of Interest Regulation* (New York: Greenwood Press, 1988).

55 *Elrod v. Burns*, 427 U.S. 347 (1976); *Branti v. Finkel*, 445 U.S. 506 (1980); and *Rutan v. Republican Party of Illinois*, 497 U.S. 62 (1990).

56 *Chicago Teachers Union v. Hudson*, 475 U.S. 292, 310 (1986).

57 *Lemon v. Kurtzman*, 403 U.S. 602 (1971).

58 See also *Torcaso v. Watkins*, 367 U.S. 488 (1961).

59 *Capitol Square Review and Advisory Board v. Pinette*, 510 U.S. 1307 (1994).

60 In *Goldman v. Weinberger*, 475 U.S. 503 (1986), the Supreme Court upheld the constitutionality of a U.S. Air Force regulation prohibiting religious headgear (an Orthodox Jew's skullcap). However, the majority opinion made much of the military's need for discipline and sacrifice of individuality for the sake of solidarity.

61 See *Goldman*, 475 U.S. 503; *Sherbert v. Verner*, 374 U.S. 398 (1963); *Thomas v. Review Board*, 450 U.S. 707 (1981); and *Hobbie v. Unemployment Appeals Commission*, 480 U.S. 136 (1987), which require exceptions for some religious practices or beliefs in unemployment compensation programs. The tension between the establishment and free exercise clauses is well illustrated by *Sherbert*. A Seventh Day Adventist could not constitutionally be deprived of unemployment compensation benefits on the basis that he took himself out of the workforce by refusing to work on his Sabbath, Saturday. But an individual refusing to work on Saturday for secular reasons could be denied the benefits. This outcome gives a special, preferential status to religiously motivated behavior. When a personnel decision is the result of the application of a general criminal law, it will presumably be valid if rationally related to the achievement of legitimate governmental objectives. But there is considerable opposition to the Supreme Court's construction of the First Amendment on this point. It raises the specter that long-standing religious practices, such as male circumcision and ritual wine drinking by minors, can be incidentally criminalized under child abuse or other statutes. See *City of Boerne v. Flores*, 117 S.Ct. 2157 (1997).

62 *Baggett v. Bullitt*, 377 U.S. 360, 362 (1964); and *Elfbrandt*, 384 U.S. 11, 19. See also *Cole v. Richardson*, 405 U.S. 676 (1972).

63 *Cole*, 405 U.S. 676.

64 See, for example, *Pickering*, 391 U.S. 563.

65 *Kewly v. HHS*, 153 F.3d 1357 (1998). Under the Whistle Blower Protection Act of 1989, the employee must show by a preponderance of the evidence that the employee's disclosure of whistle-blower information was a contributing factor in the agency's adverse personnel action against the employee. If the disclosure was a contributing factor, then the burden shifts to the agency, and the agency must prove by clear and convincing evidence that it would have taken the same personnel action in the absence of the disclosure.

66 A good source on whistle-blowing, which includes a state-by-state analysis, is Marcia Miceli and Janet Near, *Blowing the Whistle* (New York: Lexington Books, 1992).

67 *O'Connor v. Ortega*, 480 U.S. 709, 723 (1987).

68 *Id.*

69 *National Treasury Employees Union v. Von Raab*, 489 U.S. 656 (1989).

70 *Mathews v. Eldridge*, 424 U.S. 319 (1976); *Cleveland Board of Education*, 470 U.S. 532.

71 *Cleveland Board of Education*, 470 U.S. 532.

72 *Id.* at 546.

73 *Board of Regents v. Roth*, 408 U.S. 564 (1972).

74 See *Rankin*, 378, 383–384: "Even though McPherson was merely a probationary employee, and even if she could have been discharged for any reason or for no reason at all, she may nonetheless be entitled to reinstatement if she was discharged for

exercising her constitutional right to freedom of expression."

75 *Codd v. Velger,* 429 U.S. 624 (1977).

76 *Cleveland Board of Education,* 470 U.S. 532.

77 *Gilbert v. Homar,* No. 96-651 (1997); U.S. Supreme Court.

78 *Cleveland Board of Education v. LaFleur,* 414 U.S. 632, 639 (1974).

79 *Kelley v. Johnson,* 425 U.S. 238 (1976); *McCarthy v. Philadelphia Civil Service Commission,* 424 U.S. 645 (1976).

80 See *Adarand Constructors v. Pena,* 515 U.S. 200 (1995) for a recent Supreme Court explanation.

81 See *U.S. v. Paradise,* 480 U.S. 149 (1987).

82 *Grutter v. Bollinger,* No. 02-241 (2003), 19–20.

83 *Id.* and *Gratz v. Bollinger,* U.S. Supreme Court, No. 02-516 (2003), 26–27.

84 See *Zobel v. Williams,* 457 U.S. 55 (1982) for a Supreme Court explanation of rational basis review.

85 *Murgia v. Massachusetts Board of Retirement,* 427 U.S. 307 (1976).

86 In *McCarthy,* 645, the Supreme Court gave very short shrift to the challenge to public human resource management residency requirements, despite the rather compelling circumstances of the employee involved.

87 President Bill Clinton's directive that federal agencies endeavor to hire welfare recipients as part of the overall welfare reform of 1996 is an example.

88 *Hampton v. Mow Sun Wong,* 426 U.S. 88 (1976).

89 *U.S. v. Virginia,* 518 U.S. 515 (1996).

90 *Shapiro v. Thompson,* 394 U.S. 618 (1969).

6

Pay and Benefits: Creating an Environment for Excellence

N. Joseph Cayer and Will Volk

Total compensation, including both direct pay and employee benefits, plays a strong role in the success of local governments in attracting and retaining high-performing employees. Local governments face many challenges in designing and delivering pay and benefit programs as the needs of employees continually change and the employment market constantly adjusts to new realities. Local governments must remain competitive in the labor market, but they are also under pressure to reduce expenditures and increase services. As with the other personnel issues addressed in this book, employee pay and benefits require continuous assessment and adjustment.

When determining pay levels, it is appropriate to make a distinction between those for existing positions and those for newly created classes of jobs, because different methods are applicable. Whereas Chapter 1 deals with pay for new job classes, this chapter covers the options available to employers to decide pay and pay raise policies for existing positions.

Establishment of pay and benefit levels

Guiding principles

- Pay and benefits should be competitive.
- Pay and benefits should be managed fairly and equitably.

Challenge

- Getting the resources to offer competitive pay and benefits, especially at the executive and professional levels

ICMA regularly surveys municipalities and counties concerning salaries of the chief administrative officer and of department heads, and it publishes the findings in *The Municipal Year Book*. Summaries of the 2008 salary data for cities with the mayor-council form of government are shown in Exhibit 6-1, those for cities with

Exhibit 6-1 Salaries of municipal officials, July–December 2008: Mayor-council form of government

Title of official	Size of municipality											
	10,000–24,999			25,000–49,999			50,000–99,999			100,000–249,999		
	First quartile	Median	Third quartile	First quartile	Median	Third quartile	First quartile	Median	Third quartile	First quartile	Median	Third quartile
Chief administrative officer	81,090	101,358	113,572	85,332	115,000	135,351	106,779	112,898	135,837	n/a	n/a	n/a
Chief financial officer	68,712	78,577	91,500	73,883	95,850	108,673	91,778	99,023	108,250	116,921	129,800	130,524
Chief law enforcement officer	70,128	83,760	95,378	86,156	95,917	107,172	90,923	101,790	116,992	n/a	n/a	n/a
Clerk	40,291	51,064	67,223	46,351	59,134	75,272	54,371	64,532	75,880	66,254	70,408	71,154
Fire chief	66,234	78,410	87,576	72,792	89,098	99,174	88,144	98,796	109,160	n/a	n/a	n/a
Human resource director	47,046	64,302	72,610	65,823	79,277	99,213	79,139	88,172	98,946	n/a	n/a	n/a
Information services director	50,323	58,720	69,764	76,788	87,848	99,049	74,654	84,094	95,800	n/a	n/a	n/a
Parks and recreation director	50,118	61,374	73,248	66,774	78,650	93,480	76,925	83,500	102,624	n/a	n/a	n/a
Planning director	54,775	65,217	82,446	63,372	77,092	94,536	77,020	86,858	95,522	96,070	100,000	115,624
Public works director	70,817	81,005	92,239	77,758	98,328	117,975	91,996	97,728	113,091	n/a	n/a	n/a

Source: Rollie O. Waters and Joyce C. Powell, "Salaries of Municipal Officials, 2008," in *The Municipal Year Book 2009* (Washington, D.C.: ICMA, 2009), 90–97. Also available at this source are additional titles and population sizes, as well as a breakdown by geographic region.

Exhibit 6-2 Salaries of municipal officials, July–December 2008: Council-manager form of government

| | Size of municipality | | | | | | | | | | | |
| | 10,000–24,999 | | | 25,000–49,999 | | | 50,000–99,999 | | | 100,000–249,999 | | |
Title of official	First quartile	Median	Third quartile	First quartile	Median	Third quartile	First quartile	Median	Third quartile	First quartile	Median	Third quartile
Chief administrative officer	99,988	112,611	131,904	125,814	141,267	155,968	135,070	149,568	166,597	163,553	180,279	202,922
Chief financial officer	72,101	85,880	97,624	95,006	108,119	117,021	101,377	109,737	124,508	113,462	123,901	141,237
Chief law enforcement officer	78,722	90,214	104,024	99,070	115,133	132,723	105,873	119,562	129,412	121,387	130,806	151,557
Clerk	48,651	57,626	69,468	57,172	71,473	85,028	62,077	74,266	84,288	78,258	89,460	101,244
Fire chief	68,886	79,410	91,952	91,514	103,899	118,137	98,921	109,160	120,697	114,513	130,522	146,157
Human resource director	59,444	71,865	83,262	80,300	92,928	104,988	89,802	100,234	111,926	103,894	114,555	132,379
Information services director	60,547	70,595	85,105	78,613	90,910	99,963	84,999	96,561	106,639	100,244	114,336	129,348
Parks and recreation director	63,973	75,383	89,030	82,954	96,508	112,483	90,020	99,923	116,791	97,524	112,043	123,845
Planning director	66,227	76,535	91,336	85,238	92,504	112,882	86,366	98,116	109,755	94,712	104,183	125,097
Public works director	71,401	87,131	97,907	96,678	108,127	124,796	105,850	114,916	127,473	117,164	125,000	131,970

Source: Rollie O. Waters and Joyce C. Powell, "Salaries of Municipal Officials, 2008," in *The Municipal Year Book 2009* (Washington, D.C.: ICMA, 2009), 90–97. Also available at this source are additional titles and population sizes, as well as a breakdown by geographic region.

Exhibit 6-3 Salaries of county officials, January–December 2008

Title of official	Size of county											
	25,000–49,999			50,000–99,999			100,000–249,999			250,000–499,999		
	First quartile	Median	Third quartile	First quartile	Median	Third quartile	First quartile	Median	Third quartile	First quartile	Median	Third quartile
Chief administrative officer	79,533	87,516	101,676	90,763	104,803	113,274	98,758	135,693	155,593	149,344	179,307	214,614
Chief financial officer	58,125	74,692	84,059	60,509	65,097	83,672	94,107	105,164	115,627	99,064	116,177	125,969
Chief law enforcement officer	46,072	62,200	74,602	67,686	72,676	82,000	94,006	101,025	110,398	107,988	128,873	151,946
Clerk	36,368	42,183	51,939	43,354	51,788	60,497	60,063	66,707	75,840	69,124	79,076	91,518
Fire chief	36,777	53,900	63,321	44,186	52,368	68,606	63,297	80,493	100,182	66,194	111,197	129,265
Human resource director	38,239	51,640	65,627	54,000	63,690	70,838	75,266	88,366	106,278	99,570	112,245	124,278
Information services director	52,339	58,471	75,720	53,000	65,520	78,418	85,870	89,227	97,922	99,299	108,276	126,617
Parks and recreation director	44,434	53,641	63,491	53,848	59,016	69,512	71,105	90,412	98,051	92,123	113,520	116,177
Planning director	41,856	51,929	67,308	58,600	69,617	81,241	74,045	94,193	107,987	88,616	107,638	118,441
Public works director	71,206	84,200	89,106	67,603	84,410	99,834	99,047	111,234	119,892	106,634	117,322	134,302

Source: Rollie O. Waters and Joyce C. Powell, "Salaries of County Officials, 2008," in *The Municipal Year Book 2009* (Washington, D.C.: ICMA, 2009), 110–116. Also available at this source are additional titles and population sizes, as well as a breakdown by geographic region.

the council-manager form of government are shown in Exhibit 6–2, and those for counties are shown in Exhibit 6–3. The tables show the first quartile, the median or midpoint, and the third quartile.

Pay is set within guidelines established by local government policy. Several criteria go into the guidelines; among them are merit or performance, labor market conditions, and comparability with other jurisdictions and the private sector, as well as collective negotiations. Because pay and benefits make up the largest share of most local governments' expenditures, they often become controversial as citizens/taxpayers look at the costs. Local government pay is public information, and taxpayers may become angry at pay they perceive to be excessive. Thus, decision makers have to consider the public mood while also dealing with employees and, in many cases, their unions.

Most positions in local government organizations are assigned pay ranges. Exceptions include positions at the very top, which may be open-ended and negotiable. Thus, most employees are placed somewhere in the existing pay plan upon joining the organization. Subsequently, much of the time administrators spend on pay issues is devoted to pay adjustments.

Pay adjustments

Guiding principles

- Pay should be competitive.
- Pay should be perceived by employees as fair and equitable.
- Pay should reward effort.

Challenges

- Managing pay within the confines of limited budgets
- Keeping both employees and taxpayers satisfied
- Finding the proper balance between across-the-board pay increases and variable pay raises based on individual performance so as to keep work motivation and productivity high
- Adjusting possibly substantial pay differences between senior and junior employees that are the result of labor market conditions at the time of hire and not of differences in performance

Types of pay increases

There is not one best practice when it comes to pay adjustments; each pay policy has its benefits and drawbacks. Thus, many employers have resorted to a mix of across-the-board and variable, individualized pay increases.

Across-the-board increases   Across-the-board pay raises provide each employee with an equal amount or percentage of pay increase, although employees usually have to perform satisfactorily to receive the increase. Across-the-board increases are predictable and easy to administer as the appropriate amount is added to each employee's pay. Many employees perceive this pay policy as fair since little judgment is required to implement it and everyone is treated the same. However, there are those who perceive it as unfair because it does not take into account differences in work effort and performance. In rare circumstances, across-the-board adjustments are made downward; in recent years, for example, some local governments dealing with fiscal stress have reduced pay across the board in an effort to reduce costs without laying off people.

The most common across-the-board increase is the cost-of-living adjustment (COLA), which helps employees keep up with increases in the cost of living or consumer price index. But in most cases, the adjustment is lower than the actual cost-of-living increase. Another type of across-the-board adjustment is the step increase. This policy allows employees to move up a step in the pay plan as long as they achieve a satisfactory performance evaluation. Local governments vary with regard to the number of steps they permit and the frequency of granting pay raises; most do it annually, but some offer other periodic increases.

Base rate adjustments   Base rate adjustments add some amount (usually a percentage) to the whole pay plan so that every position in the organization is adjusted. Thus, every employee receives the adjustment.

Lump-sum adjustments   Some local governments offer lump-sum payments as well; these may be given as loyalty pay or longevity pay in which every employee who has been with the organization for a certain period of time receives a lump sum at the end of each year. In some jurisdictions, these adjustments can amount to tens of thousands of dollars for some employees. The lump sum may also be based on performance so that an employee may receive money one year for outstanding performance and not receive it again.

Performance pay   Public employers are increasingly adopting performance-based pay systems. This shift from across-the-board adjustments is grounded in the recognition that it is important to make a pay distinction for superior performance, and it flows from a growing belief that all employees, and particularly top performers, want to work in an environment where results matter. Some argue that this concept is even more important during times when local governments have limited payroll dollars to allocate to raises and need to reward those workers who contribute the most to the success of the organization.

Performance pay mechanisms can take a variety of forms. The most common distinction is between merit pay, which is added to the base pay and permanently increases the paycheck, and bonus pay, which is a one-time payment. Other options include percentage increases based on how the employee is rated on previously agreed-upon factors against a three-, four-, or perhaps five-level rating scale. Some employers consider the employee's position in the salary range. This approach suggests that high performers who are being paid less because of their lower rank should receive a proportionally larger increase than a more modest performer whose salary is already in the upper portion of the range.

Key to the success of any such program is, first and foremost, the full commitment of the governing body and the jurisdiction's top management to the concept and elements of the system. Open communication and consultation with employees, as well as clarity of expectations and system objectives, are also essential. The most technically sophisticated system will have little chance of success if one or more of these prerequisites are overlooked. (For more on performance pay, see Chapter 3.)

Market-based pay   Market-based pay establishes levels according to the rate of pay for comparable positions in the labor market. Sometimes local governments negotiate specific pay with individuals they want to hire and thus pay the market price. More commonly, comparability pay studies are done to see what the going rate is for all positions. Comparability studies may be very informal, such as inquiring what the going pay rate is among other local governments, or they may be very formal, using data from the U.S. Department of Labor and other sources. The relevant market for comparison varies greatly by jurisdiction and type of position. For clerical staff, the typical comparison group is the local market. For more technical or higher-level positions, however, the appropriate comparison group may be the regional or national or even the international labor market. For example, many police and fire organizations typically set pay and promote from within. Especially in high-population growth areas, local governments increasingly have recruited from national labor pools and have had to adjust pay to be competitive.

When the market is surveyed to attract a specific person or to be competitive for a specific class of jobs, challenges arise concerning internal pay equity. People who are already employed in the organization will likely become resentful of those whom they perceive as being better paid. It is a challenge to manage the system and find the funds to make periodic pay adjustments that do not hurt morale.

Gain sharing Gain sharing provides rewards to employee teams for improvement in productivity or savings to the organization. Generally, every team member gets an equal share of some portion of the savings generated by the group. The intent is to develop team cohesion as well as to improve performance.

Skill/competency-based pay Skill- or competency-based pay gives employees a bump in pay for gaining or having specific skills. Many local governments pay people a bonus for having language skills other than English that permit them to communicate with non-English-speaking individuals in the community. The concept can be applied to any skill that is in particular demand by the jurisdiction and is hard to find in the labor force.

Single-rate pay While salary ranges are the predominant methodology for managing employee pay, there are jobs and work flow circumstances where a fixed dollar amount represents a more effective compensation approach. Limiting pay opportunity to a single rate should be considered whenever the tasks that constitute the job do not permit or require performance variation or discretion, or whenever there is effectively no learning curve. This can be the case when output is driven by an established work flow (e.g., assembly line work) or when full performance proficiency can be achieved in a very short period of time. In those instances a market rate is determined and remains in place until competitive factors suggest a change.

Hybrid pay delivery (step, merit, nonbase, etc.) There is no single-pay delivery approach that meets all employer/employee needs all the time. Factors that would be affected by a change in pay delivery, such as the employer's need to limit payroll growth, generational considerations, area pay practices (important in union interest arbitration), composition of the workforce (management versus line staff), ease of communication, and payroll system limitations, should be identified. Employers must carefully develop and evaluate their pay objectives and consider which or how many of the pay delivery options might best achieve the results that they and their employees are seeking. Since there is no single approach or combination of approaches that can be labeled "best practices" and adopted permanently, it is important to articulate the concept of flexibility in policy or pay philosophy well in advance of any actual design or rollout process.

An example of a hybrid approach might consist of a merit-only system, in which a total of 3 percent of an employee's base salary is available for payment in a given year. But in the hybrid approach, only 2 percent is added to the employee's base salary, and this new, higher base salary is then used to compute future percentage increases. The remaining 1 percent is paid out as a lump-sum bonus at the beginning or perhaps the end of the payroll year and is not considered in any future pay adjustment calculation.

Another mix of pay options could combine across-the-board COLA or step increases with individualized pay raises based on performance. It might be a morale booster when all employees see a raise in their paychecks, while superior effort and performance are recognized as well.

Collective bargaining   In collective bargaining, the employer and representatives of the employees negotiate to determine pay changes. In local governments with collective bargaining, a process for deciding about many personnel issues is done through negotiations. Employees choose a union or other organization to represent them in the negotiations. (See Chapter 4 for more on union issues.)

Structure of benefit plans

Guiding principles

- Benefits should be structured in a way that the public employer can stay competitive in the labor market.
- Benefits should be adapted to the needs of employees.
- Benefit plan designs should consider future workforce demographics.
- Benefit plan designs should recognize increasing fiscal constraints and avoid future unanticipated financial liabilities.

Challenges

- Offering competitive benefits and meeting the needs of a diverse workforce while staying within budget
- Managing the administration of a great variety of possible benefits

Local government employers need to inventory what types of benefits they offer and how those benefits fit together to serve the needs of all their employees. Some benefits are mandated by federal or state law; others are optional. The appropriate balance between mandated and optional benefits presents another issue for the employer.

Mandated benefits

Mandated benefits include Social Security, unemployment compensation, and workers' compensation, as well as family and medical leave. Many of these benefits emerged out of the New Deal programs of the 1930s and are often referred to as social insurance programs. Family and medical leave is the latest to be added to the mandated benefits.

Social Security   Social Security provides retirement income for employees and income security for individuals unable to work because of injury or illness. Survivors of employees who paid into Social Security are also covered. For nearly sixty years, local governments could participate in Social Security on a voluntary basis, but in 1991, legislation required that state and local government employees not covered by a public retirement system be included in Social Security.

A challenge for local governments is how to integrate Social Security and local retirement pension packages, especially as concern over the long-term solvency of Social Security grows. One solution that has been suggested is to develop formulas to incorporate Social Security benefits into retirement pensions, but so far, no formal action has been taken. Local governments can choose to include the Social Security benefits as part of their overall retirement benefit plans; but because the national government keeps changing the base salary for Social Security contributions and benefits, it is difficult to develop a formula. Some jurisdictions include Social Security when explaining their complete benefits portfolio to their employees.

Unemployment compensation Unemployment compensation, also part of the Social Security Act of 1935, offers temporary income to individuals who have been laid off or, in certain instances, quit their jobs, as long as they actively seek employment. Beneficiaries receive a fixed level of income for some specified number of weeks. Employers and the national government contribute to the fund that supports the program.

Workers' compensation Workers' compensation provides part of the wages, as well as medical and rehabilitation benefits, to employees who are unable to work because of work-related injuries. The major challenge for employers is controlling abuse by a small number of employees who take advantage of the system. (This problem is addressed more fully in Chapter 5.)

Family and medical leave The Family and Medical Leave Act of 1993 (FMLA) established the newest mandated benefit. All employers with at least fifty employees must provide up to twelve weeks of unpaid leave for the birth or adoption of a child; foster care; care of a sick spouse, child, or parent; or the employee's own serious health condition during any twelve-month period. In 2002, California became the first state to adopt a paid family leave plan providing employees with up to 55 percent of their pay for six weeks. It should also be noted that FMLA provisions were expanded in 2008 to provide leave under certain circumstances to families of military service members.

Among the challenges for local government employers has been reconciling the requirements of the FMLA with other requirements, such as those of the Fair Labor Standards Act (FLSA) or accommodations under the Americans with Disabilities Act (ADA) and other federal laws, as these regulations have been interpreted. (For more on the FMLA and ADA, see Chapter 5.)

Optional benefits

Local government employers offer many benefits not required by law, hoping to attract and retain high-performance employees. Health care plans and retirement pension plans are offered by almost all local government employers; 87 percent of state and local government employees received health care benefits in 2007 and 89 percent participated in retirement plans;[1] similarly, 61 percent earned vacation leave and 87 percent had sick leave benefits.[2] Educational leave and tuition reimbursement for job-related courses and workshops are common. Some local government employers also offset their employees' child care and elder care expenses.

Because the list of discretionary benefits constantly changes and employees have different needs depending on their family circumstances, many employers have created a system called a cafeteria plan (see page 194). In this plan, the employer establishes a fixed dollar amount of benefit expenditures per employee and permits the employee to determine how to spend part of the allocation. For example, a local government might allocate some portion of each employee's health benefits to single health coverage, some to long-term disability, and some to life insurance, leaving the remainder to the individual employee to use to upgrade health insurance, purchase dental insurance, purchase additional life insurance, or take as taxable income.[3] In most cases, employees can pay for additional coverage beyond what the employer provides.

Health care   Health care plans are among the most commonly offered benefits provided by local government employers. Contemporary health care plans cover many types of health care needs, but that has not always been the case. Traditional plans included only medication and hospitalization to treat physical illness and maintain physical health. Plans gradually added mental health care and limited dental coverage. In 2007, 87 percent of state and local government employees had access to health care benefits, 55 percent had access to dental care benefits, 34 percent had vision care, and 86 percent had outpatient prescription drug coverage.[4] Local governments also learned that preventive health measures could help contain the growing costs of health care coverage and thus began to focus on prevention. Today prevention measures include regular physical exams, wellness programs, nutrition counseling, encouragement of healthy lifestyles, exercise, and stress reduction.

Health care plans are among the most costly benefits provided and those costs are continually increasing. Estimates of the level of expenditure vary widely, but in 2007 about 17 percent of the gross domestic product, representing approximately $2.4 trillion, was spent on health care.[5] The average premium for employer-sponsored health care rose to $4,704 for single coverage and $12,680 for family coverage in 2008, up 119 percent since 1999.[6]

Traditionally, local government employers offered indemnity plans in which employees were free to choose their medical services and providers. The plans paid for specific services rendered for given maladies, and payments were generally made directly to the service provider, such as the physician or hospital. Some argued that such plans fostered abuse by encouraging the use of possibly unnecessary procedures because they would be covered. Thus, to contain spiraling costs, employers switched to health maintenance organizations (HMOs) and preferred provider organizations (PPOs). Under these plans, the employer contracts with the HMO or PPO to cover employee health care costs. The employee selects a particular group practice (HMO) or a particular physician who is under contract with the PPO. The HMO or PPO agrees to provide services according to some fixed cost. Employees may be required to pay some agreed-upon fee (co-payment) depending on the service received. Employers have found that costs continue to increase, but at a slower rate with HMOs and PPOs than with the traditional indemnity plans.

Continually growing health care costs prompted local governments to ask employees to share in the cost of premiums. Increased deductibles and co-payments help reduce the overall cost to the employer while increasing the cost to the employee. Employers may also offer more than one option to employees.

ICMA found in 2007 that 99 percent of local governments surveyed were offering health insurance to their employees, with PPO plans being offered by 74 percent, HMO plans by 40 percent, and indemnity plans by 9 percent.[7] Thus, employees can choose which plan they prefer, but they bear more of the expense as the cost of the plan increases. For example, the indemnity plan is most expensive for the employee, whereas the HMO is least expensive.

A variation on this theme is the "tiered network" concept: providers are grouped into tiers, typically based on cost, efficiency, quality of care, and favorable contract terms between the insurer and the provider. Those providers that have the highest quality at the lowest cost can offer patients the most favorable co-pay and coverage arrangements, and it is the patient who considers these factors when selecting a health care provider. This type of plan arrangement is typically included in the concept of consumer-driven health plans (CDHPs) discussed in detail below.

Consumer-driven health plan "Consumer-driven health plan" is a broad term used to describe health insurance plans that have a high-deductible medical plan paired with a health savings account (HSA) or a health reimbursement account (HRA) component. In this kind of plan design the employee is asked to assume greater responsibility for the management of health care expenses, and the employer provides access to funds to help the employee meet these expenses. The careful consideration of which plan components to offer (beyond what is required) is important to ensure maximum benefit to the employee.

HSAs permit employees to set aside pretax money to spend on out-of-pocket medical expenses. If not spent, the money rolls over to the next year and, upon termination of employment, any remaining monies are paid to the employee. Approximately 17 percent of local governments offered HSAs to their employees in 2007.[8] In contrast, HRAs are a mechanism for employers to provide employees with funds to pay for qualifying out-of-pocket health care expenses. Upon termination of employment, unused monies may be retained by the employer or paid to the employee.

The key consideration in all CDHP arrangements is that the employee is asked to have a greater understanding of, and take greater responsibility for the expenditure of, health care dollars. This is a significant shift from traditional plan designs in that costs are transparent to the end consumer of health care products and services.

Voluntary Employee Beneficiary Association A Voluntary Employee Beneficiary Association (VEBA) is a mechanism for establishing individual employee accounts to pay expenses and benefits as defined in the plan document. These accounts can be funded by the employer and participating employees through payroll deductions and by cashing out sick leave, vacation leave, or other accrued leave when employees separate from employment. Creating and maintaining a VEBA trust can be complex, and working with a benefits consultant is advisable.

Other insurance Disability insurance constitutes another form of insurance benefit. Most local governments provide short-term disability coverage at no cost to the employee and make long-term disability coverage available at the employee's expense. Group rates allow the employee to purchase the coverage at lower rates than if purchased individually. Many employers also purchase life insurance policies for their employees, usually in an amount equivalent to a single year of salary with the option for employees to purchase additional coverage at group rates.

Health insurance coverage under COBRA

The Consolidated Omnibus Budget Reconciliation Act (COBRA) requires local governments with twenty or more employees to offer continued coverage to former eligible employees and their dependents under the jurisdiction's group health plan. The table below identifies the qualifying events that determine eligibility and length of coverage. It is the employer's responsibility to inform the employee, spouse, and dependents about their COBRA rights when they become eligible for the plan. The former employee becomes responsible for paying both his or her own and the employer's shares of the premium cost. The employer may charge an additional 2 percent administrative fee.

Qualifying event	Persons covered	Length of coverage
Termination of employment	Employee, spouse, dependents	18 months
Reduction of work hours	Employee, spouse, dependents	18 months
Employee's death	Surviving spouse, dependents	36 months
Employee's divorce or legal separation	Former spouse, dependents	36 months
Former employee's Medicare entitlement	Spouse, dependents	36 months
Change in dependent status	Former dependent	36 months
Employee disability	Employee, spouse, dependents	29 months

Source: Consolidated Omnibus Budget Reconciliation Act of 1985 (P.L. 99-272, April 7, 1986; 42 U.S.C. § 300bb). In 2004, the Department of Labor released final regulations and model forms governing the notice requirements for continuing health care coverage under COBRA. To comply with the regulations, which generally went into effect for plan years beginning on or after January 1, 2005, employers had to modify their COBRA forms and procedures, as well as the COBRA provisions of their health plan's summary plan description.

Legal insurance is another employee benefit program offered increasingly by local government employers. Although government employees are usually indemnified for actions within their authority and undertaken in good faith, employers may offer coverage for nonwork-related legal expenses. Employers generally offer this type of coverage at group rates for purchase at the employees' expense.

Leave Local governments offer many types of leave to their employees, including holiday, vacation, sick, and family care leave. In most jurisdictions, employees receive national holidays, and some jurisdictions offer special holidays such as Statehood Day. Holiday leave totals ten to twelve working days a year in most local governments. Paid vacation leave typically amounts to a week or two in the first few years of employment. After five years or so, employees receive gradually increasing vacation time up to some maximum amount, such as four weeks per year.

Virtually all local government employers also offer sick leave, normally based on the amount of time worked. Commonly, employees accrue a day a month or so, which they use as needed. As a rule, they may accrue only a certain amount of sick leave and must use it by a certain date or lose it. In some jurisdictions, unused sick leave may be paid out in cash, particularly if the employee leaves the organization, or may be converted to vacation leave at a 4-to-1 (or other) ratio once the employee's unused sick leave reaches a certain level. Some jurisdictions also allow employees to share their unused sick leave with other employees who need it, either through a pool arrangement or by direct donations.

Family care leave has replaced maternity and paternity leave. Family leave other than that required under the FMLA also may be offered for such things as bereave-

fyi

Bereavement

In the United States, bereavement leave is generally quite limited and permitted only for the period of the funeral. For instance, California allows its state employees the equivalent of only twenty-four work hours of leave (with an additional sixteen hours if it is necessary to travel some distance). Many policies are also limited in terms of the qualifying relationship with the deceased and thus exclude aunts, uncles, and close friends. As with family and medical leave, bereavement leave is usually either unpaid or counted against an employee's regular leave time. If an organization allows flextime or compensatory (comp) time, most employees are willing to make up this time. These accommodations are usually minor to the employer, but they may loom large in an employee's perceptions and communicate a true concern by the organization for his or her welfare.

Requests for extended bereavement leaves, defined as leave for medical or family care under the Family and Medical Leave Act of 1993, seem to be growing. Employees taking extended bereavement leave may also claim temporary disability (especially for episodic depression). Medical problems should be verified through affidavits of physicians or clinical psychologists.

Supervisors have a responsibility to handle bereavement in the workplace with tact. When a supervisor finds that someone significant to an employee has died, the supervisor should

- Respond immediately to the news
- Avoid platitudes or statements that may offend the employee, who may not share the supervisor's theology
- Inform the employee's co-workers
- Ease the employee back to work
- Check with the employee periodically (every two weeks)
- Refer the employee to bereavement groups
- Watch for signs of depression or sleep disorders that can affect job performance.[1]

Most supervisors underestimate the time that an employee needs to return to full performance. The workplace culture expects people to carry a stiff upper lip, but it may take weeks, months, or a year or more before the employee is operating at 100 percent.

Source: Theodore Pedeliski.

1   Philip M. Perry, "How to Deal with a Grieving Employee," *Law Practice Management* (April 1996): 44-49. For a series of brochures providing helpful advice for handling grief in the workplace, write to the Hospice Council of Metropolitan Washington, 1377 K Street, N.W., Suite 66, Washington, DC 20005.

ment or special occasions involving children; however, these provisions are usually very limited. Some jurisdictions offer personal leave amounting to a day or two a year, which the employees may take for any reason as long as they plan it in advance. Many employers have introduced personal leave to curb abuse of sick leave. Because leave policies have become complex and abuses have led to inequities for employees, many employers have developed comprehensive approaches to leave policy, sometimes called paid time-off (PTO) arrangements or unileave. Comprehensive leave policies establish a set number of leave days, which the employee can use for vacation, sick, or other leave. Typically, the employees accrue leave time according to the length of time they are employed by the jurisdiction. More detail on this approach is provided later in the chapter.

Leave for military service has taken on new importance because of the military actions abroad. National policy requires employers, including local governments, to guarantee full reemployment rights to employees who take leave for military service. Upon their return, these employees are entitled to their former positions with full seniority or to a job of similar pay, rank, and seniority. They also must receive any pay increases, promotions, or other benefits that they would have received if their employment had not been interrupted. (See Chapter 5 for information on the Uniform Services Employment and Reemployment Rights Act of 1994.)

Family care As noted previously, the FMLA mandates certain leave for family care, but many local government employers also offer other forms of leave. As child care is an issue for young families, some local governments provide child care subsidies, and even more employers offer elder care programs for employees with elderly parents or other family members. These services (especially child care) may be offered on premises, but most plans provide for some subsidy.

Employee development Local government employers have long recognized that to keep up with changing circumstances, fiscal constraints, and demands for improved services, they must provide for the continuous development of their employees. This can involve internal or external programs. Training and development opportunities, offered internally, are common in larger jurisdictions. These opportunities include programs that typically focus on the knowledge and skills that employees need to perform their jobs effectively, and workshops that can be used for a variety of learning outcomes, ranging from updating basic computer skills to reviewing changes in law and policy affecting employees' work. In some cases, the training and development opportunities are also available for broader professional and personal development issues.

Smaller jurisdictions can make use of external training and development opportunities offered by professional associations, universities, and consulting firms on topics of relevance to local government employees. Most employers provide funds for such programs, offering tuition reimbursement for job-related classes or degree programs that will enhance the skills and abilities of their employees. Professional conferences permit employees to maintain currency in their fields and also allow for interaction with peers from across the country; professional organizations often use their annual conferences to conduct training and development sessions. Employees may attend these conferences and qualify for reimbursement. (See the online supplement for details on technical assistance providers and educational opportunities.)

Increasingly, local governments are allocating a certain number of dollars to individual employees for training and development purposes. Employees are able to choose which approved programs best suit their needs and use the money accordingly. The resources for such programs benefit not only the employees in their personal growth but also the employers by ensuring that employees keep abreast of new developments. But well-trained and well-educated employees are more marketable, and employers also have to keep up pay and other benefits to remain competitive in the labor market. Employers who offer tuition reimbursement may want to contractually obligate the employees who make use of the program to either stay with the agency for a number of years or repay the tuition costs to the employer upon leaving.

Employee assistance Recognizing that performance on the job is affected by the well-being of the employee, many local governments provide services to assist employees in dealing with stress. Originally, employee assistance programs (EAPs) were developed to provide counseling for substance abuse problems. Subsequently, the programs grew to cover almost any personal problem that leads to stress and that might affect concentration on the job, from family issues to legal and financial problems. While some local governments offer in-house EAPs, many provide access to professional consultants under contract. Employers recognize that it is more cost-effective to help and retain a good employee than it is to recruit and train a new one. EAPs also often offer training on strategies for stress management to help reduce illness, accidents, and absenteeism related to stress.

Employee wellness and health promotion   Wellness programs can help employees stop smoking, lose weight, or get regular exercise. Healthier employees are less likely to use sick leave or develop medical problems that will increase the organization's health care insurance costs. Awards and other forms of recognition are sometimes used as incentives, and some employers allow employees to convert unused sick leave to cash.

Flexible schedules and telecommuting   Some local government employees enjoy flexible work hours or the right to telecommute—that is, to work at home and stay in touch with the office via computer and telephone. Flextime helps the employee who has family obligations that make an 8-to-5 schedule difficult or who just likes working other hours. When some employees come in earlier than the traditional schedule and some stay later, the local government may be able to offer the public extended office hours. Telecommuting enables employees to work at home and maintain family obligations; it also reduces travel to and from work, thus helping to reduce air pollution and traffic congestion. The local government may choose to provide work-related equipment such as computers that employees need to work at home.

Housing and moving incentives   Moving expenses are commonly offered to managerial and professional employees who are recruited from other areas. Housing allowances are often provided to top-level managers. However, some local

---

fyi

The family-friendly workplace

Since absenteeism and tardiness can be caused by family obligations, creating a family-friendly workplace can reduce attendance problems. Some employers allow employees to participate in student-teacher conferences during work hours or to take their children to medical appointments. More comprehensive family-friendly personnel policies allow for job sharing, part-time employment, flextime, compressed workweeks, and paid time off for personal and family responsibilities. Public employers with flextime and comp-time programs have found that employees are quite willing to make up time lost in dealing with a family emergency. Another experimental accommodation allows employees with child care or nursing demands to carry out their job functions by working out of their homes or telecommuting.

However, telecommuting raises its own problems.[1] Under the Fair Labor Standards Act (FLSA), there are currently no regulations that deal with record keeping and monitoring of employees who are covered by overtime provisions and who also telecommute. Employers are well advised to take steps to reduce their legal exposure under the FLSA. The employer should implement a written policy against covered employees working overtime unless they obtain prior express permission from a supervisor.

Source: Theodore Pedeliski.

1   Deborah A. Sudbury and Douglas M. Towns, "Traps for the Unwary: Employment Law Implications of Telecommuting," *Employee Relations Law Journal* 23 (Winter 1997): 5-29.

governments also offer housing allowances to attract and retain police and fire department personnel, especially in high-cost areas, or to encourage police personnel to live in neighborhoods where their presence may help to reduce crime or contribute to redevelopment efforts.

Uniforms For some employees, uniforms or a uniform/clothing allowance may be provided to offset the cost of required dress standards.

Awards Award programs represent another type of benefit. Employees receive awards for suggestions that lead to the improved performance of the organization. Typically, local governments pay some percentage—perhaps 10 percent—of the first-year savings arising from the employee's suggestion. Theoretically, award programs help maintain and improve morale.

Retirement pensions Like health care, local government pensions represent one of the most costly employee benefits. Pension costs as a percentage of total compensation declined to 5.8 percent in 2001, down from 9 percent in 1996, but since 2001 this percentage has been rising.[9] While most employers offer a specific retirement investment plan, many also allow the employees to choose from among approved financial consultants who can design an investment option for individual employees.

Retirement benefits were originally developed as defined benefit plans. They guaranteed the employee a fixed benefit based on the employee's age and number of years of service. Traditionally, these plans were based on a pay-as-you-go approach, which requires the jurisdiction to raise the money to pay for the benefits as employees retire and start drawing pensions. However, pay-as-you-go led to many problems for local governments because, during election years, local political leaders often found it tempting to promise increased retirement pensions, knowing that someone else would have to come up with the money when the bills came due. Political leaders also often bought labor-union peace with agreements to increase retirement pensions. During the 1960s and 1970s, it was common for local governments to agree to generous pension plans. During the 1980s, however, many of those jurisdictions faced severe financial strain as the costs of the pensions came due at the same time that citizens were voting to cut taxes and, thus, the revenue to pay for the increased costs.

As a result, local governments explored other options, the most important of which is the defined contribution plan. In this plan, the employee's ultimate pension is based both on the amount of money invested by and for the individual employee and on the earnings on that investment. Accounts are set up in the name of each employee, and money is contributed to the account usually by both the employer and employee. Additionally, the employee's earnings on the investment are credited to the account. At retirement, the employee receives a pension based on the amount in his or her account. (See Exhibit 6–4 for a comparison of defined benefit and defined contribution plans.)

With the defined contribution plans, forward funding (in which money is set aside and invested before obligations are incurred) replaces pay-as-you-go so that the costs to the local government are more predictable. But these plans have not been universally embraced, largely because public pension funds have a reputation for being poor performers; historically, the investment strategies of fund managers

Exhibit 6-4   A comparison of defined benefit and defined contribution plans

	Defined benefit	Defined contribution
Investment account	Plan level	Individual employee
Employee benefit	Specified in advance	Depends on account value
Employer cost	Depends on various factors	Specified in advance
Investment decision making	Employer	Employee
Objectives		
Funding certainty	Plan liabilities change on the basis of changes in actuarial assumptions (e.g., future salary increases, investment earnings, employee turnover).	Employer liability is fulfilled annually as contributions are made to employee accounts.
Predictable costs	Annual cash expenditure for plan varies from year to year on the basis of actuarial assumptions (see above).	Annual cash expenditures are more predictable as they are based on employee salaries.
Recruitment tool	Benefits are not portable and may not be so appealing to an increasingly mobile workforce.	Benefits are portable and may be more appealing to an increasingly mobile workforce.
Rewards for long-term employees	Benefits are typically based on final year(s) salary, rewarding long-service employees.	Benefits are based on accumulated contributions and earnings.
Lower administrative expenses	Expenses include actuarial evaluation in addition to record keeping and investment management.	Expenses are generally lower than for a defined benefit plan because no actuarial evaluation is necessary.
Reduced investment risk	Investment risk is assumed by the employer. Adverse experience increases employer funding costs.	Investment risk is assumed by the employee. Adverse experience does not increase employer funding costs.
Unlimited benefit potential	Benefits paid at retirement are predetermined by the plan's benefit formula.	Benefits paid at retirement are not limited by a formula. There is a potential to earn greater benefits through superior investment results.
Ease of understanding	Benefits are based on variables that are difficult to predict (e.g., future earnings and years of service at retirement).	Benefits accumulate each year, and contributions are generally based on a percentage of earnings. Participant statements present benefits accumulated to date.
Access to benefits while employed	Benefits may not be withdrawn under any circumstances during active employment.	Benefits may be withdrawn under certain circumstances provided that Internal Revenue Service guidelines are followed.

Source: Adapted from Kathleen Jenks Harm, "Defined Contribution Retirement Plans," *MIS Report* (October 1996): 2.

Health insurance and pensions: What Americans want in a job

Americans ranked health insurance as the most important factor in choosing a job, followed by job security, clear policies and procedures, and retirement plans, according to a national poll conducted by Princeton Survey Research, Inc., and released by the Center for State and Local Government Excellence (SLGE) in 2008.

Two forces make it increasingly difficult for governments to remain competitive in attracting and retaining talent: (1) state and local workers are older and more educated than private sector workers and (2) fiscal pressures have grown, particularly to fund retiree health care and pension benefits.

Information about promising practices and reliable data about benefits can help employers make informed decisions about what changes make sense for their organizations. What do we know?

While pension assets and other retirement savings reflect market values, it is important over time to have a disciplined approach to fund retirement obligations. State and local government pension plans were well funded before the financial meltdown in late 2008. In an SLGE study of eighty-four locally administered pension plans, Boston College researchers found that local plans had accumulated assets to cover about 85 percent of future benefit payments accrued by present and past employees and that 69 percent of local governments were making their full annual required contributions to the pension plans.[1]

Health insurance coverage poses more challenges, particularly for retirees. Many states and localities face substantial unfunded liabilities for their retiree health care. In 2006, the annual cost to state and local governments for retiree health care averaged about 2 percent of employee salaries. The General Accounting Office estimated in 2008 that if employers continue to fund these obligations on a pay-as-you-go basis, their costs will rise to 5 percent of salaries by 2050.[2]

Now that the Governmental Accounting Standards Board Statement No. 45 (GASB 45) requires states and local governments to report their unfunded liability for retiree health care and other post-employment benefits, governments are examining ways to reduce their costs or limit the subsidy for future retirees. In a survey conducted for the SLGE, five states reported that they have established a trust to fund retiree health care; fifteen other states indicated that they were likely to do so. To control costs, seventeen states expected to limit the subsidy for future retirees while three states said they were likely to eliminate subsidies for current retirees. "A large majority of states have introduced disease management programs . . . and conduct claims payer audits."[3]

Administrators seek to retain attractive benefit packages because they know how important benefits are in recruitment, retention, and retirement planning. Keeping abreast of promising practices and reliable data can help them make sound decisions.

Source: Elizabeth K. Kellar, executive director, Center for State and Local Government Excellence.

1 Alicia Munnell, Jean-Pierre Aubry, and Kelly Haverstick, "The Funding Status of Locally Administered Pension Plans," Center for State and Local Government Excellence, *Issue Brief* (October 2008): 6, slge.org (accessed March 27, 2009).

2 U.S. General Accounting Office, *State and Local Government Retiree Benefits: Current Funded Status of Pension and Health Benefits,* GAO-08-223 (Washington, D.C.: GAO, January 2008).

3 Dennis M. Daley and Jerrell D. Coggburn, *Retiree Health Care in the American States* (Washington, D.C.: Center for State and Local Government Excellence, December 2008), 2, slge.org (accessed March 27, 2009).

have been very conservative. More recently, however, some public investment fund managers have engaged in speculative ventures or politically motivated investment strategies that were unsound, and some states have used pension funds to balance budgets or reduce taxes. On top of that, the performance of the funds depends on the fluctuations of the financial markets. For all these reasons, employees may be mistrustful of defined contribution plans. With good management, however, such a plan can benefit employees and employers alike.

Most states operate retirement systems, which local governments are required to join or for which they are eligible. Thus, the operation of the fund is handled at the state level, and the local government functions within state requirements. The statewide systems help to alleviate some of the fiscal problems that local governments have encountered with their own funds. For example, after many local government systems in Massachusetts found themselves in serious financial difficulties, a statewide system was created that allows local governments to pool resources so that they can forward fund their pension plans. This means that money for pensions is invested during the tenure of the employee, and when the employee retires, payments are made from this pooled fund rather than from the current operating budget.

Demographic changes present challenges to retirement systems. Longer life spans and early retirement place strains on the funds. The aging of the population and questions about the solvency of Social Security have created concerns about the ability of retirement systems to meet their obligations and of retirees to receive adequate pensions. The concerns are particularly important for those with pay-as-you-go systems, but others are affected as well. How to integrate Social Security income into the retirement pension planning provides another challenge to the local government employer.

Post-employment health care savings   The Post-Employment Health Care Savings Plan (PEHCSP) is a savings account for employees to fund their health care expenses when they leave employment. Amounts contributed to the plan are tax free, interest earned is tax free, and payments, which may be used to pay medical and long-term care premiums as well as approved out-of-pocket medical expenses, remain tax free. Some employers provide added contributions on employees' behalf, depending on the level of the other benefit plan contributions being provided, including the conversion of paid time-off (PTO) hours. To conform to Internal Revenue Service regulations, employees have no individual choice on the amount of their contribution into the plan. Contribution amounts or sources in the case of PTO are determined by the employer and are the same for all members of an identified employee group.

Deferred compensation   Many employers also permit employees to defer some compensation. The federal government, through the Internal Revenue Code (IRC), allows employees to shield up to a maximum of $16,500 in 2009 for employees age 49 or under and $22,000 for those 50 and over.[10] The amount that the employee wants to set aside is deducted from his or her pay before taxes are calculated. The deferred compensation can be invested in options chosen by the employee. Taxes are paid at the time the employee starts taking payouts from the investments, typically at retirement.

The total compensation package

Guiding principles

■ Benefits must be considered part of the total compensation package and expressed in terms of their aggregate cash value to the employee and their total expense to the employer.

■ Flexibility should be built into the plans to accommodate employees' different and changing needs.

Many compensation programs were designed at a time in the past when most families had one breadwinner, usually the husband and father. These programs rarely consider today's more common two-wage-earner, single-parent, or single-with-no-dependents employees. Moreover, they rarely address changes in need as employees age, lose dependent coverage, or plan for retirement.

To better accommodate these considerations, local government employers have in recent years established plans that blur the line between pay (direct compensation) and benefits (indirect compensation). While traditional pay systems focus almost exclusively on cash compensation and employees often view benefits in noneconomic terms, employers recognize the need to control ever-increasing staff costs by expressing these expenses in terms of their aggregate cash value to the employee and the corresponding bottom-line expense to the employer.

Recognizing, communicating, and permitting a degree of employee control over the form in which the aggregate income is paid is the principle at the heart of the total compensation concept. Full expression of this principle includes permitting employees to opt out from available plans in exchange for higher cash compensation; to shift income from the paycheck to higher-cost medical or dental plans; or perhaps to purchase additional time off, consistent with established plan rules as well as with accounting, actuarial, and tax considerations.

Flexible benefit plans

A more limited form of a total compensation plan is one that focuses primarily on choice within the benefits arena. Such plans often are referred to as flexible, or "cafeteria," benefit plans. The key elements that define a cafeteria plan are that (1) participants are employees and (2) participants may choose from a "menu" of options consisting of cash and "qualified benefits."

Tips for the successful implementation of a cafeteria plan

If you are considering the establishment of flexible benefit arrangements, it is advisable to seek assistance from a consultant experienced in designing and establishing these kinds of plans. Initial consultant efforts would determine and evaluate

☐ Specific objectives that the organization is seeking to achieve

☐ The range of plan options the organization may be prepared to consider

☐ The present components of the organization's benefits plan

☐ Organizational readiness for this concept

☐ Plan administration and cost considerations

☐ Typical pros and cons of establishing a more flexible compensation or benefits arrangement.

Tradable plans In a typical cafeteria arrangement, the value and equivalency of tradable plans, stated in terms of dollar cost, internal tender (flex bucks/flex credits), or other related concepts, are established. Employees then have the opportunity to "purchase" the level of benefits they want and perhaps receive any value not spent, either in cash as a lump sum or staggered in their monthly paychecks. Normally these plans require some level of basic participation in at least the medical plan. Currently, most cafeteria plans are limited to the following options:

- Medical/dental, eye care, hearing care, etc.
- Group term-life insurance
- Short-/long-term disability plans
- Group legal services
- Cash or IRC-eligible deferred compensation plans
- Vacation or PTO plans.

A sample flexible benefits plan configuration is presented in Exhibit 6–5, pages 196–197.

Flexible spending plans Flexible spending plans, also referred to as "income reduction plans," provide employees with a choice between taxable cash and nontaxable compensation in the form of payment or reimbursement of eligible expenses. The employee funds this plan by voluntarily making nontaxed payments into it. These payments represent a reduction in the employee's taxable income. Participants may use this money to pay medical and dental insurance premiums, and eligible medical and child care expenses. Medical savings accounts are an example, but they have unique rules regarding forfeiture, among other things. A recent development in these plans is to provide a debit card to access these flexible spending funds; in this way, many out-of-pocket costs are eliminated, and the administration associated with processing reimbursements is significantly reduced.

Paid time-off plans Traditional paid vacation, sick leave, and bereavement leave plans have been in place with most employers for decades. Increasingly, these plans are being replaced by PTO arrangements, which combine vacation, sick leave, funeral leave, and occasionally holidays into a single plan. Usually the total number of days available under PTO plans is less than the sum available under the previous policies. This, however, is a function of the specific provisions in place, jurisdiction time-off philosophy, and employee time-off usage trends.

A key reason for this shift to PTO plans is the highly structured nature of the traditional arrangements, which typically incorporate extensive rules and procedures. Sick leave rules in particular require supervisors to make highly subjective judgments, and the actual use of the sick leave benefit varies greatly within the typical employee population. For these reasons, it is virtually impossible to achieve equity and consistency across the workforce in the provision of this particular benefit.

A key feature of PTO plans is the time-off approval process. Although sick leave ultimately ought to be available only when the employee is sick, this is often not the case. Supervisors become entangled in questions that they are ill equipped to handle and that lend themselves to inconsistent application. Time off under PTO plans, on the other hand, is typically subject only to nonintrusive notice/request/ approval procedures that have been developed consistent with labor contracts or other related policy considerations. A sample PTO policy and plan configuration is

Exhibit 6-5   FlexComp Program–Dakota County, Minnesota

Overview of program components

Medical plans

Employees choose from three different medical plans. All are open access plans that include in- and out-of-network benefits. The employer contribution is based on the premium for the base plan and is identical for all three plans. This results in employees paying additional premium costs if they elect the costlier plan or receiving premium savings if they elect the cheaper plan.

HealthPartners Distinctions Plan (Base Plan) ranks providers, clinics, and hospitals in two tiers. Tier 1 includes the providers and facilities with the best cost and quality and has the lowest co-pays. Out-of-pocket costs are determined by the provider/facility (tier) chosen.

HealthPartners HRA Plan combines a high deductible medical plan with a tax-free reimbursement account (HRA) that is funded by the employer ($500 for single and $1,000 for family). This plan has the lowest level of benefits.

HealthPartners Choice Plan is a preferred provider plan that offers the highest level of benefit.

Dental plans

Employees may choose from two dental plans, a preventive plan or a comprehensive plan. Both plans include in- and out-of-network benefits. The employer contribution toward dental coverage is a flat $25/month, regardless of the plan and coverage level selected.

Preventive Dental Plan provides 100% coverage for preventive care received from a network provider. There is no coverage for restorative, major services, and orthodontia.

Comprehensive Dental Plan covers preventive, restorative, and major services. Orthodontia coverage is not included.

Life insurance plans

Basic Life Insurance and AD&D provides $50,000 life insurance and $50,000 AD&D coverage at no cost to the employee.

Employee Supplemental Life: Employees have a one-time opportunity to purchase $40,000 of life insurance without providing evidence of insurability. With evidence of insurability, employees may purchase supplemental life insurance in $5,000 units up to a maximum of $300,000. Premium rates are based on the employee's age.

Spouse Supplemental Life: Employees have a one-time opportunity to purchase $10,000 of spouse life insurance without providing evidence of insurability. With the spouse's evidence of insurability, employees may purchase spouse supplemental life insurance in $5,000 units up to a maximum of $150,000. Premium rates are based on the spouse's age.

Child(ren) Supplemental Life Insurance: Employees have a one-time opportunity to purchase $10,000 of child(ren) life coverage without providing evidence of insurability. The unit rate for $10,000 of child(ren) life is $2.00 per month regardless of the number of children covered.

Flexible spending accounts

Health care and dependent day care flexible spending accounts allow employees to set aside pre-tax dollars for eligible medical and/or child care expenses. During the annual open enrollment period, employees elect the amount to be deposited into their account(s) for the year. Employees receive tax-free reimbursements from their accounts after incurring eligible expenses. The pre-tax premium account plan allows employees to pay their portion of medical and/or dental premiums with pre-tax dollars. Enrollment in the pre-tax premium account plan is automatic. Employees choosing not to participate must opt out.

Short-term disability plan

Short-term disability insurance is a "replacement of income" benefit that pays 60% of salary if the employee is injured or disabled and medically unable to work. Benefits begin when the elimination period is completed and continue for the first 180 days of missed work. Premiums are paid by the employee and are based on current salary. Premium costs are determined by the elimination period elected during the annual open enrollment period.

Exhibit 6-5 FlexComp Program–Dakota County, Minnesota *(continued)*

8-day elimination period option

15-day elimination period option

30-day elimination period option

75-day elimination period option

Long-term disability plan

Long-term disability insurance is a "replacement of income" benefit that pays 40 percent or 60 percent of salary if the employee is injured or disabled and medically unable to work for more than six months. Premiums are paid by the employee and are based on current salary and the percentage level elected during the annual open enrollment period.

40 percent benefit level

60 percent benefit level

Long-term care plan

Long-term care provides coverage for extended personal care for basic living activities like bathing, eating and dressing due to accident, aging or illness. Premiums are paid by the employee. Coverage is available to employees and retirees, spouses, parents and parents-in-law, grandparents and grandparents-in-law.

Flex leave (paid time off)

Flex leave can be used for any purpose, subject only to non-intrusive request/approval procedures. An employee's flex leave accrual rate is based on years of service.

Flex leave conversion

The flex leave plan discourages unnecessary time off by providing annual conversion incentives. During the open enrollment period, employees may convert flex leave to wages and/or deferred compensation. To be eligible, employees must have a balance of 60 hours of flex leave at the end of the third payroll quarter and must have used 60 hours of flex leave during the first three payroll quarters. Eligible employees may convert up to 20 percent of their flex leave balance to deferred

compensation and/or up to 100 hours of flex leave to wages to offset the cost of their benefit elections.

Holidays

Employees have ten paid holidays per year.

Wellness credit

The Employee Wellness Program is designed to maintain and improve employee's personal health, reduce health care premium costs, and improve employee morale. Each year, a $60 wellness credit is paid to employees who have met specific wellness-related criteria throughout the year.

Employee assistance program (EAP)

The employee assistance program offers support, information, and resources to help employees and their family members through challenging times. The program provides free counseling for up to four sessions per problem, per year.

Post Employment Health Care Savings Plan

The Post Employment Health Care Savings Plan is a tax-free savings account for employees to fund their health care expenses when they leave employment. Amounts contributed to the plan are tax-free, interest earned is tax-free, and payments, which may be used to pay medical and long-term care premiums as well as approved out-of-pocket medical expenses, remain tax-free. To conform to IRS regulations, employees have no individual choice on the amount of their contribution into the plan. Contribution amounts are determined by the employer and are the same for all participants.

Eligibility for part-time employees

Part-time employees are eligible for the entire FlexComp Program. The employee must consistently earn enough wages to pay the required payroll premium deductions. The employer contribution towards a part-time employee's benefits is pro-rated based on hours the employee is budgeted to work.

Note: The Dakota County flexible compensation program was begun in 1992. Since then it has been adopted in a number of other jurisdictions. There is little question that this approach represents the direction of benefits programs both private and public. The county received an achievement award for the FlexComp Plan from the National Association of Counties (NACo) in 1998.

provided in Exhibit 6–6, and questions and answers regarding flex leave are presented in Exhibit 6–7 (see pages 199–202).

Insured versus self-insured arrangements

While some significant opportunities can be gained through self-insured arrangements (primarily with medical or dental plans), such an approach should be considered with caution. This is particularly true for smaller jurisdictions—that is, those with fewer than 750 to 1,000 plan participants (not the same as the number of employees). As the term suggests, the jurisdiction serves as the "insurance company" with all the corresponding risks and rewards. Size is significant with respect to (1) financial capacity and (2) the number of plan participants over which risk can be spread. The volatility in the benefits market in recent years has made self-insurance somewhat unattractive when compared with rate guarantees available in most commercial insurance markets. This consideration, as well as the continuing consolidation of providers, suggests that only a larger employer or a consortium of smaller organizations might continue to benefit from essentially eliminating the insurance company profit portion from the costs of providing the plan in question.

The key advantages of self-insurance include the potential cost advantage noted above as well as substantial opportunity to design and configure the various elements of the plan. Coverage levels, cost-control provisions, administrative service arrangements, funding mechanisms (e.g., a trust arrangement), and provider options all represent available possibilities for flexibility or varying approaches that would benefit both employer and employee.

Benefits continuation

When an employee's career ends by termination, resignation, or retirement, the employer must generally address an array of benefit elements—some statutory, others most commonly a function of jurisdiction policies and past commitments.

Key among the benefit continuation elements is compliance with COBRA, which enables separating employees (and certain dependents or former dependents) to remain on the jurisdiction's medical and dental plans, as well as its vision and drug plans and flexible spending arrangements (FSAs). Plan participation is typically at the full employer group rates. This may represent a less costly option than purchasing individual coverage. Since COBRA provisions are complex, some employers retain third-party administrators to ensure the complete management of this statutory requirement. In the absence of a third-party administrator, the jurisdiction should develop detailed processes to meet COBRA requirements. Additionally, since some states have adopted more comprehensive benefit continuation provisions, jurisdictions are advised to seek out the necessary information to determine the extent of any state requirements that must be met.

Other benefit plans may also come into play when an employee separates from employment. Depending on specific plans and provisions, various issues would need to be resolved at the time of separation, such as funding the jurisdiction's PEHCSP or deferred compensation plan by cashing out of PTO or other accrued leave time, establishing mechanisms to apply these funds toward health care premium payments, or otherwise launching employer provisions that may apply to the disposition of remaining employee funds. Clear communication of these provisions, including survivor considerations, becomes important because employee monies—in some cases significant amounts—may be involved.

Exhibit 6-6   Flex Leave Plan document

Introduction

It has been a continuing objective of Dakota County to provide equity, consistency and flexibility in the delivery of benefits alternatives to County Staff. Where appropriate, certain benefits have also been designed to incorporate employee tenure so as to recognize and reward loyal service to the County. These considerations are particularly significant in the accrual, utilization and administration of paid time off.

While traditional paid vacation, sick leave and bereavement leave have been in place for many years, those programs are highly structured, with extensive rules being applied to the actual use of the benefit. With sick leave in particular, these rules often inject the employer into employees' personal lives and require supervisors to make highly subjective judgments. Utilization of sick leave also varies greatly within the employee population and it is, therefore, virtually impossible to achieve equity across the work force in the provision of this particular benefit.

The Flex Leave Plan replaces county policies on vacation, sick leave and funeral leave and combines these benefits into a single plan. All eligible employees accrue flex leave based on tenure. Plan provisions discourage unnecessary utilization by providing cash and savings incentives.

Flex Leave can be utilized for any purpose, subject only to normal, non-intrusive request/approval procedures consistent with policy and labor contracts.

With the adoption of this plan, Dakota County firmly accepts and endorses the principles of equity, consistency, flexibility and the recognition of tenure in the delivery of this benefit.

Policy

It is the policy of Dakota County to provide employees necessary paid time away from work. This policy is implemented by means of the Flex Leave Plan, which covers all paid leave previously available under the county's vacation, sick leave and funeral leave policies.

Flex leave can be utilized for any purpose, subject only to necessary request/approval procedures consistent with policy and labor contracts.

Accrual rates (new hires)

Years of service	Annual accrual rate
0–5 years	160 hours/20 days
6–10 years	192 hours/24 days
11–15 years	240 hours/30 days
16 or more years	304 hours/38 days

Nonunion employees hired prior to September 6, 1992, will accrue flex leave at the rate established under previous vacation and sick leave policies until such time as the flex leave provisions are equal to or greater than the previous combined vacation and sick leave provisions.

Use of flex leave

Flex leave is accrued on a per pay period basis and may be used subsequent to the pay period in which it was earned. Nonemergency use must be requested in advance per departmental policies. Emergency use may require documentation of the emergency. Probationary employees may use no more than 16 hours of flex leave during the probationary period. Maximum carry over from one year to the next is 125 days/1,000 hours. Employees who are eligible to participate in the county's post employment health care savings plan will have the cash equivalency of hours in excess of 1,000 deposited in the Minnesota State Health Care Savings Plan (HCSP) according to the provisions in the post employment health care savings plan.

(continued)

Exhibit 6-6 Flex Leave Plan document *(continued)*

Annual conversion options

Employees with a minimum flex leave balance of 60 hours at the end of the 3rd payroll quarter may convert (subject to maximum deferral regulations as stated in IRC [Internal Revenue Code] Section 457) up to 20 percent of their flex leave balance each year, to the County's deferred compensation plan if they have used a minimum of 60 hours of flex leave during the first three quarters of the current payroll year. Conversion of flex leave to deferred compensation will be effective the following year. Employees may additionally convert up to 100 flex leave hours to wages to offset the cost of benefits enrollments provided they maintain a minimum flex leave balance of 40 hours after the conversion has occurred. Employees who have terminated their county employment and qualify as Dakota County retirees may convert flex leave to deferred compensation, subject to maximum deferral regulations as stated in IRC Section 457, on their final paycheck, prior to receiving their severance payment.

Termination benefits

An employee's flex leave balance becomes available upon termination. The County's post employment health care savings plan provisions will apply if the terminating employee is eligible to participate. The following chart provides the details concerning the severance benefits for terminating employees.

If the terminating employee	Severance payment
Qualifies for the post employment health care savings plan	• Post employment health care plan provisions apply. • Flex Leave termination conversion option applies.
Does not qualify for the post employment health care savings plan <u>and</u> • *Does not qualify as a Dakota County retiree and* • *Participates in Flex Leave, and* • Has an Extended Sick Leave Bank	• Flex Leave is paid in full. • One-half of sick leave to a maximum of 400 hours is paid.
Does not qualify for the post employment health care savings plan <u>and</u> • *Qualifies as a Dakota County retiree and* • *Participates in Flex Leave, and* • Has an Extended Sick Leave Bank	• Flex Leave is paid in full. • One-half of sick leave to a maximum of 400 hours is paid. • Unpaid extended sick leave hours will be used to create an account from which medical, dental and life insurance premiums may be paid until it is exhausted or until the retiree dies, whichever comes first.
Does not qualify for the post employment health care savings plan **and** • Participates in Flex Leave, and • Does <u>not</u> have an Extended Sick Leave Bank	• Flex leave is paid in full.
Does not qualify for the post employment health care savings plan **and** • Does <u>not</u> participate in the Flex Leave Plan	• Vacation and sick leave hours are paid per union contract.

Eligibility

All nonlimited, full-time and part-time Dakota County employees are eligible to participate in the Flex Leave Plan beginning September 6, 1992. Nonlimited, part-time employees accrue flex leave on a pro-rata basis.

Exhibit 6-6 Flex Leave Plan document *(continued)*

Participation

Effective January 1, 1994, all Dakota County employees not covered by a collective bargaining agreement shall participate in the Flex Leave program.

Employee groups covered by collective bargaining agreements must negotiate participation in the Flex Leave program through the collective bargaining process.

All non-union employees hired on or after September 6, 1992, shall participate in the Flex Leave program.

Current vacation/sick leave balances

Existing vacation and sick leave balances shall be converted to the Flex Leave program in the following manner. Unused vacation balances shall be converted to the Flex Leave Accounts of participating employees. New flex leave hours, as accrued, shall be added to the converted vacation balance.

Sick leave hours will be converted to the Extended Sick Leave Bank hours.

Extended Sick Leave Bank

For employees hired before September 6, 1992, total unused sick leave hours shall be frozen at the balance in effect at the time of conversion. This account shall become the Extended Sick Leave Bank and may be used for future illness or disability.

In the event of illness, injury or disability, the first 16 hours of absence in each plan year must be taken from the Flex Leave Account before accessing the Extended Sick Leave Bank. Subsequent absence (due to illness, injury, or disability) within that plan year may be taken from the Extended Sick Leave Bank or the Flex Leave Account, at the employee's choice.

Employees receiving workers' compensation may use the Extended Sick Leave Bank to return to 100% of their current salary.

Exhibit 6-7 Flex leave questions and answers

Q: Do the following answers on flex leave apply to union employees as well as to non-union employees?

A: Bargaining units will need to negotiate implementation of the Flex Leave Plan. While implementation dates will vary, it is anticipated that the general provisions of the Flex Leave Plan description and the following questions and answers may apply to some union employees beginning in 1993.

Q: Since the accrual rate for flex leave is slightly less than the combined vacation and sick leave accrual rate, will I lose days when I enroll in the Flex Leave Plan?

A: No. Employees will remain at their current accrual rate until the Flex Leave Plan accrual rate catches up with them. For example, employees with 3 years of service are currently accruing 24 days of combined sick and vacation leave per year. When they enroll in the Flex Leave Plan, they will continue to accrue at the rate of 24 flex leave days per year until they have completed 10 years of service.

Q: Will my Extended Sick Leave Bank be stored as hours or dollars?

A: Extended sick leave will be stored as hours. The value of your Extended Sick Leave Bank hours will be determined by your rate of pay at the time those hours are used.

Q: How will I keep track of the hours I have in the Extended Sick Leave Bank?

A: An employee's current Extended Sick Leave Bank balance will be stated on each paycheck stub under the heading "EXTED/SICK BAL."

(continued)

Exhibit 6-7   Flex leave questions and answers *(continued)*

Q: What are the requirements to access the Extended Sick Leave Bank?

A: Each payroll year, after employees have used 16 hours of flex leave (for any purpose) they are eligible (if sick) to use hours from the Extended Sick Leave Bank. County policy for using sick leave will continue to apply for accessing the Extended Sick Leave Bank.

Q: Can an employee who is receiving workers' compensation use the Extended Sick Leave Bank to obtain 100% compensation?

A: Yes. If an employee has an Extended Sick Leave Bank, it can be utilized to receive 100% wages while off work due to a work-related injury. This is consistent with current County policy.

Q: Is there a requirement that the flex leave balance be exhausted before an employee is eligible to receive short-term disability (STD) or long-term disability (LTD) benefits?

A: Effective March 1, 1993, employees are not required to exhaust their flex leave to be eligible for STD or LTD.

Q: How will planned flex leave and unplanned flex leave be determined and recorded?

A: A major Flex Leave Plan objective is to encourage the advance planning of absences from work. The Flex Leave Plan description requires that "non-emergency (planned) use be requested in advance" and that "emergency (unplanned) use may require documentation." A central focus of the Flex Leave Plan is to provide employees with adequate time off work while assuring efficient departmental coverage through providing adequate advance notice. Employees are expected to provide as much notice as possible when requesting time off work. For flex leave to be considered "planned," an employee should give the supervisor advance notice—equal to the amount of requested time off, up to 5 days. Department rules and requirements concerning employees' absence from work will continue to be applied.

Supervisors may deny a specific request for non-emergency flex leave to assure necessary departmental workload coverage. It is expected that unplanned absences will vary based on individual needs and departments ability to accommodate employees requests while maintaining efficiency.

Both planned and unplanned flex leave will be recorded on the employee's time sheet, which will remain in the department.

Q: How will prior county employment affect my flex leave accrual rate?

A: "Limited" employees who are hired as "nonlimited" employees and who have not had a break in service will automatically have the "limited" aggregate years of service credited to them. Individuals who have had prior employment with the County and have been re-employed may be eligible for restoration of those previous years of service per current County policy.

In both instances, this restoration of service applies to the benefit accrual date only. An employee's benefit accrual date is defined as the date that determines the rate at which flex leave is accrued.

Q: What is the flex leave accrual rate for nonlimited part-time employees?

A: Flex leave will accrue at a pro-rated amount based on the actual hours paid. This is consistent with current County vacation and sick leave policy.

Q: What will happen if I have used most or all of my flex leave and then get sick and need to be away from work for 2 weeks?

A: One of the basic concepts in the Flex Leave Plan is to encourage employees to plan ahead whenever possible. Since the possibility always exists that a person may become sick and need time off work, employees are expected to take this into consideration when using their flex leave. If an employee does not have flex leave hours or Extended Sick Leave Bank hours available and is absent from work, the time off work will be considered unpaid.

Administrative issues

Plan administration often is overlooked when the establishment, expansion, or redesign of the benefits program is being discussed. This oversight can result in employee concerns because of unmet needs or in employer surprise when the workload and corresponding costs of the plan are fully understood. Administration represents the significant but often hidden cost that at some level is unavoidable. Even when insurance agents purport to handle all plan activities, there remains a substantial effort necessary to the effective delivery of the employer plans. Often this effort requires staff time, as well as the availability of data management systems and procedures to ensure both the smooth implementation and communication of the plan and the capacity to ultimately process claims. As with other aspects of the benefits program, however, a range of options is available.

While some benefits support comes from resources internal to the organization, many administrative tasks can—and some should—be left to outside contractors. Key among those best contracted out are claims administration. Although available benefits software has made the task dramatically less difficult, heavy claim loads are anything but routine. Plan interpretation can pose regular difficulty, and the speed with which claims are resolved, as well as the perceived fairness and consistency of this process, sets the tone for the overall program. Any employer would be well advised to ensure that these tasks are handled in the most effective manner possible, whether internally or through contracted services. Many employers use electronic options for premium payment and vendor interfaces. Employees sign up for their desired benefits and access the benefits online, often directly from the vendor. This arrangement eliminates the need for an employer to process benefit requests and claims, thus saving the employer money in the long run.

Purchase and design considerations

Guiding principles

- Small governments should employ a benefits consultant.
- Small jurisdictions need to develop the expertise to handle, or seek expert advice for, the proper content and oversight of the contract.

Challenge

- Managing the contracting process and working with the benefits consultant to achieve local government goals

Use of consultants

The growing complexity of even the most basic benefit programs makes retaining specialists experienced in the planning, design, purchase, and evaluation of the plans unavoidable. That is particularly true in the smaller jurisdictions that simply cannot afford to retain this level of expertise in-house. Employers should develop the contractual skills needed to work effectively in this arena by learning how to select a qualified consultant and manage the output from this relationship. The chief executive of the jurisdiction should take ownership of the project and focus on understanding each step in the process, questioning the consultant as necessary, to ensure that all jurisdictional objectives in employing the consultant are met.

Caution

- Do not assume that once a consultant is hired there is nothing left to do but receive the work product.

- Do not purchase a "black box," the contents of which are known only to the consultant.

The RFQ/RFP process

While specific requirements differ, a jurisdiction is normally subject to a structured process when it enters into a contract for group insurance for its employees. This process is generally one of two types:

Request for quotation Sometimes referred to as a "request for competitive bid," a request for quotation (RFQ) involves the development of a bid specification that details the exact service or product being sought and that is advertised or communicated to the relevant industry segment. There is typically a threshold cost below which such a process is not required (e.g., $10,000), and the contract normally is awarded to the lowest responsible bidder. This is the most common approach to the purchase of benefit products that are relatively uniform across the market and for which the selection decision will be based almost solely on the price of the product—for example, group term-life insurance.

Request for proposal When the jurisdiction is establishing or renewing a plan that is subject to vendor or employer design variations, the request-for-proposal (RFP) approach is typically used. In contrast to an RFQ or competitive bids, this process normally focuses on the provision of services (e.g., medical care for employees) in which the level of the service provided and the mechanisms for providing it may differ significantly from vendor to vendor.

Applicable statutes, jurisdiction policies, or labor contracts often establish the nature or extent of the changes that can be made to plans as a result of vendor- or employer-generated variations from one plan configuration to the next. The aggregate value of the benefits, as certified by an actuary, often cannot be reduced, but variations in the specific level or type of coverage being provided are commonly permitted.

Insurance agents

It is common practice in smaller organizations to purchase components of benefit programs from local insurance agents. Other jurisdictions have found it to be cost-effective to retain a consultant to manage the purchase process directly with carriers. The actual rates for a given coverage often can be less with this second approach.

Tips for a successful bidding process

- ☐ Make sure that the bid specification is comprehensive.

- ☐ Ensure that the product or service being described in the request for competitive bids is, in fact, what the jurisdiction is seeking.

- ☐ Follow a strict bid administration process.

Caution

When bidding the design and purchase of a benefits plan, avoid

■ Being inconsistent when communicating with potential vendors

■ Revealing one vendor's information to another vendor

■ Opening bids before the submission deadline.

Although insurance agents suggest that they handle plan administration when the program is purchased from them, the carriers' own administrative staffs provide a significant amount of assistance to employers; thus, agents may be duplicating services already in place or adding steps to the process and thereby adding to the cost.

Communicating the benefits program

Guiding principle

■ Plan benefits should be effectively and clearly communicated to all employees so that they can make the best decisions for their individual situations.

Challenge

■ Communicating the full value of the benefits program to employees

The very nature of most benefit programs obscures their true value to the employee and their true cost to the employer. It is therefore in the interest of the jurisdiction to fully communicate the plan(s) so that employees recognize the significance of what is available as well as whatever additional compensation the benefits program represents. This is particularly true when a flexible benefits plan is being contemplated since such a plan requires choices that could have a significant impact on the employee and his or her family. The only way to avoid the waste that comes from either indifference to or misapplication of the benefits dollar is through well-planned, adequately funded, professionally delivered, ongoing communication. Effective written communications include materials that carefully and completely describe the plan in plain language and that are presented to employees in small increments to facilitate understanding. New employee orientation provides a good opportunity to begin the process of communicating the value of benefits.

Individual benefit statements

A common method of more fully communicating both the range of benefits available and the value of selected plans is the individual benefits statement. This statement is generally prepared through the application of specialized computer software and is provided to employees on an annual basis. It itemizes in detail the actual dollar value of each element of the benefits program, including items that typically are not fully acknowledged by employees. Among the less understood benefits are employer FICA (Federal Insurance Contributions Act) contributions; workers' compensation and unemployment compensation contributions; pension plan contributions; and the value of PTO, vacation, sick leave, and holidays. A number of consultants specialize in preparing the annual individual benefits statement. Their services include communications planning, data gathering, statement design, distribution to employees, and ongoing maintenance.

Online benefit communications

A relatively new method of communicating benefits is providing employees with online access to their individual records, including balances in savings plans and pension plan information. Online programs have interactive capabilities so that employees can develop "what if" scenarios and better visualize how their current choices may translate into short- and long-term results, as well as how different choices may affect them in the future. This type of approach is particularly important when employees are considering the implications of flexible benefit choices or are planning for retirement. Online communication programs hold the promise of greatly enhancing the tools available to employers, and of providing employees with a simple and reliable financial planning mechanism that permits them to accept the greater responsibility inherent in the delivery of a modern benefits program. Web-based delivery of employee benefits continues to expand, reflecting a trend toward self-service in managing human resource functions.[11]

Open enrollment

A key opportunity for communicating available benefit choices is the annual open enrollment process. In most plans, this event provides employees with the opportunity to rethink their choices, enroll in plans that they may have previously declined, or purchase higher levels of coverage.

In preparation for the process, employers should carefully review available communication channels and seize the opportunity to hold group meetings and encourage face-to face dialogue. The result can often be dramatic, both in the employer's understanding of employee needs and expectations, and in the employees' comprehension of the existing choices and the related costs to the employer.

Evaluation of benefit programs

Guiding principle

- Demographic and societal changes make it necessary to constantly reevaluate benefits.

The benefit needs of employees change constantly, challenging the local government employer in many ways and creating the need for new approaches to benefits. This is partly the result of changing demographics, but it is also the result of societal transformations, such as the changing structure of families. Dual-career couples have somewhat different needs than the traditional family of the 1940s and 1950s. Some elements of standard benefit packages may actually be redundant when both members of the couple are employed outside the home, requiring employers to allow an employee to opt out of a particular coverage if the spouse has similar coverage. Yet allowing employees to opt out of traditionally required coverage, such as health care, can make contracting for and administering the benefit even more complex.

As noted above, the aging of the workforce also creates challenges. As people now live longer, many employees have responsibilities for elderly relatives. Older employees need different benefits than do younger employees: older employees usually use health care services more intensively, while younger employees have more need for child care and education benefits.

Increasing numbers of unmarried-couple households have led to pressure for domestic partnership benefits, which are highly controversial for many local governments. The controversy arises because most people associate domestic partner-ship with homosexual couples, although the reality is that unmarried heterosexual couples far outnumber homosexual couples. Gradually, local governments are moving to provide domestic partnership benefits, and this move brings with it implementation challenges, especially in defining what constitutes a domestic partnership.

Cafeteria-style benefit plans appear to be an answer to the challenges brought about by changing demographics. The cost resulting from the increased complexity of administering cafeteria benefits is offset by the savings that come from not pay-ing for benefits that are not used by some employees. Typically, benefits represent approximately 30 percent of total compensation costs of local governments. The cafeteria plans provide alternative approaches to particular benefits—for instance, giving employees a choice of health care provided using indemnity, HMO, or PPO plans.

Many local governments are experimenting with consortia or cooperative approaches with other governmental jurisdictions: by pooling resources and numbers of employees, local governments can often obtain better bids or negoti-ate better terms for the provision of some of their benefit programs. Costs can also be reduced by lowering the number of people eligible for coverage. Thus, many jurisdictions are dropping part-time and retired employees from eligibility for health care. Retirement costs may be reduced by raising the retirement age. Also in use are two-tiered benefit plans, in which current employees retain the level of benefits in place when they were hired, but new employees receive a lower level of benefits.

Regardless of the approaches they use, increasing numbers of local government employers are also asking their employees to pay part of the cost of their benefit programs. Generally, local governments have been generous in fully funding most benefits and in offering a wider range of benefits than is typical among private sector employers, especially smaller ones. Yet they also seem to be less successful in controlling costs, which might be related to the tendency of government to be somewhat more socially conscious in its policies. In some places, local government employees have developed an entitlement mentality regarding benefits, and this mentality is usually encouraged by the employers themselves.

Employee participation in the design of benefit plans is another way of getting employees to accept responsibility for their benefits. Participation gives employees an understanding of the cost factors involved in alternative plans, which can lead to wiser use of benefits. One way to engage employees in the design and evaluation process is to survey them on benefits issues. A few questions from such a survey are presented in Exhibit 6–8 (see pages 208–209).

Evaluation questions

The effective design and delivery of any benefits program must be grounded in careful consideration of the answers to the following key questions:

1. What benefit plans currently exist?
2. Why does each plan exist?
3. What specific objective is each plan designed to achieve?
4. To what degree is the plan achieving its objective?
5. What are the needs of the workforce?
6. What are the needs of the jurisdiction?

Exhibit 6-8   Sample employee benefits survey

The following text and questions are excerpted from a sample survey instrument published by Richard E. Johnson in Flexible Benefits: A How-To Guide (see source note below). The complete survey is several pages long.

This survey is an effort to learn your opinions about your benefits. _____ must regularly make tough decisions about how to best spend its benefits dollars and (administration/personnel) wants to know your views to help in the process.

   It is important that you answer the questions honestly so we get a clear sense of your opinions about the benefits here. So that you feel free to answer openly we do not want you to put your name on the questionnaire. For your further protection, seal your completed questionnaire in the envelope provided and (provide instructions for returning the questionnaire to a specific office).

   No one at _____ will ever see a completed questionnaire. Instead, _____ will get a report from _____ summing up how groups of people feel about various issues.

   While we can't promise that everyone's ideas can be used in planning changes, (personnel/administration) wants to be as responsive as possible to your opinions and concerns on these important issues.

	(1) Strongly agree	(2) Agree	(3) Disagree	(4) Strongly disagree
I know where to get the information I need regarding my benefits.	☐	☐	☐	☐
Employee medical claims are paid quickly and fairly.	☐	☐	☐	☐
I'd rather work at this company than any other company in the area.	☐	☐	☐	☐
Increasing my direct pay is more important to me than improving benefits.	☐	☐	☐	☐
The benefits here are as good as at other companies in the area.	☐	☐	☐	☐
The company's paid time-off policy is fair.	☐	☐	☐	☐
Company-paid disability insurance won't give me enough income if I become disabled for a long period of time.	☐	☐	☐	☐
I don't understand how the paid time-off policy works.	☐	☐	☐	☐

   Before you answer these next items, we would like to tell you about two possible new employee benefits. These plans are available due to some recent laws passed by Congress. The (administration/personnel) is considering them, but first we would like to get your opinions.

   Pretax savings plans let you deposit some of your pay in a company-sponsored saving account but before you pay income tax on it. The idea is to leave it there until retirement (or in case of a few specific emergencies which stop your income). Since retired people may have less tax taken out of their income than when they were working, they gain by having "sheltered" that money from taxes during their working years, *plus* those pretax dollars have been growing through investment. Congress hoped that these plans would encourage people to set aside some of their own money for retirement.

   Health care reimbursement funds also let you set aside your money before taxes are deducted, in this case for use in paying health care costs that are not covered by insurance. For example, if you need eyeglasses or a routine physical, your expenses can be paid from the money you have in the fund. Since you never pay income tax on this money, it's "worth more" when you use it to pay for these medical expenses. While there's a good deal more to these plans, please answer the following items as best you can, based on what you know at this point.

Exhibit 6-8   Sample employee benefits survey *(continued)*

	(1) Strongly agree	(2) Agree	(3) Disagree	(4) Strongly disagree
I would consider putting some of my pay into a pretax savings plan.	☐	☐	☐	☐
The pretax savings plan sounds like a good way to save for retirement.	☐	☐	☐	☐
It would be a real advantage to me to be able to "shelter" some of my income from taxes.	☐	☐	☐	☐
I like the idea of taking some personal responsibility for my retirement income.	☐	☐	☐	☐

Source: Reprinted with permission from Richard E. Johnson, *Flexible Benefits: A How-To Guide,* 5th ed. Copyright 1996, International Foundation of Employee Benefit Plans, Inc., 18700 West Bluemound Road, P.O. Box 69, Brookfield, WI 53008-0069; 414/786-6710, ext. 8240. All rights reserved. Statements of opinions expressed in this article are those of the author and do not necessarily represent the views or positions of the International Foundation, its officers, directors, or staff.

7. How do current plans relate to these needs?
8. Are costs in line with what the jurisdiction can afford?
9. Is the overall benefits plan competitive?
10. How well do employees understand the benefits program?
11. How easily can employees and beneficiaries receive answers to their questions?

The most important issues concern the needs of employees and the employer. Because of changing demographics, competitive pressures, and budget limitations, the answers to the questions are not static. They evolve, and the benefits program should evolve with them.

Strategies for the future

In the future, five key strategies can reshape a benefits program.

Help employees be mentally and physically fit   EAPs and unpaid personal leave programs beyond FMLA and independent of child care considerations fall into this category. These programs have seen increased implementation and spending since the terrorist attacks on September 11, 2001. Wellness programs help employees make healthy lifestyle choices, and discounted memberships to fitness centers can be available for little or no cost. These programs pay dividends that include reduced medical plan premiums, reduced absenteeism, increased productivity, and reduced turnover.

Establish programs that help employees care for dependents   In recent years this area has developed more rapidly than any other. Programs such as dependent care spending accounts are in place in many jurisdictions and are very popular. Other benefits, such as well baby care and child care referrals and resources, have also become more common. Elder care services and resources are among the fastest-growing benefits today. A 2003 article by the American Association of Retired Persons (AARP) reported that nearly 22 million American workers are caregivers of parents and other loved ones.[12] These employees need help balancing job and family care responsibilities. Most employers already offer some form of job flexibility. However, additional programs, such as estate planning, long-term care insurance, and access to geriatric counselors and social workers, as well as educational materials for employees, should be strongly considered.

Make work more flexible   Technology has made work truly portable, and employees can be instantly accessible from almost anywhere. Employers needing to do more with less continue to find new ways to embrace flexible work arrangements. Web-based access to the workplace can make the virtual office a reality.

With the large number of baby boomers nearing retirement, it will become increasingly necessary for both the employer and the employee to develop forms of phased retirement. This will provide employers with a ready pool of knowledgeable employees for an extended period of time, and will significantly reduce the stress often associated with leaving one's "productive years" behind. Some employers are developing plans that ease employees into retirement over a number of years; some are even looking to the post-retirement population as a recruitment resource.

Provide mechanisms that save time   Time is the twenty-first-century employee's most valuable commodity. Programs that reduce or eliminate the many small, time-consuming tasks of modern life are growing in popularity. They can range from providing employees with resource lists for home maintenance or housekeeping services to providing valet services at reduced costs. Well-conceived benefit programs and, specifically, programs that save time can be very attractive to employees.

Support employees through their financial life cycle.   Benefits such as long-term care, legal services, housing assistance, dependent care, group rates on auto and homeowners' insurance, retirement planning, and tuition reimbursement rank high among employees' priorities. However, the importance of these priorities to the individual employee changes over time. For example, a young employee new to an area may be more interested in housing assistance than in long-term care, yet long-term care may be a very important benefit to another employee in the later years of his or her career. Since the passage of the Long Term Care Security Act, signed into law in 2000, and the changes in many state tax codes, long-term care insurance has seen a growth rate of 18 percent. As baby boomers age and employers offer this benefit via payroll deduction, this trend should only continue.

More than ever, employees need to be educated on their investment and retirement opportunities. Recent business scandals have created a new awareness that employees must take active, personal responsibility for their financial future, and employers are expected to provide the necessary planning tools.

Section 529 plans, in which employees can put aside savings for higher education and incur no federal tax on earnings, remain popular. These plans are open to residents of any state and can be purchased by parents and grandparents. While they do not directly offer these plans, employers can provide information and education to their employees about them.

Similarly, voluntary programs that offer group rates and payroll deductions for auto/home insurance, legal services, supplemental life insurance, and other services generally cost the employer little, yet the convenience factor to the employee is significant. Group purchasing can also reduce employees' fees for health clubs, movie theaters, and other entertainment.

As the cost of mandated benefits rises, employers may not want to add optional benefits. But voluntary programs can signal to employees that the employer cares about their personal well-being. Maintaining a caring organizational culture while insisting on high performance standards can foster loyalty and group cohesion. Top performers may be less inclined to leave government service, and public employers may find it easier to promote an environment for excellence.

Notes

1 "National Compensation Survey: Employee Benefits in State and Local Governments in the United States, September 2007," 1, bls.gov/ncs/ebs/sp/ebsm0007.pdf (accessed March 26, 2009).

2 Ibid., 24.

3 Ibid., 30.

4 Ibid., 10–11.

5 National Coalition on Health Care, "Health Insurance Costs" (2008), nchc.org/facts/cost.shtml (accessed March 26, 2008).

6 The Kaiser Family Foundation and Health Research & Education Trust, "Employer Health Benefits: 2008 Summary of Findings" (2008), 1, ehbs.kff.org/images/abstract/7791.pdf (accessed March 26, 2009).

7 Evelina Moulder, "Local Government Employee Health Insurance Programs," in *The Municipal Year Book 2008* (Washington, D.C.: ICMA, 2008), 3, 4.

8 "National Compensation Survey: Employee Benefits in State and Local Governments," 27.

9 "Compensation Costs in State and Local Governments, March 1999 to March 2001," *Facts from EBRI* (September 2001), ebri.org/publications/facts/index.cfm?fa=0901fact (July 26, 2003); see also Donald Boyd, "Retiree Pensions and Health Benefits: State and Local Governments Face New Budget Challenges," *2006 Rockefeller Institute Reports on State and Local Government Finances* (April 2006).

10 Internal Revenue Service, "IRS Announces Pension Plan Limitations for 2009" (October 16, 2008), irs.gov/newsroom/article/0,,id=187833,00.html (accessed March 26, 2009).

11 CedarCrestone, "CedarCrestone 2008–2009 HR Systems Survey: HR Technologies, Service Delivery Approaches, and Metrics" (2008), cedarcrestone.com/whitepapers/CedarCrestone_2008-2009_HRSS_WP.pdf (accessed March 29, 2008).

12 American Association of Retired Persons, "Caregiving," aarp.org/life/caregiving/Articles/a2003-10-27-caregiving-balancingwork.html (accessed March 29, 2009).

7

Employee Responsibilities: Setting Expectations

Don A. Cozzetto, Theodore B. Pedeliski, Jonathan Tompkins, and Jonathan P. West

The employment relationship can no longer be viewed as a simple wages-for-work bargain. Over time it has evolved into a highly complex web of mutual rights and responsibilities. Employees now enjoy many statutory rights, such as the right to be protected from racial or sexual harassment. In addition, public employees are protected by constitutional rights, such as the right to due process in adverse personnel decisions. Beyond these legal safeguards, workers also expect to be compensated fairly and to be treated with respect.

But with rights come responsibilities. In their role as employers, local governments have a right to expect workers to perform assigned tasks dependably and to behave in ways that promote the attainment of organizational objectives, and workers in turn are responsible for doing so. Ensuring that employee responsibilities are fulfilled is every bit as important as ensuring that their rights are protected. These rights and responsibilities are often expressed in an organization's code of ethics. Without the full cooperation and productive efforts of their workers, local governments cannot carry out their mandated purposes effectively and efficiently.

This chapter reviews basic employee responsibilities and emphasizes the importance of communicating workplace expectations to employees as clearly as possible. Attorneys often advise managers that they are more likely to prevail during the appeal of an adverse personnel decision when workplace expectations have been clearly communicated to employees. But the truth is that clarifying and communicating expectations is simply the sensible thing to do. Workers cannot be expected to direct their efforts toward the realization of organizational objectives if they have no clear sense of the mission and values of their departments, the way their work efforts contribute to mission attainment, or the way their personal and interpersonal behaviors contribute to or detract from organizational effectiveness.

Expectations of attendance

Guiding principles

- Employees must understand that regular attendance is a basic expectation.
- Repeated absenteeism must be met with counseling and discipline.

Regular attendance is expected of most employees. If they are not at the office or in the field attending to their assigned duties, the ability of the agency to fulfill its mission is severely compromised. Excessive absenteeism has traditionally provided just cause to discipline or terminate employees, and judges and arbitrators have repeatedly affirmed this.

Absenteeism may have any of several causes. The employee may have a drinking problem or may abuse drugs. The employee may have physical or mental disabilities that have an intermittent effect on both work function and attendance. The employee may not consider work responsibility or regular attendance an important priority, or may consider them secondary to family responsibilities, personal business, or even recreational events.

Organizations invest a great deal in their employees as they are recruited, trained, and developed. Because most employees soon become highly valuable human resources, the wise supervisor will not be too quick to discipline or discharge. The reasons behind a poor attendance record should be investigated, counseling sessions held, and referrals made to employee assistance programs when warranted. In many instances, the causes of excessive absenteeism can be addressed successfully without having to resort to discipline or discharge. However, the prudent supervisor will document every instance of absenteeism or tardiness in case it becomes necessary to justify a disciplinary action to a judge or arbitrator.

Attendance and discretionary leave

Organizations that allow employees to use their leave time for discretionary activities with proper notice have noted an increase in requests for day and short leaves. This technically does not become a problem for the agency until the employees

Caution

Government managers should not discourage the use of sick leave for bona fide illnesses, but they are responsible for ensuring that sick leave is not abused by employees. Managers should keep an eye out for patterns of absenteeism or lateness that merit intervention in order to determine the cause and to counsel the employees affected. Some patterns might include

- Employees who are habitually late or absent following weekends or holidays
- Employees whose absenteeism or lateness seems to be associated with a period of great personal stress
- Employees who leave during the day to conduct personal errands (going to the bank before it closes, completing a business deal, seeing a lawyer or other professional)
- Employees who appear to be taking "elective sick leave" for minor annoyances or borderline health problems
- Working parents who elect to use their sick leave for situations covered under the Family and Medical Leave Act (FMLA) (because sick leave is paid and FMLA leave is not).

have exhausted their leave time and none is left for necessary and nondiscretionary leaves. As both public and private organizations move toward more flexible work periods, the tensions will increase between employees who seek more flexible work schedules and accommodations to their life circumstances, and employers who must maintain an orderly work schedule for all employees. (See Chapter 6 for more on leave policies.)

Attendance and family and medical leave

Since 1993, both private and public employers have been bound by the Family and Medical Leave Act of 1993 (FMLA) (see Chapter 5) to allow eligible employees to take leaves of absence for medical reasons that apply to themselves, their spouses, their children, or their parents. The act also permits employees to obtain intermittent leave in limited increments of time.

The FMLA, as well as the Americans with Disabilities Act (ADA), establishes a new set of expectations for employees, employers, and supervisors. Agencies are expected to be accommodating to genuine family and health needs. Employers may not terminate an employee for excessive absenteeism during the period in which he or she is exercising a family or medical leave right.[1] However, employees also have obligations to comply with certain expectations:

- *Notice.* The employee must provide the employer with reasonable notice of his or her intention to take FMLA leave (thirty days' advance notice for foreseeable leave and as soon as practicable for more immediate needs). The employee must also obtain the consent of the employer to take FMLA leave. (In California and Wisconsin, state laws allow the worker to simply notify the employer.)
- *Substitution of leave.* The employer may require the employee (with notice) to substitute any accrued paid vacation leave, personal leave, or sick leave for any part of the twelve-week period of FMLA leave.
- *Certification.* The employer may require the employee to submit certification from a health care provider stating the date on which the medical condition commenced, the probable duration of the condition, and supportive medical diagnoses and facts.

Both employer and employees are expected to be able to work out new work schedules, new productivity goals, compensatory work times, use of substitutes, and revised vacation schedules.

Tips for dealing successfully with attendance problems

Supervisors and managers must

☑ Document all incidents of absenteeism and lateness for each employee

☐ Inform employees about attendance policies, including when the workday begins and ends; make sure employees understand these policies; and impress on employees the requirement to give prior notice of absences and report unavoidable lateness

☐ Inform employees with emerging patterns of absenteeism or lateness about the burdens they create and the disciplinary measures that may be applied

☐ Work with employees to modify schedules or make up time that may have been lost.

FMLA intermittent leave provisions create special problems for employers who have devised no-fault or paid time-off absenteeism policies. Under such systems, employees can take a certain number of days off with reasonable prior notice to the employer. Warnings and disciplinary actions are triggered after the number of grace days allowed within a twelve-month period is exhausted or if the employee does not provide notice. Progressive sanctions can apply, rising ultimately to suspension and termination. Under the FMLA, an employee who has exceeded the maximum number of grace days cannot be denied intermittent or block leave if he or she has demonstrated eligibility for such leave.[2]

Workplace conduct

Guiding principles

- Civility is a two-way street.
- Order and decorum are essential to morale and work productivity.

Employees should be informed that threats, vulgarities, personal insults, and deprecatory statements will not be tolerated.[3] They should also be informed that the public workplace is subject to public scrutiny and public expectations. Employers must remember, however, that civility is a two-way street. Employees develop their own perceptions of proper employer behavior, and they may consider some supervisory behaviors unacceptable (see the "Caution" sidebar below).[4]

Alcohol abuse

Alcohol abuse presents special problems because the recovering alcoholic may be covered by the ADA.[5] However, regardless of the disabling character of the physical condition, the employee is still held to expectations of proper conduct both in the workplace and off duty. The focus on proper workplace conduct should include work-related behaviors (attendance, punctuality, productivity, and customer service) as well as civility. Criminal conduct off duty may constitute grounds for sanctions for a recovering alcoholic just as it would for someone not classified as an alcoholic. It is the conduct that is the issue.[6]

Caution

The following behaviors on the part of supervisors can have a negative effect on employees' conduct:

- Ignoring an employee's complaints or questions
- Criticizing or chastising an employee in front of other employees
- Not believing an employee's story ("My battery went dead and the tow service didn't come for two hours")
- Failing to give recognition for work well done
- Failing to go first to the employee who has become the object of an investigation
- Not expressing sympathy for or interest in an employee's personal burdens
- Not being totally professional in dealing with employees.

Some local governments have implemented a zero-tolerance policy for employees, especially law enforcement officers, who appear for work while under the influence of alcohol. This policy applies even if the employee's blood alcohol level is lower than the threshold for a driving violation.

Off-duty behaviors raise questions, however, because they may have only a tangential relation to job performance and they involve very private choices. The distinction between workplace and private environment may blur when members of a workplace get together for social events. Excessive drinking and inappropriate conduct by employees in such a context may be the occasion for concern and action by managers.

When a jurisdiction bans off-duty public consumption of alcohol by police officers, it treads on some very private ground. Do off-duty social sessions involving department members carry an unintended public message? Would such a ban apply to police having alcohol with their meals in restaurants? Protection of employees' conduct involving alcohol (or tobacco use) is extended in about half of all states; they have laws prohibiting employment discrimination when an employee is engaging in "any lawful activity" or "using any lawful product." While these laws do protect social drinkers and smokers in their off-duty behaviors, they also restrict employers in dealing with employees who are unable to perform their jobs when health problems associated with that activity arise.

Drug abuse

Many local governments follow the lead of the federal government to create a drug-free workplace using a three-pronged approach: detection, rehabilitation, and educational awareness.

Drug testing can be initiated before hiring and can continue after employment begins. The pre-employment examination, seen as a basic condition for employment, screens out users of drugs without consideration of the applicant's on-the-job performance. While it does involve an intrusion into the applicant's privacy, applicants have advance notice of the test and can avoid that personal cost by not applying. And in point of fact, the very process of being considered for a position carries with it an expectation of reduced privacy since a prospective employer scrutinizes the applicant's full employment history and all job-related variables.

fyi

Drug-free workplace

Following terms of the Drug-Free Workplace Act of 1988, public organizations are required to

- Publish a policy statement notifying employees that it is unlawful to possess, manufacture, dispense, or use a controlled substance in the workplace
- Specify actions (including the possibility of termination) that will be taken if the policy is violated
- Establish a drug-free awareness program that requires employees to be informed of
  - The dangers of drug abuse in the workplace
  - The person's responsibility in maintaining a drug-free environment
  - The availability of counseling, rehabilitation, and employee assistance programs.

Post-employment drug (or alcohol tests) can be administered

- As part of a periodic medical examination
- As part of an investigation of an accident involving the employee
- If there is reasonable suspicion, based on certain facts, that the employee is using drugs (as indicated by impairment)
- Randomly if the employee is in a position with a zero tolerance for drug or alcohol impairment.

Interpersonal relationships: On and off duty

Guiding principles

■ Employers need to make their employees aware of the possibility that workplace relationships can lead to sexual harassment claims and resentment among co-workers.

■ In adopting policies affecting the marital activities of workers, the public employer ought to have a legitimate governmental interest in mind for the courts to sustain such policies.

Challenges

■ Developing fair workplace policies that protect consenting adults who date or fraternize against sexual harassment claims without fostering employee resentment, impeding normal co-worker interaction, or violating employees' privacy

■ Deciding whether there is a clear nexus between an employee's off-duty activity and the employee's job performance or the proper functioning of the public agency

Dating and romance

The workplace is a popular arena for interpersonal relationships: friendships, domestic partnerships, and romances. Over the past decade, public employers have been developing policies that deal with dating and fraternization issues.

The development of these policies is a natural extension of the development of guidelines and training programs to deal with sexual harassment. Employers have discovered that when workplace relationships turn sour or involve exploitation, the victimized employee may initiate sexual harassment claims. Workplace romances between employees and superiors, however consensual in character, may raise the same issues of pressure and exploitation that come up in cases where the advances are unwelcome. Romantic alliances between employees in power-differentiated positions may also engender feelings of resentment among other co-workers and give rise to cases of "reverse sexual harassment," in which employees who may qualify for advancement or job rewards feel that they were passed over in favor of the employee who has a special relationship with the superior.[7]

Court decisions of the 1970s affirmed the power of agencies to put moral litmus tests on employment, generally accepting at face value the agency's concern for "moral discipline" and a proper public image. For many years the courts also limited fundamental privacy rights to legal marriage relationships. By 1985, however, a federal court ruling on the discharge of a police officer for cohabiting with a woman not his wife adopted a different analysis of the privacy interests involved. The court found that a concern for "community morals" was insufficient to allow

Tips for policies on personal relationships in the workplace

☑ Recognize that the public agency has no legitimate interest in interfering with co-worker relationships other than ensuring that the relationship does not affect employee morale, employee productivity, or agency functions.

☑ Restrict dating between co-workers in power-differentiated relationships.

☐ Maintain an open-door policy to allow employees involved in a supervisor-subordinate or other power-differentiated relationship to discuss their situation with appropriate managers. Supervisors should usually let employees take the first step toward such a discussion unless other employees express concern.

☐ Encourage employees to report to appropriate managers or supervisors any relationships that cause them concern.

☐ Ensure that one of the involved parties does not have decision-making authority over the terms and conditions of employment of the other party and does not have a role in the latter's performance appraisal process.

☐ Allow for reasonable attempts to accommodate the interests of the couple and co-workers through modification of work schedules, restructuring of jobs, and arrangement of job transfers.

☐ Give all employees full notice of the policy and make compliance a condition of employment.

☐ Specify what sanctions come into play if violations occur. For instance, if a violation has led to favoritism, bias, preferential treatment, harassment, or disruptive incidents, disciplinary action up to termination may be taken.

Source: Adapted from Dan J. Schaner, Exhibit 1: Model Co-Worker Dating and Fraternization Policy, in "Romance in the Workplace: Should Employers Act as Chaperons?" *Employee Relations Law Journal* 20 (Summer 1994): 66-67.

public employers to discipline workers for engaging in extramarital sexual activity, given the fact that the activity did not have any effect on the ability of the parties to perform their jobs.[8] The key question that public employers must address in the case of nontraditional lifestyles pursued by employees is whether there is a clear nexus between the off-duty activity and the employee's job performance or the proper functioning of the public agency.

Since the 1980s public employers have retreated from penalizing employees who are cohabiting. This has paralleled the repeal in several states of statutes that criminalize adultery and fornication. But new issues have emerged with same-sex relationships. In 1997 the federal Court of Appeals for the Eleventh Circuit dealt with a public employment issue that involved homosexual marriage and religious liberty.[9] The attorney general for the state of Georgia withdrew an offer of employment after discovering that the job candidate had gone through a religious marriage ceremony that had joined her and another woman in marriage. The rejected candidate filed suit, alleging that the employer had interfered with her constitutionally protected rights of intimate association, religious exercise, and expressive association. The public office justified the withdrawal on grounds that the same-sex marriage would raise issues in conflict with current interpretations of Georgia law and would interfere with prosecutorial actions. In addition, the attorney general stated that he simply could no longer "trust" the candidate. The circuit court decided that no fundamental rights were abridged by the office and gave great weight to the fact that a prosecutor's office must have full discretion in hiring those employees in whom it can place its full confidence.

Nepotism

Concerning themselves less with off-duty relationships than with on-duty relationships, a growing number of employers, especially those in the public sector, have implemented nepotism rules.[10] These rules follow the general trend toward regulating interactions between related employees who work together in power-differentiated positions. In other words, one member of a working couple cannot be in a supervisory position over another or affect the terms and conditions of the other's employment.

For instance, if one member of a couple is a supervisor, he or she shall not in any way participate in the evaluation or determination of salary levels or conditions of employment of the other member. The fact that a supervisor's name appears on a document relating to the terms and conditions of the spouse's employment can be regarded as a prima facie conflict of interest.

Nepotism rules also prohibit one member of the same immediate family from working in such proximity to the other that interference in job performance might result. The rules require that when these close relationships occur in the workplace, one of the couple (usually the less senior employee) must be transferred or discharged. These nepotism rules have come at a time when more women are entering the workplace and more workers are marrying people they meet at work.

Couples adversely affected by the nepotism rules have challenged these policies, arguing that the policies violate not only their fundamental and constitutional right to marry,[11] but also the Fourteenth Amendment equal protection clause through the disparate impact these rules have on women in the workplace. In 1995, federal courts ruled on three separate cases that challenged nepotism rules.[12] In one case in which one spouse was a nurse employed by a hospital and the other was a helicopter pilot employed by an air-ambulance service under contract with the hospital, the employer went so far as to call for the transfer of the married employee. In each of the three cases, the federal courts affirmed the power of the public entities to restrict the working conditions of married co-workers. The courts decided that, while there is a fundamental right to marry, the test of a policy is whether it creates a direct legal obstacle that would actually forbid employees from marrying.

Policies affecting the marital activities of workers are also covered by the rational-basis test. That is, such policies will be sustained if they can be shown to advance a legitimate governmental interest, such as minimizing workplace conflicts, decreasing the possibility of sexual harassment claims, or ensuring the equitable treatment of all employees.

Relationships between life-sharing workers are to be assessed by the same rules as those between married workers: managers should maintain an open-door policy and make accommodation efforts (see the tips box on the previous page). The employer's reactions toward peer-level romantic relationships should also be limited to those situations that affect employee morale, employee productivity, or agency functions.

Use of public property: Computers and the Internet

Guiding principles

- Agency policies must clearly spell out the boundaries of what personal use of government equipment can be allowed.
- Rules must be enforced equally for all job classes and ranks.

Challenge

- Deterring Internet abuse while allowing exploration and creative use of the Internet to improve government functioning

In government, both managers and rank-and-file employees uphold a public trust. In some jurisdictions, the political culture may tolerate some use of public properties for personal use. This practice is seen as part of the perquisites of office. But in the past several years, employers have moved toward a no-tolerance policy for the personal use of public properties, a policy that extends to all ranks of employees.

The workplace environment is replete with items that can be used for personal benefit. From phones, photocopiers, and computers to office supplies, the employee is constantly tempted to use these items for personal needs because they offer convenience. Thus, agency policies must clearly spell out the boundaries of what can be allowed in terms of personal use. The agency is also responsible for educating its employees as to the more stringent expectations that are found in the public sector as opposed to private corporations, where personal use of equipment and resources may be allowed as a job perquisite. Isolated incidents of misuse can not only erode a climate of trust and integrity but also become epidemic.

Probably the most acute problem involving the use of public property is the use of agency computers and their online capabilities. The term *personal computer* is often taken literally, even though the equipment is public and its intended use is for government business only. Computers can be used for cruising the Internet not only for work-related information but also for personal applications. Some employees may use their e-mail privileges for communication of the most personal nature or may waste time talking in chat rooms. Abuse rises to a more serious level when employees use these channels of information to access and download pornographic or hate material. The intrusion of such material into the workplace sows the seeds for harassment and discrimination suits. Employees may also post or download material that violates copyright laws. In 1997 Congress passed the No Electronic Theft Act, which makes it a federal crime to distribute or even possess unauthorized copies of copyrighted material even when no profit is involved.[13] Employees should also be warned to be careful in posting information that may provide grounds for defamation suits.

Because the First Amendment prevents government from stifling free speech, government has little control over employees who establish their own Web pages on their home computers. Although these Web pages represent an employee's own expressive activity and do not tie up the employer's equipment, they are certainly not private. Rather, they become accessible to everyone and thus may become an issue for the local government if the Web site reveals conduct that is not in the interest of the agency.

At present, the law is unsettled in terms of restrictions that can be put on public employees' use of the Internet. A 1998 decision by a federal district court in Virginia struck down as unconstitutional a Virginia law that prohibited state employees from

Tips for successful online policies

☐ Create a policy that prohibits use of work time or agency equipment or resources to access adult or other information that has no relation to work responsibilities and that may disrupt the workplace.

☐ Distribute written and electronic copies of the policy to all employees and take steps to update it regularly.

☐ Inform employees if the agency plans to monitor Internet usage. The agency should follow through on its monitoring even that means only occasional spot checks.

☐ Consider letting employees surf the Web on their own time if they stay within written guidelines.

☐ Trust employees to use common sense when working with the Internet just as they are trusted in the use of any other agency property or resource.

Source: Ian Logan, "You Are Being Watched," *PC World* 15 (November 1997): 245-253.

accessing sexually explicit material on state computers except when agency heads had certified that such material was required for bona fide state projects.[14] The judge found that the law restricted employees' ability to "read, research, and discuss" controversial topics that were a matter of public concern. However, the court did recognize that the state is entitled to guard the productivity of its employees against distraction and has a right as well as a legal duty to avoid the creation of a hostile work environment. The court noted that the statute involved was not sufficiently inclusive, that it ignored the limitless variety of disruptive computer activity (e.g., accessing online video games, chat rooms, shopping sites, and use of e-mail for non-work-related topics), and that it left open the question of valid restrictions on computer or Internet abuse under regulations that are carefully tailored to target disruptive activity rather than content of information.[15] Two years later, however, the decision was reversed. In that case, the judge ruled that the state's restriction on sexually explicit materials on computers that are owned or leased by the state is constitutional because it regulates state employees' speech only in their capacity as state employees and thus is consistent with the First Amendment.[16]

E-mail should be recognized as an open letter box. Managers as well as employees should be aware that everyone can read everyone else's mail. Public managers, especially those in states that have open-records and open-meeting laws, should also recognize that their files are open. In one state, the attorney general ruled that e-mail discussions and straw votes on a personnel decision were open records.[17] As a result, the press published messages exchanged between members of a state board, splashing colloquial speech, personal characterizations, and confidential remarks across news pages. Exhibit 7–1 is a sample county e-mail policy.

Different approaches have been suggested to deter or sanction Internet abuses. These approaches can include blocking sites (which is expensive and not fully reliable) and monitoring employees. Monitoring can prevent some Internet abuses, but it must be approached thoughtfully. For one thing, it demands a great deal of time from supervisors, and the costs may outweigh the benefits. For another thing, it is regarded as an invasion of workplace privacy and can thus foster resentment and the motivation to move on to another employer. For tips on discouraging Internet abuse, see the tips box above.

Exhibit 7-1   Sample policy for employee use of e-mail

The county e-mail system is county property and may be used for county business. The system is not to be used for employee personal gain or to support or advocate non-county-related business or purposes. All use of the e-mail system is subject to management access pursuant to the following policy.

1. Incidental and occasional personal use of e-mail is permitted, but such messages will be treated no differently from other messages. Any personal message can be retrieved by the county even though it has been deleted from an individual's in-box. Assume that any e-mail message you are drafting will be made public, and draft it accordingly.

2. No computer system is completely secure. The e-mail system is not intended to transmit sensitive materials such as personnel decisions, legal opinions, or confidential material that may be more appropriately communicated by written memorandum or personal conversation.

3. Employees may not intentionally intercept, eavesdrop, record, read, alter, or receive another person's e-mail message without proper authorization in accordance with this policy.

4. This policy applies to all employees, contractors, part-time employees, volunteers, or other individuals provided with access to the county's e-mail system as necessary for business with the county.

5. Employees' e-mail communications should be routinely and regularly deleted from their in-boxes.

6. Under no circumstances shall any employee use the e-mail system for messages that could reasonably be considered as injurious or offensive to others on the basis of race, sex, age, sexual orientation, religious or political beliefs, national origin, or disability. Inappropriate e-mail messages can give rise to claims of discrimination, harassment, defamation, emotional distress, and copyright infringement.

7. Solicitation of funds, political messages, and harassing e-mail are prohibited.

8. Use of the county e-mail system for personal business, whether profit or nonprofit, is prohibited.

9. The county may access e-mail messages within the county system of all individuals covered by this policy for any purpose not specifically prohibited by law. If practicable, employees will be notified in advance of such access or receive notice within a reasonable time after the access. Employees will be notified of date of access, purpose of access, and identity of person who accessed the information, and information obtained.

10. Employees are informed that their department managers or county commission may disclose to parties within or outside the county the contents of e-mail sent to and between individuals covered by this policy without the permission of the individuals if it serves the interests of the county or the public.

Source: Adapted from the policy of Grand Forks County, North Dakota.

A lawyer for the Electronic Frontier Foundation has diagnosed much of the trepidation about Internet misuse as "fear of the future." A prudent approach may be simply to monitor the functioning of the offices to see if productivity or agency focus are affected in any way. In general, adaptation will eventually lead to better-functioning agencies.[18] Certainly, the online capabilities of Web pages and e-mail put an agency into more direct contact with its clients and members of the public.

Confidentiality

Guiding principle

- Public employees have an ethical obligation to guard the confidentiality of personal information under their control.

One of the primary expectations attached to a position involving information management is that confidentiality will be preserved. Public agencies develop and record a wide range of information on individuals and businesses that is essential to the execution of government functions. These records include personal and financial information on clients, convicts, patients, wards, recipients of public payments, contractors, parties under regulation, and public employees. Public agencies have an ethical obligation to keep this information confidential and restricted to those with a bona fide need to know. Thus, the local government must provide employees with policies and procedures based on relevant state and local laws regarding confidentiality of and open access to public records.

The increasing reliance on computerized information networks makes it more difficult for managers of public records to keep these records confidential. Employees should be thoroughly briefed on security measures involving passwords, blocked information, read-only access rules, and restricted access to printers. The faxing of information to other parties—even to allied agencies—should be strictly controlled.[19]

Confidentiality of records needs to be especially protected where release of information could reasonably be expected to constitute an "unwarranted invasion of privacy." Although this is a subjective concept, a number of states (e.g., California and New York) have specified what constitutes such an invasion.[20]

Political activity

Guiding principle

- Managers and supervisors should not abuse their power and bring political activities into the workplace.

Challenge

- Becoming thoroughly familiar with the political activity laws of both the state and the local jurisdiction

At the federal level, the Hatch Act of 1939 was for decades a major restraint on federal employees' involvement in political activity.[21] Apart from voting, most forms of political participation were closed to federal employees. An amendment passed by Congress two years later extended the act to state and local workers whose agencies' activities were federally funded. In 1993 Congress passed the Hatch Act Reform Amendments, which substantially relaxed the restrictions on political activity and stipulated that employees should be encouraged to exercise fully and freely and without fear of penalty or reprisal their right to participate or refrain from participating in the political process of the nation.[22] Actually, the amendments reflect the rules on the political activities of public employees that have evolved at the state level and have been codified in "little Hatch Acts." These state laws vary widely but focus on managers and supervisory personnel more than on rank-and-file workers. They particularly focus on deterring abuses of power that involve power-differentiated relationships.

Statutory prohibitions on political activity or influence in administration

- Any use of authority to coerce or influence an agency action or decision
- Any requirement or pressure from a superior to an employee to contribute to any political fund
- Any personnel action that includes a condition that an employee give or withhold political contributions
- Any recommendations or job evaluations that are based on political affiliations or political opinions expressed by the employee
- Any provision of lists or names of employees to any political candidate or organization
- Any direct or indirect offer to a government employee of an increase in compensation or salary by any person seeking elected or appointed office.

In addition, all state political activity statutes implement what is known as politics-workplace separation. Some states indicate that there should be no solicitation of election campaign contributions on public premises,[23] no political activity during working hours, and no political activity by an officer or public employee while in public uniform.[24] However, no simple guidelines can answer all the questions about the proper bounds of political activity by government employees. It is, for instance, unclear whether a public employee can engage in political activity on behalf of a spouse, or whether the officer of an agency can be a delegate to a party convention or a campaign manager for another candidate. Managers must become thoroughly familiar with the political activity laws of their states and their local jurisdictions.

Off-duty activities

Guiding principle

■ A government employee should be proscribed from holding a second job only if it directly conflicts with the employee's public duties.

A complex question for managers in the public sector involves whether managers themselves or their employees may hold other offices, private or public, or engage in other employment. This issue covers a wide range of circumstances:

- A public employee seeking to hold a political office, such as a seat on a city council or school board
- A public employee holding a directorship in a corporation—for instance, serving on a bank's board of directors
- A public employee offering his or her talents as a consultant in a particular field of expertise or running a consultation service out of his or her home
- An appointee to a public executive position completing terms of contracts he or she entered into before being appointed
- A public employee substantially augmenting his or her income with honoraria from speaking engagements
- An employee taking a part-time job outside normal work hours
- A public professional donating his or her services to a cause.

These situations are covered by common law and by explicit constitutional and statutory provisions that vary from state to state. In addition, home-rule cities may develop their own rules with regard to the outside income activities of municipal employees. There might be provisions on this topic in an organization's ethics code as well.

According to common law, the holding of one office does not, in itself, disqualify an officeholder from simultaneously holding another job or contract, provided that there is no conflict of interest in the functions of the two offices and that one office does not extend its regulatory net over the other.

State constitutions and statutes are more explicit in barring dual activities. The most common restriction aims to preserve a separation of powers by preventing a person who has a position in one branch from holding a position in another branch that can make policy or exercise authority over the first position (one cannot be superior and subordinate at the same time). Thus a police officer—an employee of the executive branch—cannot hold a position in a legislative forum, city council, or state legislature. Some states at one time forbade state employees, including university faculty members, from serving as state legislators. Those statutes are now generally being relaxed to allow employees to take leaves of absence from their employment while a legislature is in session.[25]

A basic problem is determining whether a government employee's outside activity gives rise to a conflict of interest or an incompatibility with the employee's primary public duties that warrants its forfeiture. A government employee should be proscribed from holding a secondary job only if that job directly conflicts with the employee's public duties. For instance, a public health inspector should not own a business he or she is required to inspect. Similarly, a police officer may be precluded from working in or operating an establishment that serves alcoholic beverages or from engaging in off-duty process serving, since those activities can involve the officer in civil disputes.[26]

---

fyi

Guidelines restricting outside employment and activity

Full-time government employees are permitted to engage in outside employment subject to the following restrictions:

- Employees will not engage in any employment, with the exception of military service obligations, that will interfere with the proper performance of city (county) employment. Employees shall report to work refreshed and ready to work.
- Employees will not accept pay or compensation from anyone for work time while they are on duty with the city (county).
- Employees will not engage in employment that would interfere with a worker's obligation to his or her primary employer (e.g., being on call to respond to emergencies).
- Employees are prohibited from working for any contractor or company that has a current contract with the city (county) or for an employer that would constitute a conflict of interest with the city (county).
- Employees will not accept or solicit private work while they are on duty or as a result of their employment with the city (county).

Source: Adapted from "Employee Reference Guide," City of Grand Forks, North Dakota, 1998.

Exhibit 7-2   Issues to be included in a professional code of conduct or ethics manual

Policies

Outside employment and activities

- Limits on off-duty earnings (not off-duty income)
- Permitted off-duty contracts, engagements for teaching and lecturing
- Research, writing, and publication of material that is agency related or that covers agency functioning
- Profits and royalties from such publication; on-duty/off-duty use of time to produce publications
- Attendance at conferences at agency expense (guided by job relatedness)
- Honoraria for engagements that are agency related and/or are for activity during agency time
- Participation in civic activities (generally encouraged but commitments may be limited in time) and use of comp time to cover such participation
- Limits on political activities

Relationships between employees of different ranks

- Exchange of gifts and gratuities between upper-level and lower-level employees; de minimus gifts (birthday recognitions, employee farewells, etc.)

- Fraternization between upper-level and lower-level employees

Conflicts of interest

- Employment of relatives
- Contracts with the city
- Use of public equipment, facilities, or personnel for private gain

Conduct

- Zero tolerance for harassment
- Zero tolerance for threatening or violent behavior

Confidentiality of information

- Adherence to open-meetings and public-record laws

Procedures

Where to seek advice
How to declare a possible conflict
Where to report improper behavior

Key ordinances and state statutes

Source: Partially adapted from Office of the Mayor, *Ethics Manual* (Orlando, Fla.: City of Orlando, 1995).

Generally, state statutes confer almost plenary powers on the local hiring and appointing authority to define and proscribe those activities that are inconsistent with the duties and responsibilities of the officers and their employees. (Exhibit 7-2 presents a list of issues that might be included in a local government ethics manual.) But once those ethics policies for local government are established, the agency or office will still need to deal with each case on an individual basis. An employee has a particular responsibility to come forward with any information on outside employment or income activity that can be considered collateral employment. The manager of the agency and the employee must review the situation together to determine the permissibility and scope of this outside activity.

The manager must then follow through with an assessment of the employee's performance to determine whether the outside activities have not only raised conflicts of interest but also negatively affected job performance (as evidenced by increased absenteeism or tardiness, decreased alertness at work, or decreased quality of performance).

Honoraria are another issue of outside activity that must be evaluated by agencies. State and local governments have expressed an interest in limiting appearances and honoraria where such activity would interfere with the government's interests as an employer. That interest includes avoidance of dual compensation for officers or employees and use of agency time to qualify for the honoraria. Ambiguous situations arise when an agency officer represents the agency or presents agency views. Some agencies require that officers turn over any honoraria to agency accounts. And officers cannot request travel reimbursements from the agency when the costs of travel are borne by those making the invitation. Again, this is one area in which an agency should have a policy in place.

Residency

Guiding principle

■ Managers should communicate any residency requirements to job candidates during their initial interviews.

Local governments have a long history of imposing residency rules on their employees.[27] These rules have taken several forms:

- Jurisdictional residency rules that require employees to live within the jurisdictional boundaries of the government for which they work
- Geographic or distance rules that require employees to live within a certain distance of their workplace
- Durational rules that require job applicants to be residents or become residents within a specified period
- Job-specific rules that apply to some classifications of employees (e.g., police, firefighters, medical emergency crews, school administrators) and not to others.[28]

Employees and their unions have challenged these rules, alleging that they are unreasonable and violate the rights of privacy and travel and a "fundamental" right to live wherever individuals may choose. In dealing with these rules, however, both federal and state courts have generally avoided the issue of whether residency is a fundamental right and instead used a rational-basis test to measure the validity of the rules. They have tended to strike down durational rules that bear no relation to the recruitment of persons with the proper qualifications. They have also struck down efforts to retroactively enforce residency rules after a period of nonenforcement. However, they have upheld rules of continuing residency, distance, and job-specific residency requirements. In short, the courts have taken a balancing approach to residency requirements, deciding in favor of the rules where the city can advance valid governmental objectives and against the rules only when the requirements impose genuine hardships on the workers.

Residency rules across the country present a checkerboard of approaches. In California, the state constitution bars jurisdictional residency rules but allows geographic residency rules. Montana and Kentucky require public employees to be registered to vote in the jurisdictions in which they work, affirming their stake in the community and their accountability to the people they serve. Michigan is one state where unions gained the right of public employees to collectively bargain residency issues. At least eleven states recognize that the residency of employees is distinctly a local issue that should be worked out with local authorities.

Since residency requirements are a condition of employment, managers should communicate these requirements to job candidates during their initial interviews. If a candidate is qualified for the position, the local government may provide listings or realtor references to assist the new employee in obtaining suitable and affordable housing within the jurisdiction.

Communicating expectations and responsibilities

Guiding principles

- All employees must be fully informed about what is expected of them in their jobs.
- The communication of rules and requirements through handbooks or manuals must be periodically reinforced with memos, fliers, and verbal reminders.
- Rules must not dominate the work process. Managers should emphasize shared principles in pursuit of the agency's mission rather than the workplace rules.

As emphasized in the preceding sections, employees have certain responsibilities to their employers. Management has the right to expect employees to attend work regularly, carry out assigned duties in a productive and cooperative fashion, ensure that work performance is not adversely affected by the use of drugs or alcohol, avoid entangling personal relationships that might undermine morale or create conflicts of interest, respect norms of privacy and confidentiality, and refrain from using public property for personal benefit.

But administrators cannot rightly and fairly hold employees accountable if they do not make their expectations known. Managing the workforce to best advantage requires the clear communication of expectations of performance, workplace behaviors, and adherence to agency objectives. These expectations can be communicated through several channels: job interviews and orientation, handbooks, memos, posters on bulletin boards, training in workshops, meetings with supervisors, and online.

Codes of ethics

Ethics codes help to communicate organizational norms and expectations for people who work both inside and outside government. Codes reflect the organization's collective consciousness and specify what is good or bad and right or wrong in an organization's behavior (see Exhibit 7–2 on page 227). Ethics codes can be categorized as aspirational, restrictive, or hybrid. Aspirational codes go beyond legal strictures and focus on norms of desired behavior, such as personal integrity or public service. Restrictive codes draw attention to permissible and impermissible behaviors, as well as to investigations and sanctions for violators. Hybrid codes combine elements of aspirational (need for fair treatment) and restrictive (avoiding conflicts of interest) provisions.[29] Specific code provisions can be further categorized as duty based, principle based, virtue based, and consequentialist, with duty as the core of the public service ethic.

Thus, codes are frequently composed of "don't" statements (don't divulge confidential information) as well as tenets listing obligations (seek no favor), responsibilities (provide clear, complete, understandable responses to the public), virtues and values (exercise compassion), and aspirations (show dedication to democratic government).[30] Code-related guidance can help signal to individuals and groups the ethical values of the organization. To be meaningful, codes should clearly state principles, expectations, and responsibilities and address potential ethical dilemmas that might confront organizational members.

An organization's code of ethics should pay attention to both the content of the document and the process of formulating that content. The process should involve open dialogue and be inclusive, transparent, and collegial. Ideally it would be developed in a participative environment with widespread employee involvement.

Among the challenges in writing a code are deciding how abstract or concrete it should be; how comprehensive it should be; whether it should apply to those in elected as well as appointed positions, and to part-time as well as full-time employees; whether it should contain principles exclusively or include behavioral guidelines as well; how and to what extent organizational members should be held accountable for its provisions; and whether it should include a strict investigative and enforcement mechanism.[31] Developing, discussing, assessing, revising, and communicating the ethical code can keep it vital and useful as a "living" document. However, some codes are written and then forgotten or benignly neglected, which spells trouble sooner or later. The principles and practices expressed in the code should permeate the organizational culture and be viewed as part of a larger system designed to promote ethical conduct.[32]

Ethics codes have been both criticized and praised. Critics complain because, among other things, codes may lack organization, precision, priorities, and clear guidance. They may also lack definitions of key terms and sanctions, and consistency of application. Further, codes can be coercive, spawn red tape, restrict options, and reduce managerial flexibility. They can be merely symbolic and ineffectual, serving as a substitute for careful thought.

Supporters, by contrast, contend that codes serve a number of useful purposes. Rightly conceived and executed, they regulate, instruct, and inspire organizational members; enable enforcement of shared standards; and alert those outside the organization of what they can expect. Advocates of codes argue that codes provide a framework for analyzing decision alternatives, encourage high standards of behavior, offer a basis for evaluating performance, strengthen organizational identity and commitment, and increase public confidence. Further, they contend that codes can deter unethical acts, raise ethical consciousness, provide protection to employees from unreasonable demands by superiors, and aid in adjudicating disputes among organizational members.[33]

Personnel policy manual

Employers should provide all employees with a handbook or manual that specifies in writing all personnel policies and rules. The handbook establishes a reciprocal set of responsibilities for employer and employee. It tells employees what is expected of them in the workplace and what they can expect from their employer in terms of fair treatment. The range of issues that demand policies in order to prevent or resolve employer-employee conflicts has grown substantially in kind and number. A comprehensive employee handbook should cover all the issues listed in the sidebar on page 231.

Conduct policies and workplace rules do not require the legal specificity used in hearing procedures but must pass a "reasonableness" test. That is, whether the local government is an at-will employer or can, under state law, terminate employees only after finding just cause (see Chapter 5), local policies and workplace rules laid out in a personnel handbook should provide "a reasonable employee" with advance notice of what would be regarded as cause for discipline or termination.

Handbooks will indicate the range of behaviors that provide grounds for disciplinary action or termination. (Exhibit 7–3 on page 232 provides an example of work rules regarding misconduct that can lead to dismissal or other disciplinary action.) Under the federal model, "just cause for termination" has been interpreted to include any conduct, on or off duty, that impairs the performance or disrupts the functioning of an agency. Certain offenses against the state or the employer, such as theft, résumé fraud, fighting, insubordination, and workplace assault, can be

Contents of a comprehensive employee handbook

- At-will employment disclaimer and acknowledgment form *(see Chapter 5)*
- Employment rights as recognized by the local government or as codified in state law or federal statutes
  - Equal employment opportunity statement *(see Chapter 5)*
  - Rights under such statutes as the Fair Labor Standards Act (FLSA), Equal Pay Act, Americans with Disabilities Act (ADA), Family and Medical Leave Act (FMLA), Pregnancy Discrimination Act, and Age Discrimination in Employment Act (ADEA)
- Agency or city procedures governing appointments, promotions, and transfers
- Pay policies (raises, bonuses, temporary increases, incentive pay, travel expense reimbursements, overtime), including method of payment, pay schedule, and final payment
- Benefits attached to employment (pension, health insurance, life insurance)
- Procedures for evaluation and review of performance
- Employee records, access, confidentiality/privacy/ application of open-records laws
- Code of ethics *(see Exhibit 7-2 for a list of issues that might be covered in a professional code of conduct or ethics manual)*
- Work rules
  - *Attendance*
    Holidays
    Vacations
    Sick leave, notice, documentation
    Personal and family leave

Bereavement leave
Jury/witness duty
Military duty
Donated time/compensatory (comp) time/ flexible time
Lunch breaks/rest periods
- *Use of equipment*
  Telephone, computers, e-mail *(see Exhibit 7-1),* software
  Agency vehicles, office supplies
- *Conduct and misconduct*
  Dress code
  No-smoking policies
  Drug- and alcohol-abuse policies
  Sexual, racial harassment *(see Exhibit 5-1 for an example of a harassment policy)*
  Fraternization policies
  Workplace civility
  Misconduct (behaviors that trigger notice, counseling, and possible disciplinary action) *(see Exhibit 7-3)*
- *Corrective and disciplinary procedures*
  Handling of complaints
  Investigations
  Notice
  Discussion, counseling, employee assistance programs
  Mediation and arbitration
  Hearings, appeals
- *Channels of communication*
  Suggestions
  Changing work rules
  Grievance procedures

prima facie evidence of just cause. But not all misconduct can provide just cause to suspend or remove an employee. Generally, the misconduct must be substantial. Occasional absenteeism, neglects of duty, rudeness, horseplay, and violations of dress codes or other work rules may not be sufficient to establish just cause.

The policies contained in the employee manual should be repeatedly communicated to employees through various verbal and written channels, such as the orientation meetings for new hires and periodic memos to all staff. Public employers who simply hand the manual to their employees and have them sign affidavits that they have received and read it are remiss in their responsibility to ensure that employees are properly informed about the rules that may be applied to them.

Exhibit 7-3   Sample work rules

[Employer] is concerned for the safety and well-being of all of its employees. For this reason, certain rules are necessary to ensure a safe work environment. The following, ranging in degrees of severity, is a partial list of categories of improper conduct that, when engaged in, shall constitute grounds for disciplinary action, up to and including immediate dismissal:

- Use of alcohol or drugs while on duty
- Unauthorized possession of a weapon on work premises
- Sleeping while on duty
- Assaulting a co-worker, supervisor, or other employee
- Punching another employee's time card
- Theft of company property
- Insubordination

- Falsifying records, reports, or information of any nature
- Any other serious misconduct that *[employer]* believes warrants immediate dismissal.

The following, ranging in degrees of severity, is a partial list of categories of improper conduct that, when engaged in, shall constitute grounds for progressive discipline:[1]

- Smoking in areas not designated for smoking
- Engaging in horseplay
- Tardiness or absenteeism
- Leaving work before scheduled quitting time
- Failure to punch time clock
- Creating unsanitary or unsafe working conditions

1   Progressive discipline means, for instance, that a first offense incurs an oral warning; a second offense, a written warning, a third offense, suspension; a fourth offense, dismissal.

Since the employee manual is vital in communicating the parameters of workplace conduct, it should itself be a model of good communication. The best-written policies are succinct and written in language that is understandable on first reading.[34] Because employees increasingly react to adverse employment decisions with litigation, and regard the manual as a definitive contract that limits the employer to the specific "causes of actions" within it, employers must avoid including language suggesting that the manual is such a contract. Rather, the manual should include a statement to the effect that the provisions within it are informational and that the city or agency reserves the right to interpret any provision and to change the policies with reasonable notice to employees. The rules should allow employers to exercise discretion in dealing with personnel problems.

Reserving some measure of discretion on conduct issues also allows supervisors to reasonably accommodate an employee's unique situation. The employee manual draws a narrow line between expectations of scrupulous adherence to work rules and relaxation of rules in special circumstances. In treading this fine line, the employer should aim at consistency. In fact, inconsistency in this regard opens the door to charges of favoritism or discriminatory and disparate treatment of employees.

Despite the counseling efforts of supervisors, disciplinary action sometimes becomes necessary (see Chapter 8). One of the primary tests of just cause is whether workers have been given adequate notice of what is expected of them and the probable consequences that will follow if those expectations are not met. This is one of the reasons that it is so important for personnel manuals to clearly set forth workplace rules and expectations. However, an employee manual containing

Caution

- Avoid legal jargon in communication information on procedures or conduct. (The following, for instance, would be considered legal jargon: "Employees filing a claim of discrimination shall refer to Section 3406 of the City Code and move to demonstrate that they are members of a protected class and establish a prima facie case of disparate treatment.")

- Avoid language that creates an enforceable contract, particularly with regard to guarantees of continued employment.

- Avoid conduct rules that precisely lay out prohibited behaviors and do not provide for sensible discretion by supervisors and administrators to deal with related behaviors that negatively affect the organization.

- Avoid draconian rules that do not allow for some flexibility and corrective action (e.g., a rule that holds that an employee who is absent for two consecutive days without giving notice to the department head shall be considered to have abandoned his or her job and is liable for termination).

long lists of do's and don'ts gives the appearance of an old-style military personnel manual, reflecting distrust of employees and a desire for maximum conformity. Such expressions of distrust and conformity are inconsistent with the contemporary view that valued human resources should be trusted, treated with respect, and given considerable flexibility in determining how best to carry out their delegated tasks.

Perhaps the best solution to this dilemma is to ensure that employees read and understand the behavioral rules set forth in the employee manual, so that disciplinary actions can be sustained, and thereafter to emphasize the shared principles that will guide pursuit of the agency's mission rather than the workplace rules. This approach is consistent with what has come to be known as principle-centered leadership.

Job interviews and orientation

Some policies in the employee manual and ethics code may need to be communicated to a job candidate in his or her interview. These would include, for instance, provisions that require an employee to live within the city. Most candidates are informed of an agency's equal employment opportunity policy during the initial interviews. And a candidate who may have a spouse or relative already employed at the agency should also be informed of the agency's nepotism policies.

A new employee's job orientation session should thoroughly familiarize the new hire with the company's workplace policies and ethics rules. This orientation should be given on the first day of employment or as soon thereafter as practicable. Both the human resource director and the supervisors under whom the employee will be working should be involved in the orientation; the presence of the supervisors shows a new employee that these managers are ready to answer questions and help him or her to succeed. As each section of the handbook and code is introduced and explained, the employee should have full opportunity to ask questions. The individual conducting the orientation should not be surprised by the naïveté of new employees, even those with degrees and professional training.

The orientation session should also clearly indicate to the employee how to use reporting and appeals channels. Each department should have a reporting procedure that provides at least two places for an employee to go with a complaint. This procedure should include a bypass channel for the employee's supervisor. An employee should not have to report harassment or abusive behavior to the harasser (see Chapters 5 and 8).

The employer should also provide for feedback on the orientation session, allowing the new employee to evaluate the session and its usefulness in a questionnaire. Typically, this would include such questions as the following:

- Did you think the orientation session was helpful in preparing you for your job?
- What part of the orientation was most useful? Least useful?
- Was any part of the orientation unclear? On what issues?
- Have you reviewed the employee handbook and ethics code? Do you have any questions about them?
- Have your supervisor and co-workers been helpful in familiarizing you with the job and your department?
- Do you have any questions about employment with the city?

Supervisors

Supervisors also play an important role in communicating expectations to employees. Supervisors represent the authority of their parent organizations and are charged with maintaining a productive and safe work environment. They therefore need to direct and control the conduct of employees through verbal guidance, written comments, rewards, and discipline. (All these supervisory activities come together in the performance evaluation process discussed in Chapter 3.) Supervisors are also the primary conduits of information both to and from employees. In a real sense, supervisors represent the personification of a department's policies; they make the pages of the employee manual and ethics code come alive.

Many supervisors consider themselves first as specialists in their own field—whether it be engineering, fiscal management, or some field of public service—and second (if at all) as human resource specialists. However, a supervisor must wear two hats. All supervisors should have special training in the whole panoply of policies, provisions, and work rules in the employee manual and ethics code.

Tips for successfully communicating expectations to employees

☐ Communicate all policies affecting the employer-employee relationship through a written employee handbook.

☐ Hold orientation sessions for new employees in which agency policies are described, explained, and discussed.

☐ Train all supervisory personnel in the agency's workplace policies and ask them to convey these policies to subordinates on a day-to-day basis.

☐ Educate employees on new policies and changes in existing policies.

☐ Use a variety of methods of communication to educate employees about personnel policies.

They should also expect continued education in changing policies. Various newsletters are published to keep human resource personnel up-to-date on developments; supervisors can be provided with subscription copies or be on a circulation list for such materials. A knowledgeable supervisory crew can be an agency's best line of defense against employee discontent or problems.

Unfortunately, in both overt and subtle ways, a supervisor can also create personnel problems damaging to the agency. For instance, a supervisor might discriminate racially in job assignments to placate prejudiced subordinates, or might use banter to reprimand male workers for workplace failings while responding to women's shortcomings in harsh or vulgar terms. In the extreme case, a supervisor might engage in sexual harassment. These possibilities make it all the more important to train supervisors well.

Changing policies

Any amendments to existing policies must be carefully drafted and communicated to employees, and all contrary language must be eliminated. In the case of changes that have their source in court decisions, the employer should wait until legal counsel has thoroughly analyzed the decisions before communicating them. Administrators should be careful in making any amendments or changes that affect or revoke benefits, such as vacation or sick leave, that an employee may have already accumulated.

Employee participation in changing work rules

While administrators bear the responsibility for formulating work rules, the input of employees can be crucial for arriving at rules that are realistic and inspire employee compliance.

Employers may set up either formal or informal procedures for employee participation in work rule formulation and amendments. A process involving changes in the rules and codes could provide for

- Appointment or election of employees to serve on policy committees
- Prepublication of changes or amendments to work rules
- Solicitation of comments from employees on changes or amendments
- Meetings for employees during which proposed rules are explained, discussed, and justified.

Involving employees in the formulation of personnel policies is important not only in identifying potential problems but also in communicating expectations. As in the initial job orientation sessions, trainers legitimize work rules and codes by explaining why the rules or provisions have been made and demonstrating their reasonableness. For instance, a requirement that city garbage workers wear protective eye gear, shirts, and steel guard shoes may seem onerous and picky, especially when those workers are sweltering for hours in temperatures around the 100-degree mark. However, reference to the injuries or health problems that result from noncompliance with such rules can provide the justification that makes them acceptable.

Discussion of conduct rules should continually emphasize the need to maintain respect for all co-workers in the organization. The objective is to develop a knowledgeable workforce with a sense of professionalism from bottom to top.

Communicating changes in rules

Once rule changes are finalized, they must be communicated to all covered employees. Proper notice of rule changes may be made via several channels:

- Loose-leaf additions to each employee's manual or code
- Publication in the department newsletter (with commentary)
- Posting on employees' e-mail
- Posting in prominent workplace locations (lunchrooms, restrooms)
- Notification included with paychecks.

Conclusion

Managers can limit disciplinary problems by leading with integrity. People in charge must be above reproach. A discovery of modern management theory is that managerial ethics matter to employees—and matter a lot.[35] Ethics matter from the perspective of the manager strengthening his or her self-respect, from the perspective of employees trusting their superiors enough to follow their lead, and from the perspective of a successful agency being able to attract and retain the most competent and dedicated public servants.

An important aspect of setting expectations is to see that messages are consistent and clear. Nothing diminishes the integrity of a manager as much as a set of mixed messages. In changing environments where both managers and rank-and-file employees are challenged to know more, to adapt technologically, to be more accountable, to be innovative, and to do more with less, the messages must be consistent and on target.

Notes

1 Robert M. Howie and Laurence A. Shapiro, "How Long Is Enough? Leaves of Absence as Reasonable Accommodation under ADA," *Employee Relations Law Journal* 29 (Fall 2003): 33–49.

2 Christopher Snow and Sarah Campbell, "Recent Changes to Federal Employment Laws Will Affect Utah Companies: Examining the ADA Amendments and New FMLA Regulations," *Utah Bar Journal* 22 (March/April 2009): 18–24; Eric Schweitzer and Luci Nelson, "Just When You Thought You Understood the Family and Medical Leave Act," *South Carolina Lawyer* 20 (March 2009): 38–43; Brian F. Jackson and Howard R. Flaxman, "Intermittent Leave and Reduced Leave Schedule: Traps for the Unwary under the Family and Medical Leave Act," *Employee Relations Law Journal* 20 (Summer 1994): 29–46. See also Richard J. Reibstein, "The FMLA and Absenteeism," *HR Focus* 73 (August 1996): 3; Robert B. Gordon and Christopher L. Ekman, "Attendance Control Issues under the ADA and FMLA," *The Labor Lawyer* 13 (Fall 1997): 393; and Arthur F. Silbergeld and Stacie S. Polashuk, "Chronic Serious Health Impairments and Worker Absences under Federal Employment Law," *The Labor Lawyer* 14 (Summer 1998): 1–22.

3 Pamela Johnson and Julie Indvik, "Rudeness at Work: Impulse over Restraint," *Public Personnel Management* 30 (Winter 2001): 457–465.

4 Kirstin D. Grimsley, "Leaner—and Definitely Meaner: The Growing Problem of Incivility on the Job Is Hurting Profits as Well as Feelings," *Washington Post National Weekly Edition*, July 20–27, 1998, 21.

5 Paul E. Starkman, "Answering the Tough Questions about Alcoholism and Substance Abuse under the ADA and FMLA," *Employee Relations Law Journal* 25 (Spring 2000): 43–77; Ann C. Hodges and Douglas D. Scherer, "The Employment Law Decisions of the October 2000 Term of the Supreme Court," *Employee Rights and Employment Policy Journal* 5 (2001): 391–449; John E. Matejkovic and Margaret E. Matejkovic, "What Is Reasonable Accommodation under the ADA? Not an Easy Answer," *Mississippi College Law Review* 28 (2009): 67–103.

6 Theresa Johnson Holt, "Alcoholism and Misbehavior: Implications of the ADA," *Labor Law Journal* 47 (November 1996): 729–734.

7 Dean L. Schaner, "Romance in the Workplace: Should Employers Act as Chaperons?" *Employee Relations Law Journal* 20 (Summer 1994): 47–71.

8 *Briggs v. North Muskegon Police Department*, 746 F.2d 1475 (6th Cir. 1984), *cert. denied*, 473 U.S. 909 (1985).

9 *Shahar v. Bowers*, 114 F.3d 1097 (11th Cir. 1997).

10 James Podgers, "Marriage Traps in the Workplace: Nepotism Rules Make It Harder for Spouses to Be Colleagues in Public Sector," *ABA Journal* 82 (January 1996): 46–47.

11 Cases supporting this position include *Ross v. Stouffer Hotel Co.*, 816 P.2nd 302 (Hawaii 1991); and *Hughes v. Lipscher*, 906 F.2nd 961 (3rd Cir. 1990).

12 *Parks v. City of Warner Robins*, 43 F.3d 609 (11th Cir. 1995); *Waters v. Gaston County*, 57 F.3d 422 (4th Cir. 1995); *Wright v. Metro Health Medical Center*, 58 F.3d 1130 (6th Cir. 1995).

13 The act signed into law by President Clinton on December 16, 1997, does not contain traditional fair-use exemptions such as those allowing photocopying by libraries and academic institutions, or quotation for the purposes of review or criticism.

14 *Urofsky v. Allen*, 995 F. Supp. 634 (E.D. Va. 1998).

15 Ibid. at 639–640.

16 *Urofsky v Gilmore*, 216 F.3d 401 (4th Cir. 2000).

17 North Dakota Attorney General Open Records and Meetings Opinion, 98-0-05 (March 3, 1998). E-mail messages are subject to open-record and records-retention laws. Straw votes conducted over e-mail raise troubling questions.

18 Quoted by John Schwartz, "New Cultural Battleground Comes with a Mouse," *Washington Post National Weekly Edition*, February 23, 1998, 22–23.

19 Kathleen A. Frawley, "Confidentiality in the Computer Age," *RN* 57 (July 1994): 59–60; and Note: "Keeping Secrets in Cyberspace: Establishing 4th Amendment Protection of Internet Communication," *Harvard Law Review* 110 (May 1997): 1591–1608.

20 For typical inventories of information given statutory protection, see California (Government) Code § 6254 (West 1997); and New York (Civil Rights) Law § 50a, New York (Civil Service) Law § R79.1, 80.8 (McKinney 1997).

21 53 Stat. 1147, 1939, 80 Stat. 525, 1966, codified in 5 U.S.C.A., §§ 7321–7323.

22 P.L. 103-94, 107 Stat. 1001, 1993, codified in 5 U.S.C.A., §§ 7321–7325.

23 See, for example, McKinney's *Consolidated Laws of New York Annotated*, Civil Service, Subdivision 3: Section 107.

24 See, for example, West's *Annotated California Code—Government* §§ 3206–3207.

25 For an earlier discussion on this issue, see Carlton J. Snow and Elliott M. Abramson, "By the Light of Dual Employment: Standards for Employer Regulation of Moonlighting," *Indiana Law Journal* 55 (1979–1980): 581–614.

26 See *Long Beach Police Officers Association v. City of Long Beach*, 759 P.2d 504 (Cal. 1988).

27 Richard A. Posthuma, "A Balanced Approach to Residency Rules for Local Government Employees," *Government Union Review* 13 (September 1992): 46–73.

28 See, for example, Brian R. Johnson, Greg L. Warchol, and Vic W. Bumphus, "Police Residential Requirements: An Exploratory Analysis," *Journal of Collective Negotiation in the Public Sector* 26 (Winter 1997): 43–64.

29 Jonathan West, "Ethics and Human Resource Management," in *Public Human Resource Management: Problems and Prospects*, 5 ed., Steven W. Hays, Richard Kearney, and Jerrell D. Coggburn (Upper Saddle River, N.J.: Prentice Hall, 2008).

30 See James Svara, *The Ethics Primer* (Sudbury, Mass.: Jones and Bartlett, 2007), chapter 5.

31 Montgomery Van Wart, "Codes of Ethics as Living Documents," *Public Integrity* 5, no. 4 (2003): 331–346.

32 See Carol Lewis and Stuart Gilman, *The Ethics Challenge in Public Service* (San Francisco: Jossey-Bass, 2006), chapter 8, and Jonathan West and Evan Berman, *The Ethics Edge* (Washington, D.C.: ICMA, 2006).

33 Mark Frankel, "Professional Codes: Why, How, and with What Impact?" *Journal of Business Ethics* 8, nos. 2–3 (1989): 109–115.

34 For a guide to the preparation of a good employee manual, see Jean d'Agenais and John Carruthers, *Creating Effective Manuals* (Cincinnati, Ohio: South West Publishing Co., 1985); also see Stephen E. Befort, "Employee Handbooks and Legal Effect of Disclaimers," *Industrial Relations Law Journal* (now *Berkeley Journal of Labor and Employment Law*) 13 (1991/92): 326–381, see "Lack of Clarity," 353f.

35 Bob Lewis, "The Ethical Manager Knows How to Apply the Right Motivational Tools," *InfoWorld* 19 (November 10, 1997): 134.

8

When Things Go Wrong

Charles R. Wise, Brian Clemow, Saranne P. Murray, Lisa B. Bingham,
Arlene J. Angelo, and Siegrun Fox Freyss

Even in jurisdictions with professional managers, well-trained supervisors, care-fully drafted personnel policies, and procedures designed to ensure that the policies are followed, things go wrong. Potential problems range from the macro level to the individual employee—from an economic recession that can reduce revenues so severely that cutback management becomes the overriding concern of the employer, to a poorly performing employee who can occupy a substantial amount of the employer's time and energy.

This chapter begins by addressing the problem of cutback management, a consequence of macrolevel circumstances. However, the bulk of the chapter focuses on the micro level. People are human, mistakes are made, and problems arise that require attention. The test of a well-managed human resource operation is not how many personnel problems arise but how effectively the employer addresses them. Where significant litigation is involved, legal counsel generally will coordinate the response. However, there are many other common personnel problems that government managers can effectively resolve merely by following a sound plan of defense.

This chapter is intended only as a first reference for local government managers who see trouble brewing. It is much more cost-effective in the long run to consult counsel early, when a problem starts to develop, and to get advice about how to anticipate a claim and prepare a defense, than to wait until the sheriff serves the jurisdiction with notice of a lawsuit.

Cutback management

Guiding principles

- Jurisdictions should have a policy on cost reductions in place before a recession and a decline in revenues occur.
- Employers should weigh the benefits and drawbacks of various cost-cutting approaches involving the workforce.

Challenges

- Finding cost-cutting measures that will bring the budget into balance while minimizing disruptions for employees
- Retaining the strongest employees and maintaining a high-performance culture despite a reduction in resources

Since payroll tends to be the largest budget item in local governments, a significant drop in revenue requires a critical look at staffing levels. Chapter 3 has a section on downsizing the workforce, focusing on how to determine whom to lay off and what documents to consult. This chapter broadens the discussion and summarizes additional cost-cutting approaches in the human resource area.

Laying off employees is one option available to employers, but it may not be the best one. A hiring freeze is often the first step: it is easy to administer and less demoralizing than other approaches in that it does not create identifiable victims. But the consequences of a hiring freeze need to be carefully analyzed and selectively overridden to ensure that mission-critical positions are filled.[1] Another consequence of a hiring freeze can be poor morale, which management needs to monitor and acknowledge. Employees may be affected by a larger workload, and they may fear, justifiably so, that a freeze may be followed by layoffs. Employers are advised to be transparent in their plans and actions, and to be vigilant about false rumors that may fill blogs and e-mail boxes.

A survey of public employers conducted by the International Public Management Association for Human Resources (IPMA-HR) in November 2008 found that a hiring freeze was the first action taken; the second was cutting costs by restricting travel and reducing training expenditures.[2]

A third option can be a freeze on any pay increases or even a pay reduction. The percentage of the pay reduction can be applied across the board or progressively, with the highest-paid executives and professionals accepting the steepest reduction. A fourth option can involve incentive pay for early retirement. This may indeed remove some of the highest-paid employees from the payroll, but there may be unanticipated consequences as well: some of the strongest, most marketable employees may accept the incentive pay, retire, and then join the corporate sector.

Furlough, a temporary layoff from work, may be the next option. Depending on the amount of money that needs to be saved, the furlough can be a few days per months or whole weeks. To keep morale up, all ranks, from the chief administrative officer on down, should participate in the furlough. And whatever benefits the employer provides, from health insurance to life insurance, should continue. The temporary layoff can also be made optional. If the family finances allow it, parents with dependent children or with elder care responsibilities may welcome a less stressful lifestyle.

When the reduction-in-force (RIF) is permanent, bumping rights may come into play. Instead of laying employees off directly, the employer may grant the targeted employee the right to bump another person in the same job class but with less seniority.

Some jurisdictions abolish programs and departments and contract the work out instead. Research indicates that in such instances, the city or county needs proper legal advice in writing the contract as well as in administering it. Well-defined, concrete services are easier to contract out and to monitor for compliance than soft services that require a lot of discretion.[3]

Finally, the employer can create an unpaid internship program and use volunteers to supplement the paid staff. The efforts of Los Angeles County can serve as a model. When an economic downturn in the 1990s made it difficult to staff departments adequately, the county's department of human resources and local universities created a partnership. The county identified work that could be done by an undergraduate or graduate student, and the universities advertised the learning opportunities and provided the interns.[4]

In general, employers should develop a cutback policy before an economic downturn requires drastic steps in order to ensure an orderly, well thought-out approach.[5] If the workforce is unionized, the collective bargaining agreement should contain provisions on how to proceed. Civil service rules and other agreements should contain guidelines as well. (Also see Chapter 3.)

Discipline and discharge of employees

Guiding principles

- The first step in discipline is a reasonably thorough yet timely investigation into the alleged employee misconduct.
- Discipline should start at the lowest appropriate level and work up to more significant penalties.
- Disciplinary action should proceed independent of any criminal prosecution proceedings.

Challenges

- Balancing the right of the employee to ventilate a perceived grievance against the interests of the public agency
- Preventing internal dissent from escalating into workplace misconduct
- Handling employee termination in a way that does not leave the organization open to liability

One of the most common personnel problems faced by public and private sector employers alike is dealing with unacceptable performance, conduct, or behavior on the part of individual employees. An appropriate response to such problems is one that focuses on correcting the problem, if possible, but that resorts to discipline and ultimately discharge if the employee fails to achieve a satisfactory level of improvement.[6]

Investigating and documenting employee misconduct

The first step in discipline is a reasonably thorough yet timely investigation into the alleged employee misconduct. When a manager takes disciplinary action prematurely, without having first conducted an investigation, that action is more likely to be overturned by a court or an arbitrator, usually because the manager missed some important facts. Ordinarily, a manager will want to hear what both the employee and witnesses have to say and determine what evidence there is before recommending discipline. If a public manager follows the steps outlined in the sidebar on page 242, it is more likely that the final disciplinary action will be reasonable and withstand scrutiny.

A gray area emerges with behaviors that may reflect dissatisfaction, disloyalty, or dissent but that do not rise to a confrontational level. These acts of noncompliant behavior can invoke the protections of the First Amendment for the expressive employee, especially if the workplace or supervisor/subordinate conflict can be characterized as a "matter of public concern." Whistle-blowers, for example, may certainly disrupt an agency with their principled disobedience, but they are protected if their revelations involve issues of public interest and agency accountability.

Managers tread a fine line in dealing with speech they find disruptive. Each circumstance requires a balancing between the right of the employee to ventilate

Steps to take before recommending discipline

For any event that may give rise to discipline, the manager should

- Interview each eyewitness
- Collect and safeguard any original documents that may be relevant and make copies for legal counsel
- Collect physical evidence (such as broken equipment or an altered time card) and store it securely, making sure that clear records of the chain of custody (the people who had access to the evidence) are maintained in order to protect against claims later that evidence was tampered with or manufactured
- Examine what discipline has been imposed on other employees who have committed the same or substantially similar acts of misconduct
- Interview the employee (in the presence of a union or other representative if *Weingarten*[1] is applicable, as discussed on page 245) to determine whether there are any mitigating circumstances or considerations specific to the employee that should be taken into account
- Inform the employee of the charges and the evidence, giving him or her an opportunity to respond or explain before discipline is imposed (see the section on *Loudermill*[2] on page 245)
- Consult with counsel about the investigation if the charges are likely to be serious and contested
- If the conduct is also subject to a criminal prosecution, collect all court documents before they are sealed as part of a plea bargain arrangement; time may be of the essence, for example, in getting access to witness affidavits that are part of the arrest warrant.

1 *NLRB v. Weingarten, Inc.,* 420 U.S. 251 (1975).
2 *Cleveland Board of Education v. Loudermill,* 470 U.S. 532 (1985).

a perceived grievance and the interests of the public agency. Since 1968, following the landmark Supreme Court case *Pickering v. Board of Education,*[7] the courts have assessed these conflicts between employees and their public employers and determined that the public employer can validly assert the following interests:

- The effect of speech on the conduct and discipline of the other employees
- The effect of speech on harmonious relations among the employee's co-workers
- The effect of speech on the employee's job performance
- The breach of relationships that require personal loyalty and confidence
- The effect of speech on the function of the agency.

A disruptive impact can be broadly interpreted to extend to effects beyond the immediate workplace, such as an undermining of confidence in the agency. More recently, the U.S. Supreme Court has given greater discretion to public supervisors in dealing with disruptive speech in the workplace. In the 1994 case *Waters v. Churchill,*[8] the Court upheld a hospital supervisor's right to fire an employee who criticized the department and her superior before trainees. Even though the disruptive statements were "surrounded by protected speech," the statements were not immunized from sanction. The Court held that the supervisor, prior to moving to terminate the individual, had conducted an investigation from which she could reasonably conclude that the statements were actually disruptive. (See Chapter 5 for more on First Amendment protections of speech in the workplace.)

Managers have a responsibility to deal with internal dissent and prevent such dissent from escalating into workplace misconduct. The open door is the manager's first line of defense. The second line of defense is early intervention: calling in an employee to discuss his or her problems. A third preventive action is keeping on top of small issues. Employees can become irritated about issues that seem minor to others, such as the location of a workstation near a draft or away from windows. In dealing with an employee's complaint, it is important to make inquiries of other employees. A manager may find that more than one employee's comfort quotient is affected.

After the employer has decided on appropriate disciplinary action, it is critically important to document for the employee's personnel file both the action and the results of the investigation that preceded it. Even a verbal reprimand can be documented through a memorandum recapping the date and basis for it. These documents can refresh a supervisor's memory if there is ever a need for testimony on the events that gave rise to the discipline. They can also provide evidence of progressive disciplinary action and establish just cause to dismiss when the employee persists in the misconduct or performance problem. Due process concerns and most collective bargaining agreements require that the employee receive a copy of any notice of discipline and of any records placed in his or her permanent file.

Progressive discipline, affirmative discipline, and just cause

One of the most widely accepted principles of personnel management is the concept of *progressive discipline*. The theory is that discipline should start at the lowest appropriate level and work up to more significant penalties. Employers should terminate employment only as a last resort, when an employee is unable or unwilling to respond to less drastic disciplinary measures. Progressive disciplinary steps might include

- Informal counseling
- Oral warning or reprimand
- Written warning or reprimand
- Minor (one to five days) suspension
- Major (more than five days) suspension
- Discharge.

Of course, it is not always appropriate to start at the lowest rung of the disciplinary ladder. For a significant offense, many employers start with a written warning or suspension, and it is generally accepted that certain major offenses (such as stealing from the employer, drinking on the job, or assaulting a supervisor) call for immediate dismissal. It may also be appropriate to skip certain steps of progressive discipline for certain offenses. For example, many employers think suspension is an inappropriate response to absenteeism since it effectively compounds the underlying problem.

A sometimes faster alternative method to progressive discipline is *affirmative discipline*. In this approach the problem employee signs a contract (also called an action plan or a plan for improvement) specifying the steps that he or she will take to overcome the problem behavior and detailing the consequences, including employment termination, in case of noncompliance. This approach puts the pressure on the employee to improve performance and show commitment to stay with the organization. The affirmative discipline approach can also be combined with features of the progressive technique, in that a verbal discussion about the performance problem can take place days or weeks before the contract is signed, and one violation of the contract may lead to a temporary suspension rather than to an immediate dismissal.[9]

Determining just cause: The Daugherty standards

- Was the employee aware (or should he or she have been aware) of the rule or standard he or she is accused of violating?
- Was the rule or standard reasonable?
- Did the jurisdiction conduct a reasonable investigation into the alleged wrongdoing or misconduct?
- Was the investigation fair?
- Has it been convincingly established that the rule or standard was violated?
- What mitigating or aggravating factors are present in the employee's work history (length of service, prior discipline, etc.)?
- Have comparable situations occurred in the past, and if so, how have the employees involved been treated?

Source: Adolph M. Koven and Susan L. Smith, *Just Cause: The Seven Tests,* 3rd ed. (Edison, N.J.: BNA Books, 2006).

The principle underlying an appropriate response to disciplinary problems is often referred to as *just cause.* This phrase is used in the vast majority of collective bargaining agreements to define acceptable disciplinary action, and it has been carried over into nonunion settings as well. To determine whether there is just cause for discipline in a given case, managers should ask themselves the questions shown in the sidebar above. These questions are sometimes called the Daugherty standards[10] after Carroll R. Daugherty, a famous arbitrator who helped popularize them. A wide range of other considerations may also come into play, depending on the specific circumstances involved.

Loudermill, the right to appeal, and other procedural issues

Before disciplinary action is taken, the employer should be aware of any procedural requirements that apply. All too frequently, even though an employee is proven guilty of an offense and the disciplinary action that is taken is appropriate, that action is nevertheless overturned because the employer violated applicable procedural protections.

In most cities and counties, disciplinary action is subject to appeal, either through a civil service or personnel appeals board, or through the contractual grievance procedure in a union contract. To be sure that the action will stand up under review, it is important not only that the offense be documented and proven but also that the punishment fit the crime. In many cases, the range of appropriate discipline for a particular type of offense may be commonly understood; in others, the employer should have established and disseminated a listing of offenses and applicable penalties. In any event, the reviewing body usually has the authority to decide not only the employee's guilt or innocence but also the reasonableness of the punishment.

In the public sector, any discipline of an employee is considered to be a government action since the employer is a governmental entity. Under the U.S. Constitution, any government action that deprives any individual, including an employee, of a property or liberty interest, such as employment, must comply with the principles of due process. One of these principles, the U.S. Supreme Court has ruled, is that an employee charged with an offense must have an opportunity to respond to the charges before he or she is dismissed *(Cleveland Board of Education v. Loudermill)*.[11] Even if the employee has a legal or contractual right to a post-termination hearing, he or she must nevertheless have a pre-termination opportunity to hear the accusations and offer an explanation or any response he or she wishes to present. This is called a *"Loudermill* hearing," after the case in which the Court first articulated the requirement.

In all likelihood, other procedural requirements are applicable as well. Most collective bargaining agreements contain such protection for union members, and often there are requirements imposed by public sector collective bargaining laws or rulings by state labor relations agencies. For example, private sector principles such as *Weingarten* rights are often carried over to public sector employees. Under the *Weingarten* doctrine, unionized employees who are required to attend interviews from which they reasonably anticipate that disciplinary action may result are entitled to union representation if they request it.[12] A federal court of appeals has extended this right to nonunion employees as well. Many municipal ordinances, regulations, and personnel rules also contain procedural protections for employees.

Specific situations requiring special consideration

Certain types of disciplinary situations call for the application of special consideration. In some cases, this is because specific legal requirements come into play; in other cases, practical concerns require a different approach from normal disciplinary situations.[13]

Sick leave abuse and other attendance problems   There are two general types of employee attendance problems with which employers often must deal. One is excessive absenteeism or tardiness; the other is misuse or abuse of sick leave or other similar benefits.

Excessive absenteeism or tardiness is generally dealt with as a matter of progressive discipline, perhaps (as noted above) skipping the suspension step of the procedure. Some employers have defined numerical thresholds for different types of discipline so that employees know that a certain number of days or occurrences of sick leave within a stated period of time will result in a specific disciplinary response. In other situations, employers impose discipline on a case-by-case basis when absenteeism becomes unacceptable by any reasonable standard. Even a single instance of sick leave abuse, however, may result in serious discipline. That is because fraudulent use of paid leave for purposes other than the employee's personal illness is a form of theft from the employer.

The key in these cases is to demonstrate that the employee knew the limitations of the employer's sick leave policies and took sick leave knowing that he or she was not entitled to do so. In any disciplinary action involving attendance problems, however, it is important to establish that the employer's expectations were clearly communicated to the employee and that the employee was unwilling or unable to meet those expectations.

Alcohol and drugs   In cases where substance abuse is involved, it is essential to draw a distinction between prohibited behavior, such as possession or consumption of alcohol or controlled substances in the workplace, and the employee's status as an alcoholic or drug-dependent person. Under various antidiscrimination statutes, it is risky for employers to discipline or discharge employees simply because of alcoholism or drug addiction. These are often considered to be illnesses that call for treatment, not discipline.[14] However, even an alcoholic or drug addict may be prohibited from possessing alcohol or drugs on the employer's premises, or from consuming or being under the influence of such substances during working hours. Discipline for these offenses should be handled in the same manner as it is in other cases, even if the employee claims to have a substance abuse problem and requests treatment.

In dealing with issues involving substance abuse, a manager must untangle the various laws and regulations that establish the public employer's obligation to its employees who demonstrate substance abuse. This includes the Rehabilitation Act of 1973,[15] the Americans with Disabilities Act (ADA),[16] and state statutes and administrative rules.

Following the federal examples of Section 501 of the Rehabilitation Act of 1973 and the Comprehensive Alcohol Abuse and Alcohol Prevention Treatment and Rehabilitation Act of 1970 and its amendments of 1979,[17] states and their subdivisions have set up evaluation and treatment programs as well as accommodations for the disability of alcoholism. The issue becomes one of establishing the parameters of accommodative and rehabilitative efforts intended to make the employee a dependable and fully functioning worker.

If the alcoholism is tied to excessive absenteeism, critical absenteeism (absence from a critical meeting or call of duty), disruptive incidents involving other employees or superiors, or job snafus, the employee's conduct or performance is what provides the grounds for discipline or termination. As long as the employee is not sanctioned "solely by reason" of his or her alcoholism, the employer may proceed.

In cases where alcohol may be the reason for an employee's poor performance, the supervisor may want to confer with the employee, pointing out the performance problems and advising about available counseling services if the performance problems are caused by personal or health issues. If the employee subsequently refuses help and his or her performance continues at an unsatisfactory level, the supervisor is to provide a clear choice between submitting to counseling and cooperating with treatment, or accepting the consequences of unsatisfactory performance.[18] It is the employee's responsibility to meet the requirements of his or her diagnosis and treatment programs. Should the employee refuse to cooperate with treatment efforts, the supervisor is justified in invoking the hard option of the choice given the employee.

Alcohol consumption may lead to criminal conduct, the most frequent manifestation of which is driving under the influence (DUI). When the conduct occurs off duty, the issue is whether the incident affects the public agency or the job performance of the employee. A DUI conviction can provide cause for dismissal if it involves criminal behavior, creates bad publicity for the organization, or compromises duties such as law enforcement.[19] Courts have noted that while an alcoholic's disability may have compelled that person to drink, it did not compel that person to drive a motor vehicle or engage in other misconduct. DUI convictions may result in the suspension or loss of driving privileges, and if a driving license is a necessary job qualification, loss of those privileges may provide grounds for at least transfer or demotion of the employee.

Employer representatives should be careful not to accuse an employee of having an alcohol or drug problem unless the evidence is overwhelming. Otherwise, the employee may claim that he or she is being discriminated against because of a perceived disability. A better approach is to offer the employee help if he or she admits to a problem, rather than requiring treatment for a problem that the supervisor has perceived but the employee has not admitted.

The ADA explicitly exempts from coverage any employee or job applicant who is currently engaging in the illegal use of drugs, and court decisions have made it clear that the ADA may not be used as a shield for illegal conduct. That is, the ADA's protection does not extend to an employee who enters a rehabilitation program only after being confronted with the fact that his or her employer is aware of illegal use. The Equal Employment Opportunity Commission construes the phrase "currently engaged in illegal use of drugs" as applying to use that may have occurred weeks or even months prior to discharge, and the ADA's protections apply to persons in long-term recovery, not to persons just entering recovery.

However, borderline cases abound. What about an employee who has successfully completed a program, relapses, and then voluntarily checks back into a rehabilitation program? While the courts have held that such a person exercises current use, administrative discretion might appropriately decide that the person should be given a second chance at rehabilitation.[20] Here again, however, a clear employer policy allowing only one opportunity for leave to undergo treatment for substance abuse may well justify refusal of a second chance.

One additional variable in these challenging cases is the coverage provided by the Family and Medical Leave Act (FMLA).[21] FMLA regulations state that when an employee takes leave for substance abuse treatment, he or she has exercised his or her right to do so under the FMLA, and the employer may not take action against that individual for taking FMLA leave. However, the door still remains open for taking action against the employee for violating a provision of the employer's substance abuse policy. This conflict has not yet been resolved by the courts.[22]

Threats and violent behavior   Threats and violent behavior on the part of an employee may give rise to legal claims by co-workers and others with whom the offending employee comes into contact. Therefore, employers in such situations must respond quickly and decisively. It may even be appropriate to remove the employee from the workplace immediately, preferably suspending him or her with pay until a *Loudermill* hearing is conducted, in order to protect others from harm and the jurisdiction from liability.

As with substance abuse, threatening or violent conduct on the part of an employee may be the result of an illness or another personal problem for which treatment is appropriate before an employer resorts to discipline. Sources of violence include competitive pressures, loss of autonomy, changing workforce demographics, domestic dysfunction, and victimization by nonemployees.[23] It is important to develop a policy and encourage a climate in which employees can communicate their concerns. There are several ways to do this. For example, an employee assistance program can provide an employee with referrals to counseling and assistance outside the workplace. An employee ombudsman program can provide confidential, in-house facilitation for work-related problems or concerns. An accessible grievance procedure is important for communicating claims of harassment or threats. If these resources are available and an employee fails to use them, the employer's position in any subsequent litigation will be stronger. An employee who declines such assistance generally cannot later claim to have been entitled to

fyi

Identifying potentially violent employees

Although there is no way of knowing for sure whether an employee may become violent, below is a list of factors or warning signals that may help an employer identify potentially dangerous employees.

- Has the employee recently had personal problems outside of work—for example, a death in the family or a divorce?
- Does the employee have a history of violent tendencies either at or outside of work?
- Does the employee have severe mood swings or suffer from depression?
- Does the employee have an alcohol- or drug-abuse problem?
- Is the employee resentful toward authority? Is the employee engaged in running conflict with a supervisor?
- Has the employee's work performance suddenly deteriorated?
- Does the employee keep to himself or herself?

Some of these symptoms (or actions) alone—particularly behavior that harms or threatens persons or property—may be grounds for dismissal depending on the situation. The risk of violence increases when several warning signals are present. An employer who suspects that an employee may be violent should contact its labor counsel, offer supervisory counseling, and consider referring the employee for professional counseling.

Source: Robert L. Levin, "Workplace Violence: Navigating through the Minefield of Legal Liability," *Labor Lawyer* 11, no. 171 (1995): 181-182.

---

treatment rather than discipline. In recent years many public organizations have adopted "zero tolerance" policies.

In assessing the conduct of employees, a manager must keep in mind the distinction between an employee's acceptable speech and unacceptable disruptive conduct. Some behaviors speak for themselves: assaults, threats, bringing a weapon into the workplace, pervasive outbursts of profanity, destruction of property, insults. They create a hostile environment, not unlike that defined by the courts in sexual harassment cases. It is an environment that makes it difficult for employers to do their jobs. The worst cases actually create a clear and present danger to other employees.

Criminal misconduct   Theft, assault, and other behavior that violates criminal statutes may also be grounds for disciplinary action. However, as discussed below, discipline is appropriate only if the conduct occurs in the workplace or has some demonstrable nexus to the job.

If discipline is appropriate, it is important to keep such action independent of any criminal prosecution that may occur. Many employers make the mistake of suspending an employee pending the outcome of criminal prosecution. The problem with this approach is that many prosecutions do not result in conviction but rather in a decision not to prosecute, or they produce some other result that does not clearly establish grounds for discipline. Unless the employer has developed and pursued its own case against the employee, it may be left with no grounds on which to base a disciplinary decision. While a city or county may be in a better position than most other employers to obtain the cooperation of law enforcement agencies, it is wise not to assume that criminal prosecution will provide a shortcut that will avoid the customary disciplinary process. If an employer does turn over evidence of criminal wrongdoing to the police or a prosecutor, it should retain copies of any documents provided for use in disciplinary proceedings.

Off-duty conduct   In many respects, government employees have greater rights than their private sector counterparts to conduct their personal life as they wish. In most situations, what a public employee does on his or her own time is not the concern of the public employer. For example, gone are the days when a public school teacher could be terminated for cohabitating with another person out of wedlock. However, discipline for off-duty conduct is justified if it affects the employee's ability to do his or her job or is directly detrimental to the government employer. For example, a police officer may be fired for selling drugs, a teacher may be fired for sexually assaulting a minor, and a social worker may be fired for welfare fraud. As in many other situations, the circumstances of the individual case are crucial in making a determination as to whether discipline is appropriate. (For more on off-duty conduct, see Chapter 7.)

Correcting problems with supervisors and managers   In many respects, dealing with disciplinary or other personnel problems involving supervisors and managers brings into play the same considerations that apply when dealing with problems involving any other employee. However, there are important differences resulting from two significant distinctions between supervisors and managers, on the one hand, and the rank-and-file employees who work under their direction, on the other hand. First, public employees who have been hired for, or promoted into, positions of significant responsibility are expected to meet a higher standard of performance and conduct than can be expected from their subordinates. Second, actions of managerial-level employees are often attributed to the municipal employer per se and therefore may expose the jurisdiction to greater potential liability than if a lower-level employee had engaged in the same conduct.

The first of these two distinctions becomes important when dealing with disciplinary offenses such as absenteeism or tardiness. For an entry-level employee, this is the classic situation that calls for progressive discipline. However, if a department head cannot get to work on time or fails to let the office know when he or she will not be in, it may be that only one warning is needed before a determination is justified that the individual is simply not suited to his or her position. In general, problems with supervisors or managers tend to be dealt with through annual performance reviews rather than through disciplinary procedures. This is particularly true when the issue involves performance on the job rather than some specific misconduct.

Another reason why the steps of discipline may be somewhat attenuated in the case of a higher-level employee is that in dealings with both subordinates and members of the general public, actions and statements of management employees may constitute, both practically and legally, actions of the jurisdiction itself. A good example of this principle is found in court decisions in sexual harassment cases in which the employer may be held strictly liable for the conduct of supervisory and managerial employees, even if the employer has no knowledge that such conduct is occurring. In dealings with third parties, members of management may be perceived to have (and may actually have) ultimate authority to make final decisions

Caution

■ A pending criminal prosecution does not make disciplinary action unnecessary. Disciplinary procedures should be pursued as well.

■ Adverse actions of management employees may constitute actions by the jurisdiction itself and result in liability for the jurisdiction.

on behalf of the government entity. Under circumstances such as these, a public employer cannot tolerate repeated errors in judgment or recurring misconduct. In certain circumstances even a nonsupervisory employee who has some authority over co-workers can create liability for the organization.[24]

Supervisory or managerial employees of municipalities and counties may also have different procedural protections from those that apply to their subordinates. In many states, supervisors do not have the right to unionize and therefore lack the substantive and procedural protections that are often included in collective bargaining agreements. On the other hand, state statutes or municipal ordinances sometimes provide special protection for certain managers and department heads. In certain states, police chiefs, fire marshals, and other selected officials have protections against arbitrary dismissal on political or other grounds. When dealing with discipline or discharge of such high-level employees, employers should check for special statutory or other protections that may apply.

Handling an employee termination   Many employers who have good grounds for dismissing an employee nevertheless get themselves in trouble because of the way in which the termination process itself is handled. This tends to happen more in private industry than in the public sector, where more procedural protections (such as *Loudermill* hearings) tend to apply. Nevertheless, it is a good idea for employers to take a few simple precautions to avoid trouble.

First, the employee should always be told the real reason for his or her termination. Some employers are reluctant to come out and say that they believe the employee has been engaged in misconduct or to openly address inadequate performance. However, if a discharge is disguised as a job elimination or other no-fault termination, the employer will have some explaining to do if, for example, the employee files a discrimination claim. The investigating agency is likely to assume that if the employer misstated the real reason for the dismissal at the time of the termination, there must have been something to hide. Even if the real reason for the discharge is not particularly well documented, it is better to face that problem head-on than to fabricate another reason for the dismissal that cannot be defended at all.

Another mistake that sometimes occurs in the termination process is not allowing for negotiation of terms that will avoid a contested case. Sometimes, simply allowing an employee the option of resigning is enough to avoid a fight. In other cases, it makes good business sense to negotiate a "separation package" that will allow the employer to implement a high-risk termination decision quietly. When terminating a long-serving employee who is in one or more protected classifications, a few months' worth of pay and benefits will be much less expensive than

Tips for successfully managing disciplinary action

☐ Determine whether in-house or outside counsel should be involved, especially if circumstances indicate that termination might be appropriate and that the employee might seek to contest the termination in an administrative, arbitral, or judicial forum.

☐ Quietly conduct a complete investigation but get facts quickly.

☐ Discreetly obtain corroborating statements from other employees as well as from those directly involved.

☐ Review the employee's personnel records during the investigation to determine whether the employee has been involved in other incidents.

☐ Do not assume that the supervisor's accusations are true. Test the veracity of supervisors' statements as well as the statements of lower-level and nonsupervisory employees.

☐ Always allow an employee who is suspected of wrongdoing to provide an explanation of events, and then interview or reinterview witnesses to determine whether the employee's explanation appears valid.

☐ Do not threaten an employee with prosecution, loss of job, or other consequences for wrongdoing. However, an employee may be told that there could be job-related consequences for not cooperating in an investigation.

☐ Do not touch employees being questioned or make threatening gestures.

☐ Do not restrain employees from leaving the room where the questioning is taking place. Never lock the door, or stand in front of or block the exit.

☐ Refrain from asking employees about private matters unrelated to the investigation of misconduct.

☐ Obtain a written consent, waiver, or release from employees before conducting polygraph exams, and use a competent, experienced examiner when such examinations are permitted by law.

☐ Obtain a signed admission, if possible, from the employee suspected of wrongdoing or misconduct.

☐ Advise the employee that he or she is not being *accused* of misconduct, but rather, that the investigation has provided sufficient information to believe that he or she has engaged in misconduct.

☐ Never state to anyone that an employee has engaged in wrongdoing unless you are required by law or a collective bargaining agreement to prove or establish that misconduct has occurred.

☐ If asked, advise the employee's co-workers that you are not at liberty to disclose the reasons for the employee's discipline or separation from employment.

☐ Do not file or institute criminal or civil charges or complaints against an employee without probable cause to believe that the employee is guilty or liable.

Source: Adapted from Ronald Green and Richard J. Reibstein, *Employer's Guide to Workplace Torts: Negligent Hiring, Fraud, Defamation, and Other Emerging Areas of Employer Liability* (Edison, N.J.: BNA Books, 1992), 105-106.

Caution

There are several ways in which a manager can get into trouble when dismissing an employee:

- Failing to tell the dismissed employee the real reason for the termination.

- Generating controversy and perhaps even a lawsuit by dismissing the employee outright rather than negotiating a quiet resignation.

- Treating the dismissed employee like a criminal and embarrassing him or her before co-workers.

- Making defamatory statements about the dismissed employee to co-workers, future prospective employers, or other third parties.

- Misleading prospective employers by providing only favorable information about the dismissed employee. It is better to limit the information given to name, rank, and period in which the individual was employed by the jurisdiction.

- Handling an adverse personnel decision in a way that raises discrimination claims.

a lawsuit, regardless of the outcome. This is particularly true when the employer has not adequately documented the problems with the individual's performance or other reasons for the discharge.

If the employer and employee decide to use a separation agreement—and it is wise to do so if the jurisdiction is to expend a substantial amount of public funds on severance pay or other benefits—it makes sense to seek legal advice in preparing the document. An important element of any such agreement is a waiver by the employee of any claims against the employer; however, there are various legal requirements that apply if such a waiver is to be valid for certain types of claims, such as age discrimination. It is becoming more common for employees who have signed a waiver of claims to later change their minds and sue their former employers, so it makes sense to have a capable lawyer review the document to ensure that it is valid and enforceable.

Another mistake to avoid is treating the discharged employee "like a criminal." Even a discharge that is completely defensible on the merits can become problematic if the employee is confronted at his or her workstation and hustled out the door as if he or she were a security risk. If such a risk in fact exists, it should be handled in more subtle ways. An employee who feels that he or she has been abused in the process of termination may sue on that basis, even if the reason for the dismissal is not contested.

Finally, it is very important to manage post-termination contacts effectively. Managers should channel all inquiries from third parties to a particular individual, perhaps themselves or a human resource professional, and should give out no information other than "name, rank, and serial number" unless required by applicable law or agreed upon with the employee. Many discharged employees have sued—not over their dismissal but over allegedly defamatory or otherwise improper statements made to prospective employers or other third parties.

On the other hand, it is important not to affirmatively mislead prospective employers since this can also lead to liability claims. Some public entities have been sued by subsequent employers of terminated employees because when those employers called for references, they were given only positive information and not warned, for example, about the employee's history of violence. Even adopting a policy of providing references only when they are positive may not avoid problems: an employee may be able to prove a pattern of practice that demonstrates no reference is the equivalent of a negative reference. This is another situation in which it would be wise to get input from an employment lawyer.

To deal with the legal ambiguity, thirty states have passed job reference immunity laws, which protect employers who provide information about current or previous employees to new employers. Usually these laws stipulate that the reference must be provided at the request of the employee or the prospective employer, and that the information has to be job related and truthful.[25] (See Chapter 5 for more on this subject.)

Investigating and responding to complaints by employees

Guiding principles

- A jurisdiction should take all discrimination and harassment claims seriously.
- If the employer can prove just cause to dismiss an offending employee, it will have a defense to most claims arising out of the dismissal.

Challenge

- Avoiding mistakes that can lead to claims arising from legitimate personnel action

Until the last third of the twentieth century, almost all personnel problems arose in the context of the employer initiating disciplinary or other action against a problem employee. More recently, however, a growing percentage of personnel problems are the result of complaints initiated by employees or applicants for employment claiming mistreatment by their potential employers, their co-workers, or even third parties. A dizzying array of new laws and judicial decisions creating new rights for both public and private employees has been promulgated in the last few decades. Employee claims have become so common that there is even a specialized type of insurance coverage—Employment Practices Liability Insurance (EPLI)—to deal with them. Examples include claims of discrimination, sexual harassment, wrongful termination, whistle-blower violations, First and Fourth Amendment violations, and related constitutional claims. Employers should be aware, however, that EPLI policies can require that the employer turn over the defense to the carrier and its counsel.

Discrimination claims

Many employees either are members of one or more protected groups—for example, women, a racial or ethnic minority group, or a protected age class—or qualify for some other statutory protection against discrimination, such as disability or religion. Therefore, whenever some adverse action is taken against an employee or applicant for employment, chances are good that he or she will have some basis on which to claim employment discrimination. Managers should be familiar with state and federal antidiscrimination legislation and the classifications that are protected in their jurisdictions.[26] (For a quick review of antidiscrimination laws, see Exhibit 5–4 in Chapter 5.)

Whenever an employee or a job applicant makes a discrimination claim, the jurisdiction should take it seriously. It is easy for an employer to assume that the complaining employee or applicant is simply using his or her age, race, sex, or other protected characteristic as an excuse for complaining about a valid personnel action. However, there are at least two good reasons not to brush aside any discrimination claim.

First, even if the action in question (e.g., a decision on hiring, firing, transfer, or promotion) was entirely justified, there may be circumstantial evidence that suggests otherwise. If a thirty-year-old is hired for a position and the other five applicants are over fifty, or if a woman is denied promotion to a level at which all the incumbents are men, the employer will have some explaining to do, even if the decision had nothing to do with age or sex. Since the motivation for an employment-related decision is not easy for either side to prove, there is a tendency to look at other circumstances to see what they suggest.

In most jurisdictions, an employer does not actually have to prove the absence of a discriminatory motive. However, if the employee can prove one or more factors that raise an inference of discrimination, the employer may be required to prove a legitimate nondiscriminatory reason for its action. Therefore, it would be a mistake for an employer to take too lightly a discrimination claim under circumstances in which it cannot easily explain its actions by objective—and demonstrably job-related—factors. For example, an employer may not impose a college degree requirement for a particular job unless it can demonstrate that a college degree is necessary for performance. Since higher-education requirements tend to adversely affect minority employees and applicants, maintenance of such standards may be discriminatory unless they can be objectively justified. (See also Chapter 2 on the validity of testing procedures and Chapter 3 on the validity of performance appraisal techniques.)

The second reason for taking discrimination claims seriously is that they may in fact be justified. In a typical municipality or county, employment-related decisions are made by many different people, not all of whom are trained in human resource issues and some of whom may harbor discriminatory feelings. Such individuals may treat certain employees differently from others. Further, even if a personnel action is taken for reasons that are entirely neutral on their face, if there is disparate impact on a protected classification (such as a college-degree requirement), a discrimination claim may be successful even if there was no discriminatory intent.

Taking a complaint seriously involves, at a minimum, conducting a thorough and objective investigation and providing a response to the complainant, preferably with as much supporting documentation as is appropriate under the circumstances. If the investigation produces evidence that suggests some justification for the complaint, it may also be necessary to follow up with prompt remedial action. This in turn involves compensation for any adverse impact the complainant may have suffered and correction of the underlying problem so that it does not recur.

A thorough investigation usually involves interviewing the complainant, those involved in making the decision that brought about the complaint, and other witnesses, who may or may not be employees of the jurisdiction. Simply asking the key decision maker to explain his or her action does not constitute a thorough investigation. Ideally, the person who is in charge of the investigation should be someone who is removed from the events and the people who are the subject of the complaint, and that person's opinion as to the appropriate resolution should be given great weight.

Whether or not the results of the investigation suggest that some remedial action is appropriate, it is important to respond to the complainant and provide as much information as possible about the investigation and its results. In many cases, the complainant is not necessarily expecting a reversal of the decision that occasioned the complaint; he or she only wants someone to review the situation and ensure that there were no irregularities. Of course, some complainants will never be satisfied with the results of an internal investigation. However, the process will almost always produce valuable information that will be useful to the employer if and when the employee or applicant pursues the claim in an administrative or judicial forum.

Sexual and other harassment

Sexual harassment is a form of sex discrimination. Sexual harassment is unwelcome attention or harassment, even if not specifically sexual in nature, that is directed only at one sex and that directly affects conditions of employment; interferes with job performance; or creates an intimidating, hostile, or offensive working environment[27] (see Chapter 5). The Supreme Court has also ruled that same sex harassment is illegal.[28]

The same principles that apply to discrimination complaints generally are also applicable to sexual harassment complaints. That is, at a minimum, the employer should provide a prompt and thorough investigation followed by a response to the employee who made the complaint, together with effective corrective action, if appropriate. However, employers are likely to deal with certain scenarios in sexual harassment cases that do not normally arise in other discrimination claims.

First, the complainant may be objecting to the conduct of fellow employees or even of third parties rather than of management. While sexual harassment usually involves conduct or statements by a supervisor toward a subordinate, it may also be offensive behavior by co-workers. This may present special problems when it comes to investigating the claim since co-workers may be reluctant to confirm complaints against their peers. Union members, for example, may be subject to more or less subtle pressure not to bear witness against fellow union members. Harassment by third parties includes such varied circumstances as the office supply salesman pursuing the purchasing agent's secretary or a taxpayer harassing a tax collector. Employers have a responsibility to take corrective action in any such circumstances.

Another problem that tends to be unique to sexual harassment cases is that victims often say they don't want the perpetrator punished; they only want him (or her) to stop. Victims may even say that they don't want the harasser to know they have complained. It is generally unwise, however, for an employer to agree to be bound by such a request. Nothing prevents the victim from later changing his or her mind and claiming the employer should have done something in response to the complaint. Further, if the harassment involves serious misconduct, the employer may be exposed to liability from other complainants, even if the original complainant never raises the issue again. If the same person harasses other employees, those employees may claim that the employer was aware of the problem and, regardless of the preferences of the original complainant, should have done something to protect others against the same conduct.

Although other forms of harassment in the workplace may not receive as much attention and notoriety as sexual harassment, they can present legal issues that are just as serious. Many employers who have policies prohibiting sexual harassment

fyi

Addressing sexual harassment

If an employee complains of sexual harassment, the employer must take these steps:

Investigate promptly

Carefully choose the investigator. Generally, employers use their human resource personnel, but the employer should make sure that an unbiased person decides each complaint. Never have the person accused of harassment conduct the investigation! Make sure that the investigator is thorough, takes good notes, and is trusted by employees.

Be discreet. Make sure that the investigation is kept confidential. This will help avoid employer liability for defaming the alleged harasser.

Gather evidence. The victim and accused harasser should both be interviewed, but separately. Ask each for witnesses and also interview those witnesses separately. Ask open-ended questions and be careful not to pressure employees into giving a desired answer. Find out the nature of the relationship between the victim and the alleged harasser, including whether any sexual relationship is or has been consensual. Determine whether the accused harasser has previously been accused of sexual harassment.

Determine whether sexual harassment occurred. Consider (1) whether physical contact occurred, (2) whether any verbal comments are offensive to a reasonable person, (3) whether the harasser has been disciplined for sexual harassment in the past, (4) whether the victim consented to the behavior, and (5) how many incidents occurred. One isolated incident may not constitute sexual harassment. However, if it

was severe, if it involved physical touching, if it involved conduct by a supervisor, or if the harasser has been disciplined for harassment in the past, it probably is sexual harassment.

Take appropriate action

Inform both employees separately of the determination. Have your sexual harassment policy handy to help answer questions that arise in these interviews. If no harassment is found to have occurred, make sure the alleged victim understands that a thorough investigation has been conducted.

Make sure the penalty fits the crime. Employers must carefully balance the rights of both employees. Appropriate discipline may include a verbal reprimand, written reprimand, order to stay away from the victim, transfer, demotion, pay cut, suspension, or termination. A meeting with both the victim and the harasser at which the harasser is merely reminded to behave is probably not sufficient; however, not all conduct warrants termination. If no sexual harassment has occurred, do not punish the accused.

Do not punish the victim. Although an employer may offer the victim a chance to transfer, the victim should not be transferred against his or her will.

Do not retaliate against the complaining employee. Even if the employer finds that no harassment occurred, neither the alleged harasser nor any other employees should be permitted to retaliate against the employee. Be aware of whether the complaining employee is disciplined, demoted, or denied benefits, and thoroughly document the reasons for any necessary action.

Source: John A. DiNome and Saundra M. Yaklin, with assistance from Caroline A. O'Connell.

also prohibit harassment based on race, religion, national origin, and so on. Complaints about such types of harassment should be dealt with in the same manner as complaints about sexual harassment.

The Supreme Court has specified under Title VII the responsibilities of employee complainants and employers in sexual harassment cases. Although employers are vicariously liable for sexual harassment by supervisors, an employer may escape liability if two conditions are satisfied. First, the employer has to demonstrate that it exercised reasonable care to prevent and promptly correct any sexually harassing behavior. Second, the employer must demonstrate that the complainant unreasonably failed to use preventive or corrective measures offered by the employer, or failed in other ways to avoid harm. The second test will normally be satisfied if the employee unreasonably fails to use the employer's procedure for registering complaints.[29]

The Court has held that when sexual harassment results in a victim's dismissal, demotion, or other tangible job impact, the employer is automatically liable. If a supervisor, however, makes harassing threats but does not carry them out, the employer may not be liable if the jurisdiction can show that it made reasonable efforts to prevent and correct the harassment and that, as above, the victim unreasonably failed to pursue the publicized and available procedures for registering complaints.[30]

Jurisdictions should adopt and widely disseminate policy statements condemning sexual harassment. Complaint procedures must be available, prompt, and effective, and jurisdictions should ensure that the procedures do not require the victim to file the complaint directly with the harasser. Training programs for employees and supervisors about policies and procedures can help insulate jurisdictions from liability for harassment.

Wrongful discharge, defamation, negligent or intentional infliction of emotional distress, and other state law tort or contract claims

As courts broaden traditional causes of action to apply to new issues, employees may also bring an increasing number of claims under state law. A single set of circumstances—for example, events leading up to dismissal of an employee—may give rise to a variety of related claims. In general, if the employer can prove just cause to dismiss the employee, it will have a defense for most of these claims. However, it is useful to understand what types of claims may arise so as to avoid unintentionally couching a legitimate personnel action in language that might trigger a claim.

Wrongful discharge is a tort or contract claim under state law that arises when the employer dismisses an employee in retaliation for some conduct that is protected by an important public policy. For example, an employer generally may not fire an employee for filing a workers' compensation claim since this would discourage employees with legitimate claims from pursuing them and would defeat the purposes of workers' compensation laws. Similarly, an employee who reports violations of state and federal law may be protected from dismissal under this doctrine, even if there is no applicable whistle-blower statute.

An employee may claim defamation if an employer publicly criticizes his or her performance or states the reasons for dismissal to a third party without the employee's consent. An employee may claim that the employer's conduct in carrying out the dismissal was egregious and abusive, and, either negligently or intentionally, caused emotional distress. In general, an employee will bring these claims in state court in a civil lawsuit seeking damages.[31]

Free speech and other First Amendment issues

While some states have adopted legislation establishing free speech rights for public (and in a few cases private) employees, free speech rights for governmental workers generally emanate from the First Amendment to the U.S. Constitution.

Free speech   Some employees may challenge adverse employment decisions by alleging that a manager violated their First Amendment free speech rights. This is more likely to occur when a manager has relied on an employee's expressive actions as a factor in discipline. The First Amendment guarantees free speech, which public employers must respect, but in the public workplace, this right is qualified in several ways. Governments may have sound reasons for wanting to limit an employee's speech, and courts have been sympathetic to several arguments. (For more on employees' rights to free speech, see Chapter 5.)

Freedom of association   As with free speech, a government employer must have valid employment-related reasons for limiting freedom of association. Generally, public employers cannot ask prospective employees what organizations they hold memberships in or who their friends and acquaintances are. Nor can the government base an adverse action against a current employee on the personal ties or associations of that employee. Membership in a subversive group is not in itself grounds for dismissal. Instead, the individual employee must have engaged in or supported some subversive or otherwise illegal action.[32] (For more on employees' right to freedom of association, see Chapter 5.)

Freedom of association may be an issue when an employee alleges that a public employer took a personnel action on grounds of political patronage rather than performance. The Supreme Court has held that party affiliation and support are unconstitutional bases for almost all public personnel actions, including dismissal, transfer, promotion, or recall.[33] However, employees in high-level policy positions and "confidential" employees are not protected.

Whether a person is occupying an exempted policy-making or confidential position is a question of law for the court, which will not determine the answer solely by the job's official designation. At least one federal appeals court has said that the judicial inquiry should be based on whether the "policymaking position authorizes either directly or indirectly meaningful input into governmental decision making on issues where there is room for disagreement on goal formulation or implementation."[34] Whether an employee is judged to be a confidential employee depends on whether he or she acted as a confidential adviser and helped "formulate plans for the implementation of broad goals" or whether the employee had "limited responsibility."[35]

Privacy issues

Searches of public employees at the workplace will be judged by Fourth Amendment standards. To determine the extent of Fourth Amendment protection, courts must establish the boundaries of the workplace and determine whether the employee had a reasonable expectation of privacy. These issues are decided on a case-by-case basis. A balancing test weighs the employee's legitimate expectations of privacy against the government's need for supervision and control. (For more on employees' Fourth Amendment rights, see Chapter 5.)

Complaints about employees by third parties

Guiding principle

- Federal criminal civil rights statutes, which can affect the employment context, apply to municipal or county employees.

Challenge

- Taking citizens' complaints against employees seriously and conducting a thorough investigation, while protecting the employees' legal rights and preserving organizational effectiveness

Most employment-related complaints are made by employees, but government employers also have to deal with complaints about employees by taxpayers, people with whom the city or county does business, and other third parties. Examples range from allegations of police misconduct made by people who are questioned or arrested, to claims that an inspector has solicited a bribe, to complaints that a town employee has been rude or abusive to a taxpayer.

As with complaints of discrimination or other mistreatment made by employees, a municipality should react to third-party complaints by conducting a prompt and thorough investigation and following up with a response to the complainant, which should include remedial action if appropriate. However, many municipal collective bargaining agreements and some municipal ordinances, personnel rules, or procedures contain specific requirements to be followed in the investigation of and response to complaints by third parties.

A good example of such employee protections is the "police bill of rights" championed by many police unions; this contains such provisions as mandatory notification of the employee who is the subject of the complaint and a prohibition against taking action solely on the basis of an anonymous complaint. Obviously a public employer should take whatever steps are necessary to comply with such requirements without jeopardizing the effectiveness of the investigation or response. Of course, if the complaint alleges criminal misconduct and the jurisdiction elects to press criminal charges, then all the usual constitutional protections apply. However, as discussed above, the employer should draw a distinction between criminal prosecution and employee discipline; the latter need not necessarily wait for or depend upon the former.

Supervisory personnel should understand, however, that under certain circumstances, employee conduct can give rise to suits by citizens that can result in liability, not only for the employee but also for the jurisdiction and the supervisor. In addition, federal criminal civil rights statutes, which can affect the employment context, apply to municipal or county employees.

On the civil side, under the federal statute 42 U.S.C. 1983, citizens may sue local government employees in federal court for violations of federal constitutional or statutory rights and seek compensatory money damages and/or injunctive and declaratory relief. Citizens may also pursue declaratory and injunctive relief directly from local governments. In addition, compensatory money damages may be sought from a local government because of the actions of its employee if the violation by that employee is found by the court to be pursuant to an "official policy" or "governmental custom."[36]

The fact that jurisdictions can be held liable for compensatory monetary damages for the actions of their employees provides an added incentive to promptly investigate charges of abuse by public employees. Failure to take corrective action in response to such charges can be introduced by subsequent plaintiffs as proof of toleration of such practices, thereby constituting a governmental custom justifying the payment of damages.[37] And even if the employee involved is excused from the suit by virtue of being judged by the court as having acted in "good faith" under the doctrine of qualified immunity, the local government will not be excused from liability. In addition, public employers may be held liable for failure to adequately train employees under some circumstances.[38] Further, a city or county may be held liable for violating a citizen's constitutional rights on the basis of a failure to train, even if no individual employee is found individually liable.[39]

With respect to finding the jurisdiction liable because the employee acted pursuant to an official policy, policy is made when a decision maker who possesses the final authority to establish public policy with respect to the action issues an official proclamation, policy, or edict.[40] Courts seek to identify which city officials speak with final policy-making authority, and the definition of the officials' functions under relevant state law drives the inquiry.[41]

A supervisor also may be held liable for the actions of a subordinate employee judged to have violated a citizen's rights. Supervisor liability may be found when the plaintiff demonstrates an "affirmative causal link" between the supervisor's inaction and harm suffered by the plaintiff.[42] Evidence of failure to investigate or address the propensities of employees to violate citizens' rights can result in supervisor liability.

Under some circumstances, local government employees can be prosecuted for criminal violation of a citizen's civil rights in federal court under 42 U.S.C. 1982. In the event of an official indictment, if the public employer decides there is merit to the charges, it can take action to suspend the employee. The employer is not required to hold a predetermination hearing in such an event, as long as the suspended employee receives a sufficiently prompt post-suspension hearing.[43]

Contested cases in the labor and employment arena

General principles

- It is important to determine insurance coverage immediately when an employment-related lawsuit or administrative proceeding threatens.
- The choice between an all-out defense and pursuit of a settlement should be made early in the proceedings.
- Employers should take administrative complaints seriously and defend them as thoroughly as they would if the claims had been filed in court.

Challenge

- Resolving a matter at the administrative level with either a favorable decision or a reasonable settlement so as to avoid costly litigation and/or a jury trial

With increasing frequency, workplace problems tend to spill over into administrative and judicial forums. In both the public and private sectors, employment litigation has mushroomed over the past few decades. Newly created statutory rights and protections, common-law developments in many states, and the creativity of plaintiffs' lawyers have all combined to foster a more litigious atmosphere. As noted above, this new environment has even spawned a new type of insurance, which specifically addresses liability resulting from employment decisions.

Regardless of whether a municipality has purchased an EPLI policy, it is wise to notify both the carrier and the broker or agent for any insurance that might possibly apply to an employment-related lawsuit or administrative proceeding. Many such claims are complex in nature and involve a variety of different causes of action or "counts." Insurance protection may not apply for some counts but may be available for others. If a jurisdiction commences its own defense without notifying the appropriate carrier, coverage may well be lost.

Caution

■ A local government can lose its insurance coverage if it begins litigation without properly notifying the relevant insurance carrier.

■ Admissions or statements by an employer in an administrative setting may later be used in a judicial setting.

Defending lawsuits in state or federal court

If it is determined that no defense will be provided by the jurisdiction's insurance carriers, the next step is to retain competent and experienced counsel. Employment defense work is now recognized as a separate specialty in the legal profession, and a city or county should not count on its corporation counsel or a general practitioner to have this expertise. In larger cities, there may even be attorneys specializing in defending against the particular type of claim involved.

Most defense lawyers will urge that a thorough investigation of the plaintiff's claims be done promptly and that an objective evaluation of the prospects for a successful defense be conducted as early as possible. Litigation is extremely expensive and time-consuming, and it is wise to make an early determination as to whether it is more appropriate to mount an all-out defense or to pursue the possibility of settlement. Once the parties are heavily invested in the outcome of the litigation, it becomes much more difficult to find a mutually acceptable compromise.

Although the steps followed in the defense of an employment-related lawsuit will vary from case to case, they usually include obtaining statements from all potential witnesses and reviewing all available documents and files for relevant evidence. Each side engages in this process initially with respect to its own witnesses and documents. However, the judicial system establishes a formal process for gaining access to the other side's witnesses and documents; this is known as "discovery." In most cases, discovery includes depositions of the other side's witnesses, interrogatories requesting answers to questions addressed to the opposing party, and requests for the production of documents and other relevant information in the possession of the opposing party.

Upon completion of discovery, and after disposal of any pretrial motions, there is usually another opportunity to consider settlement before going to trial. In most cases, the trial is the most expensive part of the litigation process, and of course it involves the greatest risk to both sides. Most lawsuits are settled before trial, and employment litigation is no exception. Public employers may be particularly well advised to consider settling cases in which a jury is involved since jurors (who are generally employees themselves) tend to be sympathetic to the employee's point of view and often think of government as having deep pockets.

If a trial cannot be avoided, the conduct of that proceeding is, of course, in the hands of the jurisdiction's attorney. However, the county or city should insist on being consulted with respect to significant strategy issues since it, of course, has the greatest stake in the outcome of the case.

Responding to complaints by or through administrative agencies

A wide array of employment-related cases arises in the context of an administrative proceeding rather than in response to (or prior to) court litigation. Examples include wage and hour problems, health and safety issues, workers' compensation claims, and, in many states, employment discrimination claims. Each state or federal agency has different substantive and procedural rules, which vary too widely to permit a meaningful survey within the confines of this chapter. However, a few general principles are worth noting.

First, employers make a mistake when they fail to take administrative complaints seriously or fail to defend them as thoroughly as they would if the claim had been filed in court. In many situations, the decision of an administrative agency carries significant weight in any judicial appeal, and if the agency decision goes against the employer, it may be very difficult to obtain a reversal in court.

Further, administrative complaints tend to be much less expensive to defend than lawsuits. If it is possible to resolve a matter at the administrative level with either a favorable decision or a reasonable settlement, the jurisdiction is generally much better served by doing so. Usually, there are more and better opportunities in an administrative proceeding to discuss the matter informally, explore the merits of both parties' positions, and structure a creative resolution that serves the interests of all concerned.

However, since many claims initiated in an administrative forum later end up in court, it is a good idea to obtain legal advice before responding to an administrative complaint. Often admissions, statements, or other evidence used in one setting can come back to haunt an employer in another. Also, a lawyer may help to ensure that all the legal issues within the jurisdiction of the administrative agency are adequately addressed. It is wise to understand these principles, and to explore their application to the particular dispute at hand, before taking steps that cannot be retraced.

Handling labor relations matters

Union-management relationships tend to be adversarial by their nature, and much of the labor relations process consists of resolving disputes and settling differences. The principles of public sector labor relations are explored in Chapter 4. This chapter focuses only on a few specific types of contested cases in the labor relations arena.

Grievances and arbitration Most union contracts contain a procedure for resolving disputes about interpretation or application of the contract's terms, as well as for appealing disciplinary decisions and other management actions. Contractual grievance procedures generally contain several steps, starting with the lowest level of management and usually culminating in binding arbitration by an outside agency. Obviously, it is wise to resolve grievances at the lowest possible level in order to minimize the expenditure of resources and disruption of harmonious working relations between labor and management.

If a dispute ends up before an arbitrator (or panel of arbitrators), the jurisdiction should treat it just as seriously, and focus just as much energy and attention on it, as it would if the case had arisen in an administrative forum. Many grievances involve potential consequences that may include thousands of dollars in back pay or a major erosion of management's right to operate in the manner it sees fit. Decisions of grievance arbitrators are generally subject to only limited review, and therefore a negative decision in arbitration may be difficult or impossible to reverse in court.[44]

Unfair labor practice charges   Most states that have public sector collective bargaining laws include in those statutes a list of practices in which employers are prohibited from engaging. Examples of conduct commonly prohibited by such statutes are failure or refusal to negotiate in good faith over mandatory subjects of employees based on union status or preference; and interference, restraint, or coercion of employees engaged in protected activities, such as forming, joining, or assisting a union. When an employee or a union claims that one or more of these prohibitions have been violated, the applicable statute usually provides a board of labor relations or other agency to which a claim of unfair labor practices can be submitted. A public employer's response to such claims should follow the same procedures and principles as outlined above in the discussion of complaints to administrative agencies.

Alternative dispute resolution: Ways to handle things that go wrong—without litigation

Guiding principle

■ Mediation, facilitation, conciliation, early neutral evaluation, arbitration, and other alternative dispute resolution methods can save the local government time and money.

Increasingly, employers use many forms of alternative dispute resolution to resolve disputes when things go wrong in the workplace. Alternative dispute resolution includes processes such as mediation, facilitation, conciliation, early neutral evaluation, arbitration, and minitrials. (For more on these alternative dispute resolution techniques, see Chapter 4.)

Mediation, facilitation, and conciliation are all consensual forms of assisted negotiation or settlement in which a third-party neutral helps the parties reach a mutually agreeable settlement; they differ in how actively the neutral tries to bring the parties together. For example, in *mediation*, the parties generally meet together across a table to exchange their perspectives on the dispute directly, before the mediator breaks them into separate rooms for individual confidential sessions called "caucuses." *Facilitation* tends to involve large numbers of parties and consists of the neutral trying to foster orderly discussion in a group meeting. *Conciliation* is used for discrimination cases under Title VII and may be done with the parties individually through telephone conversations. In all three processes, the neutral has no power to impose a settlement or outcome upon the parties; only the parties themselves may do that if they reach agreement.[45]

Early neutral evaluation and arbitration are adjudicatory proceedings in which the parties to a dispute hire a private judge to decide the case for them. Like advisory arbitration, *early neutral evaluation* provides a nonbinding decision. *Binding arbitration*, common in labor relations contracts but finding increasing use in the nonunion sector, involves a private judge rendering a final and legally enforceable decision on the dispute.[46]

Employers interested in using alternative dispute resolution have a wide range of choices and resources. There are government and private providers of alternative dispute resolution services—for example, the Federal Mediation and Conciliation Service and the American Arbitration Association. These third-party providers will supply lists of mediators, arbitrators, fact finders, or other neutral evaluators upon request. In addition, many states have state boards of mediation and arbitration with panels of mediators, arbitrators, and fact finders. Sometimes these panels are empowered to hear disputes regarding particular categories of public employees, such as state employees, municipal employees, or teachers. There are also numerous mediators and arbitrators in private practice. Listings are available from the Association for Conflict Resolution, or from the ABA Section for Dispute Resolution, the fastest-growing section of the bar. Both are headquartered in Washington, D.C. Many communities also have community mediation centers that will provide free or low-cost mediation services for employment disputes.

Many nonunion employers are adopting binding arbitration for all employment disputes as a means of avoiding the uncertain outcome of a jury verdict.[47] In *Gilmer v. Interstate/Johnson Lane Corporation*,[48] the Supreme Court held that it would enforce a pre-dispute agreement to arbitrate an age discrimination claim. Arbitration can provide a timely and cost-effective means of resolving employee claims arising out of discipline or dismissal. However, dispute resolution plans should contain certain procedural safeguards for employees if public employers expect them to be enforceable in court. These safeguards include a right to counsel, reasonable discovery, and participation in selecting the arbitrator, and are described in detail in "A Due Process Protocol for Mediation and Arbitration of Statutory Disputes Arising out of the Employment Relationship."[49] This document does not have the force of law, but it is an effort by the dispute resolution profession to regulate itself, and federal courts of appeals have noted that they will examine employers' plans for these safeguards in considering whether to enforce the arbitration agreement.[50]

Even if an employer does not have a dispute resolution plan in place before things go wrong, the municipality or its counsel may wish to suggest one or more means of dispute resolution before proceeding to litigate a dispute.[51] However, increasingly, employers are designing conflict management systems to handle the wide variety of employment disputes before they turn into formal complaints or litigation. These systems are most effective if they provide for early intervention and multiple points of access, and if they progress from the most informal, cost-effective alternative dispute resolution methods that concentrate on disputants' interests to the more formal, quasi-adjudicatory processes to determine disputants' rights.

Civil service commissions or appeals boards

General principle

■ Public employees have the right to a hearing and to appeal any adverse personnel decision.

As part of their due process rights, public employees have the right to a hearing and to appeal any adverse personnel decision. In jurisdictions where few grievances arise, an appeals board can be appointed on an ad hoc basis; on the other hand, a city or county with a steady stream of complaints may want to have a permanent appeals board. To ensure political balance on the board, management and labor usually receive the same number of positions to fill while one person has to be acceptable to both sides. For instance, two members of a five-member board may be appointed by management and two members by labor, while the fifth person is jointly appointed by management and the union. In appointing commission members, officials should aim for balance in expertise, appointing some members with a legal background and others with a background in human resource management.

Notes

1 Gerald J. Miller and James H. Svara, *Navigating the Fiscal Crisis: Tested Strategies for Local Leaders,* a white paper prepared by the Alliance for Innovation (Washington, D.C.: ICMA, January 2009), icma.org/documents/ Navigating_Fiscal_Crisis_%28Final%29_ 1-25-09.pdf (accessed May 25, 2009).

2 International Public Management Association for Human Resources (IPMA-HR), "Hiring Freezes Taking Place Now, Layoffs Next Year," press release (November 18, 2008), ipma-hr.org/content.cfm?pageid = 759 (accessed May 25, 2009).

3 ICMA has useful tools for successful contract negotiations and contract administration: see icma.org/main/topic.asp?hsid = 1&tpid = 16&stid = 18.

4 County of Los Angeles, "C-Beep [Community-Based Enterprise Education Program]," dhr.lacounty.info/CBEEP.asp (accessed May 25, 2009).

5 Miller and Svara, *Navigating the Fiscal Crisis,* 10.

6 For a more detailed guide to preventing specific kinds of lawsuits, see James G. Frierson, *Preventing Employment Lawsuits: An Employer's Guide to Hiring, Discipline, and Discharge* (Edison, N.J.: Bureau of National Affairs [BNA] Books, 1994).

7 *Pickering v. Board of Education,* 391 U.S. 563 (1968).

8 *Waters v. Churchill,* 511 U.S. 661 (1994).

9 Jonathan Tompkins, *Human Resource Management in Government* (New York: HarperCollins, 1995), 311–312.

10 Enterprise Wire Co., 46 *Labor Arbitration Reports* 359 (1966): 362–365. See also Adolph M. Koven and Susan L. Smith, *Just Cause: The Seven Tests,* 3rd ed. (Edison, N.J.: BNA Books, 2006); and Marvin Hill Jr. and Anthony V. Sinicropi, *Remedies in Arbitration,* 2nd ed. (Washington, D.C.: BNA, 1991): 139–141, 522–556.

11 *Cleveland Board of Education v. Loudermill,* 470 U.S. 532 (1985).

12 *NLRB v. Weingarten, Inc.,* 420 U.S. 251 (1975); *Epilepsy Foundation of Northeast Ohio v. NLRB,* 268 F. 2d 1095 (2001).

13 For a detailed discussion of different bases for discipline and discharge and ways that arbitrators treat them, see Norman Brand, ed., *Discipline and Discharge in Arbitration* (Edison, N.J.: BNA Books, 1998).

14 For more complete information on this issue, see Frank Elkouri and Edna Asper Elkouri, *Resolving Drug Issues* (Edison, N.J.: BNA Books, 1993); and on disability discrimination claims more generally, see Robert L. Burgdorf Jr., *Disability Discrimination in Employment Law* (Edison, N.J.: BNA Books, 1996); James G. Frierson, *Employer's Guide to the Americans with Disabilities Act* (Edison, N.J.: BNA Books, 1995); and Tia Schneider Denenberg and Richard V. Denenberg, *Alcohol and Other Drugs: Issues in Arbitration* (Edison, N.J.: BNA Books, 1991).

15 Section 501 of the Rehabilitation Act of 1973, 29 U.S.C. § 791.

16 Americans with Disabilities Act, 42 U.S.C. § 12101, et seq.

17 42 U.S.C. § 4551 et seq.

18 *Federal Personnel Manual Supplement 792-2, Alcohol and Drug Abuse Programs* (1980), 7. This manual provides an extensive statement of reasonable accommodation duties to alcoholic employees.

19 See *Maddox v. University of Tennessee,* 62 F.3d 843 (6th Cir. 1995).

20 Jonathan R. Mook and Erin E. Powell, "Substance Abuse and the ADA: What Every Employer Should Know," *Employee Relations Law Journal* 22 (Autumn 1996): 57–78.

21 Family and Medical Leave Act, 29 U.S.C. § 2601, et seq.

22 Ibid., 65.

23 Tia Schneider Denenberg and Richard V. Denenberg, "Workplace Violence and Dispute Resolution," *Dispute Resolution Journal* 51 (January–March 1996): 6–16.

24 *Mack v. Otis Elevator Co.,* 326 F.3d 116 (2d Cir. 2003), *cert. denied, Otis Elevator v. Mack,* 540 U.S. 1016 (2003).

25 "Thirty States Have Job Reference Immunity Laws," *IPMA News* (November 1997): 6.

26 For a primer on equal employment opportunity law, see Nancy Sedmak and Chrissy Vidas, *Primer on Equal Employment Opportunity,* 6th ed. (Edison, N.J.: BNA Books, 1994); for more comprehensive material on employment discrimination law, see Barbara Lindemann and Paul Grossman, *Employment Discrimination Law,* 3rd ed. (Edison, N.J.: BNA Books, 2002).

27 For a sexual harassment primer that is good for supervisory training and reference, see Barbara Lindemann and David D. Kadue, *Primer on Sexual Harassment* (Edison, N.J.: BNA Books, 1992); for a more detailed analysis of the developing law of sexual harassment, see Barbara Lindemann and David D. Kadue, *Sexual Harassment in Employment Law* (Edison, N.J.: BNA Books, 1992), and Lindemann and Grossman, *Employment Discrimination Law.*

28 *Oncale v. Sundowner Offshore Services,* 523 U.S. 75 (1998).

29 *Faragher v. Boca Raton,* 524 U.S. 775 (1998).

30 *Burlington Industries, Inc. v. Ellerth,* 524 U.S. 742 (1998).

31 For more information on these and related claims, see Ronald M. Green and Richard J. Reibstein, *Employer's Guide to Workplace Torts: Negligent Hiring, Fraud, Defamation, and Other Emerging Areas of Employer Liability* (Edison, N.J.: BNA Books, 1992), and Frierson, *Preventing Employment Lawsuits.*

32 *Scales v. United States,* 367 U.S. 203 (1961).

33 *Rutan v. Republican Party,* 497 U.S. 62 (1990).

34 *Lohorn v. Michal,* 913 F.2d 327 (7th Cir. 1990); *Nekolny v. Painter,* 653 F.2d 1164 (7th Cir. 1981).

35 *Elrod v. Burns,* 427 U.S. 347 (1976).

36 See, for example, *Pembaur v. City of Cincinnati,* 475 U.S. 469 (1986).

37 *Monell v. Department of Social Services,* 436 U.S. 658 (1978).

38 *City of Canton, Ohio v. Harris,* 489 U.S. 378 (1989).

39 *Fagan v. City of Vineland,* 22 F.3d 1283 (3d Cir. 1994).

40 *Jett v. Dallas Independent School District,* 491 U.S. 701 (1989).

41 *McMillan v. Monroe County, Alabama,* 520 U.S. 781 (1997).

42 *Shaw v. Stroud,* 13 F.3d 791 (4th Cir. 1994).

43 *Gilbert v. Homar,* 520 U.S. 924 (1997).

44 For a comprehensive reference on arbitration, see Edward P. Goggin and Marlin M. Volz, eds., *Elkouri and Elkouri's How Arbitration Works,* 6th ed. (Edison, N.J.: BNA Books, 2003).

45 For a more detailed discussion of mediation, see Christopher Moore, *The Mediation Process: Practical Strategies for Resolving Conflict,* 3rd ed. (San Francisco: Jossey-Bass, 2003).

46 For a more detailed discussion of mediation and arbitration of nonunion employment disputes, see Jack T. Dunlop and Arnold M. Zack, *The Mediation and Arbitration of Employment Disputes* (San Francisco: Jossey-Bass, 1997).

47 Ibid.

48 *Gilmer v. Interstate/Johnson Lane Corporation,* 500 U.S. 20 (1991).

49 American Arbitration Association, "A Due Process Protocol for Mediation and Arbitration of Statutory Disputes Arising out of the Employment Relationship," in *Guide for Employment Arbitrators 1,* Publication No. AAA219-10M-8/96 (1996): 19–24.

50 See, for example, *Cole v. Burns International Security Services,* 105 F.3d 1465 (D.C. Cir. 1997).

51 For more information on designing a conflict management program for employment disputes, see David B. Lipsky, Ronald L. Seeber, and Richard D. Fincher, *Emerging Systems for Managing Workplace Conflict: Lessons from American Corporations for Managers and Dispute Resolution Professionals* (San Francisco: Jossey-Bass, 2003); and Cathy A. Costantino and Christina Sickles Merchant, *Designing Conflict Management Systems* (San Francisco: Jossey-Bass, 1996).

For Further Reading

Preface

James, Kay Coles. "The HR Paradigm Shift and the Federal Human Capital Opportunity." *Public Manager* 30 (Winter 2001–2002): 13–16.

Riccucci, Norma M., and Katherine C. Naff. *Personnel Management in Government: Politics and Process.* 6th ed. Boca Raton, Fla.: CRC Press, 2008.

Introduction

Cohen, Steven, and William Eimicke. *Tools for Innovators: Creative Strategies for Managing Public Sector Organizations.* San Francisco: Jossey-Bass, 1998.

Deci, Edward L., and Richard M. Ryan. *Intrinsic Motivation and Self-Determination in Human Behavior.* New York: Plenum Press, 1985.

Freyss, Siegrun Fox. "Local Government Operations and Human Resource Policies: Trends and Transformations." In *The Municipal Year Book 2004*, 17–25. Washington, D.C.: ICMA, 2004.

———. "Municipal Government Personnel Systems: A Test of Two Archetypical Models." In *Local Government Management: Current Issues and Best Practices,* edited by Douglas J. Watson and Wendy L. Hassett. Armonk, N.Y.: M. E. Sharpe, 2003.

———. "Professional Norms and Actual Practices in Local Personnel Administration. A Status Report." *Review of Public Personnel Administration* 13 (Spring 1993): 5–28.

Gill, Robert P. "Essentials of Workforce Planning." *IPMA-HR News* (February 2004).

Goleman, Daniel. *Working with Emotional Intelligence.* New York: Bantam, 1998.

Gottfried, Frances. *The Merit System and Municipal Civil Service.* New York: Greenwood Press, 1988.

ICMA. *Local Government Online: Putting the Internet to Work.* Special Report. Washington, D.C.: ICMA, 2000.

International Personnel Management Association (IPMA). *Workforce Planning Resource Guide for Public Sector Human Resource Professionals.* Alexandria, Va.: IPMA, 2002.

Kaplan, Robert S., and David P. Norton. *The Balanced Scorecard: Translating Strategy into Action.* Boston: Harvard Business School Press, 1996.

Karoly, Lynn A., and Constantijn W. A. Panis. *The 21st Century at Work: Forces Shaping the Future Workforce and Workplace in the United States.* Santa Monica, Calif.: Rand Corporation, 2004.

Mosher, Frederick C. *Democracy and the Public Service.* 2nd ed. New York: Oxford University Press, 1982.

Moulder, Evelina. *Compensation and Benefits for Local Government Employees: Programs and Practices.* Special Data Issue no. 6. Washington, D.C.: ICMA, 2001.

———. *Recruiting and Selecting Local Government Employees: Programs and Practices.* Special Data Issue no. 5. Washington, D.C.: ICMA, 2001.

Muirhead, Lindsay. "HR Transformation in the Public Sector." *IPMA-HR News* (November 2008): 8–10.

Osborne, David, and Ted Gaebler. *Reinventing Government: How the Entrepreneurial Spirit Is Transforming the Public Sector.* Reading, Mass.: Addison-Wesley, 1992.

Riccucci, Norma M., ed. *Public Personnel Administration and Labor Relations: An ASPA Classics Volume.* Armonk, N.Y.: M. E. Sharpe, 2007.

Senge, Peter M. *The Fifth Discipline: The Art and Practice of the Learning Organization.* New York: Currency Doubleday, 1994.

Shafritz, Jay M., Albert C. Hyde, and Sandra J. Parkes, eds. *Classics of Public Administration.* 5th ed. Belmont, Calif.: Wadsworth/Thomson, 2004.

Smith, Russell L. "The 'Electronic Village': Local Governments and E-Government at the Dawn of a New Millennium." In *The Municipal Year Book 2002,* 34–41. Washington, D.C.: ICMA, 2002.

Thompson, Frank J., ed. *Classics of Public Personnel Policy.* Belmont, Calif.: Wadsworth, 2003.

Van Riper, Paul P. *History of the United States Civil Service.* Evanston, Ill.: Row, Peterson, 1958.

Woodward, Ann. "Engaging Frontline Workers in Times of Organizational Change." *Public Administration Review* 69 (January/February 2009): 25–28.

Chapter 1 Planning and paying for work done

Abosch, Kenan S., and Janice S. Hand. *Broadbanding Design: Approaches and Practices.* Scottsdale, Ariz.: American Compensation Association, 1994.

Beyerlein, Michael M., Susan Freedman, Craig McGee, and Linda Moran. *Beyond Teams: Building the Collaborative Organization.* San Francisco: Jossey-Bass/Pfeiffer, 2003.

Brown, Preston "Tim," and Susan K. Cavanaugh. *Building Successful Organizations: A Guide to Strategic Workforce Planning.* Washington, D.C.: National Academy of Public Administration (NAPA), 2000.

Bryson, John M. *Strategic Planning for Public and Nonprofit Organizations: A Guide to Strengthening and Sustaining Organizational Achievement.* San Francisco: Jossey-Bass, 1995.

Bryson, John M., and Farnum K. Alston. *Creating and Implementing Your Strategic Plan: A Workbook for Public and Nonprofit Organizations.* San Francisco: Jossey-Bass, 1996.

Cavanaugh, Susan Knighton. *The Case for Transforming Public Sector Human Resource Management.* Washington, D.C.: NAPA, 2000.

Condrey, Stephen E., ed. *Handbook of Human Resource Management in Government.* San Francisco: Jossey-Bass, 1998.

Gordon, Gerald L. *Strategic Planning for Local Government.* Washington, D.C.: ICMA, 1993.

Harris, Patricia A. *Total Quality Management: Strategies for Local Government.* Washington, D.C.: ICMA, 1993.

ICMA. *Compensation 2004: An Annual Report on Local Government Executive Salaries and Fringe Benefits.* Washington, D.C.: ICMA, 2004.

Johnston, William B. *Civil Service 2000.* Washington, D.C.: Hudson Institute, 1988.

Judy, Richard W., and Carol D'Amico. *Workforce 2020: Work and Workers in the 21st Century.* Indianapolis, Ind.: Hudson Institute, 1997.

Kawecki, Charles, Kristi Cameron, and Joan Jorgenson. *Revisiting Civil Service 2000: New Policy Direction Needed.* Washington, D.C.: U.S. Office of Personnel Management, 1993.

Kiyonaga, Nancy B., ed. "Special Issue: Workforce and Succession Planning." *Public Personnel Management* 33 (Winter 2004): 357–496.

Klingner, Donald E., and John Nalbandian. *Public Personnel Management: Contexts and Strategies.* 4th ed. Upper Saddle River, N.J.: Prentice Hall, 1998.

Lawler, Edward E., III. *Rewarding Excellence: Pay Strategies for the New Economy.* 2nd ed. San Francisco: Jossey-Bass, 2000.

Mears, Peter. *Organizational Teams.* Delray Beach, Fla.: St. Lucre Press, 1994.

Mohrman, Susan Albers, Susan G. Cohen, and Allan M. Mohrman Jr. *Designing Team-Based Organizations: New Forms for Knowledge Work.* San Francisco: Jossey-Bass, 1995.

Moulder, Evelina. "Police and Fire Personnel, Salaries, and Expenditures for 2003." In *The Municipal Year Book 2004,* 123–176. Washington, D.C.: ICMA, 2004.

NAPA. *Modernizing Federal Classification: An Opportunity for Excellence.* Washington, D.C.: NAPA, 1991.

National Commission on the State and Local Public Service. *Hard Truths/Tough Choices: An Agenda for State and Local Reform.* Albany, N.Y.: Nelson A. Rockefeller Institute of Government, 1993.

Nutt, Paul C., and Robert W. Backoff. *Strategic Management of Public and Third Sector Organizations: A Handbook for Leaders.* San Francisco: Jossey-Bass, 1992.

Pierce, Jon L., John W. Newstrom, Randall B. Dunham, and Alison E. Barber. *Alternative Work Schedules.* Boston: Allyn and Bacon, 1989.

Pynes, Joan E. *Human Resources Management for Public and Nonprofit Organizations.* 2nd ed. San Francisco: Jossey-Bass, 2004.

Risher, Howard. "The New Compensation Model." *IQ Service Report.* Washington, D.C.: ICMA, December 1998.

Risher, Howard, Charles H. Fay, and Associates. *New Strategies for Public Pay: Rethinking Government Compensation Programs.* San Francisco: Jossey-Bass, 1997.

Rothwell, William J. "Knowledge Transfer: 12 Strategies for Succession Management." *IPMA-HR News* (February 2004): 10–11.

Salaries 2004. CD-ROM. Washington, D.C.: ICMA, 2004.

Sumser, Ray. *Broadband Pay Experience in the Public Sector.* Washington, D.C.: NAPA, 2003.

Tompkins, Jonathan. "Strategic Human Resources Management in Government." *Public Personnel Management* 31 (Spring 2002): 95–109.

Chapter 2 Recruiting for a high-performance workforce

Arthur, Diane. *The Employee Recruitment and Retention Handbook.* New York: AMACOM, 2001.

Brice, Maurice. *Diversity: A New Direction.* Washington, D.C.: NAPA, 2002.

Buford, James A., Jr. *Personnel Management and Human Resources in Local Government.* Auburn, Ala.: Auburn University Press, 1991.

Daly, Peter H., and Michael Watkins. *The First 90 Days in Government: Critical Success Strategies for New Public Managers at All Levels.* Boston: Harvard Business School Press, 2006.

Equal Employment Opportunity Commission. "Uniform Guidelines on Employee Selection Procedures." 29 *Code of Federal Regulations* § 1607 (1997).

Fisher, Cynthia D., Lyle E Schoenfeldt, and James B. Shaw. *Human Resource Management.* 5th ed. Boston: Houghton Mifflin, 2003.

Heneman, Herbert G., and Timothy A. Judge. *Staffing Organizations.* 4th ed. Boston: McGraw-Hill, 2003.

Katznelson, Ira. *When Affirmative Action Was White: An Untold History of Racial Inequality in Twentieth-Century America.* New York: W. W. Norton, 2005.

Kellough, J. Edward. *Understanding Affirmative Action: Politics, Discrimination, and the Search for Justice.* Washington, D.C.: Georgetown University Press, 2006.

Lord, J. Scott. "Internal and External Recruitment." In *Human Resource Planning, Employment, and Practice,* edited by Wayne F. Cascio, 73–102. Washington, D.C.: Bureau of National Affairs, 1989.

Schmidt, Frank L., and Deniz S. Ones. "Personnel Selection." *Annual Review of Psychology* 43 (1992): 627–670.

Chapter 3   Maintaining a high-performance workforce

Aamodt, Michael C. *Applied Industrial/Organizational Psychology.* 4th ed. Belmont, Calif.: Thomson/Wadsworth, 2004.

Ammons, David N. *Municipal Benchmarks: Assessing Local Performance and Establishing Community Standards.* 2nd ed. Thousand Oaks, Calif.: Sage, 2001.

Carnevale, David G. "Human Capital and High Performance in Public Organizations." In *Public Personnel Administration: Problems and Prospects.* 3rd ed., edited by Steven W. Hays and Richard C. Kearney. Upper Saddle River, N.J.: Prentice Hall, 1995.

———. *Trustworthy Government: Leadership and Management Strategies for Building Trust and High Performance.* San Francisco: Jossey-Bass, 1995.

DeLeon, Linda, and Ann J. Ewen. "Multi-Source Performance Appraisals: Employee Perceptions of Fairness." *Review of Public Personnel Administration* 17, no. 1 (1997): 22–36.

Denhardt, Robert B. *The Pursuit of Significance: Strategies for Managerial Success in Public Organizations.* Belmont, Calif.: Wadsworth, 1993.

Edwards, Jack E., John C. Scott, and Nambury S. Raju, eds. *The Human Resources Program—Evaluation Handbook.* Thousand Oaks, Calif.: Sage, 2003.

Ferris, Gerald R., Sherman D. Rosen, and Darold T. Barnum. *Handbook of Human Resource Management.* Cambridge, Mass.: Blackwell, 1995.

Glaser, M. "Tailoring Performance Management to Fit the Organization: From Generic to Germane." *Public Productivity and Management Review* 14, no. 3 (1991): 303–319.

Goleman, Daniel. *Emotional Intelligence.* New York: Bantam Books, 1995.

Gore, Al. *From Red Tape to Results: Creating a Government That Works Better and Costs Less: Reinventing Human Resource Management.* Vice President's Report, National Performance Review. Washington, D.C.: U.S. Government Printing Office, 1993.

Gravett, Linda, and Robin Throckmorton. *Bridging the Generation Gap: How to Get Radio Babies, Boomers, Gen Xers, and Gen Yers to Work Together and Achieve More.* Franklin Lakes, N.J.: Career Press, 2007.

Holzer, Marc, and Kathe Callahan. *Government at Work: Best Practices and Model Programs.* Thousand Oaks, Calif.: Sage, 1998.

ICMA. *Employee Performance: Appraisal and Management Training Package.* Washington, D.C.: ICMA, 1997.

———. *Performance Appraisals for Local Government Employees: Programs and Practices.* Washington, D.C.: ICMA, 2001.

Ingraham, Patricia W., James R. Thompson, and Ronald P. Sanders, eds. *Transforming Government: Lessons from the Reinvention Laboratories.* San Francisco: Jossey-Bass, 1998.

Klagge, Jay. "360-Degree Sociometric Feedback for Individual and Organizational Change." *Public Administration Quarterly* 19, no. 3 (1995): 352–366.

Lawler, Edward E., III. *Treat People Right: How Organizations and Employees Can Propel Each Other into a Virtual Spiral of Success.* San Francisco: Jossey-Bass, 2003.

Lovrich, Nicholas P. "Assessing the Performance of the Individual on the Job." In *Handbook on Public Personnel Administration and Labor Relations,* edited by Jack Rabin, Thomas Vocino, W. Bartley Hildreth, and Gerald J. Miller. New York: Marcel Dekker, 1983.

———. "Performance Appraisal: Seeking Accountability and Efficiency through Individual Effort, Commitment, and Accomplishment." In *Public Personnel Administration: Problems and Prospects.* 3rd ed., edited by Steven W. Hays and Richard C. Kearney. Upper Saddle River, N.J.: Prentice Hall, 1995.

Meyer, Herbert H., Emanuel Kay, and John R. P. French. "Split Roles in Performance Appraisal." *Harvard Business Review* (January–February 1965): 123–129.

Mohrman, Allan M., Susan M. Resnick-West, and Edward E. Lawler III. *Designing Performance Appraisal Systems: Aligning Appraisals and Organizational Realities.* San Francisco: Jossey-Bass, 1989.

Nalbandian, John. "Performance Appraisal: If Only People Were Not Involved." *Public Administration Review* 41, no. 3 (1981): 392–396.

Noe, Raymond A. *Employee Training and Development.* 2nd ed. Boston: McGraw-Hill/Irwin, 2002.

Perry, James L. "Compensation, Merit Pay, and Motivation." In *Public Personnel Administration: Problems and Prospects.* 4th ed., edited by Steven W. Hays and Richard C. Kearney. Upper Saddle River, N.J.: Prentice Hall, 2003.

Risher, Howard, Charles H. Fay, and Associates. *New Strategies for Public Pay: Rethinking Government Compensation Programs.* San Francisco: Jossey-Bass, 1997.

Roberts, Gary E. "Developmental Performance Appraisal in Municipal Government: An Antidote for a Deadly Disease?" *Review of Public Personnel Administration* 15, no. 3 (1995): 17–43.

———. "Linkages between Performance Appraisal System Effectiveness and Rater and Ratee Acceptance: Evidence from a Survey of Municipal Personnel Administrators." *Review of Public Personnel Administration* 12, no. 3 (1992): 19–41.

———. "Maximizing Performance Appraisal System Acceptance: Perspectives from Municipal Government Personnel Administrators." *Public Personnel Management* 23 (December 1994): 525–549.

Roberts, Gary E., and Tammy Reed. "Performance Appraisal Participation, Goal Setting and Feedback: The Influence of Supervisory Style." *Review of Public Personnel Administration* 16, no. 4 (1996): 29–60.

Shareef, Reginald. "Skill-Based Pay in the Public." *Review of Public Personnel Administration* 14, no. 3 (1994): 60–74.

Smith, Sharon L., and Ronald J. Stupak. "Public Sector Downsizing Decision-Making in the 1990s: Moving beyond the Mixed Scanning Model." *Public Administration Quarterly* 18 (Fall 1994): 359–379.

Waldman, David A., Leanne E. Atwater, and David Antonioni. "Has 360-Degree Feedback Gone Amok?" *Academy of Management Executive* 12 (May 1998): 86–94.

Yammarino, Francis J., and Leanne E. Atwater. "Implications of Self-Other Rating Agreement for Human Resources Management." *Organizational Dynamics* 25 (Spring 1997): 35–44.

Chapter 4 Labor-management relations and collective bargaining

Bogue, Bonnie G., Carol Vendrillo, and Liz Joffe. *Pocket Guide to Workplace Rights of Public Employees.* 2nd ed. Berkeley: Institute of Industrial Relations, University of California, 2005.

Coleman, Charles J. *Managing Labor Relations in the Public Sector.* San Francisco: Jossey-Bass, 1990.

Coulson, Robert. *Labor Arbitration: What You Need to Know.* 5th ed. New York: American Arbitration Association, 2000.

Cozzetto, Don A., Theodore B. Pedeliski, and Terence J. Tipple. *Public Personnel Administration: Confronting the Challenges of Change.* Upper Saddle River, N.J.: Prentice Hall, 1996.

Fisher, Roger, William Ury, and Bruce Patton. *Getting to Yes: Negotiating Agreement without Giving In.* 2nd ed. New York: Penguin Books, 1991.

Keane, William G. *Win! Win or Else: Collective Bargaining in an Age of Public Discontent.* Thousand Oaks, Calif.: Corwin Press, 1996.

Kearney, Richard C., with David G. Carnevale. *Labor Relations in the Public Sector.* 4th ed. New York: CRC Press, 2009.

Rubin, Barry, and Richard Rubin. "Labor-Management Relations: Conditions for Collaboration." *Public Personnel Management* 35 (Winter 2006): 283–298.

Smith, Ralph R. *Practical Guide to Interest-based Bargaining.* 2nd ed. Huntsville, Ala.: FPMI Communications, 2000.

Chapter 5 Employee rights: Avoiding legal liability

Center for Personnel Research. *Employee Handbook Toolkit.* Alexandria, Va.: International Public Management Association for Human Resources (IPMA-HR, formerly International Personnel Management Association), 2003.

——. *Employee Handbooks.* Alexandria, Va.: IPMA-HR, 1998.

Condrey, Stephen E., ed. *Handbook of Human Resource Management in Government.* San Francisco: Jossey-Bass, 1998.

Lee, Yong, and David H. Rosenbloom. *A Reasonable Public Servant.* Armonk, N.Y.: M. E. Sharpe, 2005.

Miceli, Marcia, and Janet P. Near. *Blowing the Whistle: The Organizational and Legal Implications for Companies and Employees.* New York: Lexington Books, 1992.

National Center for HIV, STD, and TB Prevention. "Updated U.S. Public Health Guidelines for the Management of Occupational Exposures to HBV, HCV and HIV and Recommendations for Postexposure Prophylaxis." Atlanta, Ga.: Centers for Disease Control and Prevention, 2001.

Occupational Safety and Health Administration (OSHA). *Guidelines for Preventing Workplace Violence for Health Care and Social Service Workers.* Document no. OSHA 3148-01R. Washington, D.C.: OSHA, 2004.

Roberts, Robert. *White House Ethics: The History of the Politics of Conflict of Interest Regulation.* Lanham, Md.: Rowman and Littlefield, 1998.

Rosenbloom, David. "Constitutional Problems for the New Public Management in the United States." In *Current Public Policy Issues: The 1998 Annals,* edited by Khi Thai and Rosalyn Carter. Boca Raton, Fla.: Academic Press, 1998.

Rosenbloom, David, James Carroll, and Jonathan D. Carroll. *Constitutional Competence for Public Managers. Cases and Commentary.* Itasca, Ill.: F. E. Peacock, 2000.

Rosenbloom, David, and Rosemary O'Leary. *Public Administration and Law.* 2nd ed. New York: Marcel Dekker, 1997.

Steingold, Fred S., Amy Delpo, and Lisa Guerin, eds. *The Employer's Legal Handbook.* 5th ed. Berkeley, Calif.: Nolo Press, 2003.

Chapter 6 Pay and benefits: Creating an environment for excellence

Beam, Burton T., Jr., and John J. McFadden. *Employee Benefits.* 6th ed. Chicago: Real Estate Education, 2001.

Black, Ann. *New Era of Benefits Communication.* 2nd ed. Brookfield, Wis.: International Foundation of Employee Benefit Plans (IFEBP), 2000.

Bureau of Labor Statistics. *Employee Benefits in State and Local Governments, 1998.* Bulletin 2531. Washington, D.C.: Bureau of Labor Statistics, U.S. Department of Labor, 2000.

Cuda, Amanda. "More Than One Way to Pay: Compensating Employees in a Tough Economy." *IPMA-HR News* (February 2009): 8–10.

Employee Benefit Research Institute (EBRI). *EBRI Databook on Employee Benefits.* 4th ed. Washington, D.C.: EBRI, 1997.

———. *Fundamentals of Employee Benefit Programs.* 5th ed. Washington, D.C.: EBRI, 1996.

Harker, Carlton. *Self-Funding of Health Care Benefits.* 5th ed. Brookfield, Wis.: IFEBP, 2003.

Harm, Kathleen Jenks. "Defined Contribution Retirement Plans." *MIS Report.* Washington, D.C.: ICMA, October 1996.

Harris, Jennifer D. *2001 Survey of State and Local Government Employee Retirement Systems.* Chicago: Public Pension Coordinating Council, 2002.

Johnson, Richard E. *Flexible Benefits: A How-To Guide.* 6th ed. Brookfield, Wis.: IFEBP, 2002.

Krass, Stephen J. *The Pension Answer Book.* Brookfield, Wis.: IFEBP, 2004.

McKay, Robert J. *Canadian Handbook of Flexible Benefits.* 2nd ed. New York: Wiley, 1996.

Moulder, Evelina. *Compensation and Benefits for Local Government Employees: Programs and Practices.* Special Data Issue no. 6. Washington, D.C.: ICMA, 2001.

———. *Local Government Health Benefits: Responses to Costs and Customers.* Special Data Issue no. 2. Washington, D.C.: ICMA, 2003.

Pacelli, Jane D. *Benefit Design in Public Employee Retirement Systems.* Chicago: Government Finance Officers Association, 1994.

Reilly, Thom, Shaun Schoener, and Alice Bolin. "Public Sector Compensation in Local Governments. *Review of Public Personnel Administration* 27 (March 2007): 39–58.

Roberts, Gary E., Jerry A. Gianakis, Clifford McCue, and XiaoHu Wang. "Traditional and Family-Friendly Benefits Practices in Local Governments: Results from a National Survey." *Review of Public Personnel Administration* 33 (Fall 2004): 307–330.

Rosenbloom, Jerry S. *The Handbook of Employee Benefits: Design, Funding, and Administration.* 5th ed. New York: McGraw-Hill, 2001.

Chapter 7 Employee responsibilities: Setting expectations

Goleman, Daniel. *Emotional Intelligence.* New York: Bantam Books, 1995.

Howie, Robert M., and Laurence A. Shapiro. "How Long Is Enough—Leaves of Absence as Reasonable Accommodation under ADA." *Employee Relations Law Journal* 29 (Fall 2003): 33–49.

Johnson, Pamela, and Julie Indvik. "Rudeness at Work: Impulse over Restraint." *Public Personnel Management* 30 (Winter 2001): 457–465.

Lewis, Carol, and Stuart Gilman. *The Ethics Challenge in Public Service.* San Francisco: Jossey-Bass, 2006.

Schaner, Dean L. "Romance in the Workplace: Should Employers Act as Chaperons?" *Employee Relations Law Journal* 20 (Summer 1994): 47–71.

Silbergeld, Arthur F., and Stacie S. Polashuk. "Chronic Serious Health Impairments and Worker Absences under Federal Employment Law." *Labor Lawyer* 14 (Summer 1998): 1–22.

Starkman, Paul E. "Answering the Tough Questions about Alcoholism and Substance Abuse under the ADA and FMLA." *Employee Relations Law Journal* 25 (Spring 2000): 43–77.

Svara, James. *The Ethics Primer.* Sudbury, Mass.: Jones and Bartlett, 2007.

West, Jonathan. "Ethics and Human Resource Management." In Steven W. Hays, Richard C. Kearney, and Jerrell D. Coggburn, eds. *Public Personnel Administration: Problems and Prospects.* 5th ed. Upper Saddle River, N.J.: Prentice Hall, 2008.

West, Jonathan, and Evan Berman. *The Ethics Edge.* Washington, D.C: ICMA, 2006.

Chapter 8 When things go wrong

American Arbitration Association (AAA). "A Due Process Protocol for Mediation and Arbitration of Statutory Disputes Arising out of the Employment Relationship." In *Guide for Employment Arbitrators,* 19–24. Publication AAA219-1OM-8/96. New York: AAA, 1996.

Anderson, Jonathan B., and Lisa B. Bingham. "Upstream Effects from Mediation of Workplace Disputes: Some Preliminary Evidence from the USPS." *Labor Law Journal* 48 (October 1997): 601–615.

Bingham, Lisa B. "Mediating Employment Disputes: Perceptions of REDRESS at the United States Postal Service." *Review of Public Personnel Administration* 17, no. 2 (1997): 20–30.

Brand, Norman, ed. *Discipline and Discharge in Arbitration.* Washington, D.C.: Bureau of National Affairs (BNA) Books, 1998.

Denenberg, Tia Schneider, and Richard V. Denenberg. *Alcohol and Other Drugs: Issues in Arbitration.* Washington, D.C.: BNA Books, 1991.

———. "Workplace Violence and Dispute Resolution." *Dispute Resolution Journal* 51 (January–March 1996): 6–16.

Dunlop, Jack T., and Arnold M. Zack. *The Mediation and Arbitration of Employment Disputes.* San Francisco: Jossey-Bass, 1997.

Elkouri, Frank, and Edna Asper Elkouri. *Resolving Drug Issues.* Washington, D.C.: BNA Books, 1993.

Frierson, James G. *Employer's Guide to the Americans with Disabilities Act.* 2nd ed. Washington, D.C.: BNA Books, 1995.

———. *Preventing Employment Lawsuits: An Employer's Guide to Hiring, Discipline, and Discharge.* Washington, D.C.: BNA Books, 1994.

Green, Ronald M., and Richard J. Reibstein. *Employer's Guide to Workplace Torts: Negligent Hiring, Fraud, Defamation, and Other Emerging Areas of Employer Liability.* Washington, D.C.: BNA Books, 1992.

Hill, Marvin F., Jr., and Anthony V. Sinicropi. *Remedies in Arbitration.* 2nd ed. Washington, D.C.: BNA Books, 1991.

Koven, Adolph M., and Susan L. Smith. *Just Cause: The Seven Tests.* 2nd ed. Washington, D.C.: BNA Books, 1992.

Lindemann, Barbara, and Paul Grossman. *Employment Discrimination Law.* 3rd ed. Washington, D.C.: BNA Books, 1996.

Lindemann, Barbara, and David D. Kadue. *Primer on Sexual Harassment.* Washington, D.C.: BNA Books, 1992.

———. *Sexual Harassment in Employment Law.* Washington, D.C.: BNA Books, 1992.

Miller, Gerald J., and James H. Svara, eds. *White Paper. Navigating the Fiscal Crisis: Tested Strategies for Local Leaders.* Tempe: Alliance for Innovation, Arizona State University, and Washington, D.C.: ICMA, 2009.

Moore, Christopher W. *The Mediation Process: Practical Strategies for Resolving Conflict.* 3rd ed. San Francisco: Jossey-Bass, 2003.

Ruben, Alan Miles, ed. *Elkouri and Elkouri: How Arbitration Works.* 6th ed. Washington, D.C.: BNA Books, 2003.

Sedmak, Nancy J., and Chrissie Vidas. *Primer on Equal Employment Opportunity.* 6th ed. Washington, D.C.: BNA Books, 1994.

Contributors

Arlene J. Angelo (Chapters 5 and 8) is a partner in the Litigation Department of Ballard Spahr Andrews & Ingersoll, LLP, in Philadelphia, Pennsylvania, and a member of the firm's Labor, Employment and Immigration Group. Her practice involves the representation of employers in a wide variety of labor and employment law matters, including labor arbitrations, negotiation and administration of labor contracts, union organizing campaigns, National Labor Relations Board and Pennsylvania Labor Relations Board proceedings, and employment discrimination claims. She also counsels clients in a broad range of human resource areas, and frequently lectures on employment and labor law topics, including sexual harassment, effective discipline, and compliance with the Americans with Disabilities Act and the Family and Medical Leave Act.

Lisa B. Bingham (Chapter 8) is the Keller-Runden Professor of Public Service in the School of Public and Environmental Affairs at Indiana University (IU) in Bloomington. Prior to coming to IU in 1989, she practiced labor and employment law as a partner in the firm of Shipman and Goodwin, LLP. In addition to five teaching awards from IU, she received the Association for Conflict Resolution's Abner Award in 2002 for excellence in research on dispute resolution in the public sector; the Rubin Theory-to-Practice Award in 2006 from the International Association for Conflict Management (IACM) and Harvard Project on Negotiation for research on conflict resolution; and research awards for conference papers from the American Bar Association Section of Dispute Resolution, the Industrial Relations Research Association (now the Labor and Employment Relations Association), and the IACM. She has coedited three books and authored over seventy articles, monographs, and book chapters on dispute resolution and collaborative governance. Together with Professor Rosemary O'Leary of the Maxwell School of Syracuse University, she received the Section of Environmental and Natural Resource Administration of the American Society of Public Administration's Best Book award for *The Promise and Performance of Environmental Conflict Resolution* (2005). In 2007, Professor Bingham was elected a Fellow of the National Academy of Public Administration. She earned her AB from Smith College and her JD with high honors from the University of Connecticut School of Law.

N. Joseph Cayer (Chapter 6) is the Frank and June Sackton Professor of Public Administration in the School of Public Affairs at Arizona State University. He is the author of numerous books and chapters on public administration and public policy with an emphasis on human resources and management, and his articles have appeared in such journals as *Public Administration Review, Review of Public Personnel Administration, Public Personnel Management,* and *Employee Assistance Quarterly.* He received his BA and MPA from the University of Colorado, and his PhD in political science from the University of Massachusetts.

Brian Clemow (Chapter 8) is a partner in the labor and employment law department of Shipman and Goodwin, LLP, in Hartford, Connecticut. He has taught public sector labor law at the University of Connecticut Law School and has chaired the Labor and Employment Law Section of the Connecticut Bar Association. He serves as labor counsel to both the executive and judicial branches of the government of the state of Connecticut.

Don A. Cozzetto (Chapter 7), president of the University of Northern British Columbia from 2003 to 2008, has also served as academic vice-president and provost at Northern State University in South Dakota (1999–2003) and, before that, as professor and dean of the College of Professional Studies at Florida Gulf Coast University. He has written extensively in the areas of personnel administration and personnel law, and with Theodore Pedeliski he coauthored *Public Personnel Administration: Confronting the Challenges of Change.* He has acted as a consultant to a number of state, county, and municipal public and non-for-profit organizations in both the United States and Canada. A native of British Columbia, he is a specialist in public administration, human resource management, and aboriginal government. He received his PhD in public policy and public administration from Virginia Polytechnic Institute and State University.

John A. DiNome (Chapter 5), a partner in the law firm of Reed Smith in Philadelphia, Pennsylvania, represents a variety of regional and national employers in collective bargaining, labor arbitration, and employment-related litigation, and he is also labor counsel for a number of municipalities, representing them in their dealings with both union and nonunion employees. He is a past chancellor of the board of trustees of the Rutgers University School of Law Alumni Association, and a member of the board of directors of Leadership Philadelphia. A frequent author and lecturer in several national education programs in the field of labor and employee relations, he has spoken extensively on all facets of private and public sector labor and employment law on behalf of numerous organizations, including the Council on Education; the International Bridge, Tunnel and Turnpike Authority; the National League of Cities; and ICMA. He received his JD with honors from Rutgers University School of Law, where he served as president of the student body.

Jenny L. Holland (Chapter 3) is a doctoral student in political science at Washington State University (WSU) in Pullman. Her research interests include American government and politics, public policy, and public administration. She has served as an intern for two members of Congress and has been a staff member on a highly contested California State Assembly campaign. As a graduate student, she has served as a research assistant and an undergraduate academic adviser, and has also worked as a researcher in WSU's Division of Governmental Studies and Services. She holds BA degrees in political science and English from California State University in Bakersfield, where she was recognized as the Outstanding Graduate for the School of Humanities and Social Sciences.

Richard C. Kearney (Chapter 4) is professor and director of the School of Public and International Affairs at North Carolina State University. He has previously served in teaching and administrative positions at the University of Northern Iowa, University of South Carolina, University of Connecticut, and East Carolina University. His research and teaching specialties are labor relations and collective bargaining, human resource management, state and local government, and public policy. His most recent publications include *Labor Relations in the Public Sector,* 4th ed. (2009); *State and Local Government* (8th ed., coauthored with Ann O'M. Bowman, forthcoming in 2010), and *Public Human Resource Management: Problems and Prospects,* 5th ed. (coauthored with Steven W. Hays and Jerrell D. Coggburn, 2009). He earned his MPA and PhD in political science at the University of Oklahoma.

Nicholas P. Lovrich (Chapter 3) is director of the Division of Governmental Studies and Services at Washington State University (WSU) in Pullman. A professor of political science and a local government specialist, he was appointed the Claudius O. and Mary Johnson Distinguished Professor of Political Science in 1998 and reappointed in 2005. He trains graduate students in public administration and criminal justice to conduct applied social science research in service to state and local government agencies, and more than a score of the doctoral students he has directed have embarked on careers in academic and public sector administration throughout the country. The editor-in-chief of the *Review of Public Personnel Administration* from 1990 to 2000, Professor Lovrich works closely with state and local government agencies throughout Washington. He earned a BA in international relations from Stanford University and a PhD in political science and public administration from the University of California, Los Angeles.

Arthur H. McCurdy (Chapter 3), a state labor relations manager for the state of Oregon, has over twenty-five years of public and private sector experience in human resource management. In the public sector, he has served as chief of the State of Montana Labor Relations and Employee Benefits Bureau. He has also taught at Washington State University (WSU) in Pullman in the Division of Governmental Studies and Services and for WSU's Cooperative Extension. Private sector experience includes positions at Nortel Networks and PacTel Meridian Systems. His BA from the University of Washington, his MA from Western Washington University, and his PhD from Washington State University are all in political science with concentrations in public administration and policy. In addition, he is a certified employee benefit specialist through the International Foundation of Employee Benefit Plans and the Wharton School of the University of Pennsylvania.

Saranne P. Murray (Chapter 8) is a partner in the labor and employment law department of Shipman and Goodwin, LLP, in Hartford, Connecticut. She is co-counsel to the National Public Labor Relations Association and has served as the principal labor relations specialist for the state of Connecticut.

W. David Patton (Chapter 2), the deputy director of operations in the Utah Department of Health, is responsible for planning, management, finance, and government relations. Previously, he was the director of the University of Utah's Center for Public Policy and Administration, which provides research, education, and consulting services to public and nonprofit organizations to strengthen administration, leadership, and public policy making; he was also a research professor in the university's Department of Political Science, where he taught in the MPA and MPP programs and directed policy research projects, leadership and management development for public officials, and public forums on important public policy issues. Dr. Patton has worked with state and local governments in the areas of agency management, labor negotiations, and policy analysis, and he was the first executive director of the Utah Policy Partnership, the policy and governance advisory group of Gov. Jon Huntsman Jr. His research interests include the tools and skills of governance and collaborative leadership. He holds degrees in economics and political science, an MPA from Brigham Young University, and a PhD from the University of Utah.

Theodore B. Pedeliski (Chapter 7) had been a professor of political science and public administration at the University of North Dakota until his retirement in 2000. His areas of expertise included American, state, and local government. He is a coauthor with Don A. Cozzetto of *Public Personnel Administration: Confronting the Challenges of Change* (1996); has coauthored articles on privacy in the workplace in *Review of Public Administration* and *Public Personnel Management;* and in 2008 he contributed a chapter on popular democracy in North Dakota to *The Constitutionalism of American States* (University of Missouri Press). He received his PhD in political science and public law from the University of Minnesota in 1972.

David H. Rosenbloom (Chapter 5) is Chair Professor of Public Management at City University of Hong Kong and Distinguished Professor of Public Administration at American University in Washington, D.C. His research focuses on public administration and democratic constitutionalism. The U.S. Supreme Court cited his book *Federal Service and the Constitution* as authority on the First Amendment rights of public employees. He served on the Clinton-Gore presidential transition team with responsibilities for the Office of Personnel Management, held membership on the Onondaga County, N.Y., Board of Ethics, and was a consultant for several federal agencies, including the Merit Systems Protection Board and the Government Accountability Office. In 1993 he appeared as an expert witness for the New York State Commission on Government. He holds a PhD in political science from the University of Chicago, and in 1994 he was awarded an honorary doctor of law degree from Marietta College in Ohio, from which he had earned his bachelor's degree.

Aleksandra Stapczynski (Chapter 1) manages her own personnel management consulting practice, Human Resources Services, Inc., in Andover, Massachusetts. With over twenty years of experience providing technical assistance to cities and towns in all areas of municipal personnel management, she has provided consulting services to more than 250 Massachusetts municipalities, delivering work products that include classification and compensation studies, salary and benefits surveys, personnel bylaws, personnel policies and procedures, performance appraisal and merit systems, job descriptions, personnel system improvements, staffing studies, and general personnel management studies. She is a former employee of the Massachusetts Municipal Association and the Commonwealth of Massachusetts Department of Revenue. She holds a bachelor's degree in government and a master's degree in public administration from Suffolk University in Boston.

Jonathan Tompkins (Chapters 1 and 7) is currently director of the MPA program at the University of Montana. His teaching responsibilities include courses in human resource management, organization theory, and research methods. He has published several articles relating to personnel administration, as well as a book, *Human Resource Management in Government.* He has also served as a consultant to several state and local government agencies. He received his PhD in political science from the University of Washington in 1981.

Will Volk (Chapter 6) is director of employee relations for Dakota County, Minnesota, the third largest county in the state with about 2,000 employees represented by sixteen bargaining units. His experience includes a number of assignments in the compensation, benefits, and staffing functions as well as management and senior management positions. He was an early adopter and developer of trust-based medical plans as well as comprehensive human capital management programs. He has also championed full merit-based compensation methodologies supported by strategic planning, goal setting, and competency-based performance management systems and tools; these elements have been consolidated into a "total compensation" concept that blends wages, time-off programs, benefits, and related plans into an integrated "FlexComp" design. Mr. Volk holds a bachelor's degree from the University of St. Thomas in St. Paul, Minnesota.

Jonathan P. West (Chapter 7) is professor of political science and director of the MPA program at the University of Miami. His research interests include human resource management, productivity, local government, and ethics. He has also taught at the University of Houston and the University of Arizona. Professor West has published eight books and more than a hundred articles and book chapters. His most recent books are *American Public Service: Radical Reform and the Merit System* (coedited with James S. Bowman, 2007) and ICMA's *The Ethics Edge* (coedited with Evan M. Berman, 2006); other books are *Human Resource Management: Paradoxes, Processes and Problems,* 2nd ed. (coauthored with Berman, Bowman, and Montgomery R. Van Wart, 2006), and *The Professional Edge: Competencies in Public Service* (2004). He is the managing editor of *Public Integrity*. He served as a management analyst in the U.S. Surgeon General's Office, Department of the Army, Washington, D.C. He earned his BS from the University of Utah, and his MA and PhD from Northwestern University, all in political science.

Charles R. Wise (Chapter 8) is professor of public affairs at Indiana University, where he teaches classes in public management, public organization, public law, and policy and democratization. Currently he is serving as project director of the Parliamentary Development Project for Ukraine, which has been working since 1994 to strengthen the parliament as a transparent, effective, democratic institution. His research and teaching interests in public law include the impact of constitutions on public administration, the liability of public officials and organizations, regulatory takings and environmental regulation, and the processes of legislation. He is a past president of the National Association of Schools of Public Affairs and Administration, which accredits MPA programs in the United States. He has served as managing editor of *Public Administration Review* and received the Mosher Award three times for the best academic article to appear in that journal. He has also served on the National Council of the American Society for Public Administration, as director of intergovernmental affairs for the U.S. Department of Justice, and as associate dean of the School of Public and Environmental Affairs at Indiana University. His master's degree and doctorate are from Indiana University.

Stephanie L. Witt (Chapter 2) is director of the Public Policy Center and professor of public policy and administration at Boise State University, where her research interests include issues in state and local government and public policy. Her most recent book is *Human Resource Management in the Public Sector* (2002), and a second book, *Public Administration: Knowledge and Skills for Public Service*, is forthcoming from Houghton Mifflin. Her work has appeared in journals such as *State and Local Government Review, Public Administration Review, American Politics Quarterly,* and *Review of Public Personnel Administration.* She received her PhD from Washington State University in 1989.

Saundra M. Yaklin (Chapter 5) is a practicing attorney with Reed Smith Shaw & McClay, LLP, in Philadelphia, Pennsylvania. She handles a wide range of employment and labor matters in both the public and private sectors, but she focuses primarily on equal employment opportunity litigation. She has coauthored articles on the Fair Labor Standards Act and has also written extensively on the Americans with Disabilities Act, sexual harassment, and other fair-employment issues. She graduated from Western Michigan University in 1987 and received her JD from the University of Pennsylvania. She is admitted to the Pennsylvania and New Jersey bars.

Index

Workforce
   aging of, 206
   generational differences in, 84–85
   importance of competent, xv
   reducing size of, 7
Workplace
   alcohol and drug abuse in, 216–217,
      245–247
   computer and Internet use in, 221–223
   confidentiality issues in, 224
   drug abuse in, 245–247
   family-friendly, 189
   infectious diseases in, 159–160

   interpersonal relationships in, 218–220
   religion in, 164–165
   smoking in, 158–159
   speech restrictions in, 126
Workplace violence
   employee discipline and, 157, 247–248
   guiding principles related to, 156
   personnel policy manual statements on,
      128
   prevention of, 156–157
   tips for avoiding, 158
   victims of, 157–158
Wrongful discharge, 257